Om Mani Padme Hum

The Sound of Silence: The Diamond in the Lotus

Extemporaneous talks given by Osho at OSHO International Meditation Resort, Pune, India

OSHO

Om Mani Padme Hum

The Sound of Silence: The Diamond in the Lotus

MACMILLAN

First published in the Indian subcontinent 2015 by Macmillan
This updated edition published 2024 by Macmillan
an imprint of Pan Macmillan Publishing India Private Limited
707 Kailash Building
26 K. G. Marg, New Delhi 110001
www.panmacmillan.co.in

Pan Macmillan, The Smithson, 6 Briset Street, Farringdon, London EC1M 5NR
Associated companies throughout the world
www.panmacmillan.com

ISBN 978-93-82616-73-3

The material in this book is a transcript of a series of original OSHO Talks, *Om Mani Padme Hum – The Sound of Silence: The Diamond in the Lotus*, given to a live audience. All of Osho's talks have been published in full as books, and are also available as original audio recordings. Audio recordings and the complete text archive can be found at www.osho.com

1 3 5 7 9 8 6 4 2

Typeset in Adobe Garamond Pro by R. Ajith Kumar, New Delhi
Printed and bound in India by Gopsons Papers Pvt. Ltd., Noida

Contents

Preface

I don't think that there will come a day when science will be able to say, "Now there is no unknown left any longer, our work is finished, we can close the shop."

Even just for argument's sake, if it can be accepted that there may be a possibility that all the unknown becomes known, then too, there is a third dimension which science has been consistently denying. And that third dimension is my work. It is the work of all the buddhas of all the ages, of all the mystics, of all those who are really concerned with the essence of existence. The third category is of the unknowable, hence the word mysticism. Hence the word mystic – it is just the polar opposite of the scientist.

Science tries to demystify existence, and the mystic tries to destroy all demystifications – and to uncover the mystery again, in its immense beauty and glory, in its wonder, and in its splendor. The mystic's work is of a totally different dimension. It is not of the brain, not of the mind – it is beyond the capacity of both.

Meditation is the way to go beyond the mind and to enter the dimension of the unknowable. And because science is not willing to accept the unknowable, it is harming the whole of humanity. Unless you accept the possibility of the unknowable, meditation is meaningless. Meditation gains meaning only if there is the third category of the unknowable, because meditation is a means to the unknowable.

If you deny the unknowable from the very beginning, you are not going to accept even the possibility of meditation. And this is the blindness of science. In other words, this is scientific superstition. Man has suffered long from religious superstitions; now he is suffering from scientific superstitions. My work is to rid man of all superstitions: scientific, religious, political. Whatever their name may be, a superstition is a superstition.

Science has no reasons, no arguments, no evidence to deny meditation, but it still goes on denying it. Its very denial is so unscientific, so laughable, so ridiculous. The scientist does not understand a very simple phenomenon: that by denying meditation, by denying the unknowable, he is denying himself.

The New Dawn
Osho

A Note about Language

Spoken Words: Osho's books are not "written" but rather are transcribed from recordings of his talks. These talks are extemporaneous, without reference to notes other than copies of questions, stories or scriptures he has been asked to comment upon, or jokes he might use to drive home a particular point. He has asked his editors to preserve that quality of the spoken word in his printed books.

Pronouns: When hearing him speak, it is quite clear to the listener that generally when Osho talks about "man" he is referring to "human beings." His use of "he" as a default pronoun simply serves an ease and flow of speaking – in no way does it imply that "she" (or "they") is being dismissed or disregarded.

Osho's unique vantage point is good to keep in mind:

A meditator is neither a man nor a woman,
because meditation has nothing to do with your body;
neither does it have anything to do with your mind.
In meditation you are simply and purely consciousness.
And consciousness is neither male nor female.

– Osho

1

Expressing the Ultimate Experience

Osho,
Would you like to say something about the famous Tibetan mantra: *om mani padme hum*?

Tibet is the only country in the world which has devoted all its genius to the inner exploration. Its findings are of tremendous value. *Om mani padme hum* is one of the most beautiful expressions for the ultimate experience. Its meaning is "the sound of silence, the diamond in the lotus."

Silence also has its sound, its music – although the outer ears cannot hear it, just as the outer eyes cannot see it. We have six outer senses. In the past, man knew only that we have five outer senses; the sixth is a new discovery. It is inside your ears; hence people failed to recognize it. It is the sense of balance. And it is the sense of balance that is affected when you feel giddy or when you see a drunkard walking.

Just as these six senses are used to experience the outer, exactly the same six senses exist to experience the inner – to see it, to hear it, to feel its utter balance, its beauty. It is invisible to the outer eyes, but not to the inner. You cannot touch it with your outer senses, but the inner senses are absolutely immersed in it.

Om is the sound when everything else disappears from your being – no thoughts, no dreams, no projections, no expectations, not even a single ripple – and your whole lake of consciousness is simply silent; it has become just a mirror. In those rare moments you hear the sound of silence. It is the most valuable experience because it not only shows the quality of the inner music – it also shows that the inner is full of harmony, joy, blissfulness. All that is implied in the music of om.

You are not to say it. If you say it, you will miss the real thing. You have to hear it, you have to be utterly calm and quiet and suddenly it is all around you, a very subtle dance. And the moment you are able to hear it, you have entered the very secrets of existence. You have become so subtle that now you deserve that all the mysteries are exposed to you. Existence waits till you are ready. In the East all the religions without exception agree on this point, that the sound which is heard in the final, highest peak of silence is something similar to om.

The word *om* is not written alphabetically in any language of the East because it is not part of language. It is written as a symbol; hence the same symbol is used in Sanskrit, Pali, Prakrit, Tibetan. It is the same symbol everywhere because all the mystics of all the ages have reached the same experience: that it is not part of our mundane world; hence it should not be written in alphabetical letters. It should have its own symbol which is beyond language. It does not mean anything as far as the mind is concerned, but it means a tremendous amount as far as your spiritual growth is concerned.

All music, particularly classical music, has been trying to catch the sound of silence, so that even people who have not entered their being can experience something similar. But similar is not the same, it is a very faraway echo. Even the greatest musician has to use sounds, but however beautifully he arranges them, he cannot be absolutely silent. He gives gaps of silence in between; the whole play is between sound and silence. Those who don't understand hear the sounds, and those who understand hear the silence: the gaps between two sounds. The real music is in the gaps.

It is not created by the musician – the musician is creating the sounds and leaving the gaps as a contrast, so that you can experience something of what happens to the mystic in his inner world. Om is one of the great achievements of the seekers of truth. There have been cases which are absolutely unbelievable, but they are historical...

When Marpa, a Tibetan mystic, died, his closest disciples were sitting all around him – because the death of a mystic is as tremendously valuable as his life, perhaps more. If you can be close to the mystic when he is dying, you can experience many things because his whole consciousness is leaving the body. And if you are alert and conscious, you can feel a new fragrance, you can see a new light, you can hear a new music.

Marpa was living in a temple when he died. On his death all his disciples became suddenly surprised; they looked all around – where is the sound of om coming from? Finally they realized that it was not coming from anywhere – it was coming from Marpa! They heard it by putting their ears to his feet, to his hands, and they could not believe that inside his whole body there was a vibration creating the sound of om. Since he became enlightened, he had been hearing that sound his whole life. And because of his constant inner experience of the sound, the sound had even entered his physical cells. Every fiber of his body had learned a certain synchronicity, the same wavelength.

It has also been experienced by other mystics. The inner starts radiating, particularly at the moment of death when everything comes to a crescendo. But man is so blind and so utterly unintelligent: knowing that the mystics experience the music of silence within them and they name it om, people started repeating om as a mantra, thinking that by repeating it they will also be able to hear it.

By repeating it you will never be able to hear it. Your mind is functioning when you are repeating it. But perhaps I am the first person to tell you this; otherwise for centuries people have been teaching, "Repeat om." That creates a false experience, and you can be lost in the false and you will never discover the real.

I say to you not to repeat it, but simply be silent and *listen* to it. As your mind becomes calm and quiet, suddenly you will become aware that like a whisper, om is arising within your being. When it arises on its own, it has a totally different quality. It transforms you.

Modern physics says that everything in the world is constituted of electrical energy. According to modern physics, even sounds are nothing but electric waves. The physicists have been working from the outside. The mystics say just the opposite, but I don't see that they are contradictory. They say that the whole existence is made up of the soundless sound om. And even electricity or fire are nothing but a certain condensed form of the sound.

In the East it has been known that there have been musicians who could create a flame on an unlit candle with their music. As the music falls over the unlit candle suddenly the flame arises. It was a test in the ancient days that unless a musician could create light, fire, flame, with his music he was still amateur. He was not recognized as a master.

The explanations of physics and the mystics look different, but perhaps there is some deeper source which can withdraw the contradiction and opposition. Perhaps it is only a different interpretation because the mystic is coming from the inside and the physicist is looking at the outside. What the physicist feels as electricity, the mystic feels as the music of the whole existence. They are both saying the same thing in different languages. If there is a choice, I would choose the mystic because he is experiencing it in his very center. His experience is not just an experiment on objects, his experience is an experiment on his own consciousness. And consciousness is the very cream of existence.

This mantra has many secrets in it. The first wordless word is *om*, and the last is *hum*. The first is the flowering and the last is the seed.

The Sufis don't use the whole name of Allah – that is the Mohammedan name for God. They simply use "Allah Hoo!" and slowly, slowly they change "Allah Hoo!" into simply "Hoo, Hoo!" They have found that the sound of "Hoo!" strikes exactly at the life source just below the navel. You were connected with your life, with your mother from the navel. Just below the navel is the source of your own life.

Just try: when you say "Hoo!" the hit is below the navel. That's what we are using in our Dynamic Meditation. It is a Sufi discovery, but it can also be done in the Tibetan way. Rather than "Hoo!" – "Hoo!" seems to be a little harsh – "Hum!" seems to be a little softer. But the softer will take a longer time to wake your energies up. It is possible that in the particular climate of Tibet, the softer was perfectly good. They did not need such a harsh sound in order to hit the life source. But in the harsh desert of Arabia is where Sufi mystics started using "Hoo!"

When I was working on the Dynamic Meditation, I had a choice to use "Hum!" or "Hoo!" I tried both and found that perhaps in India, "Hoo!" is better than in the colder heights of Tibet where things are bound to be different. Just "Hum!" is perfectly right for them. "Hum!" is the hit to create om in you.

If you hit the seed of your life, it starts disappearing into the soil and green leaves, sprouts start growing. Between the two – *om* and *hum* – is *mani padme*. I don't think anyone has been able to express the ultimate experience, the ultimate beatitude, better than *mani padme*. You have to visualize it. The lotus flower in the East is the biggest, most beautiful flower. And if you put diamonds on the lotus flower in the early morning sun, you will have a tremendously beautiful experience: the lotus flower with diamonds.

It is very difficult to say anything about the ultimate experience, but Tibetan mystics have tried the best. Many things have been said about it, but "diamond on the lotus" seems to be the best expression. Because it is the greatest, most beautiful experience, and they have chosen two of the most beautiful things of the ordinary world: the lotus and the diamond. It is just a visual expression of the beauty that you come to see within yourself.

This mantra *om mani padme hum* has a whole philosophy within it. Start with *hum*, the last word, and the first will arise on its own accord. And when your inner being is filled with the sound of silence, you will also have the beautiful experience of seeing a lotus with a diamond in the early morning sun. The diamond is radiating. The lotus is so soft, so feminine, so delicate – it has no comparison with any other flower. It became so important to the mystics.

You must have seen Gautam Buddha's statues sitting on a lotus. They are showing symbolically that he has reached the ultimate; his own inner lotus has flowered. And not only the lotus has flowered, the diamond hidden behind it, inside it – as it opens its petals, you find a Kohinoor. The diamond has a quality, that's why it has been chosen. It is symbolic of eternity. The diamond is forever, it knows no death; it is immortal. The experience is beautiful and eternal.

Unfortunately, Tibet has fallen into darkness. Its monasteries have been closed, its seekers of truth have been forced to work in labor camps. The only country in the world which was working – a one-pointed genius, all its intelligence in the search for one's own interiority and its treasures – has been stopped by the communist invasion of Tibet.

And it is such an ugly world that no one has objected to it. On the contrary, because China is big and powerful, even countries which are more powerful than China can ever be, like America, have accepted that Tibet belongs to China. That is sheer nonsense – just because China is powerful and everyone wants China to be on their side. Neither the Soviets nor America have challenged the claim of China. Leave America and the Soviets aside – even India has not objected. It was such a beautiful experiment, and Tibet had no weapons to fight with, no army to fight; they had never thought about it. Their whole thing was an introverted pilgrimage.

Nowhere has such a concentrated effort been made to discover man's being. Every family in Tibet used to give their eldest son to some monastery where he would meditate and grow closer to awakening. It was a joy to every family that at least one of them was wholeheartedly, twenty-four hours a day, working on the inner being. The family was working, so they could not give all their time; they had to create food, clothes, shelter, and in Tibet it is a difficult matter. The climate is not very helpful; to live in Tibet is a tremendous struggle. But still every family used to give their first-born child to the monastery.

There were hundreds of monasteries. And those monasteries should not be compared with any Catholic monasteries. Those monasteries had no comparison in the whole world; they were concerned with only one thing: to make you aware of yourself. Thousands of devices have been created down the centuries so that your lotus can blossom and you can find your ultimate treasure – the diamond. These are just symbolic words, but the destruction of Tibet should be known in history, particularly when man becomes a little more aware and humanity a little more humane.

The greatest calamity of the twentieth century is that Tibet has fallen into the hands of materialists who don't believe that you have anything inside you. They believe that you are only matter and your consciousness is only a by-product of matter. And all this is simply without any experience of the inner – just logical, rational philosophizing.

Not a single communist in the world has meditated, but it is strange that they all deny the inner. No one thinks about how the outer can exist if there is no inner. They exist together, they are inseparable. The outer is only a protection for the inner because the inner is very delicate and soft. But the outer is accepted and the inner is denied. And even if sometimes it is accepted, the world is dominated by such dirty politicians that they use even the inner experiences for ugly ends.

Just the other day, I came to know that America is now training its soldiers in meditation so that they can fight without having a nervous breakdown, without going mad, without feeling any fear – so they can lie down in their ditches silently, calm, cool and collected. No meditator may have ever thought that meditation can be used for fighting wars, but in the hands of politicians everything becomes ugly – even meditation. Now the army camps in America are teaching meditation so that their soldiers can be more calm and quiet while killing people.

But I want to warn America: you are playing with fire. You don't understand exactly what meditation will do. Your soldiers will become so calm and quiet that they will throw away their weapons and they will simply refuse to kill. A meditator cannot kill; a meditator cannot be destructive. So one day they are going to be surprised that their soldiers are no longer interested in fighting. If a man knows something of meditation, war, violence, murder, the massacre of millions of people is not possible. Then he also knows not only himself, he knows the other whom he is killing. He is his brother. They all belong to the same oceanic existence.

The Soviet Union is also interested in meditation. But the purpose is the same – not realization of yourself, but making you stronger so that you can kill and bomb, use nuclear weapons and missiles to kill whole nations. But unknowingly, they are both going on a dangerous path. It is good, they should be helped. Once meditation spreads among their soldiers, those soldiers will become sannyasins! So I am immensely happy that although their idea is different, they don't know anything about meditation. They have only heard that it makes people calm and cool so they can fight without any fear, without looking back. Meditation gives them a feeling of immortality; hence their fear will disappear.

But meditation not only gives them the experience of their own immortality – it also gives them the experience that *everyone* is immortal. Death is a fiction. Why unnecessarily harass people? They will be living, you cannot kill them. Not even your nuclear weapons are going to kill them. In the Gita, Krishna has a beautiful statement: "*Nainam chhindanti shastrani; Naham dahati pavakahr.* Neither can any weapon destroy me nor can any fire burn me." Yes the body will be burned, but I am not the body. Meditation gives you the feel, for the first time, of your authentic reality.

If humanity were a little more aware, Tibet should be made free again because it is the only country which has devoted almost two thousand years to doing nothing but going deeper into meditation. And it can teach the whole world something which is immensely needed.

But Communist China is trying to destroy everything that has been created in two thousand years. All Tibet's devices, all their methods of meditation, their whole spiritual climate is being polluted, poisoned. And they are simple people; they cannot defend themselves. They don't have anything to defend themselves with – no tanks, bombs, airplanes, army. An innocent race which has lived without any war for two thousand years. It disturbs no one; it is so far away from everyone that even to reach there is a difficult task. They live on the very roof of the world. The highest mountains, eternal snows, are their home. Leave them alone! China will not lose anything, but the whole world will be benefited by their experience.

And the world will *need* their experience. The world is getting fed up with money, power, prestige, all that scientific technology has created – people are getting fed up. They are finished with it. People in the advanced countries are no longer interested in sex, are no longer interested in drugs. Things are falling away, and a strange despair like a dark cloud is descending on the advanced countries – one of deep frustration, meaninglessness, anguish. They all need a different climate of meditation to dispel all these clouds and bring a new day into their lives again – a new dawn, a new experience of themselves, a discovery of their original being.

Tibet should be left as an experimental lab for man's inner search. But not a single nation in the world has raised its voice against this ugly attack on Tibet. And China has not only attacked it, they have amalgamated it into their map. Now, on the modern Chinese map, Tibet is their territory.

And we think the world is civilized, where innocent people who are not doing any harm to anyone are simply destroyed. And with them, something of great importance to all humanity is also destroyed. If there were something civilized in man, every nation would have stood against the invasion of Tibet by China. It is the invasion of matter against consciousness; it is the invasion of materialism against spiritual heights.

The word *mantra* is untranslatable in English, in any Western language, but its meaning, its significance, can be explained to you. A mantra is not just something to chant. It is not chanting. A mantra is something to let sink deep in your being, just as roots go deep in the earth. The deeper the roots go in the earth, the higher the tree will go in the sky. A mantra is something like a seed to be allowed to go deep in your being, so that it can send its roots to the sources of your life and finally to the universal life. Then its branches, its foliage will go high in the sky, and when the right time comes, when the spring comes, it will be filled with thousands of flowers.

Unless a tree blossoms, it knows no blissfulness. It goes on feeling something is missing. You may have all the pleasures, comforts, luxuries of the world, but unless you know yourself, unless your inner lotus opens, you will go on missing something. You may not be certain what you are missing but a feeling that something is being missed, that "I am not complete," that "I am not whole," that "I am not what existence wanted me to be." This "missing" feeling goes on nagging everyone. Only the expansion of your consciousness will help you to get rid of this feeling, this nagging, this anguish, this angst.

Even people like Jaspers, Kierkegaard, Heidegger, Marcel, Jean-Paul Sartre, the highest geniuses of the West, are agreed on a few things: that life is nothing but boredom, anxiety, anguish, that life is accidental, it has no significance; that it is absolutely futile to search for any blissful space because there exists none. And when great philosophers like these agree on such points, the ordinary masses simply follow them.

Whatever they are saying is absolutely wrong because none of them has ever meditated, none of them has entered his own subjectivity. They are just in their heads. They have not even moved to their hearts, what to say about their being? What to say about their disappearing into the universal?

Unless you disappear into the universal ocean just like a dewdrop, you will not find significance. You will not find your real dignity. You will not find that existence showers so much joy and so much celebration on you that you cannot contain it; you have to share it. You become a rain cloud which is so burdened with rain that it has to shower. A man of deep insight, a man of intuition, a man who has reached his being becomes a rain cloud. He is not just a blessing to himself, he becomes a blessing to the whole world.

This Tibetan mantra *om mani padme hum* is a condensed form of the whole inner pilgrimage. It says how to start, what will happen when the flower opens, and what will be your ultimate experience of your inner treasures.

Eastern languages are very rich in the sense that they have made very condensed statements which can be unfolded into big scriptures. The reason was that when these mantras were created there was no writing. People had to remember them. When people have to remember them, you have to be very telegraphic, as condensed as possible. Once writing came into existence, that condensedness disappeared. Now you can explain with page after page of writing. But have you ever thought that when you receive a long letter, the longer the letter, the less is the meaning? But when you receive a telegram, naturally, just eight or ten words, the meaning is immense and the impact is immense. These are telegrams. They can easily be remembered, they can be passed from one generation to another generation without any fear that they will be distorted.

You have not to repeat the mantra, you have to understand its meaning and let that meaning sink in you. Sitting silently, be utterly quiet, unmoving. Watch your mind. A few thoughts will be there, but as you become silent those thoughts will disappear, and suddenly you hear a humming sound all around you. That humming sound is not made by you. It is at the very center of existence. It is the sound of the skies. It is the sound of space. It is the sound of the universe; it is its indication of aliveness. It is vibrating with dance and music. This om is perhaps the greatest symbol in the whole world.

> Osho,
> Can it be that crying is my celebration at the moment? When I look at you, my heart is turning inside out and a whole monsoon is breaking loose, leaving me helpless. Who is it that is crying?

It looks a little strange but it is true: you can transform anything into a celebration. Just as you can transform any celebration into a miserable affair – it all depends on you.

I have heard…

In a small school the drawing teacher made a painting on the board. He was a good painter, and he was showing his students that just by a little touch the artist can change the whole meaning of the painting. It was a portrait of a man, very sad. He touched the lips and immediately the sadness disappeared from the painting – the man was smiling. And as the man started smiling, the whole painting had a different perspective.

Just then a little boy stood up and said, "This is nothing."

The painter said, "What do you mean by saying that this is nothing?"

He said, "My mother, just by giving me a slap, changes the whole world! I may be smiling and when she hits I start crying, and when I look all around it looks so sad. You need a brush and the painting and all this; my mother needs nothing."

You are saying, "Can it be that crying is my celebration...?" If you feel blissful in crying, there is no harm. It is perfectly beautiful. Tears can be of joy, of love. Tears can show that you are overfilled with something that starts flowing through the tears. It need not be sadness, it need not be mourning; it can be festivity. It all depends on you. And you have to feel what it is because you will be absolutely certain whether your tears are coming out of frustration, sadness, failure, or they are coming out of love, joy, gratitude, prayer. Tears are one of the most mysterious things you have. They can have all the colors of the rainbow. It depends on your consciousness what colors you give them.

I have heard a very beautiful story...

It is Julius Caesar's birthday, and after breakfast the Roman senators are eager for him to take a chariot ride with them to view their present to him.

Caesar is delighted to find the whole of the driveway to the imperial palace is lined with crucified Christians. As they drive along, Caesar brings the procession to a sudden halt. "That man there!" he cries. "He must be alive – his lips are moving. I want to hear what he is saying."

The senators raise Caesar on their shoulders. "Closer, closer!" he shouts. "I can't hear."

Finally, with his ear almost touching the man's lips, he hears, "Happy birthday to you."

One can change every situation. Now he is being crucified, but he has no complaint. Within minutes he may be dead, but his heart wants to say, "Happy birthday to you."

And he must have embarrassed Caesar; he must have created a deep impression on him. From that day onward, Christians were not crucified again in Caesar's time. He felt so humble. He felt so sorry about what he was doing to these beautiful people, who are capable of rejoicing in his birthday and they are being crucified as a present. It all depends on you.

Old man Finkelstein suspects that his butler has been stealing cigars and shouts to him in the next room, "James, you have been stealing my cigars." There is no answer so he repeats it louder. There is still no answer, so he goes into the next room and confronts his servant. "James," he says, "didn't you hear me speaking to you just now?"

"No, sir," replies the butler, "there must be something wrong with the acoustics."

"Really," says Finkelstein. "Well, you go next door and say something and we will see whether I can hear it."

James goes into the next room and yells out at the top of his voice, "Some fat son-of-a-bitch has been screwing around with my wife."

He then returns. "Did you hear me, sir?" he asks nonchalantly.

"You are right, James" replies Finkelstein, blushing, "I could not hear a word. Have a cigar."

If you are feeling blissful, peaceful, silent in your crying, in your tears, and if after the tears you feel relaxed, relieved of some burden, it is perfectly good. Don't try to stop it because humanity has been given such wrong training about so many things that it has not left any human being natural. Everyone has become artificial, and particularly men. Every society has forced them not to cry, saying that it is against your manliness.

It is okay for women to cry and weep. They don't belong to your status, they are second-class citizens. But you, being first class, should show your strength. Your tears expose your weakness. But if you go on for thousands of years teaching every child such nonsense, he starts holding his tears back. No one wants to be exposed as a weakling. But the simple truth is that nature has given you exactly the same glands for tears as nature has given to women.

And if nature is listened to, then stopping your tears is a dangerous thing. It is not only tears that will be stopped – you will become less sensitive, you will become less loving. You will become harder, you will become cruel, you will become a sadist. This will be the outcome of a simple thing. You will go neurotic, psychotic. Four times more men end up in insane asylums than women. The reason being that women know how to cry and weep. They know how to let their burdens and tensions be relieved through tears. Man goes on accumulating and one day it is too much. Either he jumps from a sixty-story building and finishes himself off…

But there are strange people…

A man jumped from the eightieth floor and passed the window where one of his friends was standing. The friend said, "Goodbye," and the man also waved his hand. And soon he was flat on the ground, finished.

People came running to his friend and said, "Have you seen anything?"

He said, "Yes."

They said, "Your friend has committed suicide!"

He said, "This is strange because just a few minutes before, he was perfectly okay. While he was passing my window, we even said hello to each other."

Man has been prevented from being natural so that he can be made into a soldier, into a harder personality, so he can be made to compete in the world. There was no need for the woman because she wasn't going to compete in the world, and she wasn't going to wars either. She could be allowed to cry and weep. It became a distinction that it is manly not to weep, not to cry. It is simply against nature. Women don't go so mad because in their tears they are throwing away all their tensions. They don't accumulate to such a point that it is beyond their capacity to control it and everything goes through a breakdown.

Exactly four times more men commit suicide, although at least forty times more women threaten to commit suicide. But they don't. Women have remained, in a way, closer to nature because they were deprived from participating in man's power struggle. This curse proved a blessing in disguise. Man made himself more and more tense, neurotic. And there comes a point where life becomes so heavy, each moment such a torture, that it is better to commit suicide.

Women just talk about it. Even if sometimes they try to commit suicide with sleeping pills – not jumping from buildings because that is dangerous – they will take just a few which will be enough to harass the husband. And will make him more henpecked because he will remain always alert that the whole neighborhood condemns him saying, "You must be treating your wife badly; otherwise why does she try to commit suicide?" The doctor is angry, and the wife is enjoying a good sleep! Once in a while a woman, just by mistake, takes too many pills. It is not really the intention, just a mistake.

It is good to enjoy your tears. And don't keep them only for tensions, anxieties, frustrations, moments of sadness. No, that is using them in a wrong way. Use them when you are in love. Use them when you are feeling peaceful. Use them when you see a beautiful sunset. What can be said to a sunset? It won't understand any language. But perhaps your tears will be understood. When you see a beautiful flower, how can you resist having a few tears that existence is so beautiful? If you see a Gautam Buddha and you don't have tears in your eyes, then you are behaving inhumanly, unnaturally. Seeing Gautam Buddha, you should be in such a celebration – at least one of us has reached the ultimate potential of his being, and he is a proof that we can also reach.

You are also saying, "When I look at you, my heart is turning inside out and a whole monsoon is breaking loose, leaving me helpless. Who is it that is crying?" – it is your original being. The false never cries. The hypocrite never cries. It is only the original, the authentic.

This is the whole purpose of the communion that is happening here: to fall in a synchronicity with my heart. Naturally your heart will have to change. It will have to take a new rhythm, a new harmony, a new wavelength. And it is natural to feel helpless because you have been told that tears are a sign of weakness, helplessness. Tears are your strength, not helplessness. Tears show that you are alive, that you have not shrunk and lost all your juice. Tears show that your heart still feels, still can dance, still can rejoice.

There is a statue of Mahavira in Rajasthan. It is very famous because it is made of a very strange stone which is not found in India, but is found in Africa. Someone must have brought that stone. But in India it has become a miracle because when it is hot it perspires; tears flow from the eyes. Naturally, the people who follow Mahavira are deeply impressed. They think perhaps he is weeping for us out of compassion.

One woman came to me and said, "I have never been impressed by anything so much as the tears coming from a stone statue of Mahavira."

I said, "You don't understand; I have seen the statue." The statue is in the middle of the lake; there is a small temple, an open temple, just pillars. And because the statue is porous, when the vapors are rising from the lake because of the hot sun – and Rajasthan is very hot, it is a desert – that porous statue goes on soaking up much of the vapor that is moving around. In summer, you will not find that statue with tears or perspiration or anything, but in winter when it is cold the vapors that it has soaked up start becoming water again. Because of the coldness, the water starts coming out of the rock.

I said to the woman, "You are impressed by it, and you are not impressed by millions of people who cry? And that stone is not doing anything as far as compassion is concerned; it is just that this kind of stone is not available in India."

She was very shocked because I hurt her religious feelings. I said, "I am not hurting your religious feelings. I am simply making you aware that if you can be so much impressed by the tears of a stone statue, what about living human beings?"

But tears are taboo. It is one of the things that have been repressed. Friedrich Nietzsche is quoted as saying that he smiles because he is afraid if he does not smile he will start crying and tears will come to his eyes. His smile is just a protection; it keeps him occupied. He remains with a false smile so that authentic tears cannot come out. Naturally, for a German, it is a question of manliness. How can a German cry and weep and have tears?

But, more or less, all men around the world are Germans. They are all male-oriented, trying to impose a supremacy of men over women. But I say unto you that your tears are far more valuable than man's domination. His supremacy is nothing. He has suffered much because of this stupid attitude. Allow those tears. They are not of helplessness, they are of tremendous joy.

And you ask, "Who is it that is crying?" – it is you in your originality, not you in your personality.

"I am leaving home," shouts Giovanni to his parents. "I want wine, women, adventure."

His old father gets up out of his chair.

"And don't you try to stop me," cries Giovanni.

"Who's trying to stop you?" exclaims the old man. "I'm coming with you!"

Just be a little more understanding of all your sentiments, emotions; they all have a certain place in the total harmony of your being. But we have been kept almost blind to our own potentialities, dimensions. Be a little more alert about everything, and remember that the natural is the superior and the unnatural is phony and American.

Rabbi Finklebaum had never gambled in his life, so one day he went to the horse races just for the experience. Before the first race he saw a priest making some strange sign over a horse and then watched the priest put ten dollars on the horse to win. And sure enough, the horse won the race. So he followed the priest and watched him make signs over another horse. This time the rabbi ran off and put fifty dollars on the horse and it won at ten to one.

Again he followed the priest and saw him make weird signs over another horse, so he went off and put all the five hundred dollars he had won on the previous race on this horse. He ran up into the stand to watch the race, hoping to make a fortune, but this time the horse he had backed fell at the first fence and died.

The rabbi ran off and found the priest. "Look here," said the rabbi, "what was the meaning of all that? The first two horses you made signs over won, and then the third one fell at the first fence and I lost all my money. What is going on?"

"I am sorry, rabbi," said the priest, "but I can't help it if you don't know the difference between a blessing and the last rites."

There is so much misunderstanding. You don't know what is real, what is unreal. You don't know what has been imposed on you by others and what you have brought from existence itself as a gift.

You have to discriminate, and always choose the natural. Even if it goes against all traditions, all religions, all cultures, don't be worried. Except the natural, there is no authentic religiousness anywhere. Except the existential, there is nothing holy that you can find in the Bible, the Koran, the Gita. Just watch – inside you is nature, inside you is the existential. Always follow it and you will never go wrong. The only authentic spirituality is to be natural, is to be in tune with existence.

2

Oneness, Bliss, and Gratitude

Osho,
Is blissfulness an expression of gratitude toward existence?

It is just the reverse. Blissfulness is not an expression of gratitude; on the contrary, gratitude is an expression of blissfulness. First comes the experience of bliss. First you attain the state of consciousness where ecstasy is natural, where your potential blossoms to its ultimate expression. A great dance arises in you, a tremendous peace and a deep silence – but it is not the silence of the graveyard, it is a silence fully alive, throbbing with a heartbeat. This whole experience is bliss. And because of this bliss that existence makes available to you, a feeling of gratitude, a thankfulness arises.

To me, this is the only authentic prayer. Not the prayers that are done in the churches, synagogues, temples, before stone statues of gods – those prayers are full of greed. They are asking for something; in other words they are complaining about something. Something is wrong in life and the god should put it right. There is no gratitude in those prayers; on the contrary, they are absolute indicators of ungratefulness.

The moment you ask for something, you are saying that what you deserve has not been given to you, that what is your birthright has not been fulfilled. You are throwing the responsibility upon existence. Rather than being grateful for what has been given to you, you are showing ungratefulness for what your greed demands, what your ambition demands, what your desires are manipulating you toward. The prayers in the so-called temples of God are not true prayers. They are full of your greed, desire, lust.

The authentic prayer arises only to the meditator. It is not toward a God – which is only a hypothesis; there is no proof for any God. Yes, there is absolute proof for godliness: a quality of divineness in the sun rising in the morning, in the starry night, in the beautiful flight of a bird on the wing, in the flowers, the trees, the oceans.

All of this vast universe is enough unto itself. It needs no God – God is only a consolation for the ignorant. The meditator encounters existence itself. His own being becomes the experience of godliness. He knows that in his own inner being he is part of eternal life. There is no death, there has never been any death. Experiencing this, there arises a dance so subtle, there arises a deep gratitude, not addressed to anyone in particular but simply addressed to the whole cosmos. It is an unaddressed gratefulness to the stars, the trees, the earth, the moon, the animals, to people. And unless you experience an unaddressed gratefulness, you don't know exactly the meaning of prayer. The word *prayer* gives a wrong connotation; it should be changed into *prayerfulness*, just as I am changing *God* into *godliness*.

H. G. Wells has written one of the most important histories of the world. And when he comes to write about Gautam Buddha, he has a tremendous statement to make. He says, "Gautam Buddha is the most godless person, yet the most godly." Gautam Buddha did not believe in any god, but he believed that everyone can become a god. To be a god is nothing but the realization of your total potential. Your seed is carrying within itself, in its womb, the ultimate flowering of the lotus paradise. There are possibilities of as many gods as there are living beings in existence, if each one comes to its ultimate expression.

The very idea of one God creating the world is dictatorial. It is the fanatic's idea; it is fascist. One God is very dangerous to all democratic values, and once we accept one God as the creator of existence, we are depriving man of his dignity, his freedom. He is reduced to a puppet. If God is the creator, you can't have any freedom. If there is a God who is ruling the world, then what freedom can you have?

In India they say that without God's will even a small leaf does not move. They think they are being very religious when they make such statements. But if without God's will even a leaf of a tree cannot move in the wind, what freedom can you have? Then we are only puppets; our strings are in the hands of an unknown God. If he wants us to be miserable, we will be miserable. If he wants us to be blissful, we will be blissful. It will not be a dignity; it will be simply that everything is in his hands. We remain beggars.

People like Gautam Buddha want you to be emperors. They give you back your dignity, your honor, your self-respect. God and self-respect cannot exist together. There is no coexistence possible.

Gautam Buddha denied God not because he was an atheist; he denied God because he was a lover of ultimate freedom. His denial has a totally different reason. Atheists have been denying God not for the freedom of man, but just to give man a licentiousness: "Eat, drink, be merry because there is no God and you need not be worried. You need not feel any responsibility toward life, toward yourself." Atheists make people irresponsible. They make people synonymous with vegetables. They deny your inner being; they deny your very spirituality.

Gautam Buddha is not an atheist. He is certainly not a theist; he does not propose any hypothetical God who has to be worshipped. On the contrary, he changes the whole dimension of religion. The people who are looking toward a God in the sky are looking outward. Gautam Buddha insists there is no God; there is no need to look outward – look inward. And if you can look inward, with your eyes closed in deep silence, you will start feeling a new quality to your life, to your existence; a quality that can only be called godliness, that can only be called divine – something more than matter. You don't end with matter.

Matter may be the foundation of life, but it is not its highest peak. Matter may be the roots of the tree, but it is not its flowers. And unless you know the flowering consciousness in you, you cannot feel bliss. Bliss is the ultimate experience of coming home, of feeling at ease with existence, relaxed, in a total unity and harmony.

The moment your heartbeat and the heartbeat of existence become one, the moment your small dance is in tune with the vast dance that goes on around you, the moment you become part of this celebration that is existence, there arises a tremendous gratitude. You don't have to do it. You simply find it arising from you, just as fragrance arises from the flowers. It is a spontaneous thing. This is true prayerfulness.

I have told you a beautiful story by Leo Tolstoy…

An archbishop of the Russian Orthodox Church was very angry because thousands of people were going to see three absolutely unknown villagers who lived on a small island in a lake. People thought they were saints.

Now, in Christianity, unless the church certifies you as a saint, you cannot be a saint. This is such a stupidity that you cannot conceive; for centuries this has been going on. In fact, the English word *saint* comes from *sanctus*. It means sanction by the church. Unless the church gives you a sanction… It is almost like getting an honorary DLitt from a university. Sainthood cannot be certified by anyone. There is no one who has the authority to certify anyone's sainthood. Sainthood is, in itself, self-evident. The moment you see it, you know it. The moment you feel it, you know it. It needs no other approval.

But the archbishop was very angry, "Without *my* permission, without *my* sanction, how have three idiots from a village become saints?" And people were not coming to his congregation; they were going to visit those faraway saints. Finally he decided to go and see for himself what was going on. He took a motorboat and reached the small island. It was so small that there was only one tree on the island, but with beautiful foliage, and all three saints were sitting underneath it.

Just by looking at them the archbishop knew, "These are absolutely uneducated villagers – who has created this rumor? How gullible people are that they are worshipping these people? And as he descended from his boat all the three villagers touched his feet. He was immensely happy.

He said, "Are you the three priests the whole country is talking about?"

They said, "We don't know. People come to us, we cannot prevent them coming. All we know is that we are absolutely contented. All we know is that there is no longer any desire, no longer any ambition. Life is just a tremendous blessing, and we are enjoying it. More than that we don't know. We are uneducated, we are villagers."

The archbishop was very happy. He said, "What kind of prayer do you do?"

Those three saints looked at each other ashamed, embarrassed. Finally one said, "It was not much of a prayer. We have created it by ourselves. We don't know what the authorized prayer of the church is, but we will tell you whatever we have been doing."

Christianity believes in the trinity of God – that God is the Father, the Son and the Holy Ghost, three together. And those three villagers said, "Thinking that he is three and we are also three, we have made our prayer: 'You are three, we are three, have mercy on us!' More than that we don't know."

The archbishop was very angry, "This is not the right thing for a Christian to do! How dare you create such a stupid prayer? I will tell you the authorized version which the church accepts."

They said, "We will be very grateful, but make it a little short because we are uneducated and we cannot remember anything long."

The archbishop said, "You will *have* to remember it!"

They said, "We will try if you insist."

The archbishop recited the whole prayer. It was *really* long, and when he had said the whole prayer one of the three said, "You will have to repeat it at least three times because we are three. Be kind and compassionate so we can remember it."

He repeated it three times, they listened silently and the archbishop was very happy. They touched his feet again and he said, "You are nice people, but remember the prayer that I have taught you." And then he left in his motorboat.

When he was just in the middle of the lake he saw something almost like a cloud, running toward the boat. He could not believe what was happening. He saw the three saints coming toward him, running on the lake. They said, "Wait! We have forgotten the prayer, so we thought it would be better to catch hold of you and ask you to repeat it at least three times more; have mercy on us."

But seeing them walking on water, the archbishop thought, "Perhaps I have unnecessarily disturbed these beautiful people."

He said, "Forgive me for interfering. Continue your old prayer, which has been heard. My prayer has not been heard yet. My prayer is nothing but my intellectual approach to a hypothetical God. Your prayer comes from your very heart. Your prayer is not to ask for something, your prayer is just a thankfulness because you are feeling so contented. You don't have anything, but you have tremendous contentment. Your bliss is enough. Whatever way you want to give thanks is up to you. There is no need for you to know about the authorized prayer. On the contrary, I'm feeling miserable. In reading the holy scriptures, in learning and accumulating knowledge, I have missed my whole life. But I cannot walk on water. Your simple prayer has been heard."

This small story from Leo Tolstoy has always appealed to me tremendously. The implications of the story are great. You need not believe in God to be religious. First you have to be religious to know something about godliness. All the religions are putting the bullock behind the cart. Hence the whole of humanity is suffering – no movement, no progress, no spiritual growth.

Your religiousness, your blissfulness, your meditativeness, your experience of your own interiority, your own subjectivity – and coming to the very center of the cyclone, you will be able to dance a prayer, to sing a prayer. It need not be anything intellectual; it has to be something coming spontaneously from your being. It will be a simple thank-you. And not to any personal god because there is no personal god – a thank-you to the whole universe. The whole universe is intelligent. The whole universe is divine.

You are asking, "Is blissfulness an expression of gratitude toward existence?" – no, it is just vice versa: gratitude is an expression of blissfulness. Without knowing bliss, how can you be grateful? Grateful for what? Put things right: first, search for those rare moments when you are in tune with existence, and seek the inner path so that you can know who you are. Knowing oneself is the whole of religion. Anything else is just a footnote.

The essential religion is simply expressed by Socrates in two words: "Know thyself." In fact, within these two words are included all the holy scriptures of the world and all the mystical experiences of people who have come to know themselves. The moment you know yourself, you have known the most precious thing in existence – your consciousness, your bliss. And you have known the most beautiful, almost unbelievable experience – what we were talking about this morning: *om mani padme hum*. You have come to experience something which can only be called "the sound of silence, the diamond in the lotus" – an experience of a beauty which cannot be seen with open eyes, a sound of silence which cannot be heard by your outer ears. But at the very center it is already present; you just have to go there.

I teach you not to be bothered by any scriptures, by any churches, by any philosophical or theological systems. Religion is a very simple and humble affair. Just go withinward. Know thyself; be thyself. And all blessings will shower on you, as if thousands of roses are showering. Only out of that experience will gratitude arise. Gratitude is not possible before experiencing something of the ultimate.

> Osho,
> Experiencing headache, I discovered my male nature. Experiencing heartache, I discovered my female nature. Is there also going to be a being-ache?

There is no such thing as being-ache. The being knows superb wholeness, health. It knows no disease, no sickness, no death. To go beyond your head and your heart is to transcend the duality of existence. This transcendence brings you to your being.

Being simply means you have dropped the ego that was part of your head. You have even dropped the separation, very subtle and delicate, that was part of your heart; you have dropped all barriers between you and the whole. Suddenly the dewdrop has slipped from the lotus leaf into the ocean. It has become one with it. In a sense you are no more and in a sense you are for the first time. As a dewdrop you are no more, but as the ocean you *are* for the first time, and this is your nature.

One of the great psychologists, William James, has contributed tremendously by coining a new word for spiritual experience – the "oceanic" experience. He is perfectly right. It is the experience of expansion, all boundaries disappearing farther and farther and farther away. A moment comes when you don't see any boundaries to you; you become the ocean itself. You are, but you are no longer in a prison. You are, but you are no longer in a cage. You have come out of the cage, you have come out of the prison, and you are flying in the sky in total freedom.

Remember one thing: a bird on the wing and the same bird in the cage are not the same at all. The bird in the cage is no longer the same because it has lost its freedom, it has lost its tremendous sky. It has lost the joy of dancing in the wind, in the rain, in the sun. You may have given it a golden cage but you have destroyed its dignity, its freedom, its joy. You have reduced it to a prisoner – it looks like the same bird but it is not. A man confined to the boundaries of the mind, the heart, the body is imprisoned, walls upon walls.

In the last prison where I was in America they had three doors. It was the most technologically modern, ultramodern; the first jail of its kind made in America. It had been opened for just three months. Everything was electronic. Those three doors were almost impossible for any human being to cross. First they were all electrified – just to touch them was enough and you would be dead. They were so high that no ladder or anything else was possible to get over them. And one after another, three in all.

They opened only by using a remote control, which my jailer used to keep in his car. He would press the button, and the first gate would open. It was almost like a mountain, so big, so high, and as the car entered, it would have to wait for the first door to come down. Only when the first door had come down would the remote control work on the second door. And when the second door had come down, the remote control would work on the third door.

When I entered that jail in Portland for the first time I said to the jailer, "Perhaps you don't know, but you have managed a perfect symbol."

He said, "Symbol of what?"

I said, "This is the situation of man: the body is the first door, the mind the second, and the heart is the third. And then behind these three doors is the poor soul."

He said, "I never thought about it. It must be just coincidence; no one has thought about it, that three doors… Why three? Why not four?" He continued, "But I don't know. I have not made it."

I said to him, "Whoever made it perhaps unconsciously felt something of the symmetry, the correspondence between the imprisonment of human consciousness and being an architect for making a prison for human beings. Once you get beyond the body – which is not very difficult because the body is very beautiful in a way, as it is still in tune with nature. Hence to go beyond it is very easy; it does not give much resistance. It is very cooperative."

The real problem is the mind because the mind is created by human society, and specially designed to keep you a slave. The body has a beauty of its own. It is still part of the trees, the ocean, the mountains, the stars. It has not been polluted by the society. It has not been poisoned by the churches, religions, priests. But the mind has been completely conditioned, distorted, given ideas which are absolutely false. Your mind is functioning almost like a mask and hiding your original face.

To transcend the mind is the whole art of meditation, and the East has devoted almost ten thousand years to a single purpose – all its intelligence and genius – of how to transcend the mind and its conditionings. That whole effort of ten thousand years has culminated in refining the method of meditation.

In a single word, *meditation* means watching the mind, witnessing the mind. If you can witness the mind, just silently looking at it – without any justification, without any appreciation, without any condemnation, with no judgment at all, for or against – simply watching as if you have nothing to do with it. It is just the traffic that goes on in the mind. Stand by the side and watch it. And the miracle of meditation is that just by watching it, it slowly, slowly disappears.

The moment the mind disappears, you come to the last door which is very fragile – and that too is not polluted by the society – your heart. In fact, your heart immediately gives you a way. It never prevents you; almost every moment it is ready for you to come to it and it will open the door toward the being. The heart is your friend.

The head is your enemy. The body is your friend, the heart is your friend, but just in between the two stands the enemy like a Himalaya, a big mountain wall. But it can be crossed over by a simple method. Gautam Buddha called the method *vipassana*.

Patanjali called the method *dhyana*. And the Sanskrit word *dhyana* became, in China, *ch'an* and in Japan it became *zen*. But it is the same word. In English there is not the exact equivalent for *zen* or *dhyana* or *ch'an*. We arbitrarily use the word *meditation*.

But you should remember that whatever meaning is given to the word *meditation* in your dictionaries, is not the meaning as I am using it. All the dictionaries will say *meditation* means thinking about something. Whenever I say to a Western mind, "Meditate" the immediate question is, "On what?" The reason is that in the West, meditation never developed to the point dhyana or *ch'an* or Zen have developed in the East.

Meditation means simply awareness – not thinking about something nor concentrating on something nor contemplating something. The Western word is always concerned with *something*. Meditation as I am using it simply means a state of awareness.

Just like a mirror – do you think a mirror is trying to concentrate on something? Whatever comes before it is reflected, but the mirror is unconcerned. Whether a beautiful or ugly woman comes before it, or no one comes before it, it is absolutely unconcerned; a simple, reflective source. Meditation is only a reflecting awareness. You simply watch whatever comes in front of you. And by this simple watching, the mind disappears. You have heard about miracles, but this is the only miracle. All other miracles are simply stories.

Jesus walking on water, turning water into wine, making dead people come to life again are all beautiful stories. If they are symbolically understood, they have great significance. But if you insist that they are historical facts, you are being simply stupid. Symbolically they are beautiful. Symbolically, every master in the world is bringing people to life who are dead. What am I doing here? – pulling people out of their graves! Jesus pulled Lazarus out after he had been dead only four days. I have been pulling people out who have been dead for years, for lives! And because they have lived in their graves so long they are very reluctant to come out. They give all their resistance – "What are you doing? This is our house! We have lived here peacefully, don't disturb us!"

Symbolically it is right: every master is trying to give you a new life. As you are, you are not really alive. You are just vegetating. If the miracles are interpreted as metaphors, they have a beauty.

I am reminded of a strange story which Christians have completely dropped from their scriptures. But it exists in the Sufi literature. The Sufi story is about Jesus…

Jesus is coming to a town and just as he enters he sees a man whom he recognizes; he had known him before. He was blind and Jesus had cured his eyes. The man was running after a prostitute. Jesus stops the man and asks him, "Do you remember me?"

The man replied, "Yes, I remember you and I can never forgive you! I was blind and I was perfectly happy because I had never seen any beauty. You gave me eyes. Now tell me – what am I to do with these eyes? These eyes are attracted toward beautiful women."

Jesus could not believe it; he was stunned, shocked. "I thought I had done some great service to this man and he is angry! He is saying, 'Before you gave me eyes, I never thought about women, I never thought that there were prostitutes. But since you have given me eyes you have destroyed me.'"

Jesus leaves the man without saying anything; there is nothing to say. And as he moves on he finds another man lying in the gutter, saying all kinds of meaningless things, completely drunk. Jesus pulls him out of the gutter and recognizes that he had given him the use of his legs back. But now he is feeling a little shaky himself. He asks the man, "Do you know me?"

The man says, "Yes, I know you. Even though I am drunk, I cannot forgive you; it is you who disturbed my peaceful life. Without the use of my legs I could not go anywhere. I was a peaceful person – no fighting, no gambling, no question of friends, no question of going to the pub. You gave me the use of my legs back, and since then I have not found a single moment of peacefulness, of sitting silently. I am running after this, after that, and in the end when I am tired I get drunk. And you can see yourself what is happening to me. You are responsible for my situation! You should have told me beforehand that if I was getting the use of my legs back, all these problems were going to arise. You did not warn me. You simply cured me without even asking my permission."

Jesus became so freaked, he left the city. He did not go any further. He said, "No one knows what kind of people I am going to meet." But as he was coming out of the city he saw a man who was trying to hang himself from a tree. He said, "Wait, what are you doing?"

The man said, "You have come again! I was dead, and you forced me to be alive again. Now I don't have employment, my wife has left me because she thinks a man who has died cannot be revived; she thinks I am a ghost. No one wants to meet me. Friends simply don't recognize me. I go into the city and people don't look at me. Now what do you want me to do? And again when I am going to hang myself you are here! What kind of revenge are you taking? Can't you leave me alone? Now I cannot even hang myself. Once I was dead and you revived me – if I hang myself, you are going to revive me again. You are so intent on making miracles, you don't even care who the sufferers of your miracles are!"

When I saw this story, I loved it. Every Christian should know about it.

There is no miracle except one, and that is the miracle of meditation which takes you away from the mind. The heart is always welcoming you. It is always ready to give you a way, to guide you toward your being. And the being is your wholeness, it is your ultimate well-being.

A policeman notices a car weaving dangerously along the road, and when he pulls it over a beautiful woman gets out. She is clearly under the influence of drink but to make sure, the cop gives her a breath test. Sure enough, she is over the limit, so the cop says, "Lady, you have had two or three stiff ones."

"My God," cries the woman, "it shows that too?"

A headache is okay, heartache is okay, but don't go beyond that. Beyond that there is no ache, no pain, no suffering. Beyond the heart is all that you have always longed for knowingly, unknowingly, searched for consciously or unconsciously.

Your journey is long. Christianity, Judaism, Mohammedanism – three religions which were founded outside India – have all committed one great mistake: they have given people the idea that you have only one life. That has created many problems.

In the East all the religions have agreed on one point, that you have been here for thousands of lives; this is not the only life you have. You have lived many lives; the pilgrimage is long, and you have been going almost in circles. So your consciousness has not grown; you are committing the same mistakes again and again. Each life is wasted almost in a repetitive way.

People say that history repeats itself. History has no business to repeat itself; it repeats itself because we are unconscious so we go on making the same mistake again and again. Our consciousness remains the same. That's why in every life we live on the same miserable plane. We never grow up.

This is time enough. You should start working deeply on your being, searching for it because once you have known your being then you are not going to be born again in a body. Then you are not going to be in another prison, you will be freed from all prisons. And this ultimate freedom is the only lesson worth learning through all these lives. But we are functioning almost in a drunken way.

Ruben Levinsky is telling his friends at the club how his five-year-old son got his nursemaid pregnant.

"But that is impossible!" cries Sollie.

"Unfortunately it is not," replies the embarrassed Ruben. "The little wretch punctured all my condoms with a pin."

It is a very strange world. I have heard a proverb, very ancient: "God made women without a sense of humor so they could love men without laughing at them."

Hymie Goldberg is sitting in a bar one night when the man sitting on the next stool slides off and lands on the floor. Feeling that there is no way the man will make it home on his own, Hymie finds his address in his wallet and decides to help him. Slipping an arm around his waist, they head for the door. But immediately the man's legs crumple and he collapses.

"You drunken bum," complains Hymie, "why the hell didn't you stop drinking sooner?" The man mumbles something, but Hymie is in no mood to listen. Feeling as righteous as Mother Teresa, Hymie throws his shoulders beneath the man and carries him home. Knocking indignantly, a woman opens the door and he strides in and dumps the man on the couch.

"Here is your husband," says Hymie. "And if I were you, I would have a serious talk with him about his drinking."

"I will," promises the woman. "But tell me," she continues, looking outside, "where is his wheelchair?"

It is a hilarious world. Everything is going on so unconsciously. The only thing worth remembering is not to lose the opportunity to develop your consciousness to the point where you have the same vision, the same clarity, the same intuition, the same understanding as a Gautam Buddha. Unless you become that much awakened, your life is going to repeat the same mistakes again and again. An unconscious man cannot be expected to change his life's course. It is only consciousness, growing consciousness, that is going to change your lifestyle.

Once you are fully awakened, enlightened, you need not come back again into another womb. The enlightened being disappears into the womb of the universe itself. Not that you are no more, but in fact you *are* for the first time – as vast, as infinite as this universe is, with no boundaries, and expanding continuously.

All your misery is because you are so vast and you have been forced into a small body, a small mind, a small heart. Your love wants to expand but your heart is too small. Your clarity wants to become as clear as a sky without clouds, but your head is too small and too crowded. Your being wants to have wings and fly across the sun like an eagle, but it is encaged – three walls around it; it is almost impossible for it to get out of this prison.

The East has been working only for one thing. That's why it has not created much science, much technology because all its geniuses were concerned with only one thing, and that was the innermost core of your being. They were not objective people. They were more and more interested in subjectivity. The East has found the golden key. It can open the doors for you of infinite bliss, of all the splendor that is hidden in existence. It can allow you to receive gifts from all dimensions.

You are not a miserable creature. You are carrying a god within you, and you have to discover this god. This is the only miracle I believe in, the only magic. Everything else is nonessential.

3

Innocence Is the Only Religiousness

Osho,

Why is childlikeness compared to meditation?

When a man is reborn, only then he understands the beauty and the grandeur of childhood. The child is ignorant; hence he is unable to understand the tremendous innocence that surrounds him. Once a child becomes aware of his own innocence, there is no difference between the child and the sage. The sage is not higher and the child is not lower. The only difference is that the child knows not what he is and the sage knows it.

I am reminded of Socrates…

In the very last moments of his life he said to his disciples, "When I was young I used to think I knew much. As I became older, as I knew more, a strange thing started happening: an awareness that knowing more was bringing me to knowing less."

And finally, when the Oracle of Delphi declared Socrates to be the wisest man in the world, the people of Athens were very happy and they went to Socrates, but Socrates said, "Go back and tell the Oracle that at least for once its prophecy has been wrong. Socrates knows nothing."

The people were shocked. They went to the Oracle, but the Oracle laughed and said, "That's why I have declared him the wisest man in the world! It is only the ignorant people who think they know." The more you know, the more you become innocent.

According to the Socratic division, there are two categories of people: the ignorant knowers and the knowing ignorants. The world is dominated by the second category. These are your priests, your professors, leaders, saints, religious messiahs, saviors, prophets, all proclaiming that they know. But their very proclamation destroys the utter simplicity and innocence of a child.

Bodhidharma remained in China for fourteen years. He was sent by his master to spread the message of meditation. After fourteen years, he wanted to come back to the Himalayas; he was old and was ready to disappear into the eternal snows. He had thousands of disciples – he was one of the rarest people who have existed on the earth – but he called only four disciples and said, "I will ask only one question: What is the essence of my teaching? Whoever gives me the right answer will be my successor."

There was great silence, tremendous expectation. Everyone looked at the first disciple, who was the most learned, most scholarly. The first disciple said, "Going beyond the mind is what all your teaching can be reduced to."

Bodhidharma said, "You have my skin, but not more than that."

He turned to the second disciple who said, "There is no one to go beyond the mind. All is silent. There is no division between the one that has to be transcended and one that has to transcend. This is the essence of your teaching."

Bodhidharma said, "You have my bones."

And he turned to the third disciple, who said, "The essence of your teaching is inexpressible."

Bodhidharma laughed and said, "But you have expressed it! You have said something about it. You have my marrow."

And he turned to the fourth disciple who had only tears and utter silence, no answer. He fell at the feet of Bodhidharma. And he was accepted as the successor, although he had not answered anything.

But he *has* answered – without answering, without using words, without using language. His tears have shown much more than any language can contain. And his gratitude, prayerfulness and his thankfulness to the master – what more can you say?

The great gathering of disciples was very disappointed because this was a man no one had ever bothered about. The great scholars have been rejected; the great knowers have not been accepted, and an ordinary man… But that ordinariness is the only extraordinary thing in the world – that childlike wonder, that childlike experience of the mysterious all around.

Remember one thing, that the moment you start knowing something you are not a child. You have started becoming part of the adult world. The society has initiated you into civilization; it has distracted you from your essential nature. When the child is surrounded by the mysterious – everything just a mystery with no answer, with no question – then he is exactly at the point the sage ultimately reaches. That's why childlikeness is compared again and again to meditation. Meditation would not have been needed if people had remained in their essential childlikeness.

Do you know the root of the word *meditation*? – it comes from the same root as *medicine*. It is a medicine. But medicine is needed only if you are sick. Meditation is needed if you are spiritually sick. Childlikeness is your spiritual health, your spiritual wholeness; you don't need any meditation.

Little Ernie wants a bicycle, but when he asks his mother, she tells him he can only have one if he behaves himself, which he promises to do. But after a week of trying to be good, Ernie finds it impossible. So his mother suggests, "If you write a note to Jesus, maybe you will find it easier to be good."

Ernie rushes upstairs, sits on his bed, and writes, "Dear Jesus, if you let me have a bike, I promise to be good for the rest of my life." Realizing that he could never manage that, he starts again, "Dear Jesus, if you let me have a bike, I promise to be good for a month." Knowing that he can't do that, he suddenly has an idea. He runs into his mother's room, takes her statue of the Virgin Mary, puts it in a shoebox and hides it under the bed. Then he begins to write again, "Dear Jesus, if you ever want to see your mother again…"

When the Goldberg family moved into their new house, a visiting relative asked little Herschel how he liked the new place.

"It is terrific!" he says. "I have my own room, Ruthie has her own room and Sarah has her own room too. But poor Mom is still in with Dad."

A few maxims for you to meditate on. Perhaps your dormant childlikeness may start becoming active.

The first maxim…

Smile – tomorrow will be worse.

Nothing makes a woman feel older than meeting a fat, bald man who knew her at school.

There are no important differences between men and women, but the unimportant ones are the most interesting.

If it can't be done in bed, it is probably not worth doing.

Success for some people depends on becoming well known. For others, it depends on never being found out.

The seven ages of women: the right age, and the six wild guesses.

A woman, generally speaking, is generally speaking.

Old age is when you put on your glasses to think.

The honeymoon is over when she stops calling you "honey" and starts calling you "listen"!

The honeymoon is over when a quickie before dinner is a drink.

The honeymoon is over when the dog brings your slippers and your wife barks at you.

If you are lonesome as a bachelor, take the big step – get a dog. The license is cheaper and he already has a fur coat.

For absolutely irrational reasons, man has been dragged into seriousness. All the religions have played their role in poisoning man. The people who are on any kind of power trip are bound to destroy man's laughter, his innocent wondering eyes, his childhood. The giggle of a child seems to be more dangerous to these people than nuclear weapons.

And in fact they are right – if the whole world starts laughing a little more, wars will be reduced. If people start loving their innocence without bothering about knowledge, life will have a beauty and a blessing of which we have become completely unaware.

Just today, Hasya brought me a letter from a sannyasin who says that for seven years he has been so cowardly because he has wanted to tell me something, but was afraid. Somehow he has gathered courage and he has written. His question is, "Whenever you quote any scientific theory, it is not up-to-date." Now, I am amazed! Do you think science can ever be up-to-date? By the time it is up-to-date it is already out-of-date. What was up-to-date yesterday, has become out-of-date today. What is up-to-date today will become out-of-date tomorrow. Seeing this stupidity, I simply dropped the idea of being up-to-date. What is the point?

And you have not come here to learn science. If once in a while I mention any scientific theory it is not to explain the theory to you, it is to indicate toward something else. It is just an arrow pointing beyond, and if you don't look at the beyond and you get entangled with the arrow, you have missed the point.

If you are so interested in science, you should go to a science college. The libraries are full, there are hundreds of universities. This is not the place for you. This is the most unscientific place you can find in the world! And when I say unscientific, I mean exactly that. Science means knowledge – this place is not for knowledge. This place is for innocence. I am not imparting more information to you. My effort is to take away your information and give you a transformation.

You unnecessarily waited for seven years. But now there is no need; the choice is clear. Here we have gathered to forget all that we know, and if you are still interested in accumulating borrowed knowledge, then I feel sorry for you.

All the religions try to insist that what they are saying is true, although all their truths have been found to be superstitions. Three hundred years ago the shift came from religion to science. And science started emphasizing that whatever *it* says is true. It was an old habit gathered from the religions. Soon they became aware that at least religion remained with the same knowledge for ten thousand years. Because the knowledge in the religious area was such that there was no way to find out whether it was up-to-date or out-of-date, whether God was still alive, or dead, or sick. So God remained. In fact, no one ever knew whether he had been born yet or not. Heaven and hell remained true for thousands of years without any change. The reason was not that they were true, the reason was that they were simply fictions and there was no way and no criterion to judge.

Science took the same attitude toward its own theories, but soon the fallacy was found. Science was not talking about fictions but about facts. And as you know more facts, you have to change your old theories every day. In fact, it is said that today you cannot write a very big, comprehensive book on science because by the time the book is complete, all that you have written will be out-of-date. You can write only papers, and that too you have to be very quick to read them in some conference or publish them in some periodical because you are not alone in the world. Many people are working on the same facts. Someone may come with a better fitting, more adequate ideology.

Albert Einstein was asked, "If you had not discovered the theory of relativity, do you think it would have ever been discovered?" And naturally the questioner was convinced that unless there is a mind like Albert Einstein, the theory cannot be discovered.

But he was shocked when Albert Einstein said to him, "If I had not discovered it, within three weeks at the most it would have been discovered by someone else. Thousands of scientific minds are working. It was just fortunate that I jumped quickly and published my research."

And strangely enough it was found that another German physicist had discovered the theory of relativity *before* Albert Einstein. But he was a lazy guy; he simply waited: What is the hurry? He was thinking that no one else was going to discover such a complicated theory. He had all the notes prepared, it was just that he had not put them together. But do you think Albert Einstein is up-to-date today? You would be wrong. In science, no one can remain up-to-date. Maybe for a few moments, a few days, a few weeks.

I am not concerned with the temporal, the ephemeral, the timely. My concern is with the eternal. And the eternal has nothing to do with science or knowledge; the eternal has something to do with the mysterious and the innocent.

Be childlike, with open eyes, without any prejudices hidden behind the eyes. Just look with clarity, and small flowers or grass leaves, butterflies or a sunset will give you as much blissfulness as Gautam Buddha found in his enlightenment. The question is not dependent on things, the question is of your openness. Knowledge closes you. It becomes an enclosure, an imprisonment. Innocence opens all the doors, all the windows. The sun comes in, cool breezes pass through. And the fragrance of flowers suddenly visits you. Once in a while a bird may come and sing a song and pass through another window. Innocence is the only religiousness.

Religiousness does not depend on your holy scriptures. It does not depend on how much you know about the world. It depends on how much you are ready to be just like a clean mirror, reflecting nothing.

Utter silence, innocence, purity... And the whole existence is transformed for you. Each moment becomes ecstatic. Small things, like sipping a cup of tea, become so prayerful, no other prayer can be compared to it. Just watching a cloud moving freely in the sky, and in innocence a synchronicity happens. The cloud is no longer there as an object and you are no longer here as a subject. Something meets and merges with the cloud. You start flying with the cloud. You start dancing with the rain, with the trees. You start singing with the birds. You start dancing with the peacocks, without moving, just sitting, your consciousness starts spreading all around you. The day you have touched existence with your consciousness, religion is born in you, and you are born again. This is your real birth. This real birth I have called sannyas.

One birth is from the mother and the father; another birth is that which happens between the disciple and the master. And the second birth opens all the doors and all the secrets to explore. Life becomes a continuous adventure, a moment-to-moment excitement, a day and night ecstasy. Neither life disappears into death, nor the day dies into the darkness of the night. Suddenly you become aware that day and night are two wings of the same bird, that life and death are two wings of the same bird. The whole sky of consciousness is yours. You don't have to be a Christian, you don't have to be a Hindu, you don't have to be a Mohammedan. You only have to be a child.

Just a few jokes, for you to laugh...

Gordon MacTavish becomes the head of the Clan MacTavish and inherits a fortune. His friends at the pub fear that his new wealth will change him. There is a big discussion at the pub when the door bursts open and in strides MacTavish, waving them all to the bar.

"When MacTavish drinks," he booms, "everyone drinks!"

When everyone has had a drink, he slaps down a dollar bill on the bar and announces, "And when MacTavish pays, everyone pays!"

Hamish MacTavish is flying from Los Angeles to New York to go to his company's annual sales meeting. He is sipping his complimentary champagne in the first-class lounge when a gorgeous blond sits down next to him. He is trying hard not to look at her ample chest, and when she says, "I know you must be wondering about my T-shirt," Hamish is very pleased to be able to look straight at her bulging breasts with the initials N.N.A. printed across them. He admits that he is curious, so she tells him it stands for the National Nymphomaniacs Association. And as it turns out, she is also going to her annual national convention.

Excitedly Hamish asks, "What kind of man do you prefer?"

"Well," she confesses, "my absolute favorite is mature American Indians." But then noticing Hamish's disappointment, she quickly adds, "But a close second, Jewish businessmen."

"In that case," says Hamish, unable to contain himself any longer, "let me introduce myself." He then raises his champagne glass and says, "My name is Geronimo Goldberg."

The young minister decides to get married. In his innocence he finds a girl who has had much experience with men. On the wedding night he gets into his pajamas while his wife strips naked and jumps into bed. Kneeling beside the bed, the minister prays, "Ah God, on this great night, give us your guidance."

"Don't worry about that," says his wife. "I'll give the guidance, just pray for endurance!"

4

The Meaning of Meditation

Osho,
What does it mean to meditate over something? I know what it means to think over something; that's what the mind is continuously doing – remembering, analyzing, planning, imagining, etcetera. I also came to know a state of meditation where the "I" is no more, where all the boundaries are lost, and just a melting into the whole, a disappearing, weightlessness, light, bliss. But what do you mean when you say to us, "Meditate over it"?

The languages of the West have no equivalent to *meditation*. It is sheer poverty of experience and poverty of language – just as in the East you will not find many words which exist in the Western hemisphere, particularly scientific, technological, objective. So the first thing to be understood is that we are trying something almost impossible. In the East we have all the three words that English has, but we also have a fourth word that English – or any Western language – has missed. And the reason is not just linguistic; the reason is because this kind of experience has not been available to them.

The first word is *concentration*. In the East we call it *ekagrata*, one-pointedness. The second word is *contemplation*. In the East we call it *vimarsh*, thinking, but only about a particular subject. Not diverting, going astray, but consistently remaining with the same experience and going deeper and more comprehensively into it. It is a development of concentration. The third word is *meditation*. In the West, since Marcus Aurelius, meditation has been in a mess. His was the first book about meditation written in the West. But not knowing what meditation can be, he defines it as a deeper concentration and a deeper contemplation. Both definitions are unjustified.

In the East we have another word, *dhyana*. It does not mean concentration, it does not mean contemplation, it does not mean meditation even. It means a state of no-mind. All those three are mind activities – whether you are concentrating, contemplating, or meditating, you are always objective. There is something you are concentrating *upon*, there is something you are meditating *upon*, there is something you are contemplating *upon*. Your processes may be different, but the boundary line is clear-cut: it is within the mind. The mind can do all these three things without any difficulty. Dhyana is beyond the mind.

This is not the first time that the difficulty has been raised; it has been raised by many people. After Gautam Buddha, his disciples reached China nearabout eighteen hundred years ago and they were faced with the same difficulty. Finally they decided not to translate the word because there is no possible translation. They used the word *dhyana*, but in the Chinese pronunciation it became *ch'an*. And when fourteen hundred years ago the transmission of the lamp reached Japan, again there was the same difficulty: What to do with *ch'an*? The Japanese had no equivalent or even a similar word for it. So they also decided to use the same word; in their pronunciation it became *zen*.

And it is a strange story that Gautam Buddha himself never used the word *dhyana* because he never used the Sanskrit language. It was one of his revolutionary steps to use the people's language, not the language of the scholars. Sanskrit has never been a living language; it has never been used by the people in the marketplace. It has been the language of the learned, the scholars, professors, philosophers, theologians. And there was a tremendous gap between the world of scholars and the world of the ordinary human being. It was tremendously courageous of Gautam Buddha not to use the language in which he was trained, but to use the language of the people. He used a language called Pali. In Pali, *dhyana* becomes *jhan*. *Jhan* and *zen* are not very far away, and *ch'an* also fits perfectly well between the two.

But the people who translated the first scriptures describing meditation thought that they understood the meaning of dhyana. Most of them were Christian missionaries, and naturally they had nothing beyond the conception of the mind. Christianity has never thought about going beyond the mind; hence the possibility does not exist for anything like dhyana. The closest they could come was *meditation*. But the moment you use *meditation*, it becomes, automatically, "Meditation upon what?" The word *meditation* is intrinsically objective. Dhyana is not.

When you use *dhyana*, it does not mean "On what?" It simply means going beyond the mind. And the moment you go beyond the mind, you go beyond all objects. You simply are. Dhyana is not a process but a state of being. Not a duality between subject and object, but simply a dewdrop slipping from the lotus leaf into the ocean.

Talking to you, when I say, "Meditate over it," I know the word I am using is wrong. But the reason that I am using the wrong word is because only the wrong people are around me! All the misfits of the world fit me very well! But you can be reminded that language should not become a barrier.

Meditation is a state. You are simply silent – no thought to concentrate on, no subject to contemplate, no object to meditate over. The other has disappeared. And remember, the moment the other disappears, you cannot exist. You are part of the other. Just as if light disappears, there will be no darkness. If life disappears, there will be no death; they are intrinsically joined together. "I" and "you" can either exist together in a certain kind of coexistence or we have to disappear and then what remains is neither me nor you. What remains is the universal energy. Meditation is disappearing into the universal.

The mind is the barrier. The more you concentrate, the more you contemplate, and the more you meditate upon something, you will never go out of the mind. And the mind is the dewdrop I have referred to. So the first thing to understand is that only in the East and particularly in India was the first word for *meditation* coined. Words are coined only when you have a certain experience which is incapable of being expressed in the existing language.

For ten thousand years, India has been pouring all its genius into a single effort, and that is dhyana. If you use the word *dhyana*, you will not ask, "On what?" The very word *dhyana* has no intrinsic duality. *Dhyana* means simply silence. Utter silence, serenity.

Your question is significant. You are asking, "What does it mean to meditate over something?" – it means nothing! Never meditate over something; otherwise it is not meditation.

You are saying, "I know what it means to think over something. That's what the mind is continuously doing – remembering, analyzing, planning, imagining, etcetera." Everybody knows that. "I also came to know a state of meditation where the 'I' is no more." My own understanding is that up to this point you were talking about your existential experience; beyond this point you are simply borrowing words which you have not experienced. You say, "I also came to know..." Who will come to know? If the "I" is there, then the "thou" is there. If the experiencer is there, then the experience is there. Still the duality exists; you have not gone beyond the mind. You have not attained what you call a state of meditation.

You say, "...where the 'I' is no more..." These are words which are beautiful and you must have loved them, but you don't know the meaning of them. This is the point I was talking about last night, when Bodhidharma chose as his successor the disciple who did not answer. Because any answer will be wrong; any answer will mean "I am still here." Any answer will mean that the mind is still functioning. Any answer is bound to be wrong. The man who was chosen as the successor had only tears of joy and fell at the feet of Bodhidharma in tremendous gratitude and thankfulness. Nothing can be said.

The moment you say something you have to use the mind, you have to use language, and then naturally all the fallacies of language and all the boundaries of the mind come in.

You say, "...where the 'I' is no more..." If you are no more, then the question should have stopped here. Now who is prolonging the question still further? You go on, saying, "...where all the boundaries are lost..." Whose boundaries? Certainly you are there, seeing that boundaries are getting lost. But if you are there, the boundaries cannot be lost. That is a contradiction in terms. You are saying, "... just melting into the whole..." Have you ever heard any dewdrop shouting to the world, "Listen, I am melting into the ocean"? One simply melts and there is nothing to say. And silence prevails.

But you go on describing all the beautiful words that you must have read, you must have heard: "...just melting into the whole, a disappearing, weightlessness, light, bliss." But to whom are all these experiences happening? You are no more! At least you are needed for all these experiences to happen. Your mind is needed, your language is needed, and again you ask. If this were an existential experience, in the first place you would not have said anything.

I am reminded of a great Zen master who was sitting on the sea beach when a king happened to pass by. He had always wanted to see the master, but there was no time – the affairs of the kingdom and the worries and the wars... So this was a golden opportunity. He stopped his chariot, got down and went to the master and asked him, "I don't have much time, but I want to know what the essential teaching is. I don't want to die ignorant."

The master remained silent.

The king said, "I can understand that you are very old and perhaps you have gone deaf."

The master smiled.

The king shouted in his ears, "I want to know the essence of your teaching!"

The master wrote with his finger on the sand, "Dhyana." He did not speak.

The king said, "But that does not make much sense to me. I have heard that word many times. Elaborate a little more."

The master said to him, "I have already fallen for your sake. Otherwise the right answer was the first, when I had remained silent. But perhaps you don't know the communion that exists in silence. Out of compassion, I wrote 'Dhyana.' Now you want elaboration. I will try." He wrote again in bigger letters, DHYANA.

The king was getting a little angry. He said, "What kind of elaboration is this? It is the same word!"

The master said, "You will have to forgive me because I cannot fall more. Just for your sake, I will not let the centuries laugh about me. No one has said anything about dhyana, and no one can say anything about dhyana."

Then what have the masters been doing down the ages? – they create devices, situations in which they hope that perhaps in a thousand people one may get an insight. Those devices are not meditation. Those devices are only to bring you to a point in your own inner space where suddenly you realize and you say "Aha!" And the moment you understand the state of meditation, all methods of meditation become futile. Those methods are just arbitrary, created out of compassion for people to whom there is no other way to communicate a higher reality than the mind.

If what you say has been your experience, then the last part will be missing. You say, "But what do you mean when you say to us, 'Meditate over it'?" – I say to you, "Meditate over it" with all the explanations that there is no "it" and there is no meditator. When I say "Meditate over it" I mean exactly the opposite: "No it, no meditator. Just be."

But language is very poor. Even the very cultured languages are poor as far as the interior space of man is concerned. They don't have any indicative words because millions of people have lived but no one has looked within. And when once in a while someone looks within, he finds a space which cannot be translated in any way. You should understand not only your difficulty – your difficulty is very small – you should understand the difficulty of the man who has existentially reached the spot which he cannot translate.

One of the most beautiful mystics of India, Kabir, was asked the same question. He laughed and said, "I cannot exactly give you an explanation, but I can give you some indication. It is like the experience of sweetness to a dumb man. He knows it, but he cannot speak it. The dumb man has no incapacity to experience the sweetness of something, but if you ask him what his experience is, he cannot express it." This inexpressibility has misguided many people. They think that a thing which cannot be expressed cannot exist. They think expressibility and existence are bound to be synonymous. It is not so.

What can you say about love? Whatever you say will be wrong. In fact, when you are in love you don't even say "I love you," because that seems so small in comparison to your experience. My own understanding is that people start saying to each other, "I love you" when love has disappeared.

The American philosopher Dale Carnegie – and a man like Dale Carnegie can be called a philosopher only in America – suggests in his book, which has sold second only to the Holy Bible, "Whenever you come home, kiss your wife and say, 'I love you.' Whenever you go out of your home, kiss your wife and say, 'I love you.'" And there are millions of idiots who are doing it! The wife knows that this is only bluffing; the man knows it is all bluffing.

When you love, love is so tremendous and so vast that you simply sit hand in hand, not uttering a single word. The actual experience of love has never been expressed by any poet and will never be expressed. Love is part of our ordinary reality, just as sweetness or bitterness is. These inner spaces of meditation are not our usual experiences, so when someone stumbles upon them he is at a loss to say what he has found.

There was a man in Japan whose name people have forgotten – they only remember the "laughing buddha" because he never said anything. Ask him anything, his answer would be the same: he would laugh. I think he was a very sincere man, utterly authentic. He did not compromise with any language, with any mind, with any expression. He simply laughed. And if you can understand through his laughter, his smile, it is up to you. Most of the people thought he was mad.

When Bodhidharma became the state of meditation, the first thing that happened to him was to laugh loudly. But Bodhidharma was a learned scholar, not like a simple, Japanese laughing buddha. He did not laugh. He was asked later on by his disciples, "Please fulfill our curiosity. When you became enlightened, what was the first thing that you wanted to do?"

He said, "The first thing? I was no longer there – a tremendous laughter, but I had not to go on laughing. Otherwise people would think me just a madman. My master's advice was, 'Even a very wise master rarely finds authentic disciples. If people start thinking you are mad, then the possibility of transforming anyone is almost negligible.' So I reminded myself: laugh within yourself as much as you can, but don't show it!"

Have you seen Bodhidharma's pictures? You can use those pictures to scare your children! No one has inquired what happened because he was a prince; this face that is depicted is not the face of a beautiful prince. But I know the reason. The reason is that he is holding his laughter inside! And because of this holding, his whole face has become distorted. His eyes are bulging. He has decided to remain serious. But I don't think anyone has ever analyzed why Bodhidharma, one of the most beautiful men, should have such a ferocious look. I can say with absolute certainty that he is in tremendous trouble. If he had laughed, you would have seen his beauty, but the master had said not to laugh, otherwise no one would take him seriously. So the poor fellow became too serious, and when you are containing a belly laughter inside you everything becomes distorted.

First you have to sort out what is your experience and what is your knowledge. Knowledge is simply bullshit. If you don't like the word *bullshit*, then you can call it *cow dung* because that is a holy thing. And as you are scraping it away, you will find something of tremendous value, of your own experience. That experience will give you the meaning of meditation. I cannot give it to you. I can only show the path, how it is gained. But to say what it is, I am as dumb as anyone else has ever been.

Wishing to surprise her husband with a new wig she has just bought, Ruthie Finkelstein strolls unannounced into his office.

"Do you think you could find a place in your life for a woman like me?" she asks sexily.

"Not a chance," replies Moishe. "You remind me too much of my wife."

So beware of wigs! And remember one thing: whatever grows within you undistorted, unpolluted, unpoisoned by the millions who are around you, trust it. That is your potential. Remember, in your potential, you will not find your self. And the moment you don't find your self, there is lightness, there is blessing, there is ecstasy, but you cannot say it. The one who used to say it is no more.

The Sufis have one of the most holy books in the whole world, perhaps the only holy book. That book has existed for fourteen hundred years. No publishing house has been ready to print it because there is nothing in it to print. It is just absolutely blank.

The first master who had the book used to hide it under his pillow. His disciples were very curious, "He says everything, but if you ask about the book he simply smiles." They tried in every way. They would leave the windows open so that in the night when there was no one around and the master took the book out to read it… They even climbed on his roof, removing a few tiles to see what was written in the book. But the master was reading next to a small candle, and it was very difficult to figure out what was there. And immediately, as soon as he became aware of anyone, he would close the book and put it under his pillow.

The day he died, no one was very interested in his death – everyone was interested in the book! They pulled the book out and they were amazed – there was not a single word written anywhere. Those who had the perceptivity could see the great compassion of the master, that he never said anything about the book. He left it for them to discover.

That book still exists – in a distorted form because one publisher in England has published it, but he was worried about who would purchase it. A pseudo-Sufi has written an introduction and its whole history of fourteen hundred years. So there is something written to be read, but that has destroyed the whole mystery of the book.

You are the mystery which cannot be contained in words. And remember it as a criterion: whatever can be reduced to language is just your mind functioning. Meditation is a state when the mind stops functioning; you are simply consciousness. Not even conscious of yourself, but pure consciousness. Not even the slightest idea that "I am this," that "I am enjoying bliss and I am enjoying ecstasy." When ecstasy comes, the flood is so big, "you" cannot remain in that flood. When blessings shower on you, you evaporate.

Gautam Buddha is right when he says, "I can only point to the moon, but don't cling to my finger. The finger is not the moon." But you will be surprised about human stupidity. After Gautam Buddha… He said, "Don't make statues of me because I am not here so that you should worship me. I am here so that I can awaken you." But his statues were not prohibited. He may not have even thought about how deep the ignorance of man is. People created temples, with a finger carved in beautiful marble, and everyone forgot the moon. People worshipped the finger and the whole point was missed! What Gautam Buddha was saying was that whatever he was doing for forty-two years continuously was nothing but a finger pointing to the moon. Leave the finger aside and look at the moon.

What I am saying to you is: don't get involved in the linguistics, in the language, in the grammar. Those are all irrelevant. Just look at the moon. Even a finger which is not very beautiful can point to the moon – words are not very beautiful, but if you are wise enough you can leave the words and listen to the essence.

But don't start believing in that essence and talking about it. Let it become your experience. And even when it becomes your experience, you will not be able to give any explanation to it. You can cry out of joy, you can laugh, you can dance; perhaps those gestures signify more beautifully than the ordinary language.

Meera danced – she is one of the most beautiful women in the world. Perhaps no other woman has reached the heights Meera reached. She was a queen, but the day the moment arrived and the space within her opened, she forgot all her palaces. She started dancing in the streets of her own capital. Naturally, the family were very disturbed – a queen dancing in the marketplace! They came to her to persuade her, but she said, "I have found something that can only be expressed by dancing. I will dance all over the country."

She danced all over the country. No one knows how many people understood the dance. She sang beautiful songs. They are not philosophical treatises, but they have beautiful gaps. If you can catch those gaps, you can enter the unknown. Her dances are a language of a totally different caliber. If you can understand her dance, perhaps something will start dancing in you. All that is needed is an openness, a receptivity, so that her dance can trigger the dormant energy in your being. And if you can also dance, you will have communicated, you will have understood what meditation is.

Here, there is not one Meera, there are many. If you cannot understand meditation here, there is not much possibility to understand it anywhere else. The world is too worldly; their antagonism toward me is because I am trying to take you away from the crowd on untrodden paths where no guide exists, no maps exist. And the crowd is worried. Whether the crowd is of Christians, Hindus, Buddhists, it doesn't matter. The crowd does not want anyone to get out of its fold because that reduces its political power.

All your religions are simply political powers – in the name of religion there is the greatest cheating and exploitation of humanity. I want to take you away from the crowd, whichever crowd you belong to. I respect the individual because only the individual can know what meditation is and only the individual can know the beauty, the ecstasy, the dance of this immensely beautiful existence. Crowds have never become enlightened, it has always been the individual. I create the individual.

Just the other day, one of my old sannyasins, Amrito from Holland, told Hasya that he is writing a book called *Years of Preparation*. He is a man of great intellectual capacity, an intellectual giant, but his heart is just like that of a small child. Because of his intellect, he has been going to all kinds of people – Da Free John, J. Krishnamurti. Whenever he hears of someone he will immediately rush there. In these ten years he must have encountered many so-called enlightened people. He had a personal interview lasting one hour with J. Krishnamurti, and he showed the script to Hasya. Krishnamurti talks about me saying, "The gentleman in Pune is just a ladder. As far as I am concerned, I am an elevator."

I have sent a message to Amrito saying that I don't think of it as a criticism of me, I accept it as a compliment! With a ladder you are free; it is not so with an elevator. In an elevator you are encaged, you cannot go anywhere, and the elevator never goes anywhere – it simply goes up and down. And for ninety years Krishnamurti was moving just like an elevator, up and down, up and down. With an elevator you are not the master; you are subservient to a mechanical device which depends on many complexities – electricity, engineering, electronics. You can get stuck in the middle and you cannot do anything.

With a ladder, you are absolutely free! You are the master. You can take the ladder wherever you want, you can leave the ladder wherever you want. The ladder will not cling to you and the ladder will not ask you for any kind of surrender. I love the idea! I am certainly an old-fashioned ladder. My whole effort is to make masters of you. Krishnamurti has not even been able to make disciples of you.

I have called Amrito tonight to ask, "What other nonsense have you been listening to from these so-called enlightened people? You are *my* disciple and you have to finish your book with my declaration that you are now a master! Without that, the book will remain incomplete. But first tell me what all these idiots have been telling you so I can answer them; otherwise your book will remain incomplete."

There was a man in Mumbai, Nisarg Datta Maharaj. No one knew this big name; he was known to the masses as "Beedi Baba" because he was continuously smoking beedies. You can find such kinds of beedi babas in every village. I think India has seven hundred thousand villages and each village must have at least one; more is possible. And Amrito wrote to me a few days ago because another young Dutchman became very involved with Beedi Baba. The man seems to be very sincere, but the trouble is that the people who come from the West have very childlike hearts, very trusting, and they are unaware that in India spirituality is just a routine. Everyone talks about great things and their lives are as ugly as possible.

When Beedi Baba said that he would speak only to this young Dutchman, naturally his ego must have felt tremendously vast. The crowd that surrounded Beedi Baba was also of the same quality – rickshaw wallahs waiting for their passengers, sitting by the side of Beedi Baba. And when he said he would not speak to anyone unless it was this Dutchman… So he spoke to the Dutchman, who has now compiled books on Beedi Baba. Now, in India it is almost parrotlike, but to the Westerner it seems to be a tremendous revelation. When Beedi Baba said, "*Aham brahmasmi*; I am God, I am that," the young Dutchman immediately wrote a book: *I Am That!* Because for the West, spirituality is a foreign affair, just as for the East, science is a foreign affair.

I have heard…

In a factory in Mumbai, they installed a very costly mechanism. It worked for two days and then stopped. It worked for two days because the expert was present, and the moment the expert was gone the mechanism stopped. They phoned the expert: "What to do?"

He said, "I will have to come and it will cost a lot of money, ten thousand dollars."

But to keep the factory closed was even more costly, so they had to concede and allow the man to come. The man came and just hit the machine and it started working! The industrialist said to him, "You are charging me ten thousand dollars, just for hitting this machine?"

He said, "It is not for the hitting. For the hitting it is only one dollar, but to know *where* to hit costs money."

When Amrito's letter came to me about this young Dutchman, saying that "Many sannyasins are going to him, and I am also going to him," I talked about it. He heard it, and he took the recording to the man. The man heard it, and he was very grateful but baffled also because he was gathering a big crowd of disciples. And because he felt baffled and he was grateful that I had talked about him, I would like Amrito, when he goes back, either to bring the man to me or send him to me. Because I know where to hit!

5

The Truth Is Always Simple

Osho,
When I heard you say that you are here for us and we are here for you, I was so touched by the simplicity and the truth of it. It went to my heart like an arrow. Oh Osho, it's all so deep.

Truth is the most obvious and the most simple thing in existence. This has created tremendous difficulty – the mind is not interested in the obvious. The mind is not excited by the simple because deep down the mind is nothing but your ego, and the nourishment of the ego comes from the challenge of the far away. The more arduous, the more torturous, the more difficult an achievement is, the more the mind becomes fascinated. It is ready to go to the farthest star, not even bothering what it is going to get there; that is irrelevant.

I remember a remark by Edmund Hillary, who was the first man to climb Everest, the highest mountain in the Himalayas. When he came down, the whole world's media was interested to know what his experience was, what he had gained. Almost a hundred years before him, hundreds of mountaineers had destroyed their lives in the same effort of achieving Everest.

Edmund Hillary could not answer. For a moment there was silence, and then he said, "Just because it is there, a challenge to humanity – that was enough for me to risk my life. I have not gained anything, I have not experienced anything."

The truth is, whenever I think of Edmund Hillary standing on Everest, alone, he looks to me to be embarrassed, utterly idiotic. In fact, he did not stay there longer than two minutes. He risked his life for those two minutes. This will give you an insight into the human mind and its workings. That which is available cannot be made an achievement. And that which is not available, the farther away it is, the more nourishment there is for the ego. The obvious, that which you already have, has no interest at all for the mind.

That's why millions of people have lived on the earth and missed their own being. They traveled far and wide, world travelers like Marco Polo, Columbus. They tried to conquer the whole world, like Alexander the Great. But they forgot one thing: they have not even known themselves; then the question of conquering does not arise.

Alexander was on the way to India when he heard about a very strange man, Diogenes, who lived just by the side of the road. Alexander had heard many stories about the man; he was a legend in his own time. He lived naked.

In India, thousands of Jaina monks have lived naked. It is easy in India, but in the West it is not so easy. But you will be surprised to know why Jainism never reached outside India – the nakedness prevented it. Buddhism spread all over Asia, to Tibet, China, Korea, Japan because they were not living naked. Mahavira was a contemporary of Gautam Buddha, but he could not move – neither have any of his disciples in twenty-five centuries moved – out of India.

But Diogenes must have been a more courageous man than Mahavira...

He lived in Greece absolutely naked. All his possessions consisted only of one ordinary old-style lamp that he carried twenty-four hours, alight, even in full daylight. Whenever he would meet anyone he would bring his lamp close to the person's face. And you could see the disappointment, the frustration on the face of Diogenes. People would ask, "What are you trying to find?"

He said, "I am simply trying to find an authentic man, a simple man, a sincere man – a man without a mask, just natural, as if he has been born just now."

The day Diogenes died, people gathered and asked, "For the whole of your life, your search has been only one. Did you succeed in finding a natural, simple, innocent man?"

Diogenes said, "Don't ask such depressing questions. All that I can say about men is that they have not stolen my lamp yet."

There were many stories about the man. Alexander stopped his army and said, "I would like to see him."

The first question that Diogenes asked Alexander is the first question every intelligent person has to ask himself. Diogenes did not waste a single moment. He said, "Alexander, you are trying to conquer the whole world. What about you? Will there be time enough after you have conquered the world to know yourself? Are you certain about tomorrow, or the next moment?"

Alexander had never faced such a man. He had conquered great kings, emperors, but he could see that Diogenes was a lion of a man. With downcast eyes, Alexander said, "I cannot say that I am certain about the next moment. But one thing I can promise you, that when I have conquered the world I would love to rest and relax just like you."

Diogenes was having a morning sunbath by the side of a river, surrounded by beautiful trees. He laughed. Sometimes I think his laughter must be still echoing. People like Diogenes belong to eternity. Their signatures are not made on water.

Alexander felt offended and asked, "Why are you laughing?"

Diogenes said, "It is so simple. If I can rest and relax without conquering the world, what is preventing you? The river is big enough and I have no objection. You can take any place you want – even if you want my place, I can change. Rest now if you ever want to rest. Relax now. Now – or remember, never."

What Diogenes was saying was absolute truth, but to a man who is on an ego trip it was too obvious, too simple. Just to relax on the riverbank does not give any nourishment to the ego. What have you conquered? What is your achievement?

People measure their own lives according to their successes, according to their money, according to their power. There is no way to measure your success if you simply settle with the obvious and the simple. The obvious is nothing but a graveyard for your ego.

Remember, truth is always simple. It is untruth that is complex. If you are accustomed to lie, you will have to have a good memory. But if you are simply stating the truth, you don't need to have any memory at all. Lies are so complex, they need a very complex biocomputer which you call memory. Truth is so simple, it does not even need to be said.

I am reminded of Lao Tzu…

Every day he used to go for a morning walk, early, before the sun had risen. Just by the side of his village there was a small hillock which was the most beautiful spot to see the sun rising. One of his neighbors asked him, "Can I come with you?"

Lao Tzu said, "Whether you can come with me is not the right question. The road does not belong to me; neither the mountains, nor the sunrise. If you can come by my side but not *with* me, everything is okay. But remember, you are alone, I am alone. Nothing has to be said; no word has to be uttered."

The man had known Lao Tzu for a long time. He agreed. But one day the neighbor had a guest and the guest was also excited and wanted to follow his host, and go with Lao Tzu on his morning walk. The neighbor explained to him, "Lao Tzu has no other conditions except that you are alone; he does not want to become a crowd. Language is prohibited. You should not say anything, and I don't think he will object."

He did not object, and the guest remembered – but how long can you remember? When the beautiful sun started rising out of the morning mist he forgot all about what his host had said to him. And he said a simple thing, which should not be objectionable. He said, "What a beautiful sunrise!" Suddenly he remembered: you are alone, you are not supposed to use words. Only mad people use words when they are alone.

They returned. Reaching the house, Lao Tzu said to his neighbor, "Please tell your guest never to come again. He is too talkative."

In a two-hour morning walk he had uttered only that small sentence, "What a beautiful sunrise!" But still Lao Tzu is right.

The guest tried to argue with him saying, "I simply expressed my feeling."

Lao Tzu said, "I was also present, I was also experiencing the sunrise and the beauty. We were all surrounded with the same blessing, the birds singing and the flowers opening. I am not blind; I also have a heart. You insulted me by saying, 'What a beautiful sunrise.' Do you think I cannot understand the beauty? And moreover you forgot your promise. You are not a man who can be relied upon, you are not a man of your word."

These strange people like Lao Tzu or Diogenes are the authentic people of the world. They have known the truth not by conquering the world, not by becoming astronauts, not by climbing Everest; they have known the truth just by sitting silently doing nothing. And obviously, the grass grows by itself!

You don't have to do a thing. And when truth comes to you in its utter simplicity, it goes deep to the very center of your being because it is not a mind fabrication; it is not a thought, it is something existential.

Your experience is perfectly true. "It went," you say, "to my heart like an arrow." Yes, it goes into the heart just like an arrow. And after such an experience, you are never the same person – you cannot be. Just think of a blind man: if his eyes can be cured and he starts seeing the light and the colors, do you think he will remain the same man as he was when he was blind? He will be a totally new person.

Perhaps you are not aware that your experience of life comes eighty percent from your eyes. Only twenty percent is divided among the other four senses. It is not coincidental that a blind man attracts your sympathy more than anyone else. A man who is deaf, a man who cannot smell, a man who cannot walk – of course they create a certain sympathy in you, but the man who cannot see takes the major portion of your sympathy.

Without knowing the reasoning, you are functioning naturally. The blind man is living only twenty percent of his life. Eighty percent of his life does not exist – no colors, no paintings, no flowers, no butterflies, not all the greenery of the world, not the mountains with eternal snows. No sky full of stars, no beautiful sunrise, no beautiful sunset. His life is reduced to such a minimum.

I have heard...

A young man had just won a lottery, and he was passing over a bridge. He always used to give some money to a blind beggar there, but that beggar was not present; someone else was present. But he was still spreading his hands asking for the money "for a blind man." So the young man gave him a rupee. The blind man immediately said to him, "It is a false coin."

The man said, "Are you blind or not?"

He said, "I used to be blind, but people were cheating me. Then I changed my profession; I became deaf and dumb."

The man asked, "And what happened to the blind man who used to sit here?"

He said, "It is his holiday, he has gone to a movie."

Unless your experiences transform you, they are not experiences. They are only clouds in your mind. If you have felt the truth, then it is going to transform your whole life. It will have its impact on your every action, on your every attitude. There is no other way to know whether a man has found the truth or not. The only way is that all his gestures, his eyes, his very presence will start affecting you in a totally different way than you have ever been affected by another being, another man.

He may not say a single word, but his silence will overwhelm you. He may not look at you, but you will not be able to forget his eyes, ever. They will haunt you, they will follow you like a shadow. His words will be just the same as your words. Dictionaries cannot make any difference, but you are not a dictionary. When a man like Gautam Buddha speaks, he uses the same words that everyone else is using, but his words have a flavor, an authenticity, a sincerity of the heart; a tremendous love and compassion which the word itself does not necessarily carry.

But if you are open, available, and if the arrow has struck you in the heart, then it opens a window that has remained closed perhaps for millions of lives. And from that small window tremendous experiences can float inward, can transform you so totally.

It is said that in the great capital of Vaishali…

There used to be a thief, a master thief. He was known as a master thief because he was never caught; in fact the situation had become such that people bragged if the master thief had entered their houses. It became something prestigious because the master thief would not go to a beggar. He would go to the emperors, to the kings, to the richest people.

Mahavira was staying in Vaishali during the four months of the rainy season. The master thief was training his son in the art of which he was the master.

The master said, "Listen, one thing: Never go to listen to this man Mahavira. Even if by chance you are passing and you hear a word or a sentence from the man, close your ears. Because just with a single word he can destroy my whole effort of making you my successor."

Naturally it created a great curiosity in the young man. The father had been training him for years, and he was so afraid of a man that just a single word from him and the whole discipline can be destroyed! The young man might never have heard of Mahavira, but his father created the curiosity. One day he went to listen to

Mahavira; he heard only one sentence and became afraid of his father because his father was no ordinary man – if he came to know, he would kill him! There is no other punishment. He heard one sentence and escaped.

That night his father was in the palace of the king, and a lot of jewelry was stolen. The father escaped. The son was not part of the stealing process, but the son was caught. He was coming from a discourse of Mahavira where he had heard only one sentence, which was absolutely meaningless. The sentence which he heard was that in heaven men and women have a few strange things about them: one is that their feet are not the same as ours. Their feet are backward; they walk forward but their feet are backward. This is not great philosophy.

But the young man was caught in place of his father because they looked alike. There was a difference in age, but in the dark night… The police used a strategy to make the young man confess. He was given so much alcohol that he fell asleep. In the middle of the night when he opened his eyes, he was in a beautiful palace, with such beautiful women – he has never seen such beautiful women – and all kinds of delicious foods, ready for him. He thought, "Perhaps I have died and entered heaven!"

Then he suddenly remembered what Mahavira was saying, that in heaven the feet are backward. So he looked at the feet – they were not backward. Otherwise he would have been caught because those beautiful women were asking him, "Tell us everything you have done in your life. You are just in the reception room of heaven, and it is customary to give your whole record before you enter heaven."

He was just going to give them an account of his whole life but he stopped. He said, "My God! If I had not heard that one sentence, I would have been finished today. Although I have not done great robberies, I have done smaller things. This has been my whole training." He simply remained silent. Asked again and again, he said, "I don't have any record. I am a man of silence, not a man of action. I am a meditator." There was no other way. In the morning he was released.

He did not go to his home, he went to Mahavira and said, "Your single sentence, which was absolutely irrelevant, has saved my life. Now this life belongs to you, not to my father. And if your single sentence can save my life, I can conceive the tremendous transformation that can happen if I understand all your words, and if I can understand even your wordless silences."

Mahavira said, "I will accept you only on one condition: go and tell your father what has happened. It is your duty. Your father also needs to be saved. What he is doing is utterly stupid."

The son was very afraid but he had to go. He told the whole story. The father was shocked at first, but then he realized the truth of it. And the story is that both became initiates of Mahavira.

A man of the qualities of Mahavira not only transforms his actions, they change automatically. His words also start growing new meanings, new fragrances. His silences are also messages.

What has happened to you is going to happen to everyone who is sincerely here to be transmuted, who is not here for any ego trip, who is here for a deeper understanding of oneself.

The miracle of the deeper understanding of oneself is that simultaneously you understand the whole mystery of existence. Just one thing to be remembered. When I use the word *understanding*, I don't mean knowledge. You feel it, you touch it, you live it. You sing it, you dance it, but you don't know it. It never becomes knowledge; it becomes your very life. You are it.

But unfortunate are those who are just curiosity-mongers, who are just beggars in a way, collecting dregs from scriptures, from other people, from the rotten old past. And then covering their ignorance with their so-called knowledge. These are the most stupid people in the world, but they dominate the world because they are knowledgeable people and knowledge gives them a certain power.

A man who wants to understand the mystery of existence has to drop the idea of power completely. He has to be utterly nonexistential, as if he is not – and all the doors suddenly open. Paradise is not somewhere else. Paradise is the moment you are available to existence in totality. On this same earth, in this same time, you have entered the lotus paradise of Gautam Buddha.

Those who teach you about a heaven above in the sky are the greatest criminals the world has known because they are depriving you of the paradise that is available herenow.

Osho,
Being with "not knowing what is" seems a better pointer now, but it is still contaminated with becoming. Can insight really stop the movement of becoming, or is this theoretical?

Deva Amrito, the question you have asked is significant for every seeker on the path. You are asking, "Being with 'not knowing what is' seems a better pointer now, but it is still contaminated with becoming. Can insight really stop the movement of becoming, or is this theoretical?" First: being *is* becoming. They are not two things.

It is the language that creates the fallacy of division. When you see a river, you don't really see a river, you see a *rivering* because the water is continuously flowing. It is never in a state of being, it is always in a state of becoming. You see a tree, you see a child, you see a bud – everything is always in a state of becoming. But the language has changed verbs into nouns. It calls flowing water a *river*. It has forgotten completely the great insight of Heraclitus: that you cannot step in the same river twice. Where are you going to find the same river twice?

But if I happen to meet Heraclitus someday – and nothing is impossible in this mysterious existence – I am going to hit him hard! Because although he has stated something tremendously beautiful, it is only half true. I would like to say, you cannot step even once in the same river because when your feet touch the surface, the water underneath is flowing. When you reach the middle, the waters on the surface and underneath are flowing. When you reach the bottom, it is not the same river that you had entered. Even once is impossible; such is the river's aliveness. Nothing is dead in existence. But language has made everything dead.

We call someone a "child" and someone a "young man" and someone an "old man" – as if there are milestones where you can say that on a certain Monday, this man became old, this child became a young man. The young child is flowing continuously into youth; the youth is flowing continuously into old age. Old age is flowing continuously into death, and death is flowing continuously into future life. There is no place where existence knows any stop – not to mention stop, it knows not even a semicolon or a comma; it is an unending sentence which goes on and on from eternity to eternity.

Amrito, you are making it a theoretical question. You want to be satisfied with being. But you don't understand the nature of being. The nature of being is becoming. Once you see the point – that the nature of being is becoming – there is no question of any conflict. You don't have to repress becoming, you don't have to force yourself into being. You can allow your being its natural course of becoming.

Who are you? – you are the being and you are the becoming; they are not two separate things. The mind has a tendency to divide things and then create categories and hierarchies, and then create problems: how to achieve this, how to achieve that.

A Zen master, Lin Chi, used to say to his disciples, "I am going to ask a question. If you answer, whatever the answer, I am going to hit you. If you don't answer, I am still going to hit you." He left no other possibility; any answer would be a wrong answer, and in being afraid that all answers are going to be wrong answers, your silence is also an answer. You are trying to be clever. And Lin Chi would not leave you alone, he would hit you in any way.

When Lin Chi's successor arrived, as usual Lin Chi said, "I am going to ask the question…"

And the successor said, "You need not. If you ask the question, I am going to hit you – whatever the question. And if you don't ask I am going to hit you."

In a gathering of disciples, this stranger… And Lin Chi hugged him and said, "So you have come! Take the seat because I am retiring."

Ed Meese comes into the Oval Office one morning and says, "Mr. President, I was wondering, sir, if it might be possible for my son to work somewhere in the White House."

"Of course," replied Reagan, "what does he do?"

Meese throws up his arms and says, "Well, actually he does nothing."

"Excellent," replies Reagan, "we won't have to train him."

Amrito, you don't need any training. Just enjoy whatever you are – being, becoming – don't miss a single point. Life appears from the outside as static. From the inside, it is a constant flux. And once you know life from the outside and the inside, the flux and the stasis are no longer different. And this is the revelation, that one becomes absolutely happy, contented, fulfilled in any situation, in any state of affairs. One has no complaint, no grudge. One is simply utterly satisfied with existence as it is.

Ronald Reagan dies and goes to hell. The Devil ushers him in and Reagan is very surprised because instead of the eternal fires he had always expected, there is only a big pool full of shit. The Devil explains that the more evil you were on earth, the more you are covered with shit here. And indeed, Reagan looks around and sees many former friends and colleagues.

One scene catches his eye. In a far corner there is a short, black-haired man with a tiny mustache whose right arm is raised to the sky in salute, and the shit only comes up to his ankles. Reagan calls to the Devil and asks, "What about this man? He was very evil on earth – why is he only covered in shit up to his ankles?"

The Devil shouts, "Hey, Hitler, when will you learn to stand on your own feet instead of always standing on the pope's head?"

6

You Are a Unique Individual

Osho,
What is total acceptance?

The very word *total* acceptance has somewhere in it the shadow of nonacceptance. Total acceptance has been preached because people are living in total rejection; whatever happens to them, they are bound to find something wrong in it.

It is something very important to understand that all our so-called religious qualities are reactions. People are violent – we create a reaction, and a philosophy of teaching nonviolence comes out of it. A man who has been violent may become intellectually convinced that it is not right. He may even strive to become nonviolent, but his nonviolence will also carry the same violent attitude.

And this is not only true about ordinary people; even someone like Mahatma Gandhi, who became the apostle of nonviolence, carried a deep-rooted violence all his life. I will give you a few examples so that you can understand.

After the spinning wheel, Mahatma Gandhi was against everything that has been developed by technology, science, and man's intelligence. History stops for him with the spinning wheel. Now, no one can see directly why this should be violent. But if man stops with the spinning wheel, almost one tenth of the population of the world will die. Certainly Gandhi is not proposing the death of one tenth of humanity, but that is the implication. And those who remain will be undernourished, hungry, starving, without enough shelter. All this is covered with a beautiful word – *nonviolence.*

In his own life, Mahatma Gandhi was as violent a man as you can find. His eldest son, Haridas, wanted to be educated and Gandhi was against anything that had come from the West. Now, this very attitude is antagonistic; it is not the attitude of a compassionate man. The compassionate man, the man of love, knows only one world. And the measure he took against Haridas was this: "If you want to be educated, you will never see my face again." Do you see any nonviolence in it?

He closed the doors to Haridas. In India, it is the tradition that when the father dies, the eldest son lights the fire of his funeral pyre. Haridas was not allowed. Gandhi had made it clear. "Either living or dead, I will have nothing to do with Haridas." And what was his crime? – he just wanted to be educated!

Gandhi had very fanatic ideas, and fanatic ideas don't go together with nonviolence. Everyone had to clean the toilet, and when I say clean the toilet you should not understand the Western toilet – the Indian toilet is the ugliest, the dirtiest. He forced his wife to carry out the cleaning of his ashram's toilets. She could not understand it. She refused. But Gandhi said, "If you refuse, then this is not your house and I am not your husband." This is suitable for a dictatorial, unloving, violent person, but not to a loving person.

Once, at a train station, Haridas was hiding in the crowd; Gandhi was passing by on the train and Haridas just wanted to see his father's and his mother's face from far away; he wouldn't allow himself to come close. Gandhi was informed by his followers that Haridas was waiting at the coming station. All the windows, all the doors of the compartment were closed, and Gandhi told his weeping wife, "Stop your tears because they show that you are not with me but with Haridas." What crime had Haridas done? He simply became educated in a contemporary way. And there are so many instances in Gandhi's life in which he is utterly violent, but the umbrella of "nonviolence" covers everything.

You are asking, "What is total acceptance?" The first thing to remember is that either acceptance is total or it is not acceptance. "Total acceptance" shows that you have repressed something deep in your unconscious and you are using your total force to keep it repressed. Acceptance should be simple. It should be spontaneous; it should not be out of a certain ideology. It should be out of your understanding. Then there is no question of total or non-total acceptance.

A clarity of vision will show you either acceptance or non-acceptance. But "total acceptance" has never been looked into deeply. Why the emphasis on "total"? The emphasis is because it is a repressive measure; you have not understood it. Hence the same things exist in many dimensions: *total* abstinence, *total* celibacy, *total* surrender. I hate the word *total*! Look into your ordinary way of life. Do you say to some woman, "I love you *totally*"? Just to love is enough, more than total. The moment you insist, "I love you *totally*," it creates suspicion. You are trying to hide something behind the great word *total*.

Acceptance is beautiful, but *total* acceptance is not. Acceptance means it is arising out of your own awareness, not out of the teachings, scriptures, and the so-called masters roaming all around the world. It is your own understanding. In fact, when it is your own understanding, even the word *acceptance* becomes futile.

This moment – this silence, the birds in the trees, the sunrays reaching you. Is there any question of acceptance? It is simply happening. It is not a theoretical mind discipline. You are not sitting here with a forced discipline. You are sitting here in this enormous silence without any effort. It is so beautiful that any effort will destroy it. Let me repeat it in another way: "Do you love with effort? Are you compassionate with effort? Are you living with effort, breathing with effort? Is there any effort in your heartbeats?"

In just the same way, the whole of life becomes a spontaneous flow. Your perceptivity, your clarity decides which direction to move. But there is no effort because effort implies you are divided – one part of you is trying to take you in one direction, another part is trying to take you in another direction. Then comes the effort. Only a schizophrenic humanity lives with effort.

I don't know any effort in my life. And I cannot conceive that a man of effort can ever be in tune with existence. With whom are you fighting? Effort is a fight. I don't give you any discipline, I don't give you any commandments. I don't want you to be anyone other than you are. It is perfectly beautiful the way you are. The day you understand it: no trees are making any effort; small bushes are perfectly happy with being small. Tall cedars of Lebanon are perfectly happy with their tallness, but there is no comparison. They don't look at the small bushes as inferior – that is their spontaneity, that is how they are. In this relaxedness comes a shadow, silently, without even making any sound of footsteps – acceptance. But I don't like the word because *acceptance* means that something in you is not accepting – maybe it is a minority part. To repress that minority part, you bring *total* acceptance.

A young man came to me some twenty years ago and said, "I want to totally surrender to you."

I said, "Then you have knocked on the wrong door – go back. The day there is no idea of total and there is no idea of surrender, my doors are open to you. I will rejoice in you as you are – not pruning your branches, molding you into a certain ideal." But all the so-called religions of the world have been doing the same. They are asking of you only one thing, "Don't be yourself, be someone else."

Just the other day, I was talking to Deva Amrito. I said to him, "These should be the last words in your pilgrimage, in your seeking for the truth." His book is going to be called *Years of Preparation*. That gives a dangerous meaning. It means you are moving to achieve something, to become something. There is a certain ideal, far away – you would like to be a Gautam Buddha, a Bodhidharma, a Chuang Tzu or a Jesus Christ. The figure may not be very clear, but there is some faraway star that you are striving to reach. I said to him, "These are my words and they should be put in quotation marks: 'All these years of preparation were futile. You are exactly the same as you have always been.'"

But there are types… People like me are very lazy. I know that this is my place; I don't go running around and then come to this seat. *Years of Preparation* – and to achieve something you have always been? And you cannot achieve anything that you have not always been.

He is a very nice heart, very childish and very loving. He told me "I am disillusioned with money, power, love, relationships." I said, "You have to be disillusioned about one more thing." He looked at me, "What else is there to be disillusioned about?"

I said to him, "This is the last disillusionment, this striving to become someone. *You are it.* Now be disillusioned that all your pilgrimage has been an exercise in utter futility. You have been standing in the same place and only dreaming of preparation. And if your years of preparation have not brought you to this disillusionment, they have been in vain."

Everyone enters the world searching, seeking; it is in a way, natural. But maturity comes when you realize, "My God, I am the one whom I have been seeking!" So the title of his book will look a little strange to the person when he comes to my conclusion in the end. Years of preparation for what? – to know that there was no need of any preparation.

I also told Amrito about a tremendously beautiful pack of cards that existed in China in the days of Lao Tzu and Chuang Tzu. It has ten cards describing the search, the pilgrimage. Those ten cards are called *The Ten Bulls of Zen*. In the first picture, the bull is lost. And naturally, the owner is looking all around in thick forest, and he cannot see his lost bull. In the second picture he finds footprints; now he has a clue. In the third picture he sees the bull – not completely, but just his tail – by the side of a huge tree. But now things are becoming more certain. In the fourth picture he sees half of the bull.

In the fifth picture he has found the bull in its completeness. In the sixth picture he holds the bull by the horns. In the seventh picture he is riding home on the bull. In the eighth picture the bull is put in his place, and in the ninth picture the man is sitting outside his house, playing a flute.

When these ten pictures were transferred to Japan, they cut out the last picture. They accepted only nine pictures. What more is there? You have come home, you are playing the flute, everything is beautiful. That which was lost has been found. But when I looked at the tenth picture I said, "These people got stuck at the ninth. The tenth is the most important." But it went against their ideological, religious, moral training. The tenth picture is of the man going toward the marketplace with a bottle of wine. The buddha has now really come home.

Unless a buddha becomes absolutely ordinary, it is still an ego trip. To be as ordinary as the trees, the birds, the animals, the mountains – no bragging about any spirituality because even the bragging about spirituality is nothing but a very subtle ego trip.

It hurts me to say to you that Gautam Buddha declared, "I am the only enlightened man in the whole history of man. My enlightenment will never be superseded" – this is the ninth picture. The same was the situation with J. Krishnamurti; he could never get out of the ninth picture. He could not become what he has always been.

The mind's ways are very cunning. It will become the richest man, it will become the most powerful man, it will become the "most" of anything. It has to be on the top. It will be difficult for you if you find a buddha in a pub, but that is the right place. He has come home, he has accepted his natural spontaneity.

Don't ask about total acceptance; rather, ask about more clarity, more spontaneity, more naturalness, and acceptance will come just like a shadow. You don't have to bother about it.

Paddy is a private in the British army during World War II. One day, the general calls him to his tent and says, "Private Murphy, you have been chosen for a very special mission. You will be parachuted at night behind the enemy lines, where you will be met by a jeep. And the driver will give you your orders."

So that night, Paddy goes up in the plane. They are approaching the enemy lines when Paddy turns to his officer and says, "But sir, I have never parachuted. What should I do?"

"Don't worry," replies the officer. "All you do is jump. Then three seconds later look up and you will see your parachute open. If it does not, just pull your emergency cord and your second parachute will open. When you land, the jeep will be there to meet you."

"Okay," says Paddy, and jumps out of the plane. Three seconds later he looks up, but nothing happens. So he pulls the emergency cord and still nothing happens. "My God," says Paddy as he rushes toward the ground. "And I bet that bloody jeep won't be there either!"

Life is, intrinsically, a tremendous acceptance without your knowing. Have you accepted your eyes totally? Have you accepted your body totally? Have you accepted your situation in life totally? This idea of total acceptance imposed on you makes you miserable because it continuously creates comparison. Someone has more beautiful eyes, someone has a stronger body, someone is more knowledgeable. You are always feeling inferior and this inferiority goes on eating your heart. You become more and more miserable, but the reason is that you have unnecessarily created it. There is no need to compare because there is no one you can be compared with. You are a unique individual. And whatever you are, that's the way existence wants you to be. Enjoy it.

Change the word *acceptance* because that is not very blissful. Acceptance is something that you have to do, what else to do? There are more beautiful people, there are richer people, there are stronger people, what to do? – accept. I don't teach you acceptance in that way. My idea of acceptance is totally different from all religions.

I declare your uniqueness. You are just yourself and there is not a single person – either in the present or in the past or in the future – who is exactly like you.

Existence gives you such a unique individuality – rejoice in it. And out of that rejoicing, acceptance will come; it is not to be bothered about. I have never felt that I have to become someone. If existence wants me to be no one, I am immensely happy.

In my childhood, my teachers used to say, "You will end up being no one." And they were right! I have ended up as no one. But I am immensely happy, and all those teachers who have been trying to be someone are all miserable. Once in a while I used to go to my village and ask them how things were going: "Because I am feeling so good being no one, and you always look miserable."

Once you start rejoicing whatever you are, life takes such psychedelic colors, your each moment becomes so juicy, your whole life becomes a celebration. Drop those ideas of total acceptance. Why should you accept? It is a very depressing idea that "I accept myself." Rejoice! Dance! Sing! Let the whole world know that you are alone and unique and no one can replace you. To me, this is the way of an authentic search of oneself. There is no comparison – there is no need.

You may be surprised to know that even the so-called great men of your history were all suffering from inferiority. Napoleon Bonaparte was not tall enough, he was only five feet five. And that tortured him all his life. His guards were taller than him. One day he was fixing a picture in his bedroom but he could not reach it. A bodyguard said, "Wait, I am higher than you, I can fix it." Napoleon Bonaparte was very angry. He said, "Change your word *higher*. Simply say you are taller!" What is the difference? The difference is, *higher* hits hard; you are inferior, lower. Say *taller* – that takes much of the pain away.

But I have always wondered: I am exactly five-five, and I have never felt any inferiority. You may be seven feet tall – that does not mean that my feet do not reach the earth. And as far as the sky is concerned, neither you reach nor I reach! So the only decisive factor is that if your feet can reach the earth, it is perfectly good.

But it is not only about one man. Abraham Lincoln was not a very beautiful man; moreover, he stuttered and he was very conscious of it because a presidential candidate stuttering, not looking beautiful, has not much chance in America. A small girl suggested to him, "Uncle, if you grow a little beard that will give a more beautiful shape to your face." According to that small girl's suggestion, he grew the beard. Abraham Lincoln did not succeed in being the president, the beard succeeded! But his whole life he was harassed, haunted by the idea, "What to do with stuttering?" He felt inferior to ordinary people.

You will find, as a great psychological insight, that all politicians are born out of an inferiority complex. Because that inferiority is such a wound, they want to prove to the world that they are not inferior. "I am the president, I am the prime minister." Any man who is happy with himself will be the last to join the line of politicians in the gutter.

The day humanity is rejoicing in itself, politicians, religions, saints, the so-called moralists will all disappear. These are ugly people who are trying to hide their inferiority by becoming something – at least pretending something. They are all hypocrites. And a world without saints, politicians, priests, the so-called learned people, will be such a peaceful world: as peaceful as a garden full of flowers, as peaceful as this morning. There is no need for any war, there is no need for any nations. There is no need for anyone to pretend to be higher, there is no need for anyone to suffer a wound of inferiority.

My whole approach is to make each individual as authentic as he is intended by nature to be. And all the problems of the world will disappear. There is no other way. These problems are created by schizophrenics, neurotics, psychotics; all kinds of madmen are posing as the richest, as the most powerful.

Just see a simple thing: in America, there are thirty million people dying on the streets because they don't have food, they don't have clothes, they don't have shelter. And exactly the same number – thirty million people – are dying in hospitals because they eat too much, and they cannot stop continually stuffing themselves. They have been forced to be hospitalized because it is impossible to control them in their homes.

It is a strange situation. Exactly thirty million people are dying because of starvation and thirty million people are dying because of overeating. Just a small understanding, and sixty million people can be saved. Both are suffering. A hospital is not the place to live nor is the street a place to live. And I take this example from America because America pretends to be the richest country, but I don't see that it has yet become even psychologically normal. The same is being repeated in other countries on a vaster scale. It seems we are dominated by a certain madness. All that is needed is to drop this madness.

The richest man in the world is in Japan; he has twenty-one billion dollars. The richest man in America has only four and a half billion dollars. But can you understand a man having twenty-one billion dollars – what is he going to do with it? It is absurd. And millions of people are dying. Ethiopia is facing again another famine which will be greater than the past one. In the past famine, one thousand people were dying every day. In the coming one perhaps two thousand, three thousand people will be dying. In the European Common Market, every six months they go on drowning so much food in the ocean – mountains of butter – and just the cost of drowning it comes to two billion dollars. It is not the cost of the foodstuff, it is the cost of carrying the food to the ocean. And just by the side, in Ethiopia people don't have water to drink, people don't have food to eat.

The situation has fallen so low that in Palestine the government was forced by the people to agree that they should be allowed to eat human bodies – of course only of those who had died naturally. But this is the beginning. What is the problem if someone has not died naturally, but has committed suicide, has hanged himself? The difference is not much. What is the problem if you can get hold of some Israeli? It is a simple question, whether to eat the dead man first or to first make him dead and then eat. For the first time in history, a government has accepted that it is no longer a crime. And this is about human beings eating human beings. What about animals?

If you look around the world it seems to be a madhouse. But the mad people are in the majority, and naturally, the maddest of them are chosen to be the presidents, to be the prime ministers.

It happened in a madhouse that the old superintendent doctor was retiring and the new doctor was going to take charge. They celebrated the occasion in order to give a farewell to the retiring doctor and to give a welcome to the person who was coming in. When the old doctor was speaking, everyone was silent – no emotions, no expression, no clapping, no laughter, as if no one was there. But when the new doctor started speaking, a tremendous change happened. People were clapping, shouting, jumping, laughing. The new doctor could not understand – what is the matter? He asked his assistant, "What is the matter?"

He said, "I should not say it but I cannot hide it either. The mad people think you look more like them. You are the right person; the older one was a little too sane."

If man accepts whatever he is and uses his capacities for creativity – and everyone is born with certain capacities, certain talents, a certain creativity – he will be immensely happy in being no one. You don't have to be happy only if you become the richest man or the most powerful man. These are the childish ways of primitive man which we have carried up to now.

I would like to say to you, drop the words "total acceptance." Instead, replace them with the simple words "rejoicing in yourself." And the moment you rejoice in yourself, the whole existence rejoices in you. You have fallen in tune with the harmonious dance that is going on all around. Only man has fallen way from being part of existence, and the reason he has fallen away from it is because he wants to be someone special. If you want to be special, you will have to accept some kind of madness.

A psychoanalyst was asked, "I have heard many times these words *neurotic*, *psychotic*, but I don't see what the difference is."

The psychoanalyst said, "The difference is very delicate. The psychotic thinks that two and two make five, and he is fanatically determined about it. No one can change his mind."

The man asked, "What about the neurotic?"

He said, "The neurotic is one who knows that two and two are four, but is very uneasy about it."

Delicate differences. Unless you rejoice in whatever you are, wherever you are, whoever you are, you are not sane. According to me the definition of sanity is: a man rejoicing in his nature.

Just not to leave you serious…

A Chinese laundryman living in San Francisco opens a savings account at the bank and goes regularly to deposit his profits.

After several months he has saved up a considerable sum. One day, he comes into the bank and says that he wants to withdraw all his money. The clerk is surprised, so the Chinaman explains that he is about to get married and go on his honeymoon. The manager is called and tries to persuade the man to just withdraw enough for his immediate requirements. He also explains that if he takes out all his money, he will lose the interest. But the Chinaman will not be persuaded and so eventually he walks out with all his money.

A few weeks later, the bank manager meets the Chinaman on the street and asks him about his honeymoon and married life. The Chinaman has only this to say, "No good. Honeymoon and married life are just like banking – put in, take out, lose interest."

7

Forget about Spiritual Goals

Osho,
It seems that an automatic process, more like a pregnancy, has taken over the steering wheel. I don't have to do a thing, though I can't stop listening. Insights present themselves even if not asked for. Is this the meaning of the expression "a good sadhana is effortless"? Please comment.

Deva Amrito, it is the right time for you to see the truth in its utter nudity. Many ears may not be ready for it. But even though they are not ready for it, they are on the way to being ready one day. Let this be a seed in them: the truth about a good sadhana is that it is no longer a sadhana at all. A "good sadhana" is still a bad sadhana.

The word *sadhana* has to be understood. It comes from the root *sadhan*; *sadhan* means methods, paths, ways, techniques. The so-called sadhanas of all the religions are just spiritual games people like to play. The word *spiritual* makes them more piously egoistic.

Someone is interested in football, someone else is interested in playing cards – these are thought to be worldly games. But as I see it, there are no otherworldly games; all games are worldly. Someone is trying to achieve more success, someone is trying to become richer, someone else is trying to be more powerful. And all these have been condemned by the so-called religions without any exception.

But when someone starts moving toward higher planes of being, then you forget completely that it is the same game, only the label has changed. It is the same ego trying to prove itself special, higher than others, better than others. It is still the same comparative mind, and the comparative mind is a mind in confusion, in a mess. A comparative mind is an insane mind.

Amrito, if you simply allow things to happen – not even choosing; whatever comes to you is deeply, respectfully and gratefully accepted as a gift from the great existence – then you have become effortless. Even a slight choice on your part – "if it would have been just a little bit different" – and you have missed the point. To see existence as it is, choicelessly, is what is meant by effortlessness. It does not mean that you don't have to do anything.

Misunderstandings are so great, and particularly in the world of seekers, that they can make an effort to be choiceless. They can make an effort to be effortless, and they will not see what they are doing. The people who have known reality not as a knowledge but as an experience, have emphasized one point tremendously – that you are already what you can ever be. Your essential reality has already been given to you. It is not going to happen in the future. It is possible you may not realize it in the present. That does not mean that it is not present, it simply means your eyes are closed. You can stand with closed eyes before a sunrise and you will remain in darkness. That does not deny the existence of the sun, it simply shows your stupidity. Just open your eyes. And in fact all that you need is already given to you.

Amrito, I am reminded of a Sufi story…

A very strange mystic, Junnaid, used to pray and every time he would pray – in the morning, evening, night – he would end his prayer with a deep gratitude toward existence: "Your compassion and your abundance of gifts to me is so much that I feel embarrassed. How am I going to repay it? I don't have anything to give you, except my empty gratefulness and my tears."

He and his many disciples were on a pilgrimage. Once it happened that for three days continuously, they passed through villages where there were fanatic Mohammedans. They would not give Junnaid and his disciples food, not even water. There was no question of shelter either. They were three days in the desert without food, water, shelter. But the prayer continued to be the same and the gratefulness toward existence did not change even a little bit.

This was too much for the disciples. When days were good, it was perfectly okay to be grateful, but they had been starving for three days, thirsty, in the cold nights of the desert with no shelter, and with no hope that tomorrow things would be better. Finally, they encountered their master Junnaid and said, "There is a limit to everything. We have listened to your prayer for years, and we thought it was perfectly in tune with existence. Existence was giving us everything. But these three days we have waited, thinking that perhaps you will stop being grateful or maybe you will even complain, but you seem to be the same. Again the same gratitude, the same tears – we can't understand it. For what are you being so full of gratitude?"

Junnaid laughed and said, "These three days were the most important in my life. These three days showed me whether I have any gratitude or not. Is my gratitude simply a bargain, a persuasion, or is my gratitude something that has grown in my heart? It doesn't matter. As far as I am concerned, I don't have a choice. Whatever existence gives me is needed by me. These three days of starvation were absolutely needed by me; it is not possible for it to be otherwise. These three days of thirst, coldness in the night, almost facing death, were absolutely my intrinsic needs. I don't know about you – my gratitude is not conditional. My gratitude is unconditional, it is not because God is good to me. It has no reason at all; it is simply my joy, my blissfulness, my prayerfulness to existence. I don't have a choice."

A choiceless awareness simply means that whatever happens to you is perfectly the right thing to have happened. You don't have any judgment about it. It does not mean that you will stop doing things; you will continue doing things, but doing your things will be more like a man flowing in the current of the river, not swimming, not swimming against the current.

The effort comes when you are against the current: existence wants you to move north and you want to move toward the south. There comes the struggle, there comes your effort, there comes your separate existence as an ego. But if you are simply flowing with the river wherever it is going, you don't have a goal because a man with a goal cannot be choiceless. You don't have a destination because a man with a destination cannot relax and cannot be choiceless. He has already chosen.

There were two temples in Japan that were traditionally antagonistic to each other. For centuries they had been fighting, arguing against each other's theology. Each of the temples had an old priest, and a young boy to serve their small needs. Both the old monks had told the boys, "You should not talk with the other boy. We are not on talking terms; we are traditional enemies." But boys are boys. They wanted to play with each other. In that lonely forest, far away from the nearest village, they were the only two people who could have some communication with each other.

One day, one boy dared to disobey the old monk. He stood by the road. He knew that every day the other boy would also come out of the temple to go to the market to fetch vegetables and other things. The boy came. The first boy asked him, very friendly, "Where are you going?"

But the other boy said, "Wherever the winds take me."

The answer was not a friendly one; the answer was not to start a conversation. The boy just said this and moved away. The first boy felt very bad and he thought that his master was right, "These people are very ugly. I was asking a simple question and he is talking metaphysics."

He went to the temple and said to the master, "Please forgive me, I disobeyed you and I have been punished already."

The master listened and said, "Don't be worried. Tomorrow you stand at the same place and when the boy answers you by saying 'Wherever the winds take me' ask him, 'If the winds are not blowing, then?' You have to stop him, you have to defeat him. It is a question of our prestige."

Early in the morning the boy was ready – he had repeated many times what he had to say. Then he asked, as the boy was approaching, "Where are you going?"

And the boy said, "Wherever my legs take me."

Now this was too much! He had crammed his answer the whole night, and now the answer is absolutely irrelevant! With great anger he went to the master and said, "Those people are really cunning. They are not people to be relied upon, they change their answers."

The master said, "I had told you before, but now you have started an unnecessary trouble. Tomorrow stand there again, and when he says, 'Wherever my legs take me' ask him, 'If you had no legs, then?'"

Ready with the answer and again the same situation, the boy asked, "Where are you going?"

And the other boy said, "To fetch some vegetables from the market."

Now, what to do with these unreliable people? Whenever you have something fixed in your mind, you are going to be disappointed by existence. The old proverb has some truth in it, "Man proposes and God disposes." But it is not that there is a God who disposes you. In your very proposition you have disposed yourself. Don't propose and there is no possibility of anyone disposing you. Don't have a goal and you will never be a failure. Don't make a destination and you will never go wrong. But to understand, it simply means you will have to go on floating with the river; whether it leads anywhere or not is not your concern. You are enjoying the moment. This very moment, with the sun shining and the birds singing and the trees around the river, is enough unto itself.

But a tremendous calamity has happened to humanity, and the calamity has been brought by your so-called religious founders, by your so-called great moral leaders, your politicians, priests, professors. For centuries these people have been telling you that as you are, you are not worthy enough. Condensed, their whole teaching is that you have to become worthy, that you have to deserve some respectability, some prestigiousness. As you are, you are empty.

They had their own vested interest in it. The moralist goes on telling you that you are immoral; you are born in sin. He creates a certain psychology of guilt. It is a strategy. Once a man starts feeling guilty, he becomes sick. He loses his dignity, his individuality, his courage. He starts looking up to someone else to lead him, to guide him because as far as he is concerned, he is born in sin and whatever he does is going to be wrong. He has lost his guts.

All your leaders are living by destroying you. They are leaders because you need someone to lead you, and to make you so condemned in your own eyes that you cannot ever think that you can stand on your own feet. And that you can declare to the world, "I am alone and as I am, I am absolutely right. This is the way existence has created me."

A tremendous revolution is needed in the world where each individual declares his individuality. But you declare yourself a Christian and you have lost your individuality; you declare yourself an Indian and you have lost your individuality. You declare yourself part of any organized ideology and you have moved into a miserable situation, out of which it is very difficult to find a way. You will be getting more and more, deeper and deeper, into the mess. Because all those people are enjoying their greatness by making you small.

I am reminded of one of the great emperors of India, Akbar…

He had a great joy in accumulating all kinds of geniuses in his court from all over the country, and he loved to ask questions and to listen to their discussions.

One day he asked a very strange question. He came to the court, and he drew a straight line on a blackboard and asked the people of his court, "Without touching this line, can you make it smaller? There is a great prize waiting for you." And he had a very beautiful diamond in his hand as a prize.

Everyone started thinking, "Without touching it, how can you make it smaller?"

Akbar had a man in his court who had a great sense of humor. Since no one else was standing up, he went to the board and drew a bigger line underneath the smaller line. Without touching it he made it smaller.

The emperor Akbar remembers the incident in his autobiography, *Akbarnama*. "Even I had not thought about it, I had just looked at small children's books and found the puzzle. I thought, this is great! Because I could not figure out how you could make it small without touching it."

But in this small incident is hidden the whole misery of humanity. You have been made small without touching.

Great stories have been propounded about Mahavira – that he does not perspire. Now, only a man who has no skin and is made of plastic can manage not to perspire, and certainly plastic was not available twenty-five centuries ago. But why create such a story? – just to make you small. You perspire, you are ordinary mortals. Mahavira belongs to immortality, he does not perspire.

I have inquired as deeply as possible: neither Krishna, Buddha, nor Mahavira ever became old. There is not a single statue, not a single picture, not a single description; they are always young. Just go into any Buddhist, Jaina, Hindu temple; it is strange that these people don't grow old. They seem to be like old gramophone records which get stuck and go on repeating the same line again and again and again. But they are kept young just to make you realize that they belong to a separate category, a higher category. They don't belong to you. A snake bites Mahavira, and instead of blood, milk comes out…

Some thirty years ago, I had come to Mumbai for the first time, invited by a conference celebrating Mahavira's birthday. Just before me, the most prominent Jaina monk described exactly this incident to prove that Mahavira is no ordinary mortal; he has come from the beyond to save you, to save humanity.

Just by coincidence I was the second speaker and I asked the monk, "Have you ever thought about it? If the milk comes from the feet, then the whole body of Mahavira must be filled with milk because Mahavira cannot know where the snake is going to bite. And milk in a man's body for forty years must have turned to curd, to butter. It cannot remain milk.

"It is true that the human body is capable, particularly the female human body, but even a woman cannot produce milk from her feet. These are only simple conclusions: either Mahavira had breasts all over the body, or he must be stinking! And the conclusion that you have drawn is that this proves him to be immortal, that he has come to save humanity."

But humanity does not seem to be saved.

I have been wondering – so many saviors! Jesus is saving humanity, Buddha is saving humanity, Mahavira is saving humanity. Where is this humanity? We never come across the saved humanity, only these people who are bragging that they are going to save.

I was sitting on the bank of the Ganges, next to the Christian College in Allahabad. I was alone, it was getting dark, the sun was setting, and a man jumped in the river. I had no idea why he had jumped; it was not my business. Then he started shouting, "Help!" Only we two were there, and there was not time enough to inquire, "Why have you jumped? If you want to be saved, you were already saved." But there was no time so I jumped, pulled him out – against his will. And that felt even more strange, that he was fighting with me.

But somehow I pulled him out of the river and he said, "What kind of man are you? I was trying to commit suicide."

I said, "If you were committing suicide, then why were you shouting 'Help, save me'?"

He said, "It is human nature. I was determined to kill myself but when the cold water… And I realized that I didn't know how to swim. I forgot all about the miseries which have driven me to commit suicide."

I said, "There is no problem."

He said, "What do you mean?"

I said, "I don't have to say anything." I simply pushed him back into the river.

He started shouting again. I said, "No more. It is your business. The first time I got trapped because I could not understand that a man who wants to commit suicide would shout for help, but now I know."

He came up one time, two times, and said, "Save me, please, I don't want to commit suicide!"

I said, "Neither do I want to jump into that cold water again! I am happy where I am, you be happy wherever you are."

First, all these people are forcing you to be sinners, immoral, unvirtuous, and then they are ready to save you. First they convince you that you are sick and then they hospitalize you. They run the hospital. All these people together, however differing in their philosophies, are absolutely in agreement on one point: that man has to be proved unworthy, undignified, undeserving. Only a humanity which has been forced into a state of having deep feelings of guilt can be enslaved by the politicians, priests, pedagogues, but the basic strategy is the same.

I am fighting against the whole human past, and I am fighting against all those who have been trying to save you. You are perfectly saved. There is no need for anyone to make an unnecessary effort to save you. You are as good as existence needs you to be. In this moment, in this place, no one else can replace you. You are irreplaceable. You are not a machine where parts can be replaced. That is your dignity.

Just the other night I was telling Amrito that there have been people like J. Krishnamurti who will not even create a disciple, and my effort is just the opposite. To me, the disciple is only the beginning of a master. My effort is to give you the dignity of being a master. And unless each of my sannyasins is a master unto himself, he is going to remain in different kinds of slaveries, consciously or unconsciously. No one in the whole history of man has tried to give man his dignity. Yes, Jesus says to people, "You are my sheep, I am your shepherd." And I sometimes wonder that not a single man stood up to say, "Shut up, please! I am also a shepherd."

Gautam Buddha's story is that he was born while his mother was standing under a *saal* tree. It is a strange way of being born, and not only that, he stood directly on the earth after coming out of the womb. Ordinarily the head comes first. Once in a while the feet also come first, but no one has ever heard that a just-born child stands on the earth and walks seven feet and declares to the world, "I am the most enlightened person in the whole existence."

My problem is that for twenty-five centuries no one has criticized this man: "What kind of nonsense...?" We have become so enslaved that we have lost the courage. Even when we see absolutely patent nonsense, we don't raise a question. We simply accept it. We are left in such a situation that we have lost all our intelligence. And the profit goes certainly to the vested interests; they would like you to remain in the same situation.

Amrito, I would like you to just forget all about spiritual growth. Forget all about spiritual goals. Existence has no goal; existence is simply a tremendous playfulness of energy, not going anywhere. Rejoice in this dance, be part of this dance, and flowers of tremendous bliss will shower on you.

No one has to lead you and no one has to save you. All those people were nothing but very subtle egoists. They have dominated humanity up to now, and this is the result that we see all over the world – just misery. People go on living because what else to do? They go on dragging themselves knowing perfectly well that in the end is the grave. Hoping, dreaming, imagining, but not living. I teach you life, and life is now and here. It is always now and always here, and except drowning yourself in life in all its dimensions, in all its colors, there is no paradise. There is nothing else but this sheer dance.

People go on changing their illusions. When they are young someone has the illusion of love; perhaps love will open the doors of all the mysteries. It opens the doors, not of the mysteries, but of the miseries. Someone is running after money. And a man like Henry Ford, when asked, "You have earned more money than anyone else in the world. Now, at the top, how do you feel?" said, "Utterly frustrated because at the top there is nothing. All that I have learned in my whole life is climbing ladders. I went on climbing hoping that on the next rung may be fulfillment, but fulfillment never comes."

I have said to Amrito that when people are finished with their worldly hopes, illusions, dreams, then they change and start hoping about spiritual growth, God, paradise. These are the same people and this is the same mind which has not learned anything at all.

Unless you are completely disillusioned – that means now you don't think of tomorrow at all – you will not know the pure truth of existence, which just exists in this moment. You will not fall in tune with it. You are always moving away, postponing. You are going, you are always on the go. It is time for you to be completely disillusioned about worldly illusions, about otherworldly illusions, about love, money, enlightenment. Just simply be whatever you are, and you have arrived home. In fact you have never left it. You have always been here.

Just to bring you back to your senses…

Grandma Feigenbaum, out walking her dog, goes into the local supermarket and leaves the dog tied to the railing outside.

Immediately, the dog is surrounded by all the neighborhood dogs who come to sniff.

A cop, standing close by, watches this and calls to the old woman, "Lady, you can't leave your dog alone like that, she's in heat."

"Eat?" says Grandma Feigenbaum. "She'll eat anything."

"No, no!" shouts the cop. "The dog should be bred."

"Bread, cake, biscuits," calls out Grandma, "she'll eat anything you give her."

Becoming frustrated, the cop yells out, "Your dog should be screwed!"

"So screw her," calls back Grandma. "I always wanted a police dog."

8

In Stillness, You Disappear

Osho,

A few weeks ago, I was awake, and suddenly there was only talking. There was no talker. For years I had listened to the statement that the observer and the observed were one. I saw there was no room, no necessity for a thinker; only consciousness and the arising of phenomena. Instead of jumping out of bed, I turned around and slept. Insight seems to be like a gentle breeze, a whisper. Will you say something about the non-dramatic quality of real insight?

Deva Amrito, J. Krishnamurti has made it known worldwide that "the observer is the observed." I want to refute him completely. The moment there is no observer, there is nothing to be observed. The observer and the observed disappear simultaneously – and there is only silence; neither the knower nor the known.

This is something very complex to understand because the mind always wants duality. With *two*, the mind is absolutely at ease. The knower and the known – and the two always create the third, the knowledge. The observer and the observed are bound to create the third, the observation. Then there is no end to this infinite regress. My own silence is: there is no observer and there is no observed. Hence nothing can be said about it. The moment you say it, you lie.

It is one of the reasons Lao Tzu never said anything, never wrote anything. He had a great following, but a very strange following. Every disciple had come to listen, to understand, to know, but Lao Tzu insistently, his whole life long, refused to say anything about truth or to write anything about truth. He was ready to talk about anything else – but the people had come to know about the truth. Finally the day came. Lao Tzu left for the Himalayas to enter the eternal peace of those beautiful mountains. But the emperor of China was also interested to know what Lao Tzu had been hiding and not telling, not even giving a hint about what truth is. He ordered all the borders to be closed to Lao Tzu saying, "He cannot leave China unless he writes something about truth."

Lao Tzu was caught crossing the border toward the Himalayas – respectfully, lovingly. The emperor was not an enemy but a disciple. The emperor himself was present because that was the route they assumed he would take toward the Himalayas. A beautiful house was made for him so that he could rest and write down his experience of truth. Unless he did it, the doors would not be open for him; he was guarded continuously. This was a strange situation; perhaps no other master has ever encountered such a situation – loaded guns in the hands of the disciples!

And we can understand the situation of the disciples. They wanted to preserve the most important experience of truth for future generations. Under compulsion, Lao Tzu closed himself in the house and wrote a small book. The first sentence in that book says, "That which can be said cannot be true. That which can be written is bound to be a lie. Remember these two statements while you read my book."

Even loaded guns cannot force a master to say something which cannot be said. When the emperor got the book, Lao Tzu was released. But he had deceived them. If you remember these statements – that truth said becomes untrue, truth expressed loses the quality of being true – and if these conditions have to be remembered while reading the book, in fact there is no point in reading it! But Lao Tzu was gone.

What had been the difficulty for Lao Tzu? Because every Tom, Dick and Harry is talking about truth. *Only* Toms, Dicks and Harrys can talk about truth because they know nothing about it. To enter that silence where the two disappear… Krishnamurti has chosen to say that when the two disappear only one remains. But that goes against all the mystic experiences of the world because if one remains, the other is just around the corner; you cannot conceive what one means if you do not have some idea of the two.

A great mystic, Shankara from India, instead of using one tried a different way. It doesn't make much difference, but it is certainly better than J. Krishnamurti's idea. Shankara says a nonduality remains. He does not say one remains because one reminds you of two. He reverses the process. He says the two are no more – that will remind you of the one. But even reminding you in an indirect way is still the same.

Perhaps Gautam Buddha comes very close to saying the unsayable, but I am saying "very close." I am not saying that he has said it – almost. He denies rather than affirms. Krishnamurti affirms that "the observer is the observed." Gautam Buddha says, "Neither is there an observer nor is there the observed." In the whole history of mankind, perhaps he comes closest. He simply denies, and his denial is such that it does not provoke the idea of one; neither the observer nor the observed. And he remains silent about what remains. Just pure silence, no one even to experience it, no one even to express it.

I repeat that J. Krishnamurti has been confusing thousands of people in his long life of ninety years. If you ask me, Amrito, I will say just be quiet about it. Let it be. Don't try to describe what it is. This is a deep itch in the mind to describe everything. Unless the mind describes it, the itch remains. It is a kind of sickness. When everything has come to a standstill, when you are not, who is going to experience? Who is going to observe, and what is going to be observed? Just a stillness, and you have disappeared in it and the observed has also disappeared in it.

This is unsayable and will remain unsayable. However close you come to it, you are still far away. My own understanding is just to avoid talking about it. Don't mention it. Experience, but there should be no experiencer. In ordinary human life, there is nothing which can be compared to this experience. That creates great difficulty. Otherwise some indications, some hints – and all kinds of ways have been tried: "It is one." "It is not two." "It is neither this nor that." Just one thing has been left, which I am trying: "It is that neither are you an observer nor is there an observed. A pure oceanic vastness, an utter silence which cannot be reduced into language in any way."

But the mind is more cunning than you understand it to be. I will read your question to show you how the mind brings everything from the back door. "A few weeks ago I was awake..." *You* were there, and you were also experiencing that you were awake. The observer was there, the observed was there. The duality was perfectly following you. "...and suddenly saw there was only talking." Still the duality – who saw the talking? You were still there, listening to the talking. Because you were listening, you thought there was only talking, but the talking cannot exist without a listener. This is something to be understood.

The moment you leave your room and lock it, do you think your clothes in the room remain the same color? The white remains white, the blue remains blue, the green remains green? You are wrong. The moment you are out of the room and there is no one to see, colors disappear. For a color to exist, the eyes are absolutely necessary. Who is going to see the color? Ordinarily we don't think so – that the moment you leave your room everything changes – but the fact is scientific, that every color disappears with you. And the moment you look through the keyhole they all come back! It looks strange, but the whole of life is such. You stand and look at the sun. There is light, tremendous beauty. But close your eyes, and for you, the sun is no longer a light, and it no longer creates colors. For you, all flowers lose their colorfulness.

It is not a new question. In India, for almost five thousand years the philosophers have discussed it, and the discussion still continues even in this century. One British philosopher, Bradley, and his colleague, Bosanquet, insisted that if a man is deaf no sounds exist for him, and if all people become deaf there will be no sounds. If all people become blind there will be no colors, flowers, rainbows, stars. It looks very illogical because the flower has its own color. It does not have.

This strange experiment has finally come to the conclusion that when you see a color as red, it is all colors *except* red. Why does it look red? – because the sunrays fall on your bodies, your flowers, your trees; every flower absorbs rays from among the seven colors of the rainbow. Perhaps if all colors are absorbed, then the flower will look black. But if the flower resists and does not allow the red to be absorbed, the flower will look red. The red is the rejected ray of the sun that reaches your eye. And if the flower rejects the whole range of seven colors then it will look white.

It is not coincidental that in all the traditions of the world, white has always been thought to be something pure – without knowing exactly why. The reasonings that science has produced are very new. But white somehow represented purity, innocence, cleanliness. And every religion has depicted the Devil as black. These are symbolic. The Devil is nothing but greed. He goes on absorbing everything; he never rejects anything. The white is non-greed. It never accumulates anything, it goes on reflecting it back to its source. The Devil is a beggar; hence he has been depicted as black. But the white is utter simplicity. These symbols have persisted for thousands of years, but their implications and their scientific reasons have become available only now.

Amrito, when you say, "...suddenly I saw there was only talking," you forgot the seer, the listener. You became so focused on listening that you forgot who is listening. This is what I call the mind's very subtle cunningness. It was still two, but it managed to deceive you as one. "There was no talker." These are the rationalizations of the mind. It said, "Look, there is only talking, no talker!" But what about the listener?

Wherever there are two, there are three. You became impressed by the fact that there is no talker and the talking is going on, and you forgot who is being aware that there is no talker. And who is being aware of the talking? You were there, perfectly there, and the duality had not disappeared. "For years I had listened to the statement that the observer and the observed were one." You have listened to that statement by J. Krishnamurti. But sometimes I feel so strange that J. Krishnamurti perhaps talked more than anyone else before him. I am saying *before* him, not after him – I am still alive; that poor fellow is dead! When he said, "The observer and the observed were one," who was making this decision? Who was being aware that the observer and the observed are one? Who was the witness?

And not a single person throughout his fifty years of continuous teaching ever raised the question: "I can understand the observer is the observed, but who is the witness?" Certainly a witness is needed, someone who is standing behind and seeing that the observer and the observed are one. Again he has fallen into the same fallacy. That's why I said I am going to refute it completely.

You say, "I saw there was no room…" Then where were you? The word *room* is very meaningful. It simply means space. People have completely forgotten the root meaning of the word *room*. When you take out all the furniture from your room, all the bookshelves, everything out, you say, "Now it looks roomier." All those things were obstructing the room. They were filling the space. If you say, "I saw there was no room" you were there, and your very presence needs a certain space. That is your room. There may not be walls to your room. Even if you make the whole sky your room – it does not matter how big the room is; if you are there, you will be surrounded by space. Without space you cannot be there. And that space is the real room.

I used to stay in a very rich man's house. He was so rich that he used to collect all kinds of junk, and in the guesthouse where I used to stay, he had put everything you can possibly conceive. When he took me to the guesthouse for the first time he said, "This is going to be your room."

I looked inside and I said, "But where is the room?" A big, beautiful piano, radios, very costly furniture, many paintings and even though television had not come to that city at that time, he had a beautiful television set. Someday, television will come. I said, "I can see so many things, they have destroyed the room completely! If you want me to stay in this place, I refuse. Take all this junk out so that I can have some room."

He could not understand me. He said, "What do you mean by room?"

I mean that *room* simply means spaciousness. The room can be bigger, can be smaller, but if you are there, your very presence creates a room around you. As far as you can see – that is the wall of your room. They will both disappear together. But then there will be no one to say, "The room has disappeared. I have also disappeared." You cannot say, "I have also disappeared." There will be no one to say anything. No room, no you, no observer, no observed. Just a pure silence without any ripples.

A famous Sufi story about Mulla Nasruddin…

Mulla was always bragging in the town's cafeteria that he is a very generous man, very compassionate. People were getting tired of it. They said, "We have listened to this so many times, but we have never seen a single act of compassion, generosity, friendliness. Prove it!"

He said, "Okay, you are all invited" – a group of a hundred people from the cafeteria – "to come to my house for dinner today. Just follow me and you will see the act."

In the heat of discussion he said this, but as he started approaching closer to the house he remembered what he had done. In the morning his wife had sent him to fetch some vegetables from the market, and the whole day he had been wandering here and there. He had not come back to the house all day. And he knew perfectly well, as every husband knows, that there is only one kind of husband in the world: they are all henpecked.

He was also aware that there was nothing in the house for one hundred people – and he had invited them for dinner! He cooled down, slowed down, and finally he said, "Listen, you are all husbands and we all know the real situation. I don't have to explain it to you. Please wait outside the door. First let me go in and find a way to tell my wife that without informing her, I have invited one hundred guests for dinner."

It was understandable. Everyone was a husband, so there was no question of not understanding it. They remained outside. Mulla Nasruddin went in, closed the door… And the wife was furious! The whole day she had been waiting, hungry because there was no food, no vegetables, nothing in the house. Mulla Nasruddin said, "That is a secondary problem. I am in a more troublesome state. First help me."

The wife said, "What is the trouble?"

Mulla Nasruddin said, "In the heat of discussion, I have invited one hundred people for dinner. They are standing outside the house."

The wife said, "My God, are you mad? There is not enough food even for two of us! Now what do you want me to do?"

He said, "Just a simple thing. Go out and ask them why they are standing there. Naturally they will say, 'Mulla Nasruddin has invited us for dinner.' Tell them that there must have been some misunderstanding because since the morning he has not been seen: 'Where did you see him? I am waiting for him.'"

The wife also felt a little weird because Mulla was standing inside the house, but there was no other way. Finally, hesitantly, she went to the door, just opened the door a little bit and asked, "Why this crowd? What are you doing here?"

They said, "We are not a crowd. We are friends of Mulla Nasruddin, your husband. And he has invited us for dinner."

The wife said, "He left the house in the morning and since then he has not returned. There must be some misunderstanding."

They said, "There is no misunderstanding. A hundred people are witnesses; he came with us and he entered this door."

The wife was at a loss what to do because the Mulla was inside. Mulla was also listening. He went upstairs and from the window he said, "Listen you fellows! Can't you understand a single thing: Mulla may have come with you and may have gone out the back door. And feel ashamed! Arguing with a poor woman!"

Sufis have used the story for centuries. These stories are so simple and so beautiful, but so pregnant with meaning.

Amrito, you say, "I saw there was no room…" It is impossible. You will have to understand Mulla Nasruddin's situation. He is denying that he is in the house. His very denial is a proof that he *is* in the house.

You cannot say, "I am not." Then who is saying it? In saying "I am not," you have proved that you are. You go on saying, "…no necessity for a thinker…" Who is thinking this "…no necessity for a thinker…"? It is certainly a thought. The necessity or no necessity are both thoughts. "…only consciousness" – but that is again a thought – "and the arising of phenomena." So everything has come back from the back door! "…arising of phenomena" – certainly you are the observer and the phenomena is the observed. The mind has come back, saying to you, "There is no necessity of thinking." But this is thinking. If you are, you cannot get rid of the other. The other will follow you just like your shadow. You may become oblivious to it, you may not see it. The mind knows very cunning ways.

And I am analyzing your question for a certain reason because it is going to be everyone's problem sooner or later. A man comes to me and says, "I experienced bliss." It is nonsense. Either *you* can be or *bliss* can be. Both cannot be together. And if there is only bliss, who is going to report it?

Lao Tzu's greatest disciple was Chuang Tzu. He was moving on the path. He was reporting his experiences every day – the arising of spiritual phenomena, experiences of light, lotuses flowering – but Lao Tzu never paid any attention to what he was saying. The only thing that Chuang Tzu could see from Lao Tzu's face was, "Don't waste my time. Just go, start meditating again."

But one day Chuang Tzu never came – he used to come early in the morning. Lao Tzu waited for him. It was time for sunset and he inquired, "Where is Chuang Tzu?"

They said, "He is sitting under a tree. From the morning he has been sitting there."

Lao Tzu said, "It seems I will have to go and see what is happening. Something is certainly happening for the first time." And he went, shook Chuang Tzu's body and said, "Aha! But keep your mouth shut! Now there is no need to come every day to me to describe all that rubbish."

Chuang Tzu fell at the feet of Lao Tzu with tears of joy and said, "Your compassion is great. How many years have I tortured you? Your compassion was so great, you never said anything. You simply said, 'Continue.' You never denied. And today you have come to me just to say, 'Aha!'" Nothing more can be said.

Amrito, you are saying, "I saw there was no room, no necessity for a thinker; only consciousness..." Why are you using the word *only*? Unconsciously you are also aware that if there is only consciousness, there is no need for the adjective *only*. You know perfectly well you were there, and all the luggage that you have been preserving in the mind was there with you. "...and the arising of phenomena. Instead of jumping out of bed, I turned around and slept." That is the only good thing you did! And if ever again such stupid things happen to you, remember – don't jump out of the bed, just take a turn and go to sleep. Sleep is far better than dreaming. Your experiences were nothing but dreams, soap bubbles, with no validity of their own.

"Insight seems to be like a gentle breeze..." Insight does not "seem to be" like a gentle breeze. It is. And the difference is great. Do you say to someone, "It seems I love you. It almost seems I love you"? Either you love or you don't. Again you have started dreaming because just turning on your side does not make much difference. You can dream facing to one side, you can dream facing to another side; there are dreamers walking in the streets who are dreaming with open eyes. Dreaming is possible in every situation. "Insight seems to be like a gentle breeze, a whisper." No. When the insight opens there is no way to describe it, you cannot say it "...seems like a gentle breeze..." or "...a whisper." It is absolute silence. A whisper is too loud, and a gentle breeze is far below.

In our ordinary experiences nothing exists that can be compared to the flowering of your insight. Those who have come to the insight have suddenly become utterly silent because they cannot find how to say it, what to say about it, whom to say it to. Who is going to understand?

Gautam Buddha became enlightened one full-moon night and for seven days he did not utter a single word. The story is so beautiful. It needs to be understood from different angles because it brings new meanings, new implications. Why did he remain silent for seven days? First, he was so overwhelmed there was no question of doing anything about it. Everything was *happening*.

He had five disciples; later on he thought, "At least I should say something to those five disciples. I was ignorant, but I pretended to be a master." And there are many who are doing the same all over the world because it is easier to be a master than to be a disciple. The disciple has to go through such a transformation.

He felt compassion for those five who had followed him, but what to say to them? Will they understand? He knew perfectly well that if he himself had not been overwhelmed with the explosion, no one could have explained it to him. He would have laughed. And he does not want to become a laughingstock, but the compassion is there – which is intrinsic as you become more and more centered, more and more yourself, more and more inseparable with existence. Compassion simply comes to you. It is not something to be cultivated, not something to be disciplined. Just as the spring comes and the flowers start blossoming, the morning comes and the trees start awakening, something spontaneous… So is compassion.

He tried hard – in what way to convey it? But all words were empty. All words were contaminated. And the problem was more complicated. He would speak the word, and something of the truth would be lost in speaking. Then the person would hear it, and whatever was left would be lost in his hearing because he was going to interpret it in his own way according to his own prejudices.

On the seventh day he decided not to speak at all. Those seven days were a continuous anguish, "I know it now, but I am absolutely helpless." The story is that five gods… In Buddhism there is not one god, there are as many gods as there are living beings because every living being ultimately has to flower into a god. As far as the question of gods is concerned, Mohammedanism, Judaism, Christianity, are very dictatorial. Their gods resemble Ronald Reagan more than anyone else. Buddhism has a very democratic idea about gods. Everyone has the potential. It is up to you when you realize it. And there is no hurry either because eternity is available.

Five gods came to Gautam Buddha and prayed to him, "It happens very rarely, in millions of years, that a man comes to this state, to this space, to this blissfulness, to this truth. And the whole existence waits that now your fragrance will raise the consciousness of all those who are ready to move, who are ready to transform, and you have decided not to speak! We have come to pray to you, please speak."

They had to argue with Gautam Buddha for many days because each argument was refuted by him. And the gods also felt that he was right that no one is going to understand, everyone is going to misunderstand. Rather than helping people, the greater possibility is that the people will stone him to death!

They were adamant. They went aloof into the forest to prepare for the final argument with Buddha, "Whatever he is saying, he is right and we cannot convince him to speak. First, the truth is unspeakable. Second, it is not understandable. Thirdly, it goes against people's ideas of truth, and that creates enmity."

I can say it from my own experience. Dale Carnegie wrote a book, *How to Win Friends And Influence People*. My own experience is in how to influence people and create enemies! I have created so many enemies around the world, perhaps no one can be a competitor to me. Twenty-five countries have passed laws in their parliaments that I cannot enter their countries. Not only can I not enter, I cannot even land my airplane at their international airports to be refueled. It takes not more than fifteen minutes. In fifteen minutes at the international airport – and I will not be coming out of the plane – their whole morality is in danger. Their thousands-of-years-old tradition is in danger. Their church is in danger. Their whole new generation can be corrupted just by my sitting in an airplane at an international airport!

The gods worked hard – how to persuade Gautam Buddha? Arguments didn't seem to lead anywhere. Finally they came the last time and said, "Whatever you have been saying to us is true. Just one more point: there are millions of people who will not understand you, and there are millions who will become antagonistic to you because your truth is going to destroy their lies. And their lies are their comforts, their consolations, their only hope. Your truth is too dangerous. We are convinced of your arguments; just one simple point: among millions of people, there may be one person… You cannot deny the possibility of one person who is just on the boundary line and needs only a little push. Are you not going to help that man to cross the boundary line?"

Gautam Buddha agreed, "There is a possibility of someone, somewhere, who is just at that point but is clinging because he is afraid of moving into the unknown. A little push, and even before he realizes it, he has opened his wings and flown into the unknown.

I will speak. I will speak to the last of my breath." And he spoke for forty-two years. He was a man of immense commitment to his promise. To the very last breath, he continued – an impossible task. To stand for truth is to stand against the whole history of mankind. To stand for truth is to stand absolutely alone against the whole world. And I am saying this from my own experience.

Just the other day I received a letter from a man who works for *Time* magazine in America. He has asked two questions – one is important for you. He says, "Your effort is to save humanity; then why have you spoken against Jesus?" In the first place, I am not making any effort to save anyone. And I have spoken against Jesus because he was giving consolation to people, saying, "I will save you." That is the most dangerous and poisonous statement. It makes you relaxed; you need not worry, simply believe in Jesus and he will save you. On the last Day of Judgment, Jesus will sort out his sheep and tell God, "These are my people. They will enter paradise, and the remaining humanity will fall into the abysmal darkness of hell for eternity." I am against such consolations.

The man seems to be a Jesus freak. He cannot even understand what question he is asking. Who is saved by Jesus? He could not save himself, and he became utterly disillusioned at the last moment on the cross. Very few people have lived in such deep illusions as Jesus Christ because he believed he is the only begotten Son of God. What happened? – God started using birth control methods? Why only one begotten son? The reality is, Jesus was not the son of his own father, Joseph. Some hooligan has played a trick on the poor innocent Mary. That hooligan has become the Holy Ghost.

If such things are holy, then what is unholy? Making other people's wives pregnant without their permission – if this is holy then there is nothing unholy in the world. But he remained with this idea that he is the only begotten Son of God and he has come to save humanity.

On the cross… Because people finally got too bored; Judea was a very small place and he was roaming around Judea saying the same thing, "I have come to save you." And everyone knew he was uneducated, uncultured. "He knows nothing of the scriptures, he is not even a rabbi; he has been working with his so-called father Joseph in his carpentry workshop, and suddenly he has become the only begotten Son of God." Naturally he irritated people, annoyed people. If you don't want to be saved, you will be annoyed if someone comes knocking on your door every day to say that he has come to save you.

Jesus was crucified for different reasons than Socrates was poisoned. Socrates was poisoned because he had a truth which made the consolation of people absolutely absurd. Jesus, on the contrary, is giving consolation. Who were the people who gathered around him? He had twelve apostles. All were fishermen, farmers, gardeners. Except Judas, no one was educated. And naturally they thought, "This is a good chance. On our own we cannot hope to be saved. This man is so authoritative, let us cling to him. There is nothing to lose."

But on the cross, even Jesus became suspicious because he was waiting – God will come sitting on a white cloud, create a miracle, save his only begotten son and prove to the Jews, "You have been wrong, you have mistreated my son." But nothing happened, not even a white cloud. He looked again and again toward the sky. There was no indication of any miracle, not even a rehearsal. Everything was silent and finally he blurted out, "Father, have you forsaken me? Have you forgotten me?" But still there was no answer. There is no father in the sky and the skies don't answer anyone.

This man from *Time* magazine says to me, "You have come to save humanity." Who gave him that idea? I don't want to save anyone. It is your business, why should I interfere in your life? Even if the interference is for the good. I can explain my own experiences, I can indicate possible ways, but I am not going to save anyone. You have to walk the path alone, without any illusions.

Yes, certainly if I find someone just on the borderline, I will push him. I am lazy, but that much I can do. I am trying to push Amrito; he is just on the borderline, but there is always a nostalgia to look backward: the beautiful experiences of the mind, and ahead is an open sky with no limits. It creates fear and trembling. But Amrito has come closer and closer to me so I am going to take the risk and push him into the unknown.

He is saying, "Will you say something about the non-dramatic quality of real insight?" In real insight there is no drama; it is absolutely ordinary. People like drama, although they know it is only drama. All the religions are creating dramas for people's entertainment. People love to be entertained. But Amrito, now there is not going to be any dramatic experience – just a push and a sound following you, "Aha!"

Milarepa has asked, "Why do you like the childlike quality? The reason is very simple. It is because they are such innocent people, so nonserious, unaware of all kinds of games people play – mundane, sacred, human, superhuman. I will give you a few examples, so that you can forget Amrito and what happened to him.

The Goldberg family is on a picnic. Hymie is standing near the edge of a high cliff, admiring the sea crashing on the rocks far below.

Little Herschel comes up to him and says, "Hey Dad, Mom says it is not safe here. So either you stand back or give me the sandwiches."

Little Ernie is at the seashore when a pretty blond comes out of the surf and finds that she has lost the top half of her bathing suit.

Embarrassed, she crosses her arms in front of her chest and hurries across the beach.

She almost reaches where she has left her towel when little Ernie asks, "Lady, if you are giving away those puppies, could I have the one with the pink nose?"

Miss Goodbody, the teacher, is approaching her classroom when little Ernie comes toward her from the other direction, deliberately winking his left eye.

"Ernest," says Miss Goodbody, quite shocked. "Are you winking at me?"

"No," says Ernie, making a left turn into the classroom, "I have just got my turn signal on."

9

The Authentic Drug Is within You

Osho,
You have now been enlightened for almost thirty-six years. How does it feel to be beyond the beyond the beyond? PS Can I meet you in the pub afterward?

Vimal, it seems you have taken too much drink because we are in the pub! This place can only be described as belonging to those who are drunk with the divine – so drunk that they have forgotten their nationality, forgotten their church, forgotten even who they are. Vimal is asking me if I can meet him afterward in the pub, but beyond this pub there is no other place so drunk with the divine dance and song. What I am teaching you is to find a source within yourself which can make you a drunkard.

The joy of this life, the bliss, the ecstasy, belongs only to those whose wine is not coming from the outside – that is very ephemeral, very temporal, made of the same stuff as dreams are made of. There is another wine which grows within you. The moment you start moving inward, there is no need for anything else to make you oblivious to all the misery that surrounds you. There is no need for any other drug.

A few idiots in the West have started calling a drug "ecstasy." Now, that is absolutely against all the laws of the world because for centuries ecstasy has been copyrighted by my people! And it is not an outside drug, it flows in the very juices of your life. You don't have to move even an inch; wherever you are, you can be surrounded by all possibilities of blissfulness. And these possibilities of blissfulness are not temporal; it is not that tomorrow morning you will have a hangover. The more you drink, the more sober, the more sane, the more alert, the more conscious you become.

Unless a drug is found within your being, you are bound to look for it somewhere else. It raises a tremendously significant question. As long as we can remember in human history… The oldest, ancientmost scripture is the Rig Veda of the Hindus, and the Rig Veda talks about a certain drug, *somrasa*.

One of the most intelligent men of our century, Aldous Huxley, became very interested in searching for what this *somrasa* was because the seers of the Rig Veda used to drink it and dance around the fire. Certainly it seems it must have been a drug, and particularly to the Western objective thinker it cannot be anything else than a drug.

Aldous Huxley experimented with all kinds of drugs and finally he decided that LSD seems to come very close to the description of *somrasa*. In the hope that in the future LSD will be more refined – because it is a synthetic drug, manufactured; hence there is every possibility to improve upon it – to take away all the ingredients which can be harmful and leave only that which brings health, wholeness, awareness, and a tremendous insight into the mysteries of existence. Hoping that someday scientists were going to discover it, Huxley had already named it "soma," just to pay respect to the ancient seers of the Rig Veda.

But Aldous Huxley was in a deep misunderstanding. The *somrasa* that is being described in the Rig Veda is certainly a drug just like marijuana which used to grow in the Himalayas. Perhaps it still grows there, but we have not been able to find the place where it grows.

And the fire they were dancing around has nothing to do with the inner fire of life. I have looked into the Rig Veda as deeply, as sympathetically as possible. The people who are talking about *somrasa* and the fire ritual were even sacrificing human beings, as well as sacrificing other animals. The Hindus, who go on continuously making trouble in this country because of their insistence that cow slaughter should be stopped, should read their ancientmost scriptures. All their priests were slaughtering cows as a sacrifice to the fire god, and they were all eating the meat of the cows. Now, these people cannot be said to be meditative. I absolutely deny the Rig Veda and the prestige that it has in the minds of men. Because people don't read it, don't analyze it, don't see its stupidities and all kinds of inhumanities.

In the Rig Veda women are just a commodity. You can purchase women in the marketplace in any auction. Even the so-called seers had many wives, and they were not even satisfied with that. That is an absolutely ugly state, that any human being reduces so many women to cattle. Over and above all that, they were continually purchasing beautiful girls in auctions.

People have forgotten – times change, words take on new colors. Now in India the word *vadhu* simply means the newly-married woman. But in the times of Rig Veda, *vadhu* meant a woman who has been newly purchased from the market. Every so-called seer had two kinds of women: one group were his wives and the other were *vadhus*. The word *vadhu* is not respectable; it simply means a prostitute, purchased – a commodity, not a human being. It can be sold at any moment.

And the miracle was that the children from the married wife would be the legitimate children, and the children from the purchased wife would not be legitimate. Man has done so much inhumanity to other human beings that it is incalculable. How can a child be illegitimate? *Parents* can be illegitimate, but a child cannot be. Every child is as innocent as any other child. It does not matter whether the child is born to a prostitute or to a purchased woman or to a married woman. In all cases the child is absolutely legitimate. But people are very cunning in throwing their responsibilities on others. Parents are never called illegitimate. Children are called illegitimate.

These seers accumulated immense wealth, had many slaves, and used to eat meat. I cannot conceive that they had found the inner ecstasy I am talking about. All the circumstantial evidence goes against them. And look at their prayers – their prayers are so stupid that one feels embarrassed that these people were called great seers. Their prayers are in the Rig Veda, and the Rig Veda consists ninety-eight percent of prayers. Only two percent can be sorted out, cleaned, interpreted in a way that makes some sense. Otherwise, ninety-eight percent of it consists of such prayers that you will not believe.

One seer is praying to God, drinking that ancient LSD of Aldous Huxley, "This time, my God, listen to my prayer: your clouds should rain only on my fields, not on the fields of my enemies. You have never listened to me, but this time I am sacrificing so many cows, so many horses, you have to listen. Give me more children, and don't give a single child to my enemies." And who are the enemies? – other seers, and they are also praying! Even prayers which look so stupid, "If you are compassionate, give me some proof: the milk in the breasts of my enemy's cows should dry up."

These are religious people? "Give me and my friends victory, and defeat to my enemies and their friends." I cannot think of these people as meditative. Aldous Huxley was absolutely wrong. *Somrasa* was nothing but some herbal drug; perhaps it may have been marijuana because it still grows in Kulu Manali and in other parts of the Himalayas. There is no need to cultivate it, it simply grows naturally. Those are the places where the Rig Veda was composed.

As far as I am concerned, my interest is that all the governments of the world, all the religions of the world, all the moral teachers of the world have been against drugs; still drugs are more predominant today than they have ever been. The more they have been condemned, prohibited, made illegal, the more attractive they have become. People used to drink and take drugs at a certain stage, but the latest information from California is that school children are taking drugs, and small boys and girls are suffering in jail because they have been found taking drugs.

It is a strange story. All the religions, governments, teachers, moralists are against drugs, and the influence of drugs goes on growing. There must be something deeper in it than people have looked into. My understanding is that unless man finds a drug within himself, which I call ecstasy, he will go on finding some kind of drug as a substitute in the outside world. Only meditation can stop a person from taking drugs. No law can prohibit them – all laws have failed. It only creates hypocrites.

I am not against ecstasy, but when I say ecstasy I don't mean the drug that is available in the market. I mean the ecstasy that you are born with, that you are still holding inside you, and have not touched. Just a little taste of it and everything else on the outside immediately becomes meaningless. You have the source of the infinite ecstasy within you.

Yes, I teach you to be drunkards, but your drink has to come from your own innermost center. And the difference can be very easily understood: every outer drug will make you unconscious, addicted, and you will need more and more of it every time because your body will become immune to it.

In India, there are still a few ancient traditions which have fallen into the same fallacy as Aldous Huxley. But they have gone farther than Aldous Huxley; they drink all kinds of alcoholic beverages, they use all kinds of drugs. A moment comes when no drug can make them unconscious, no drug can bring them what they have been trying to find – a way to forget themselves, to forget this miserable world, to forget all these people. The last resort is that there are ashrams in Assam; they are the only remnants of a very long-standing tradition. They keep cobra snakes as a last resort. When no drug affects you, the cobra is allowed to bite you on your tongue. Only then do you feel a little shaken, but the miracle is that the cobra dies! The man is so full of poison, but the poor cobra was not aware; otherwise he would have escaped.

I have been concerned about why man has remained so interested in poisons. The reason is not too far away to see; you just need clarity. Man is so miserable that he cannot live consciously with this misery. He needs a few gaps, at least a few holidays from this miserable anguish, anxiety, and all kinds of tortures. Drugs have been a tremendous help. But not only the chemical drugs – Karl Marx is right when he says that the religions of the world are nothing but opium for the people. These religions have also proved to be consolations. They have also given hope, they have also given a certain future and taken away your consciousness from the present and its misery. That's the function of any drug.

My effort here, Vimal, is to make you drop all future, all hope, all illusion, and just relax in the moment knowing perfectly well that this is the only moment which exists. All else is either memory or imagination. One who is in the present immediately drowns in his own well of something which is not poisonous, but is certainly ecstatic. And once you have known your own source, there is no need to go anywhere, to any pub or to any church or to any temple.

The young doctor, inexperienced with operations, is instructed to stand at the head of the patient so that without getting in the way, he can watch the expert do an abdominal operation. He is also instructed not to speak, but after a while he can't resist, "How's your end, sir?" says the young man.

"All right," says the expert, looking up, "why?"

"I only wondered, sir," says the young man, "because my end's been dead for ten minutes."

As he was told not to speak, he remained silent! The man is dead and the surgeon goes on operating.

There are a few things which all traditions have prohibited people to say, and it needs immense courage to go against the whole tradition of mankind. For example, everyone has been told not to support any kind of drug in any way, and people have remained silent. I have not come across a single statement in which someone has dared to say that the predominance of drugs shows something immensely significant, and it cannot be simply outlawed; it cannot be simply prohibited. But I want to say it.

Let it be on record: unless man finds the authentic drug which is in his own being, there is no force on the earth which can prohibit alcohol, marijuana, hashish, LSD. More and more drugs will be coming in, and the miracle is that the people who are trying to prohibit these things – ninety percent of them are themselves using them.

Just a few days ago in America there was an international conference of homosexuals, and one MP from England represented the homosexuals of England. He is a member of the parliament, and certainly he is a homosexual; otherwise why should he be their representative? And in the conference he said, "You must be thinking that I am a strange person, being a member of parliament and representing the homosexuals, but I want you to know that at least fifty-six members of the parliament in England are homosexuals." They may not have the courage to come out – and these people will make laws against homosexuality!

Perhaps you have never thought about the fact that Jesus continued to drink alcohol, but no Christian has the guts to say that a man with the qualities of Jesus should not drink alcohol. Only if he has not found the alcohol within is there a possibility to search for alcohol without. Every night it was party time – and it is strange that even after two thousand years, people drink alcohol in the name of Jesus. Naturally, if Jesus can be an alcoholic then why make it a prohibition? If even Jesus needs it, I don't think anyone can be in a position who does not need it.

I have heard about a strange ritual that happens every year in the Vatican...

The pope comes out in all his regalia, with the cardinals following, and the rabbi from Rome comes with a big scroll. He hands over the scroll to the pope, the pope looks at the scroll, gives it back to the rabbi and everyone wonders what the matter is: "What is written on the scroll?"

Finally one young man dared to ask, "It has been going on for two thousand years; now we should at least know the content of the scroll. The whole ritual. And there seems to be no meaning."

The scroll was opened for the first time, and it was found that it was the bill for the Last Supper! And the question is, "Who is going to pay it?" Obviously, Jesus was a Jew – the rabbis should pay it, but the rabbis had denied Jesus, they crucified him. They don't accept him as one of them; the pope should pay it. But the discussion is such that there is no way to decide. Jesus is a Jew and of course his followers are Christians – and why should Christians pay for a Jewish party? So every year the bill comes, the bill goes back.

Vimal, the way to understand me is to always remember that I am insisting – from every corner, in every possible way – only on a single target, and that is your innermost being. Whatever I may have said… Never be too much concerned with what is said. Be concerned about what it indicates.

I want you to drop all games – worldly games, spiritual games, games that the whole of humanity has played up to now. These games keep you retarded. These games hinder you from growing into consciousness, into your own ultimate flowering. I want to cut away all this rubbish that prevents you. I want to leave you alone, absolutely alone, so that you cannot take anyone's help, so you cannot cling to any prophet, so that you cannot think that Gautam Buddha is going to save you. Left alone – utterly alone – you are bound to find your innermost center.

There is no way, nowhere to go, no advisor, no teacher, no master. It seems hard, it seems harsh, but I am doing it because I love you, and the people who have not done it have not loved you at all. They loved themselves and they loved to have a big crowd around themselves – the bigger the crowd, the more they feel nourished in their egos.

That's why I called even enlightenment the last game. The sooner you drop it, the better. Why not just simply be? Why unnecessarily hurry here and there? You are what existence wants you to be. Just relax.

Farmer Giles is worried about the performance of his prize bull. He doesn't seem to be interested in the cows anymore. So he goes to the vet who prescribes a course of pills for the bull.

A few weeks later, a friend comes by and asks Farmer Giles how the bull is getting on.

"Just great!" says Giles. "The vet gave me these pills for the bull and from the first day the old fellow has been unstoppable! In fact, I am making a fortune; the local farmers can't get their cows 'round here fast enough!"

"Great!" says his friend. "And what are these pills then?"

"Well," says Farmer Giles, "they are great big green ones – and they taste just like peppermints."

Osho,

Has Jesus ever laughed? Irven M. Resnich reports on the controversy between philosophy and theology about laughter; Aristotle, in his second book of poetics, raised laughter to the standard of an art, whereas Christian theology has been against laughter since the days of the Bible. For monks, a life of penance does not allow laughter. Basilius Caesarea and Hugo of St. Victor totally condemned laughter; in some monasteries it was only tolerated if it did not spread.

The question came up of whether laughter darkened the human nature of Jesus. According to Christian tradition, Jesus himself never laughed, although the philosophical traditions of Aristotle, Quintilian, Porphyry and Boethius, emphasize that laughter is a typically human

> ability. The clergymen gave various answers, but many of them pointed out that a lot of saints had never laughed either, and that Jesus, as a human being, was of course able to laugh, but he voluntarily renounced it. Not a theologically satisfying solution.

Doctor Amrito, only on one point do I agree with Christian tradition: Jesus certainly never laughed. As far as I can see, he had nothing to laugh at. First, he is a bastard. Others may have laughed, but you cannot expect Jesus to laugh. Jesus was a poor carpenter, undernourished – laughter needs some overflowing energy. And to look at Jesus' statements, he seems to be a crackpot. Crackpots never laugh. They have to keep their seriousness. Laughter brings you down to the status of ordinary humanity. Those who want to pretend to be special – how can they laugh? Such a mundane activity. All these controversies are absolutely futile. I will give you a few reasons to contemplate which will make you clear why he did not laugh:

An ancient tradition says, "Before Jesus Christ, no one knew what a headache looked like."

True misery for a man is when there are no more problems to be solved.

And Jesus had no more problems to be solved. He was the only begotten Son of God. He knew everything. Not a single time in his whole life – which was not very long, just thirty-three years – did he ever say, "I don't know" about anything. He knew everything, and whenever a person is so knowledgeable, laughter becomes impossible.

Women do have a sense of humor – look at their boyfriends!

Poor Jesus was never chosen by a woman to be her boyfriend. And still you want him to laugh? You are expecting too much from a poor carpenter. His teaching life was only three years, from thirty to thirty-three. And in those three years his whole effort was to frighten humanity as much as he could because his whole business depended on people becoming afraid of hell. That was the fundamental psychology he was working on. But when you are teaching people about hell, laughter will not fit in.

There is always more hell that needs raising.

And in three years how much hell can you raise? You may not be aware, it is an unrecorded fact but passed on by word of mouth, from generation to generation, that when Jesus used to threaten people with hellfire, women in particular used to faint. Men started trembling, perspiring. Now, this is not a situation for anyone to laugh, and particularly Jesus himself.

A man can learn much by imitating the behavior of a duck – keep calm and unruffled on the surface, and paddle like crazy underneath.

Jesus managed it perfectly well. All that unruffledness, all that seriousness is just on the surface – underneath he is also paddling like crazy, but you cannot see it. So no one has ever observed him laughing.

It is said, a change of trouble is as good as a vacation.

He never changed anything. In those three years of his teaching, he continuously insisted on the same thing. There is a contemporary parallel – J. Krishnamurti. He managed for a longer time than Jesus. He started teaching when he was twenty-five, and he went on teaching till he died at the age of ninety. No one has ever seen him laughing. In fact, if you are laughing and by chance you come across him, you will stop. Just his face…

He used to come to India once or twice a year, and he used to speak only in three or four places – Delhi, Mumbai, Varanasi, Adyar in Chennai. I had told my sannyasins everywhere to always sit in the front row, and the moment he would see my sannyasins with their red clothes and *malas*, he would completely forget what he had come to teach. He would become so angry. His people came to me to say, "This is not right; he is getting old, he may have a heart attack. You are making such trouble for him that wherever he goes, he finds sannyasins sitting in the front row. Then he forgets everyone else, he forgets what he has come for, what the subject was that he was going to teach. And furious, so furious that he starts hitting his own head!" Now, seeing such a man, can you laugh?

The happiest time in anyone's life is just after their divorce.

But that time never came in Jesus' life. I have tried to find something the poor fellow might have laughed at, but there was nothing in his life. Sitting on a donkey, moving with twelve fools – you are a laughingstock, you cannot laugh.

And it is not only true about Jesus. It is true about almost all your saints – Christian, Hindu, Buddhist – it doesn't matter to what church they belong. The saint is not supposed to laugh. The reason is simple: the saint is supposed to be working hard, moving toward the ultimate goal of life. There is no time for laughing. The whole thing is too serious. And because ordinary human beings laugh, obviously, the logic is clear: if you want to prove that you are extraordinary, you have to stop laughing. You have to stop doing many things which ordinary people do. You may even start doing things which are absolutely stupid and idiotic, but you have to be certain only about one thing – that ordinary people don't do those kind of things.

You will see saints standing on their heads. Now, if existence wanted you to stand on your head, the feet would have grown out of your head. But any kind of nonsense – Mahavira used to pull out his own hair. He wouldn't allow even a small razor to shave his head – every ordinary human being is doing that. And because he was pulling out his hair, thousands of people would gather to see this tremendously sacred event. If you look at your saints and their histories, you are bound to come to the conclusion that almost a hundred percent of them needed psychiatric treatment. But we have lived under their influence, and they have such a long tradition that its burden is heavy on our hearts, too.

He has been warned that Paddy is a bit of a fool, but the postmaster decides to hire him anyway because the post office is really short-staffed. His first day on the job, Paddy is given the work of sorting letters, and to everyone's surprise, he separates the letters so fast that his motions are literally a blur.

Very pleased about this, the postmaster approaches him at the end of the day.

"I want you to know," he says, "that we're all very proud of you. You're one of the fastest workers we've ever had."

"Thanks a lot," replies Paddy, "and tomorrow, I'll try and do even better."

"Better?" asks the postmaster, astonished. "How could you possibly do better?"

"Well," says Paddy, "tomorrow I'm going to read the addresses."

All kinds of idiots have become your saints. In fact, a man who is intelligent is not going to become one of your saints because to be a saint literally means to be a slave of the crowd. The crowd dictates. The crowd tells the saint how he has to live, what he has to eat, where he has to sleep. The saint is simply the slave of a vast crowd and because he obeys, the crowd pays him with deep respect.

And remember one thing, that in life everything needs a certain qualification, except being a saint! For that, no one is asked for any qualification, no interview.

Pope the Polack goes to the optician for an examination. "I want to make a few tests," says the optician, "so cup your hand and put it over your right eye."

The pope cups his left hand and places it on his forehead.

"No!" says the optician. "Cup your hand and cover your eye." This time the pope cups his right hand and covers his forehead.

In desperation, the optician takes a large paper bag and places it over the pope's head.

Then, he cuts out a hole in the bag over his left eye. Before he can ask the pope to read the chart, he sees his eye is full of tears. The optician immediately cuts a hole in the bag over his right eye, and tears fall from both the pope's eyes.

"For God's sake!" shouts the optician. "Why are you crying?"

"Ah!" sobs Pope the Polack, "I was really hoping for something more stylish."

10

Freedom to Be Yourself

Osho,
Are idiots born or trained?

It is a complicated question. Almost ninety percent of idiots are trained. Ten percent are born. And the ten percent are born because of those ninety percent who have been trained. Man, from his very beginning has lived a very weird life – weird in the sense that it needs idiots. If you don't have idiots, you will not have wise men; if you don't have the idiots, you will not have the so-called giants of intellect. It is almost a necessity that the category of idiots should remain.

No one has looked into the deeper layers of how the society has functioned up to now. But the way it has functioned can only be described as utterly criminal. The society needs categories, hierarchies. Up to now it has been a competitive society, and the very idea of competition is dangerous to human beings. You call one man an idiot only in comparison – in comparison to someone who seems to be intelligent.

A small boy told me…

I was a guest in his house. I was sitting in the garden in the evening and he was the only child of the family. He was not more than six years old. I asked him, "What is your name?"

He said, "As far as my name is concerned, up to now I used to think that my name was 'Don't!' Now I have started going to school, and there I discovered that that is not my name."

He is saying something tremendously important. Whatever a child is doing, adults are there to say, "Don't do it!" No one is allowed to blossom according to his own intrinsic nature. And that is the fundamental cause of creating so many idiots in the world. But they are serving a certain purpose. If people were allowed to blossom according to their nature, without any comparison and without any ideals and without enforced discipline, do you think anyone in the whole world would have accepted Adolf Hitler as a leader? Just look at your leaders.

In America, the average American is sitting glued to his chair in front of the television set. The television has become his whole life. Now television can be used in a dangerous way, and it is being used. Ronald Reagan would not have been able to become the president of America if there were no television. Television has changed the whole structure of the American mind. Now the leader need not be wise, but he has to be photogenic. Now, what has being photogenic to do with being a president? He has to be a good showman, an actor. Ronald Reagan understood the situation. He was a third-rate actor in Hollywood, a cowboy actor. I don't think any society would have chosen him to be the president, but television changed the whole situation. He could act on television and fulfill a new desire in the people, that the president should look strong, authoritative, and be able to look at least handsome.

And this he learned when Richard Nixon was defeated by Kennedy. Nixon was not aware that now the contest is not one of intelligence; the whole area of contest has changed. Kennedy looked younger – well dressed, well spoken, although some ghost writer had written his speeches and he had rehearsed them. With both men on the television screen, the comparison was very simple. Nixon looked lousy, his clothes were not up to date. He had never thought that these things mattered. He had not rehearsed what he was going to say. That used to be the way – a more spontaneous person was always thought to be more intelligent. To be photogenic is one thing; to encounter people directly is a totally different thing.

Nixon was defeated and his advisors suggested to him that he would have to change a few things. He had to become a little more photogenic, with a better hairstyle, better clothes: "And spontaneous speeches won't do; you will have to rehearse them. There is no need for you to create your own speeches, there are far better writers – let them write the speech." And the second time, he came on television as a totally different personality. The same Nixon appeared now to be matured, capable, and he was chosen.

When Nixon was chosen as president, Ronald Reagan tried to be the governor of California. He was immediately chosen because the other contestants had no idea that they had to be a showman, had to be an actor. These have never been the qualities of leaders. Once he was governor, he knew that the presidentship was not far away. And he became the president.

The people who are continuously watching television... And seven and a half hours average per day is not a small amount of time, it is one third of your life. You are being imposed on by continuously repeated ideas, personalities. People have forgotten to read; there is no time. In America people read only trashy novels – that too when they are traveling on a train or in an airplane.

In America, the beautiful hardbound book has disappeared. Who is going to purchase it? Cheap literature cannot create a Leo Tolstoy, a Dostoevsky, a Maxim Gorky. In a certain way, television has introduced a new kind of primitiveness because the primitive man depended only on his eyes – whatever he saw, that was his only knowledge. If you look into small things, you will be surprised that before the fountain pen came into existence, people had beautiful handwriting. Tremendous effort was made to write beautifully because it was signifying your personality, your intelligence, your aesthetic sense. But the moment the fountain pen came in, beautiful handwriting disappeared.

Right now you still have memories; soon you won't have. Everyone will be carrying their own computer, which can be carried in the pocket and which can contain all the knowledge contained in all the libraries of the world – you just have to know how to make it function. Man will fall tremendously as far as intelligence is concerned, memory is concerned. Everything that comes into existence brings changes so silently that you don't see them.

The idiots have been an absolute necessity for a few people to proclaim their egos, for a few people to rise high and become Nobel Prize winners. Just think for a moment. If everyone was living according to his own nature, not trying to be someone else, a tremendous intelligence would explode within you. It is something of the fundamental law of life and existence. It is good that flowers don't listen to your teachers, your leaders, your politicians. Otherwise they would say to the roses, "What are you doing? Become a lotus!" Roses are not so foolish. But if, just for argument's sake, roses start trying to become lotuses, what is going to happen? Two things are certain: there will be no roses because their whole energy will be involved in becoming lotuses, and the second thing, a rosebush cannot produce a lotus. It is not in the inbuilt program of its seed.

Have you ever come across a tree that you can say is an idiot? Or that it is very intelligent, a great giant, and deserves a Nobel Prize? Man has been distracted. Everyone – from your parents to your teachers, the school, the college, the university, your religion, your preachers, your neighbors – is trying to make you someone else, whom you cannot become. You can only become yourself, or you can miss and become just an idiot.

I call this whole history of mankind a long, unjustified crime against every human individual. It has served the vested interests: the people who are in power; the people who are scholars, which is another kind of power; the people who are rich, which is another kind of power. They wouldn't like everyone to be centered in himself because a man centered in himself cannot be exploited, cannot be enslaved, cannot be humiliated, cannot be forced to grow a cancerous sense of guilt. These are the reasons humanity has not been allowed its growth.

In Japan they have very ancient trees, four hundred years old. And they think that it is an art because the tree's height is only six inches and it shows signs of old age. But a special strategy has been used, the same that has been used against humanity. They are rooted in pots, but the pots don't have any bottom. So their roots are continually cut, and if the roots cannot go deep the tree cannot go high. There is a certain balance. The highest tree needs very deep roots to stand; otherwise it will fall. If you go on cutting the roots, the tree goes on becoming old, but it does not grow higher to its natural intrinsic capacity. I don't consider this an art, it is a crime against poor trees.

But the same crime has been committed against man. Your roots are being continuously cut. And that creates a retarded humanity.

Turgenev has a beautiful story, *The Fool*...

A sage comes to a village, and a man comes to him with tears in his eyes and says, "I don't know how to get out of this suffering. My whole village thinks I am an idiot. If I say something, they immediately condemn me, criticize me. If I don't say anything they laugh and say, 'What can he say? He is an idiot.' I am in such a fix. Hearing that you are a sage, I have come for some advice."

The sage said, "Don't be worried. A very simple technique will change the whole situation within a month. And after one month I am coming back again on the same route, so I will be able to see whether the change has happened or not." He gave the man a very simple technique.

The technique was, "Don't make any statement on your own. Just wait for someone else to make the statement. Someone says, 'How beautiful the sunset is!' That is the point – immediately jump and ask him, 'What is beautiful in it? Define it! Explain! Do you know what beauty is? And if you don't know what beauty is, how can you say that the sunset is beautiful? Before anything can be called beautiful, beauty has to be defined.'"

But even the greatest poets, philosophers – particularly those philosophers like Croce who have been dedicated to a single object, aesthetics – have not been able to define what beauty is. Although everybody knows, but to know is not enough.

Everyone knows what is good, but if the question is raised, "Define it!"… An English philosopher, perhaps one of the most intelligent Englishmen of this century, G. E. Moore, has written a book, *Principia Ethica*. The whole book is devoted to a single question: What is good? And in two hundred and fifty pages of very arduous, very subtle, logical argumentation, the concluding remark is that good is indefinable.

Naturally, after one month when the sage came back, the idiot had already become the wisest man in the village because he had stopped everyone. You say something, he would criticize it and ask for fundamental definitions. You could say a woman is beautiful and he would ask, "What is beautiful in that woman? – bones? A long nose? Stinking perspiration? What do you consider beauty?" There was no way to answer, and when people saw that they could not answer, they immediately started thinking that the man had been absolutely misunderstood. "He is not an idiot, he is a great thinker, a wise man, more intelligent than anyone else."

The sage was very happy and said, "Are you happy now?"

The man said, "I am absolutely happy."

The sage said, "Always remember, never make a statement on your own. Just wait; when someone is going to say something – criticize. Someone talks about God – criticize, ask for the evidence, ask for proof. And there is no proof and no evidence. Just remember one thing: never make a statement on your own; otherwise they will immediately jump on you and you will be an idiot again."

From the very childhood, every child is condemned – whatever he says, whatever he does, it is never right. Naturally he becomes afraid of saying anything, of doing anything on his own. He is appreciated if he is obedient, he is appreciated if he follows the rules and the regulations made by others. Everyone appreciates him. This is the strategy: condemn the man if he is trying to stand on his own feet and appreciate the man if he is just an imitator. Naturally his inner seed, his potentiality, will never have a chance to grow.

I am reminded of my own childhood…

The thing had become so ancient that no one even questioned it. If I was sitting silently, someone – and in India there are still big families, joint families; in my family there were at least fifty people – was bound to come by and ask, "Why are you sitting silently?"

Strange, I cannot sit silently, and if I make a noise and jump around the house, "Are you mad? Why are you jumping around the house?" Seeing the situation I decided that it would be better to begin the fight from the very beginning. Because once you get caught with these people it will be very difficult to come out of the crowd.

My father was amazed and said, "You never answer the question. On the contrary, you ask another question."

I said, "I have figured out that when I am sitting silently and you ask, 'Why are you sitting silently?' I will not answer. I will ask, 'Why should I not sit silently? *You* have to answer. You are a grown-up man, experienced – I am just a child. You answer me: Why should I not sit silently?'"

By and by, the whole family understood, "You cannot get any statement from this boy. He immediately turns the question around and you are in trouble." They stopped asking me anything.

The situation came up; I might be sitting somewhere, and my mother would say, "I don't see anyone in the house" – and I was sitting in front of her! "I need vegetables; someone should go and fetch vegetables."

I would say, "If I see someone, I will inform you." I was taken to be almost absent. And I proved it – because unless you prove it, it is very difficult. In the beginning they used to send me saying, "Go to the market. It is the season of beautiful mangoes – bring mangoes."

I would go to the shop selling the worst mangoes and ask, "Just give me the worst ones and charge me for the best ones."

Even those shopkeepers were amazed. "What kind of customer are you?"

I said, "What kind of customer? You have seen many customers; I am a unique customer."

And the man was perfectly happy to give me the rotten and charge the price for the best. I would come home and give those rotten mangoes and say, "These are the best, and I have paid for them." And they were stinking. My mother would say, "Just throw them out!"

I said, "Why throw them out? There is a beggar woman, I can go and give them to her."

Even the beggar woman would not accept them. She would say, "Never come to me because whenever you come you bring something rotten. Throw them to the dogs."

And I was very surprised that even dogs were afraid of me. If I would throw something to them, they would escape!

Slowly the family settled saying, "It is better to let him be, whatever he is. One thing is certain, he is not going to be anyone special in life."

They were right. I have proved their prophecy. I am no one special in life.

But who cares about being special? I am myself and that's enough, more than enough. Each moment of my life I had to struggle to protect myself; otherwise everyone is ready to cut your roots. I was expelled so many times from the schools, colleges, universities. From the very first day I entered high school… And the first period was history. The man, the teacher – very senior, very experienced – started talking about history. I said to him, "Please wait for one moment. Have you made any history?"

He said, "What kind of question is this? I teach history."

I said, "I have not come to learn about idiots like Genghis Khan, Tamerlane, Nadirshah. If you can teach me how to create history, only then I can be your student. But you don't have any idea how to create history. You are simply a parrot repeating all kinds of rubbish – which is not to be repeated to children because it will get stuck in their minds. You are an enemy."

He said, "This is strange. I cannot tolerate your presence in my class."

I said, "You will not have it – I will stand outside the class, which is not your domain, and from the window I will create as much trouble as possible."

He came out, tried to persuade me, "Join some other subject. Why harass me? I am an old man. Can't you find someone else?"

I said, "This is not the first time. When I went to the geography class the same thing happened. What concern have I to know where Constantinople is? And why should I bother about it? If you cannot teach something sensible, at least sit silently and let everyone else also sit silently."

The geography teacher said, "Then who is going to give the examination?"

I said, "The examination about what?"

He immediately took me to the principal and said, "I cannot accept this student."

The principal was in difficulty. He said, "No teacher is ready to accept you. Where should I send you?"

I said, "You are not doing much, just sitting in your principal's office. I can also sit here and if you have something sensible to say, you can say it. Or if I happen to discover something sensible, I will say it. Otherwise, silence is perfectly good."

The principal said, "Have you come here to learn something?"

I said, "No, I have come here to be myself. If you teach me and help me, support me and nourish me to be myself, then I can remain in this school; otherwise I will find some other school."

But that went on and on. I was expelled from colleges and the principals said to me, "We feel guilty for expelling you because you have not done anything wrong. But you are a little strange."

The first college I entered, I wanted to learn logic. And the old professor, with many honorary degrees, with many books published in his name, started talking about the father of Western logic, Aristotle.

I said, "Wait a minute. Do you know that Aristotle writes in his book that women have less teeth than men?"

He said, "My God, what kind of question is this? What has it to do with logic?"

I said, "It has something very fundamental to do with the whole process of logic. Are you aware that Aristotle had two wives?"

He said, "I didn't know – where are you getting these facts from?"

In Greece it was traditionally known for centuries that women were bound to have everything less than men. Naturally, they couldn't have the same number of teeth as men.

I said, "And you call this man Aristotle the father of logic? He could have at least counted – he had two wives available, but he did not count. His statement is illogical. He has simply taken it from the tradition, and I cannot trust in a man who has two wives and writes that women have less teeth than men. This is a male chauvinistic attitude. A logician has to be beyond prejudices."

Seeing the situation, the professor threatened the principal that either I should be expelled from the college or he was going to resign. And he stopped coming to the college. He said, "I will wait three days."

The principal could not lose an experienced professor. He called me into his office to say, "There has never been any trouble with that man, he is a very nice man. Just on the first day – what have you done?"

I told him the whole story and I said, "Do you think it deserves expulsion from college? I was asking absolutely relevant questions, and if a professor of logic cannot answer, who is going to answer?"

The principal was a good man. He said, "I will not expel you because I don't see that you have done anything wrong. But I cannot afford to lose the professor either, so I will make arrangements for you in another college."

But the rumor about me had spread in all the colleges. The city I was in had almost twenty colleges and finally it became a very prestigious university just by combining those twenty colleges. He sent me to another principal with a letter of recommendation, but he must have phoned him to say, "Don't believe in the letter of recommendation. I had to write it because I have to get rid of that student. He is not wrong, but he is absolutely individualistic and that is going to create trouble."

I went to see the other principal, and he was waiting. He said, "I can admit you only on one condition: that you will never attend the college."

I said, "Then what is going to happen for my examination?"

He said, "I will give you the necessary percentage for being present in the college, but this is a secret pact between me and you."

I said, "It is perfectly good – anyway your professors are out of date. But can I enter the library?"

He said, "The library is perfectly okay, but never attend any class because I don't want to hear from any professor the complaint that you are creating trouble."

And I have never created any trouble! I was simply asking questions which... And if they were really gentlemen they would have said, "I will find out. For the time being, I don't know."

But this is the most difficult thing in the world to say, "I don't know."

As I approached the university, strangely enough, my first encounter was with the vice-chancellor. He was speaking on a series of Gautam Buddha. It was the first day, and he said, "I always feel a sadness in me that I was not born in the times of Gautam Buddha; otherwise I would have gone to him and sat at his feet." And he was an old man. He had been the head of the history department at Oxford. After retiring from there, he was chosen to be the vice-chancellor of this university.

I stood up and said, "You will have to consider again."

He said, "What do you mean?"

I said, "In your own time, there have been J. Krishnamurti, Sri Aurobindo, Ramana Maharshi. Can I ask, have you gone and learned anything from these people? And if you have not gone to these people, on what authority are you saying that you feel a certain sadness that you were not born in the times of Buddha? I can say with an absolute guarantee that you would not have gone to Gautam Buddha either."

There was utter silence in the auditorium. But the vice-chancellor was certainly a gentleman. He said, "I understand your point and I take my words back. I know Sri Aurobindo, but I have never gone to him. I know Ramana Maharshi and I have not gone to him. I know J. Krishnamurti, but I have not gone to him. You are right. See me afterward."

I went to see him. He said, "It was perfectly good that you encountered me, but don't do this thing to any other professor because people are not courageous enough to accept their ignorance. They don't have guts to say, 'I don't know.' As far as I am concerned, I am immensely grateful to you because it must have been an unconscious thing in me. I was not lying, I was just feeling that when Gautam Buddha was alive I would have gone to be showered by his blessings, by his presence. But you have put me right. I would not have gone."

It is very difficult to find human beings in society who will allow you the freedom to be yourself. That has created a retardedness all over the world. Nations need idiots – otherwise, who is going to fight the wars? The world needs idiots – otherwise, how are people going to become richer and richer on the labor, on the blood of others? This civilization needs as many unintelligent people as possible – otherwise, who is going to be a Catholic, who is going to be a Protestant, who is going to be a Hindu, who is going to be a Mohammedan?

The whole structure of society has been managed in such a way that very few people exploit millions of people. And they have given consolations to those who have been exploited saying, "It is because of your past life's evil acts." You don't know anything about your past life; now, this is a good consolation: "What can I do?" Or they say, "This is a fire test of your faith in God. Be contented as you are and you will be rewarded a thousandfold beyond death." Either religions have taken refuge in the past – Jainism, Buddhism, Hinduism are all past-oriented. Or the other three religions – Christianity, Mohammedanism, Judaism – have taken refuge beyond death.

There is not much difference. All that is happening is happening *in life* and they are postponing it. Either before birth or after death, the strategy is the same. The whole point is that you should allow people to exploit you, you should allow people to drink your blood, with the deep contentment that "this is how things are." I want to say to you very emphatically that all these religions have played into the hands of the vested interests. All your priests are nothing but in the service of your politicians.

The whole history of mankind has been a disaster. And unless we start revolting as individuals, dropping all nationalities, all religions, all races, and declare that this whole globe belongs to us and all the lines of the map are bogus and false; unless individuals start changing the whole educational system...

The educational system should teach you the art of living, it should teach you the art of loving, it should teach you the art of meditation, it should teach you finally the art of dying gloriously. Your education system is not educational. It only creates clerks, stationmasters, postmen, soldiers, and you call it education. You have been deceived. But the deception has been going on so long that you have completely forgotten. And you are still going on in the same old rut.

I raise my hand against the whole past of mankind. It has not been civilized, it has not been human. It has not been in any way helpful for people to blossom; it has not been a spring. It has been a calamity, a crime committed on such a vast scale. But someone has to stand against it, and someone has to make the point that we disown our past. And we will start living according to our own inner being and create our own future. We will not allow the past to create our future.

Hymie Goldberg buys himself a fancy pair of Italian shoes in a Beverly Hills boutique, and wears them home to show them off to Becky.

Becky does not appear even to notice the new shoes, so Hymie waits until she is in bed and then walks in, stark naked except for the shoes.

Posing, he exclaims, "It is about time you paid some attention to what my prick is pointing at!"

Looking down at the shoes, Becky replies, "It is too bad you didn't buy a hat!"

In the middle of his sermon the priest stops, sniffs the air, and then holding his nose, calls the head usher to the front.

"Please go through the church," says the priest, "and see if some stray dog stole in, stooled, and then stole out again."

The usher immediately begins his inspection and after some minutes comes back to make his report.

"No, Father," he says, "I did not see where some stray dog stole in, stooled, and stole out again. But I did see some very positive signs where some creeping cat crept into the crypt, crapped, and crept out again."

I would like you to accept only one prayer, and that is laughter because when you are totally laughing you are in the present. You cannot laugh in the future and you cannot laugh in the past. All those people who have created this retarded humanity have taken away all juice, all laughter, all smiles, and dragged everyone into being inauthentic. And if you are inauthentic, insincere, you can never grow the seed that has been given to you by this great compassionate universe.

An unshaven, dirty, bedraggled panhandler, with bloodshot eyes and teeth half gone, asks Paddy for a dime.

"Do you drink, smoke, or gamble?" asks Paddy.

"Mister," says the bum, "I don't touch a drop, or smoke the filthy weed, or bother with evil gambling."

"Okay," says Paddy, "if you will come home with me I will give you a dollar."

As they enter the house, Maureen takes Paddy aside and hisses, "How dare you bring that terrible looking specimen into our home!?"

"Darling," says Paddy, "I just wanted you to see what a man looks like who doesn't drink, doesn't smoke, and doesn't gamble."

Life should not be a serious thing. It should be a deep playfulness, a fun. And every individual should be allowed absolute freedom to be himself. The only restriction would be that you cannot interfere in another individual's life sphere – it may be your wife, it may be your husband, it may be your child, it does not matter. A tremendous respect for the individual is to me the essential core of being truly religious. Be yourself and let others be themselves, and this life, this planet, can become the lotus paradise herenow.

But something has to be done and done very soon because all those idiots are preparing for a global suicide. Unless you revolt against the past, and the whole heritage of the past, you cannot save humanity, these beautiful trees, these birds singing, this small planet which is the only one to have developed to the stage of being conscious. Scientists guess that there may be millions of other planets in the universe, but there is not even a single piece of evidence yet.

The only evidence of life growing to this stage of consciousness – of love, of silence, of experiencing the cosmos – has happened on this small earth. At any cost, this earth and the people of this earth have to be saved from the calamity that is coming from your whole past. An absolute discontinuity is needed; all history books should be burned. The whole educational system should be centered on playfulness, love, freedom, consciousness, and a tremendous respect for everything that is alive. This is my vision.

The time is very short. Those idiots have been working for thousands of years and they have come to a point where they are capable of destroying this earth seven times. So much destructive force is accumulating that unless a few individuals gather courage and revolt against all that is past… I am not telling you to choose, to choose that which is good and leave that which is bad. They are altogether; you cannot do that. The past has to be simply erased, as if we are on the earth for the first time and there has been no history. That is the only possibility to create a beautiful world full of love, full of fragrance, with deep respect for everyone. The past has lived centered on hate. The future can live only if it is centered on love. The past has been unconscious. The future can only be conscious.

To many this may seem almost an impossible dream. But remember, whatever you are is not because of the politicians, is not because of the priests. Whatever you are, if some flame is still alive in you it is because of the poets, the dreamers, the mystics. We can either die with the past or we can be reborn with a new future.

Revolutions have failed; hence I talk about revolt. Revolution means a crowd, a class, fighting against the ruling class. But they have failed because of an intrinsic necessity: if you fight with the ruling class you will have to use the same means to fight, and the moment you are in power you will start doing the same nasty things to humanity as your predecessors.

Revolt has a beauty because it is individual. And there is nothing to fight with – one has simply to throw off the whole past from one's consciousness. Clean yourself and become Adam and Eve again. Disobey God again. Only then is there a possibility for this vision to become a reality. Don't be concerned about the whole world. If we can create the idea of revolt in a small minority in the world, that will do. A single seed can make the whole earth green, and a single man in revolt can create a totally new world, a totally new humanity.

I am not in favor of any organized revolution because all organizations basically destroy the individual. I am in favor of the individual and his dignity. There is no one above the individual. We have to take this tremendous quantum leap, from organized living to individual flowering. It is possible. If it is possible for me – because I don't belong to any religion and I don't belong to any nation and I don't belong to any kind of organization – it is possible for you too. And if this fire of individuality spreads, it can become a wildfire because deep down every individual is suffering. He wants to revolt against all that has been repressed, all that has been imposed on him.

You will not find a better moment. This century is coming to its end – one thing is certain, the old world cannot continue to live. All the prophets have been declaring the end of the world with the year 2000. None of them has said a single word about what happens beyond this century.

I want it to be clear to you, to my people around the earth, that the old world does not mean the planet. The old world means the old structure of humanity – it is going to die. But if we can save a few individuals, a new beginning is very close. Rather than being concerned with the old, rejoice for the new.

As far as I am concerned, I am absolutely certain that in moments of crisis – and this is the greatest crisis man has ever faced – people gather courage and take a quantum leap into something absolutely unknown. You are here from different lands, from different races, from different organizations; you will be spreading all over the world. You are going to be my ambassadors. They can prevent me from entering their countries, but they cannot prevent my ambassadors. So I am going to declare soon, in all the countries, that my ambassadors will be propagating the birth of a new man and a new world.

11

Never Go Against Your Nature

Osho,
Is enlightenment beyond the nature of things?

Enlightenment *is* the very nature of things. But it has never been said that way; on the contrary, people's minds have been corrupted by creating a goal against nature, giving it beautiful names, "*super-nature*." And man was caught in this because of a very simple reason: the nature of things is already where you are.

It is not an excitement, it is not a challenge and it does not call on you to prove your ego. It is not a faraway star. The mind wants something very difficult for its nourishment, something almost impossible. Only if you can achieve the impossible can you feel you are someone special.

Enlightenment is not a talent. It is not like someone being born a painter, a poet, a scientist – those are talents. Enlightenment is simply everyone's very source of life. You don't even have to go out of your house to look for it. Going out of your house to look for it, you have missed it. And no one knows when you will be able to come back home.

Enlightenment is nothing but realizing the fact, "I am that which I have always wanted to be, and I have never been anything else and I cannot be anything else, ever." The very definition of nature is that you cannot go beyond it. You can make the effort and create misery, anxiety, anguish, but you cannot go beyond it. It is you. How can you go beyond yourself? It is your very life source, your very existence. Wherever you go, you will be it.

There have been records of people whose first experience of themselves was just a belly laughter. Seeing the absurdity of what they were trying to do – they were trying to be themselves! That is the only impossible thing in the world because you are already it – how can you try to be it?

But the priests, the so-called religious leaders, and all those who have wanted you to be enslaved have given you ideals. They have told you, "Unless you behave in a certain way, you are wrong." Unless you do the things that they prescribe, you are not good. No one ever asked these people, "Who has given you the authority to decide for others? If you think something is good, do it, but you have no right to tell anyone else to follow you."

The great corrupters, the great poisoners are the people who have created a following. Because following simply means you are being put into an absurdity against yourself: you are being told that you have to be someone that you can never be. This has created tremendous misery in the whole of the world.

Unless we see the roots, this misery cannot disappear. We can go on increasing our gadgets, our technology, but the misery continues. It is not that only the poor man is miserable; my own experience is that the poor man is less miserable than the rich man. The poor man at least has hope; the rich man is living hopelessly. Now he knows that he has done all he could, and his life is as empty as ever – perhaps emptier. And death is coming closer; every moment life is becoming shorter and he has wasted it in accumulating money, power, prestige. He has wasted his life in being a saint, praying before man-manufactured gods. And all this has been done so that you can never simply be just yourself.

I teach you only a simple morality, and that is to never go against your nature. Even if all the buddhas of all the ages are standing against it, don't pay any attention. They have nothing to do with you. They did what they felt was right for them, you have to do what you feel is right for yourself. And what is right? It cannot be defined by any scripture. It cannot be defined by any outer criterion.

There is an intrinsic criterion to be understood: that which makes you happier is good. That which makes you blissful is the only morality. That which makes you miserable is the only sin. That which takes you away from yourself is the only thing to be avoided. Just rejoice in yourself and you are enlightened. You have always been enlightened, there is no way to be unenlightened.

I have tried in many ways, but I have to concede to you that I have failed. I could not become unenlightened. In whatever position, doing whatever kinds of things, I was surprised that whether I go north or I go south, I remain enlightened!

In Japan, they have a very beautiful doll – perhaps they are the people who make the most beautiful dolls. And this doll is no ordinary doll. In Japan its name is *daruma*, but it is the Japanese distortion of the name of Bodhidharma – the doll is made according to Bodhidharma's insight. The doll is heavy in the legs and very light toward the head. So you can throw it anyway you like, but it always goes into the lotus posture. You cannot do anything to it. People may have forgotten; it has become just a doll for children to play with. But it represents what I am saying and what Bodhidharma was saying: "There is no way for you to be unenlightened." Who has put this idea in your mind that you have to become enlightened?

Miss Prim, the elderly spinster, is giving an introductory talk at the girl's college. "Now, girls," she says, "whenever you go out, remember: no smoking in the streets, no bad conduct in public, and when men bother you, ask yourself, 'Is an hour's pleasure worth a lifetime of disgrace?' Now, girls, are there any questions?"

A voice from the back of the hall cries, "How do you make it last an hour?"

There are people around you driving you crazy. Otherwise everything is perfectly as it should be. This is the most perfect world, nothing is missing. But a few crackpots cannot sit at ease unless they drive a few other people to run after shadows which can never be realized. And the more they feel they cannot be realized, the more meaninglessness, the more hopelessness, the more the feeling of utter emptiness – and a sadness settles and becomes thicker as time passes by.

Never accept any criterion that makes you miserable. Never accept any morality that makes you feel guilty. Never accept anything that is trying to enforce something upon you that is against your simple nature. Just be yourself and you are perfect.

Move away from yourself and you are in for great trouble. Everyone is in trouble. My own experience of coming in contact with thousands of people is that I have never seen a man who is really miserable. On the contrary – I have seen people enjoying their misery, exaggerating their misery. One feels immensely compassionate that people who could have blossomed into beautiful flowers are shrunken. They have lost the way to their own home, and everyone is trying to help them to go somewhere else: "Become a Buddha, become a Jesus, become a Moses." But no one ever says to you, "Just be yourself."

What connection exists between you and Moses? What are the ties between you and Jesus Christ? But people are worshipping, praying, hoping that someday they will become the ideals of their imagination. Naturally they are always failures. You are a roseflower and you are going to be a roseflower. Let the whole world condemn or appreciate – it does not matter.

Once a man takes this stand that "I am going to assert myself" – and it has nothing to do with the ego, it is simply protecting yourself against a criminal world, corrupted for thousands of years.

You have every right to protect yourself, not to be poisoned. And there will not be any need in you for any god, religion, moral code, methodology, any effort to become enlightened. Just being natural is more than you can ever imagine. Except man, the whole of existence is enlightened. No one is trying for anything else; everyone is at ease, at home with the universe.

One of the great scientists, Julian Huxley, has a certain hypothesis – there is no way to prove it, but it seems to have certain significance. After his whole life's research he concludes, "It seems something has gone wrong in the very mechanism of man. Because no tree seems to be anxious, no animal commits suicide in the wild, no animal becomes a homosexual in the wild." But something strange happens in zoos. When animals are kept in a zoo, they start getting some great qualities of your humanity – they become homosexuals. Animals have even been found to commit suicide in zoos. They become perverted, they start doing things which none of their ancestors have ever done, in millennia. What happens in the zoo? – they become part of the human society. They start imitating human beings. They become distorted, they become unnatural.

As far as I am concerned, except man, the whole existence is perfectly healthy, perfectly at ease. Julian Huxley's idea has some pragmatic value. It may not be possible to prove what has gone wrong because man is a very complex mechanism. But something certainly has gone wrong. In my vision, it is not something hereditary that has gone wrong. It is something that happens to every child again and again because every child is born into a society which is not sane. And he has to learn the ways of the people who are insane. By the time he is capable of some intelligence, he is already poisoned. It is already too late, he has become an imitator.

Children are innocent. They come into the world without any idea of what is going to happen. Naturally, finding themselves surrounded by people, they start imitating them. That is their way of learning. But in this very process of imitation and learning, the great mistake happens which Julian Huxley thinks is genetic. It is not genetic, it is cultural. It is because of the grown-ups. The child has no other way; he has to learn from people who are sick. And these sick people will not tolerate anyone who is not sick.

Anyone who is healthy, anyone who is sane is going to be hated, is going to be poisoned, is going to be stoned to death. Because the crowd has to choose between two things. Either this single individual is right, then the whole crowd and its whole history is wrong. Or if the whole crowd and its long past, which it calls its "golden past," is right, then this man has to be erased because it is a constant question mark.

It is not without reason that Socrates is poisoned. Socrates is intolerable. His very presence hurts you because his height, his intelligence, his honesty, all prove you to be hypocrites. Certainly the crowd is not willing to accept a single man's standard against the whole history of mankind. It is better to destroy this man, to get rid of this man. He is a constant nagging; he is telling you that you are dishonest, that you are living in lies, that your gods are false, that your hopes are nothing but consolations, that you are trying to hide your nudity.

You know perfectly well that behind your clothes, you are a totally different person. These people are reminders, and it hurts to be reminded of your dishonesty to yourself. It hurts to know that your love is not love but jealousy; it is a diluted form of hate. It hurts to know that your gods are absolutely bogus, that they are your own creation; your holy scriptures are as unholy as a book can be. The easier thing seems to be to remove any man like Socrates and be at ease with your misery, and again start making efforts to become enlightened.

It is a very strange situation. Whenever someone is natural and is enlightened, you destroy him and then you try to find out how to become enlightened. Perhaps your quest of how to become enlightened is nothing but a very cunning strategy to postpone enlightenment. In fact, even to say postponement is not right. You are enlightened and you are trying not to be enlightened. Your whole effort of being a Catholic, a Protestant, a Hindu, a Mohammedan, is nothing but a device not to recognize your enlightenment.

When Socrates was poisoned, Athens was a city state, a direct democracy. Every citizen except the slaves had the right to vote and every decision had to be made by the whole city. The chief justice who was going to decide whether the majority of Athenians were in favor of poisoning Socrates or in favor of saving him, was very puzzled. He must have been a man of some intelligence. He saw that Socrates was a simple, innocent, almost childlike person. He had not committed any crime, he had not done any harm to anyone. And that's what Socrates had appealed to the court, saying, "Just tell me, what is my crime?"

There was no crime, there was no charge against him. The chief justice whispered in his ear, "Your crime is that you are a natural being. I cannot say it aloud because I know if they cannot forgive you, they cannot forgive me either. But I have immense respect for your innocence and I don't want a man like you to be destroyed. You are an exception, but you prove the rule that every man can be so innocent and so sincere and so alive and so joyous. I give you three alternatives:

"First is that Athens is a city state; its laws are not applicable outside the boundary of the city. The simple thing is for you to move outside the city. You can open your school, your academy, and those who love you will come there. And I know for certain that the younger generation is immensely impressed by you. It is the older generation..."

But in the past, the older generation was always the majority because out of ten children, nine used to die within two years of their birth. Now the situation has reversed: out of ten children only one child dies, nine go on living. For the first time it is the young people that are the majority in the world. In the past, young people were never in the majority. They were always a minority group.

The chief justice said, "Simply move out of the city."

Socrates said, "That will be cowardly. As far as death is concerned, it is going to come sooner or later. I am already old enough. But I don't want future generations to remember that Socrates moved out of Athens because of the fear of death. Please forgive me, I cannot go out of Athens."

The chief justice said, "Then the second simple thing will be to stop teaching. Live in Athens, but don't talk about your truth. And don't talk about people being sincere and authentic."

Socrates said, "You are asking me to do things which I cannot do. What is the purpose of my living if I cannot blossom into my absolute potential? When a tree blossoms, flowers are bound to be there and the fragrance is going to reach those who are receptive. I will continue to speak and I will continue to talk about truth. And I will continue to provoke people to be natural and not to become hypocrites according to the so-called religions."

The chief justice said, "I am helpless. Then the third alternative is that you have to accept the poison. Because the majority, although they have no evidence against you, simply say that your very presence is corruptive. Your very presence is destroying the youth; your very presence is taking the youth away from the old path trodden by the ancients. Your presence is making individuals assertive, giving them courage to be free and to stand alone even if it is against the whole society."

Socrates said, "There is no problem about poison. That I can accept. I am dying for a beautiful cause. I lived in absolute glory and I am dying with a crescendo."

And while he was lying in the bed and the poison was being prepared, the man – who had prepared poison for many other prisoners – was trying to delay because he also felt, "The man is absolutely innocent. If I can give him a few minutes more to live… I am a poor man, I cannot do anything more." So he was preparing the poison as slowly as possible.

But Socrates would come to the door and say to the man, "You are not being sincere, you are cheating. The orders are that as the sun sets, the poison should be given to me. And the sun has set and you have not prepared the poison. I feel you are trying to give me a few more minutes, but there is no point. I am ready to go into the unknown. Life, I have known enough. Don't delay; let me go into the unknown mysteries of death."

He was one of the most sincere men in the sense that he never said anything about beyond death. He always said, "First let me die. Unless I know, I cannot say anything about beyond death. Those who have said something are all lying, deceiving, cheating because they are still alive and they don't know anything about death. Don't force me to be in the same company. I will say only that which is my experience."

He told the man who was preparing the poison, "Be quick, because my disciples are waiting. Perhaps I can give them a few indications about death as it is experienced."

The poison was given – and this is when Socrates comes into his purest awareness. He said to his disciples, "I don't feel anything up to my knees." He pinched himself and said, "The poison has worked up to my knees. But one thing you should remember: the knees are gone, but I am as complete and entire as I have been before. Nothing has been taken away from me." And then the whole of the legs, and then the hands… And then the breathing started slowing. And Socrates said, "Perhaps I may not be able to say anything more. I want you to know that almost all of my body is dead. Just the last few breaths… And I will be gone. But I am as entire and as total and as whole as I have ever been. My awareness is crystal clear."

This shows the sincerity of the man. Only such a man can say that your source of life belongs to eternity, it doesn't die with your body. It only changes house. You have been here always, and you will be here always. You are part, an essential part, inseparable part of this immensely beautiful dancing existence.

Just be natural so that you can remain in tune with existence. So that you can dance in the rain, you can dance in the sun, you can dance with the trees, and have a communion even with the rocks, the mountains, the stars. Except this, there is no enlightenment. Let me define it. Enlightenment is to be in tune with existence.

To be in tune with nature – the very nature of things – is enlightenment. Against nature there is only misery – and misery created by yourself. No one else is responsible for it.

Two Irish leprechauns arrive at the convent door and ask to speak to the Mother Superior. They are led to her office, where one of them respectfully asks, "Excuse me, your holiness, but are there any leprechaun nuns at this convent?"

The Mother Superior looks shocked and assures him that there are not. The little guy then asks if there are any leprechaun nuns in the neighborhood. Again the reply is no.

The leprechaun then asks, "Begging your pardon, Holy Mother, but would you know of *any* leprechaun nuns *anywhere*?"

The nun shakes her head, at which the little man turns and shakes his friend by the shoulders. "You see! You see!" he cries, "I told you, you fucked a penguin!"

This is prayer time…

Old man Finkelstein tells Ruthie that he is going into town to apply for an old age pension. Ruthie says, "Sam, you don't have a birth certificate; how are you going to prove your age?"

"Don't worry Ruthie," says old man Fink and he leaves for town.

Sure enough, he is back in a few hours and reports that he will get his first check on Monday.

"So how did you prove your age?" asks Ruthie.

"Easy," says Fink, smiling, "I just unbuttoned my shirt and showed them all the gray hairs on my chest."

"Well, while you were at it," snaps Ruthie, "why didn't you drop your pants and apply for total disability?"

At a doctors' convention, a conversation is taking place in the pub at the end of the day's activities.

An Israeli doctor says, "Medicine in my country is so advanced that we can take an eyeball out of one person and put it in another and have him looking for work in six weeks."

A German doctor says, "*Ja*, that's nothing. In Germany, we can take a lung out of one person and put it in someone else and have him looking for work in a month."

A Russian doctor says, "In my country, medicine is so advanced that we can take half a heart from one person, put it in another, and have them both looking for work in two weeks."

An American doctor, not wanting to be outdone, says, "That's nothing. We can take an asshole out of Hollywood, put him in the White House, and have half the nation looking for work the next day!"

12

Against all American Tradition and Pride

Osho,
I can relate to the taste of good German chocolate, but what about the taste of enlightenment?

The mind has an incurable disease. The name of the disease is duality. It does not matter what the mind is focused on, it immediately creates a division – in the knower and in the known, in the observer and in the observed, in the subject and in the object; in short, between I and thou.

One of the most prominent thinkers of the twentieth century was Martin Buber, and his contribution is of great importance. He has condensed his whole philosophy into a book called *I and Thou*. And he has given the philosophy the name, "dialogue."

As far as the mind is concerned, what he is saying is true and relevant. But the mind is not the ultimate judge of existence. I had written a letter to Martin Buber when he was alive. I was very young, but I pointed out to him that a real dialogue is not between I and thou, the real dialogue begins when the I and the thou start merging and melting. The dialogue can even be silent, but its basic requirement is that the division should not be there. He did not reply. I wrote to him again and told him, "Not replying to me shows that you yourself are not convinced of what you are saying."

You are asking, "...what is the taste of enlightenment?" – there is no taste because you are alone. At the most, in language we can say there is a certain sensitivity, a fragrance, but it is not separate from you. It is you yourself. The taste and the taster need to be separate, and in enlightenment the only barrier is separation.

Just the other day I received another question from the same insane Catholic man from the staff of *Time* magazine saying, "You teach love, you teach compassion – then why did the people of Oregon in America become your enemies?" Ordinarily, I don't reply to people if I see that they are basically insane. And the question shows insanity absolutely clearly. If he were intelligent enough, first he should have asked, "Jesus also preached love, compassion, forgiveness – then why was he crucified by the Jews?" If his question were relevant and had not come from a Catholic prejudice, he would have seen the contradiction. And certainly the people of Oregon have not crucified me yet.

Moreover, I was only a tourist in America. Jesus was a Jew, belonged to the same people, was born among them, brought up by them. Whatever he was saying was not contradictory to the Jewish scriptures. In fact, he was trying to argue for the Jewish tradition; still the people of Judea crucified him. And this fellow, after two thousand years, has the guts to ask me, "If you teach love, if you teach compassion, then why were the people of Oregon not friendly to you?" The fact is that we have lived a past so insane, so insecure, that we are afraid of strangers. America could not find a stranger man than me. I was not part of their world, I did not believe in their values. I was really making a commune absolutely against all American tradition and pride.

I am basically against marriage; obviously the question of divorce does not arise. I am against the accidental birth of people because that is the basic cause for the earth being burdened with the retarded. I am in absolute agreement that love should be just play; the moment you start producing children it becomes business. And I cannot agree to produce this kind of humanity. I was teaching that whenever a couple… Of course unmarried because the law has nothing to do with your love. Love should be a freedom between two people, and if love disappears from even one person they have to separate, as friends, with gratitude for all the beautiful moments they lived together. Loving affairs that end up in the courts are absolutely ugly.

When a couple wants more than love, wants a child, the decision has to be made by medical science, not by them. Because neither the father nor the mother knows what the outcome is going to be – Adolf Hitler, Ronald Reagan? These idiots could have been avoided.

In a single lovemaking, the man releases almost one million sperm and from that point starts your ugly civilization. All those one million sperm have a life span of only two hours; within two hours they have to reach the mother's egg. You have seen marathon races, but you don't understand that the real marathon race is for the poor sperm. It is so small you cannot see it with your naked eye. In relation to its size, the track that it has to pass to reach the mother's egg has been calculated as almost two miles. In those two miles, one million people are struggling for survival. It is absolutely understandable that the wiser ones will stand by the side, and the idiots will do everything to reach the mother's egg. It is not a coincidence that the world is full of retarded people. And once a single sperm reaches the mother's egg, the egg closes; the remaining one million people are defeated. They have to die, there is no way for them to stay alive.

It is almost amazing that a few wise people have also reached the mother's egg. It seems just accidental. A Gautam Buddha or a Bertrand Russell – perhaps they got into the crowd and could not get out of it. The crowd is not small; they were simply pushed by the crowd – perhaps some idiot was pushing them from behind. I cannot conceive them to be so competitive that they would have reached on their own. Some accident, perhaps just chance that they entered the track first because one million people cannot enter the track simultaneously. And there is no referee to give them a signal, "Go!" So a few enter first, a few later. It seems to be just chance.

If you look at humanity, how many people of any worth have you created? And how many people have lived without any dignity, without any joy? I am in absolute agreement with scientific determination, and not to leave it – because this is the most important thing – to the idiots themselves. They can be eliminated, but then we will have to think in a totally new way. We will have to manage our lives not according to the old, which was not management but an absolute chaos.

It is not necessary that your sperm will have an Albert Einstein, a Rabindranath Tagore, a Picasso. I don't see any reason why we cannot have banks in the hospitals, medical colleges, where people can contribute their sperm just as they contribute blood. Now science is ready to read the intrinsic program of the sperm: how long it will live, whether it will be strong or weak, whether it will suffer diseases, whether it will be intelligent, whether it will have a certain genius. This is an old stupidity that your child should be only from your sperm. You can choose from the sperm bank. You can choose if you want a scientist if you want a poet of the qualities which only very few people have attained in the whole of history; if you want a painter; if you want an absolutely healthy human being, intelligent, beautiful.

And rather than you injecting it, let medical science inject a single sperm so there is no possibility for any Ronald Reagan to reach the mother's egg. These people have to be eliminated completely. They don't have a place in the future vision of mankind. Just think of a world of utterly talented people, healthy, with a longer life span, creative, sensitive. We can make this world really a garden where every plant blossoms, releases its fragrance, joins the dance that is existence.

This man's question reminded me how blind people can be and never be aware of their blindness. Jesus is crucified – that is perfect – and after Jesus, the Christianity that he unknowingly produced has burned thousands of living beings alive. No other religion is as criminal as Christianity, but this man cannot see that. He can see only enough to ask why I was not liked by the people of Oregon. It simply shows that the people of Oregon are the most retarded people in the world. After Oregon I have been trying to find someone who can defeat them, but I have not been able to find anyone. They are absolute idiots.

Just because they were afraid of me and my people – afraid because things happened when we purchased the land in Oregon. The land was for sale for almost forty years, and no one had purchased it at any price because it was only a desert. What are you going to do with a desert of one hundred twenty-six square miles?

I wanted to make the point that the people who surrounded that desert were not inventive, not intelligent – because we changed that same desert into an oasis, and that hurt the Oregonians. When we purchased the land they laughed. They used to come and say, "What are you doing? You can pour in millions of dollars; this desert is not going to produce anything." And we made the desert one of the most beautiful places you can conceive. That became a wound in the hearts of the Oregonians.

And the United States Attorney blurted out after deporting me... He was asked by a reporter in a press conference, "Why haven't you jailed Osho?"

He said, "There are three reasons. One, our priority was to destroy the commune."

That shows the reason – why should they destroy the commune? We had made a desert into a living place. Five thousand sannyasins were living there; we made roads, we made dams, we had grown sufficient food for ourselves. We made all kinds of arrangements – a small oasis. We had fifteen thousand specially-made tents which could be air-conditioned, which could be heated so that they could be used around the year. Each celebration day – and the celebrations used to last for three weeks – there were twenty thousand people from all over the world. Oregon was shocked, they could not believe it. We had every facility. There was not a single beggar – and the people who come to me are, of necessity, bound to be the most intelligent ones. The unintelligent cannot even conceive of what I am saying.

There was a heart surgeon who was known all over the country. We had our own hospital, the most qualified doctors, nurses. We had our own school, and I had made it a point that the children should not be part of the family, they should be part of the commune. Their fathers and mothers could meet them, could invite them for a visit, but they could not prejudice their minds. Those children were growing – for the first time in the whole of history – without being conditioned that they were Christian, that they were Hindu, that they were communist. No conditioning – we were allowing them to grow to whatever their inner potential is.

I don't believe in poverty. And the man from *Time* magazine has asked, "If you love people, and you are compassionate, why did you have ninety-three Rolls Royces?" But he is not aware that I don't have a single cent. Those ninety-three Rolls Royces had come from people who loved the commune. Of course, no one can use ninety-three Rolls Royces simultaneously, and they were all the latest model, the same model. I am not mad! It was just because of the gratitude of my sannyasins that they did not want to use a car that I was using. But they had their own cars.

The commune had two hundred cars of its own, one hundred buses of its own, four airplanes and a small airport of its own. We changed the whole shape of the desert, and everyone was working not as a laborer but out of love, out of creativity. And even after working the whole day, people were dancing in the evening; late in the night you could hear the flutes, the guitars. This was the pain in the neck of Oregonians: "We have been living here for three hundred years and we could not make any use of this land.

Within five years these people have changed the whole face of it." We created the most luxurious commune that has been ever created. The whole commune was centrally air-conditioned. We were not at all concerned with America or with Oregon. The nearest Oregon town was twenty miles away from us and people were so happy in the commune, no one wanted to go anywhere. Finally we had to get rid of so many cars, airplanes because what is the point? No one wants to go anywhere.

And the poor fellow is still haunted by my ninety-three Rolls Royces. He does not think for a moment that I have not kept any Rolls Royce from those ninety-three; I have not even looked back toward them. I never went to the garage. They were not mine.

But he is asking the question, "When the whole world is poor, how could you manage to live comfortably in a commune?" What do you mean? If the whole world is sick, do we also have to be sick? If the whole hospital is filled with sick people, do you want the doctors and nurses also in the beds?

I am absolutely against poverty. That became the problem, that I had abolished poverty in the commune. And what can be done in one place can be done in every place because it is the same earth – *better* earth. The commune became their priority – to destroy it so no one could compare, and no one could ask why America has thirty million beggars.

We had absorbed three hundred beggars from America into the commune. And the beggars themselves told me, "For the first time we have recognized that we are human beings because no one here treats us the way we have been treated our whole life – like stray dogs. For the first time we have felt that we are also human beings, and a tremendous dignity and self-respect has arisen in us."

Now, this was the problem. If the commune was going to become well-known all over America, the American politicians would have been in tremendous difficulty. Hence the Attorney General – who is a close friend of Ronald Reagan… They have been educated in the same schools, same colleges, and they were also working in Hollywood together. And as Ronald Reagan became the president, he immediately called his friend to be the Attorney General of America.

The second reason the United States Attorney gave was, "We did not want Osho to remain in jail because we were afraid that would make him a martyr." You can see the meaning hidden in it – the desire was there, but because of the fear that if they kept me in jail, then sannyasins all over the world were going to protest, were going to become stronger, were going to be in every way against the American domination of the world.

And the third thing is really hilarious. He said, "And moreover, the third thing is that we don't have any evidence for the charge that Osho has committed any crime." Now the US Attorney says he doesn't have any evidence against me! Then why am I being punished with a fine of almost half a million dollars? Why have I been harassed into six jails unnecessarily? Why was I arrested in the first place under the threat of loaded guns, and without any arrest warrant? Why wasn't I allowed bail?

The female magistrate who did not allow me bail behaved so strangely. I had never expected a woman to behave that way. For three days continuously the government attorney tried and failed to prove that there was any reason for my arrest. The question of bail does not arise – in fact the people who arrested me should have been punished! And the government attorney accepted in his final statement the concluding line, "We have not been able to prove anything against Osho." But the female magistrate, and that was such a surprise to me said, "You may not have been able to prove anything, but I have reasons of my own and I am not going to give him bail."

I have respected women more than any man in history, but unfortunately I have to exclude this magistrate in Carolina from my respect. And she must have suffered a deep guilt because what was she doing? I was told by my jailer – he was on the point of retirement, he had a lifetime of experience – that he could not believe it either. He said, "I have never seen such a case. When you cannot produce any evidence and still you refuse to give bail, this is unheard of!" And he told me that the reason was that the woman was being bribed from the White House. She was just a magistrate, and she had been bribed that if she refused me bail, she would be made a federal judge.

She must have felt a deep guilt for this promotion. Just the other day I came to know that she is suffering from cancer, and is on her deathbed. That guilt must have created the cancer; otherwise the woman was perfectly healthy, in fact healthier than ordinarily you expect women to be. I feel sorry for her. She got the promotion, but in a wrong direction.

My chief attorney Niren is here – he is my sannyasin. He has been going through all the jails where they mistreated me in every possible way. And they are lying; I have to speak with Niren about the points where they are absolutely lying. I have an inner, intuitive guarantee that in the Oklahoma jail I was poisoned, poisoned with thallium, which has shown its effects over the last two years. It remains deposited in the body and becomes active over a period of time. But it has to be given in small doses; if you give it in a big dose, then the effects will be immediate. This was the reason why the bail was refused and I was dragged for twelve days from one jail to another jail.

And in Oklahoma – Niren has been there – they simply denied that I had been in that jail. I knew that's what they were going to say. I reached Oklahoma in the middle of the night; it was purposefully arranged so that the whole airport was dark and there was no traffic, and still they were afraid that someone might see me. They took me out through a secret door, out of the airport.

At the airport, the man who was passing on the responsibility for me to the US Marshall whispered in his ear while he was driving. But I was sitting just behind him, and what he whispered made me certain about my intuitive feeling. The man said, "Remember, this guy is world famous and all the world media are focused on him, so don't do anything directly. Be very cautious whatever you do." Now these words indicate with absolute certainty that they were ready to do something, and the instruction was given – it has to be done in such an indirect way that no one will ever be able to find...

But I was not alone in the car. Another prisoner, a woman, was also sitting by my side. I said to her, "Listen carefully to what is being said." Niren has to find that woman because all records have disappeared – records about me, records about that woman, because she will be the witness. When Niren reached there he found that there was no record on their computer. They have their records on the computer since 1986. He had to force his way, insisting, "I have an absolute guarantee that he has been in this jail and I want to look into the records in your basement."

In the middle of the night they took me through the back door into the jail. There was no one else, they eliminated any kind of witness, but existence has its own ways. The US Marshall who brought me insisted that I could not write my own name, I had to write the name of David Washington. I should be called David Washington while I am in the jail, and I have to respond to this name.

I said, "I am not going to write anyone's name. You are forcing me to do something illegal and unconstitutional, for which you will suffer one day."

He was also tired; it was the middle of the night, and for half an hour we struggled. He said, "You are a strange person, I want to go home!"

I said, "You can go to hell! But I am not going to write David Washington."

Then he said, "I will fill in the form." And he filled in the form – my understanding was that this would be an absolute proof. He filled in the form and I signed my own signature. He looked at my signature; of course he could not understand it. No one can understand what I write.

He asked me, "What have you written?"

I said, "It seems it is David Washington."

Niren found the document and he has brought a photocopy of the document, but my signature is missing. Still, that document indicates one thing: "David Washington, Rajneeshpuram, Oregon." And that is in the handwriting of the US Marshall of that jail. My feeling is they have simply destroyed the form on which I have signed, knowing that it will create difficulty, and they have filled in another form. I would like Niren to go back to Oklahoma because the question is very simple: on this form there is no signature, either of Osho or at least of David Washington. Some signature is needed, otherwise what is the value of this record?

I entered the jail, that is certain now. That "Rajneeshpuram" they have forgotten is enough proof. Niren has to take whatever he has managed to get to the experts. Whose handwriting is that? He has to insist on getting the signature because I *have* signed it; so either they are hiding the original and they have managed another, or they have destroyed it. But the man has to be caught.

And these people go on lying. The US Marshall said to Niren, "I treated Osho the best. In no other jail was he treated the way I treated him." In fact the truth is that I was treated the worst in Oklahoma. And I have witnesses. Just by chance they put me in an isolation cell with a small window – and the glass of the window was completely dark, so dirty you could not figure out what was beyond the window. But just across from me there was another person. I don't know him, but one thing is certain. He was an orthodox Hindu sannyasin because he had orange robes. And his face – I tried in every way to clean the window to see that man, and just a few days ago that man was here. Perhaps he may still be here. He told Anando, "I am a witness that Osho was brought to Oklahoma and was put in the cell just across from me."

Niren has to find the girl, who was released that very night. She is a fat girl, nearabout thirty years of age – but a courageous one; almost a jailbird. The way she was behaving in the jail was as if it were almost her home. Niren has just to advertise in Oklahoma and the girl will respond.

Niren has also to ask the pilot of the plane because there is only one US Marshall's plane – that makes things simple. They all became very friendly to me – the pilot, the copilot, and a woman who was serving food to the people. They all felt that this was strange because "From North Carolina it is only five or six hours' flight to Oregon, and you are being tortured unnecessarily for twelve days! There is no rationality in it." So he has to interview those people about whether they had dropped me in the middle of the night at the Oklahoma airport. And particularly the woman because she was very concerned about my well-being. There was no vegetarian food but she managed some fruits, some juices, and she was sorry, saying, "We never thought that in America such uncivilized behavior, such undemocratic behavior, is still prevalent."

And when these government people say things to you – I have to listen to Niren's interviews; he has brought all the tapes – don't trust them. Because in those twelve days they were all lying to me. Every time I was taken from one jail to another jail they would say, "You are going to Oregon." And I would end up somewhere else. It continued for twelve days – free travel all over America! I enjoyed it. I became convinced that if this is the situation of the country proclaimed to be the most democratic, what will be the situation of other countries?

Just by chance Niren met Judge Leavy, who finally gave me the punishment of four hundred thousand dollars and deportation for five years from America. And fifteen years in jail if I come back to America and commit any crime. Then there will be no trial; I will be jailed. It will be enough if someone complains against me.

Niren met him on the plane and for two hours they were together. Niren asked him, "You were watching Osho for three days; millions of people see something in his eyes – have you looked into his eyes?" And Judge Leavy was lying because I was looking into his eyes and he was avoiding; he has not looked into my eyes. And even if he had looked into my eyes, he would not find anything. He has lived with criminals his whole life. He knows the eyes of crime, he does not know the eyes of innocence.

I had my cap, and he said to Niren, "I hesitated whether to tell him to remove the cap or not" – because this stupid idea exists in America that to wear a cap in the courtroom is insulting to the court. My own understanding is that to cover your head is a respectful gesture. A court has to be a temple of justice. But he said, "Finally I asked him to remove his cap." I removed the cap and with the removal of the cap I removed all my respect for American courts and the American constitution.

I am not fussy about small things. But from that moment, whatever I have heard about Judge Leavy became absolutely absurd. He is not a man of justice. He knew perfectly well that I have not committed any crime, and he punished me. Four hundred thousand dollars, knowing perfectly well that I don't have a single cent, and he deported me without any reason. I looked at the man... He will suffer for it. Perhaps he has also been bribed in the same way because now he has moved from the federal court to a higher court. Just one step more and he can move to the Supreme Court. If he is a man of any guts, he should admit that he was not concerned with justice, he was concerned with his own promotion.

I can understand Niren's difficulty, but you have to gather courage and you have to encounter these people. When Judge Leavy said, "I did not see anything in his eyes," you should not have remained silent. Because if a blind man cannot see the sun, that does not mean the sun is not there, or if a man who is interested in climbing ladders cannot see the roses, it is not the fault of the roses. To see the sublime, to see the divine you have to be unprejudiced, you have to be open and receptive. I also watched him for three days – just a dead man with no guts, hoping for perhaps just one more promotion. He may not have seen anything in my eyes, but I have seen even into his soul.

According to me, our judges are greater criminals than our criminals. Moving from one jail to another jail, I have seen such innocent people. But I have not seen anyone who can be called innocent in the courts, in the officers, in the marshals, in the judges. They are all playing into the hands of those who can give them a little more prestige, a little more respectability. I would like Niren to tell Judge Leavy that what I have seen in him is just a dead soul – utterly ugly, criminal, without any guts; just a greedy person and nothing else.

Enlightenment is not something separate from you. What is the taste of innocence? What is the taste of silence? What is the taste of purity? You cannot taste them because they are not objects. You are the taste! And when everything else has disappeared in your utter aloneness, a merger, a meeting with the cosmos happens. You cannot call it a taste, the word *taste* is too small. It certainly creates a dance in every cell of your being, in every fiber of your being. It transforms you from base metal into gold. But it is not a taste, it is a transformation. You cannot describe it, you can only enjoy it.

Now it is time for prayer...

How long a minute is depends on which side of the bathroom door you are on.
This is the whole of Albert Einstein's philosophy of relativity!

When you read a biography, remember that the truth is never fit for publication.

Truth is so simple, there is no sensation in it. No publisher is going to waste money in publishing truth. Thousands of papers, magazines, weeklies, are full of untruth. The more untruth, the greater their subscription rate, the more they are read. But remember, for this untruth we are destroying beautiful trees around the world.

The quickest way to make antifreeze is to hide her nightdress.

Prepare for eternity: tidy up your room.

To live to be a hundred, first you have to live to be ninety-nine and then be very careful for a year.

When a woman steals your boyfriend, the best revenge is to let her live with him.

If you are not confused, you are not paying attention.

There is only one way to handle a woman. The trouble is, no one knows what it is.

If you are single, all the good men are married. If you are married, all the good men are single. If you are over sixty-five, all the good men are dead.

Misery to a woman is an alive secret and a dead telephone.

There is nothing like good food, good wine and a bad woman.

Love may be blind, but it knows its way around in the dark.

You have not lived until you die in California.

A wedding is a ceremony where a man loses control of himself.

Success is relative. The more success, the more relatives.

It is better for a woman to be beautiful rather than intelligent, because men's eyes function better than their brains.

A sexy blonde with a stunning figure boards a bus and finding no empty seats, asks a gentleman for his, explaining that she is pregnant.

The man stands up at once and gives her his seat, but can't help commenting that she does not look pregnant.

"Well," she replies with a smile, "it has only been about half an hour, and it really makes me very tired!"

Paddy is obsessed by golf – it has become his only topic of conversation.

Maureen is slowly going bananas with the constant discussion of birdies, drivers and sand traps, his golf clubs, his caddies and his scores.

Finally at dinner she snaps, "I am tired of you talking about golf twenty-four hours a day! I don't want to hear about it at this meal!"

"But what shall I talk about then?" asks Paddy.

"About anything," says Maureen. "Talk about sex for goodness' sake!"

"Okay," says Paddy, "I wonder who my caddie is screwing these days?"

After the prison riot, the head warden calls the three ringleaders into his office and says, "Now then, I would like to know two things: First, why did you revolt? And second, how did you get out of your cell?"

One of the men steps forward and says, "Warden, we rebelled because the prison food is so awful."

"I see," replies the warden. "And the cell, what did you use to break the bars?"

The prisoner steps back in disgust and says, "This morning's toast!"

13

The Inner Is as Real as the Outer

Osho,
In the West, celebration is associated with the American idea of having a good time which is synonymous with noise, loud music, watching movies, smoking, sex, and the release of energy as such. While silence and serenity are automatically associated with boredom and excessive accumulation of energy which results in tension and anxiety. Could you say something about silence and the celebration of life?

The question you have asked has many implications. It is not a single question; it is one question consisting of many questions of importance. I would like to go into each dimension of the question; only then you may be able to find the answer.

The first thing to remember is that man consists of two worlds, one that leads outward and one that leads inward. Man is a duality. He is a body and a soul. And because of this tremendous duality, all the problems of the world have arisen. The duality is not a simple one. It is what I have called a "gestalt duality." In a gestalt duality you can never see both worlds together; if you choose to see one you have to forget about the other. As an example, I have told you about a small children's book where they have a picture made of simple lines, but in those lines there are two possibilities. If you fix your eyes on the picture, either you can see an old woman or you can see a beautiful young girl. You can see each separately. If you go on staring at the old woman, suddenly you will find a strange change: the old woman has disappeared and a beautiful young girl is in front of you.

If you still persist in staring... Because the eyes are not meant to stare; naturally, they are continuously moving. Movement is intrinsic to your eyes. They get tired of staring at something, they are always in search of something new. And because of this, soon you will find the young woman disappearing and the old woman replaces her again. They are both made of the same lines, just different combinations, but you cannot see both together. That is impossible. If you see the young woman, where will you find the lines that make the old woman? If you see the old woman, you don't have extra lines to create the young woman. You can see each separately, but you can never see them together. This is gestalt duality, and this is the reality of man.

The East has seen man only as a soul, a consciousness, an inward-looking being. And because it has chosen one gestalt, it has to deny the other. That's why for centuries in the East the mystics have consistently been denying the reality of the world. They say it is just a dream, it is maya, illusion. It is made of the same stuff as dreams are made of. It is not really there, it is only a mirage, only an appearance. The East has denied the outside – *has* to deny, because of the inner necessity of the gestalt duality.

The West has chosen the outside world and has to deny the inner world: man is only a body – physiology, biology, chemistry, but not a consciousness, not a soul; the soul is only an epiphenomenon. And because only the outside is real, it was possible for science to develop in the West. Technology, thousands of gadgets – possibilities to land on the moon, and the vast universe that surrounds you. But knowing all this, there has been a deep emptiness in the Western mind. Something is missing.

It is difficult for the Western logic to pinpoint what is missing, but it is absolutely certain that something is missing. The house is full of guests but the host is missing. You have all the things of the world, but *you* are not. The outcome is tremendous misery. You have all the pleasures, all the money, all that man has ever dreamed of, and at the end of centuries of effort, suddenly you find you don't exist. Your inside is hollow, there is no one.

The East has also faced its own misery. Thinking that the outside is unreal, there is no possibility of scientific progress. Science has to be objective – but if objects are only appearances, illusions, there is no point in dissecting illusions and trying to find out the secrets of nature. Hence the East has to remain poor, has to remain hungry, has to remain under all kinds of slavery for centuries.

These two thousand years of slavery are not just an accident. The East was prepared for it. It has accepted it – in a dream, what does it matter whether you are a master or a slave? What does it matter if in a dream you are being served with delicious food or you are hungry? The moment you wake up, both dreams will prove invalid. The East has consented to remain starved, hungry, enslaved, and the reason is that it has chosen a different gestalt: the inner is the real.

The East has learned ways to be silent, to be peaceful, to enjoy the bliss that arises as you drown deeper into your interiority. But you cannot share it with anyone else; it is absolutely individual. At the most you can talk about it. For thousands of years the whole East has been talking about spirituality, consciousness, enlightenment, meditation, and on the outside has remained a beggar, sick, hungry, enslaved.

Who is going to listen to these slaves and their great philosophies? The West has simply laughed. But the laughter has not been only on one side. The East has also laughed, seeing that people are accumulating things and losing themselves. We have lived in a very strange, schizophrenic state of mind for thousands of years.

You are saying, "In the West, celebration is associated with the American idea of having a good time..." That brings me to another implication. Only a miserable man needs a good time. Just as a sick man needs medicine, a miserable man needs a good time; it is a very cunning strategy to avoid your misery.

The misery is not avoided; you only forget that you are miserable for the time being. Under the influence of drugs or under the influence of sex or under the influence of your so-called "having a good time," what are you actually doing? – you are escaping from your inner emptiness. You are getting involved in any kind of thing. The one thing you are afraid of is your own self.

It has created a certain madness. And because everyone in the West is in the same boat, it becomes very difficult to recognize. Millions of people are watching football – and you call these people intelligent? Then who are you going to call retarded? Not only are these people immensely involved in games like football, they are jumping, shouting, fighting. There are no stadiums big enough to accommodate the whole country, so everyone is sitting glued to his chair in front of the television. They are doing the same stupid acts – sitting in their chairs, shouting…

I know a man who became so mad he destroyed his television because his team was losing! I was staying with the man and I asked him, "Are you ready to go to an insane asylum? In the first place, football should be for children. You have passed that age long before, but mentally your age is not more than twelve or thirteen years. And what you have done with the television makes me suspect that not only are you retarded, you are insane too."

Just last year, the University of California made a survey, a whole year's survey about boxing matches. Each time there are boxing matches – which are ugly, inhuman, animalistic – the rate of crime in the whole state of California rises by thirteen or fourteen percent. And that rise remains after the matches are finished; it goes on lingering for at least one week. Slowly, slowly it comes back to normal.

People start murdering, people start committing suicide, people start raping; all kinds of crimes suddenly start growing. Still, boxing is not condemned by any country as a criminal game which should be stopped immediately. If any government tries, the whole country will stand up against the parliament and protest because boxing is such a "good time." Two idiots are doing things on your behalf. You also wanted to do the same things, but you kept yourself in control. Now it is "having a good time" because someone else is doing it and your own repressed energies are expressed. It is something to be understood. Why should you be interested in two people behaving barbarously, harming each other? Certainly you also have the same desires. Perhaps you don't have the guts.

But it is something much more complicated. The whole West has become slowly, slowly just an observer. Someone else makes love in the film, someone else fights in the boxing matches, someone else plays football, and deep down you get identified with these people. It is good that it is kept dark in movie houses because I have watched people crying in a movie house, knowing perfectly well that it is an empty screen and a film is being projected. I have seen people laughing, I have seen people standing up, thrilled, and I have always wondered... It seems that man has left everything to the professionals and he has become just a watcher.

Obviously the professional can do the thing better than you can. But remember, things are not going to stop here. In one existentialist novel, the writer has a very definite clarity about the future: that soon only servants will be making love. Why should you bother? – you can pay the servant. But why should your wife bother? She can also pay another servant.

I am reminded of a very rich man who was bothering and torturing his psychoanalyst...

In the West, the psychoanalyst is the highly paid professional; hundreds of dollars per hour. Very few people can afford to be mad. But this man used to talk for two, three hours. The patient on the couch talks and the psychoanalyst listens, but there is a limit. The man was driving the psychoanalyst mad because it was the same story every day. And he could not stop him because he was paying so much; he was his best client.

Finally he thought of a plan and said to the man, "Because of you, I cannot see my other patients. A simple device will be very helpful. I will leave my tape recorder. You talk to my tape recorder as long as you want. And in the night I will listen to whatever you have said to the tape recorder more silently, more attentively than I can in the office because I am worried about other patients who are waiting." The rich man immediately agreed.

The psychoanalyst was not thinking that he would agree so easily. The next day when the psychoanalyst was entering the office, the rich man was coming out. He said, "What is the matter? Where are you going? What about your session today?"

The rich man said, "The session is over because I have also worked out a plan. I talk to my tape recorder in the dark night, in the silence, without any disturbance of you and your presence. Now my tape recorder is on the couch talking to your tape recorder. Why should I waste my time?"

People have become so outward that they cannot sit silently even for a single moment; that is the most difficult thing in the world. People are fidgeting. What is the fear? – the fear is that you may encounter your emptiness and once you encounter your emptiness, your life will lose all interest, all juice, meaningfulness, significance. Everyone is running from himself. And this running from themselves people call "having a good time."

Western man's life can be divided in two parts – and I have moved around the earth and watched all kinds of idiots. These are the two parts. First is having a good time and second is having a hangover. By the time the hangover is over, the time comes for having a good time. They go on between these two in a vicious circle, wasting their lives and reaching nowhere. Reaching the grave cannot be called reaching somewhere. It simply means that now the wheel is so tired and so bored with having a good time and suffering hangovers that it wants to rest inside a grave. People rest only in their graves. Outside of the grave, there is no time to rest.

In the East, we chose the opposite gestalt. We found treasures, mysteries, secrets, but the difficulty with the inner is that you cannot materialize it. You cannot prove it in a court; you cannot even have a witness. Except you, you cannot allow anyone else into your inner world. Naturally, in the East slowly, slowly individuals became isolated. These isolated individuals were constantly harassed by the crowd, by the marketplace. They wanted their inner silence, their inner serenity, their calmness, undisturbed. The conclusion was to renounce the world, move to the Himalayas or deep into the forest where you can be absolutely yourself.

But both the alternatives are choosing half the man. And the moment you choose half the man, you are going to fall into some kind of misery. The miseries may be different, but misery is absolutely guaranteed. The East is miserable because of its Gautam Buddhas, Mahaviras, Bodhidharmas, Kabirs. It is in misery because of its greatest inner explorers. And the West is in misery because of its Galileos, Copernicuses, Columbuses, Albert Einsteins, Bertrand Russells. These are the great people of the West and the East, and all these great people have chosen man in his half. To choose man in his half has been the root cause of human misery up to now.

I teach you the whole man. The inner is real – as real as the outer. And the outer is as significant as the spiritual. You have to attain a certain balance; a balance in which neither the inner predominates nor the outer, but both are equally complementary to each other. This has not happened up to now. But unless this happens, there is no possibility for any humanity to exist in the world.

The West is dying of its own success. The East has already died of its success. It is a very strange story that people have died because of their victories – choosing half is dangerous. But choosing the whole needs courage, insight and overwhelming understanding. And a mobility: just as you come out of your home and go back inside the home, your coming out of your being and going into your being should be as simple as that.

Whenever you are needed in the market, you should be in the market with your totality. The market cannot destroy your soul. And anyone who has preached to the world to renounce it was against humanity. Neither does going inward, being in a meditative silence, take away anything from the outside world. You don't have to condemn it, and you don't have to declare it illusory. It should have been so simple to see, that I am amazed why thousands of years have passed, and still it is not a recognized fact around the whole world.

I am reminded of a great Indian mystic, Adi Shankara…

He is one of the proponents of the philosophy that the world is absolutely illusory. One morning he is coming out of the Ganges, after taking his early bath before going into prayer. The sun has not risen yet. It is dark. He is coming up the stone steps in Varanasi and a man touches him. It would not have been much of a trouble, but the man simply said, "Forgive me. I am not supposed even to come close to you. I am a sudra, an untouchable. Even my shadow is evil."

Shankara was very angry. He said, "I will have to take another bath to purify myself." But he was not aware who the man was.

The man said, "Before you take another bath, you will have to answer a few questions. One question is: If the outside is unreal, do you believe me to be a reality? I am certainly outside you. And if the outside is unreal, then what is the reality of the pure River Ganges of the Hindus? It is also outside. And what do you think about your own skin? Is it inside or outside? Unless you explain it to me, I am going to remain here. You can take as many baths as you want; I will touch you again and again."

Hindus don't like to talk about the incident. And Shankara does not seem to be an honest man because after this incident he continued to preach that the outside is illusory. Every day you need outside food and every day you need outside water, and still the outside is illusory? It is such pure nonsense that it is time to condemn all these people who have renounced the world and who have been teaching the world that the outside is nothing but a dream.

I cannot believe it – if the outside is unreal, whom are you teaching? If the outside world is unreal then what are you renouncing, where are you going? – to the Himalayas? The Himalayas are as much outside as M.G. Market!

And the same kind of stupidity has been dominating the Western mind. A scientist is perfectly rational when he is working in his lab on objects, but the moment you ask him about himself, he starts saying that there is no one inside. He cannot see what an irrational statement he is making. If there is no one inside, who is working in the lab? If there is no one inside, who is watching, calculating, coming to conclusions? The science is true and the scientist himself is saying that he is not true.

These two idiotic ideologies have destroyed the whole of humanity – its peace, its love, its grandeur, its dignity. It has to be restored. I deny Adi Shankara and I also deny Karl Marx in the same breath. I am against the atheist and I am against the theist because both are trying to divide reality, which is indivisible. The outer cannot exist without the inner. Neither can the inner exist without the outer. They are both two sides of the same coin.

But believe it or not, there is not a single statement in the whole history of man declaring that man is one; that the outer and the inner are not contradictory but complementary, that they cannot exist in separation, that they are supported by each other and they should be used together. Only then can man rise to his real heights and blossom into his ultimate flowering.

You are asking, "...associated with the American idea of having a good time which is synonymous with noise, loud music, watching movies, smoking, sex, and release of energy as such." This is half the people who have chosen to be extroverts and have forgotten their own inner center. But they are getting fed up with it. Now the greatest philosophers in the West like Søren Kierkegaard, Martin Heidegger, Karl Jaspers, Marcel, Jean Paul Sartre, are all in absolute agreement that life is meaningless, that it is nothing but boredom. And the only conclusion out of all these philosophies is a very simple one: except suicide, there is no way. But there are wonders and wonders – of all these great philosophers I have named, none have committed suicide.

It reminds me of a great Greek philosopher, Zeno, who was teaching the same thing two thousand years ago. He lived a long life, he died when he was ninety. He was such a convincing, impressive personality that thousands of people committed suicide because they could not prove what the meaning of life is. If there is no meaning, then you are simply a coward and you go on dragging yourself – gather courage and commit suicide! When he was dying, a man asked him, "Zeno, following you, thousands of young people have committed suicide. A question arises: Why did you not follow your own philosophy?"

But philosophers are basically very clever people. Zeno said, "I had to suffer life just to teach people the truth." He has been a martyr because he lived for ninety years! You should worship him because he lived so you could commit suicide.

All these five great philosophers of the West – and these are the topmost – are not interested in committing suicide, they are only interested in writing about boredom, meaninglessness, anguish, angst. They all come to the conclusion that suicide seems to be the only way out, but no one gets out of the way.

The West has reached, by its own success, the ultimate failure. And this failure of nerve is very dangerous because they are in control of enormous destructive power – nuclear weapons. They can destroy the whole planet not only once, but as many times as you want. Ordinarily every human being dies only once, except Jesus Christ. But the politicians and the scientists of the West have been making arrangements for everyone to die seven times.

I don't think anyone is going to have seven resurrections. One time will do – perhaps once in a while, somewhere, some Jesus Christ… But even Jesus Christ cannot survive seven times. There are people who suspect – and I am one of them – whether he even survived one time. I have been to his grave. His grave is in India, at Srinagar in a small village, Pahalgam. In the Kashmiri language *pahalgam* means the village of the shepherd. Jesus used to call himself the shepherd. He escaped; it was not resurrection. He had never died in the first place.

The Jewish cross is a very crude instrument for killing a person. For a healthy young man like Jesus – he was only thirty-three – it would have taken at least forty-eight hours of being on the cross before he would have died. It is because crucifixion on the Jewish cross kills you very slowly, it does not kill you immediately.

There was a conspiracy between the disciples of Jesus and Pontius Pilate, who was not a Jew. The land of Jesus, Judea, was under the Roman Empire; it was an enslaved country. Pontius Pilate was the governor, the Roman governor. He had no interest in killing Jesus. In fact, he could not conceive why the Jews were so insistent to kill this innocent young man who had not committed any crime at all. Pontius Pilate was a politician; he could not arouse the whole of Judea against the Roman Empire just because of a young man. But he managed an agreement with the disciples that Jesus would be crucified on Friday – as late as possible, because as the sun sets on Friday, Jews stop every kind of work. And certainly Jesus would have to be taken down from the cross before sunset. He was only on the cross for six hours, and then he was put in a cave which was guarded by Roman soldiers.

The conspiracy worked perfectly well. During the night, Jesus was removed. And as he recovered, he was taken out of Judea because the Jews would have crucified him again. The only place where he could find people who would understand his language, people who belonged to his race, was Kashmir. Kashmir is basically Jewish, and you will be surprised to know that when Moses took the Jews out of Egypt, one of the tribes of the Jews got lost in the desert. It took forty years for Moses to find the promised land; which is nothing but a desert land, and the Jews have never been able to forgive Moses. He gave them Israel, which is not in any way like the promise he made to them. They were torturing him continuously, "Where have you brought us?" In forty years of wandering in the desert, almost ninety percent of the original people had died – the third generation was now with Moses. And Moses lost all contact with his own people because these new people had no idea what Moses had done. They had only complaints against him.

Somehow he managed to convince them saying, "This is the promised land. Remain here and I will go back to find the tribe that has been lost in the desert." That tribe had reached Kashmir – and Kashmir seems to be far closer to the promised land Moses was talking about because there is no place on the earth which is more beautiful than Kashmir. Kashmir has both graves of Moses and Jesus because Moses came in search of the tribe and found it in Kashmir. And after Judea, there was only one place – Kashmir – where Jesus could have been welcome.

He remained there – a long life, one hundred and twelve years. And you can see the Kashmiris: you can see Pandit Jawaharlal Nehru, Indira Gandhi. Just look at their noses and you will be convinced that they are Jews. Mohammedans converted the Jews, but because they also accepted Moses and Jesus as prophets, they left those two graves without destroying them. They also left a family of caretakers, which is still Jewish. Those are the only two graves in the whole of India on which there is an inscription in Hebrew. The family that has been taking care of those two graves is the only family Mohammedans have left unconverted. They are still Jews, for so long a time. And the inscription on the graves is so clear. It says "Joshua" which is the name of Jesus in Hebrew.

Jesus never knew that he would be known to the world as Jesus. His parents, his friends, his followers knew him as Joshua. The inscription says, "Joshua, the Messiah, lived in this place with his followers, a long life of one hundred and twelve years." And because of him, the village is still called Pahalgam.

But the politicians are ready to destroy the whole planet seven times. This is the success of the Western approach of taking the outside man as the whole reality. And nothing better has happened in the East. Almost fifty percent of the people in the East are hungry, starved, undernourished. By the end of this century at least five hundred million people will die, only in *this* land; I am not counting people who are going to die in China, Taiwan, Korea, Japan. Just in this country five hundred million people are going to die within ten years. The earth cannot support this huge humanity which goes on growing, unless we also start being scientific, being technological.

Even now, science is capable to support a humanity seven times bigger than the present one. Right now, there are five billion people in the world. Science has the capacity now for seven times more people to live comfortably – but science cannot do it on its own. It needs scientific minds, it needs people who are technologically expert.

My own understanding about the East is that even if people come from the West, well-educated in science and technology, their old stupidities continue inside their being. I have seen DSc's worshipping before a monkey god, Hanuman. I cannot believe my eyes! Sometimes I think it would have been better to be blind. These people who are worshipping monkey gods, elephant gods – these people don't have scientific minds. They may have had a scientific education, which is a totally different thing.

To know about science is one thing and to be creative about science is another thing. To know about meditation is one thing and to meditate is totally different. The West needs a more meditative mind and the East needs a more scientific mind. Then we will be able to create a humanity which can live without poverty, without hunger – a healthier, longer life, which you cannot even think of.

The scientific calculation is that the present body we have is capable of living at least three hundred years – just the right food, right medical care, right ecological environment and these people can live for three hundred years. I cannot conceive what treasures will be revealed if a Gautam Buddha can live three hundred years, if

Albert Einstein can live three hundred years, if Bertrand Russell can live three hundred years.

Up to now the way we have lived is such a sheer wastage. People who are trained, educated, cultured become old and die at the age of seventy. New visitors, absolutely uneducated, barbarous, go on coming from the wombs. This is not a very scientific way of arranging the world. You have to force people to retire, and these are the people who know. And you have to employ people who know nothing.

Men's lives should be made longer and birth control should be stricter. A child should be born only when we are ready to allow a Bertrand Russell to leave the world – only a replacement, and unless we can find a better replacement we are not going to allow Bertrand Russell to leave the world. And there is every possibility to find a replacement because we can read the whole program in the genes: all the possibilities that a person is going to pass through. Whether he is going to be a painter of the quality of Picasso or he is going to be a poet of the genius of Rabindranath Tagore; how long he is going to live, whether he will be healthy or sick. Not only can we read the future program of the genes, we can change the program also. From the very beginning of his life, the sick person can be made to live a healthier life and the idiots can be avoided, the retarded can be avoided.

Existence gives everything with such abundance that if you don't choose, things are going to be a chaos. Every single human being… A male, if he has not been corrupted by religions, will have an opportunity to give birth to a child at least four thousand times. And each time he releases one million sperm. That means each human male can create a whole India! Such abundance simply means you have to be very choosy. Naturally, in this crowd you cannot find many Rabindranaths. Rabindranath himself was the thirteenth child of his parents; before him, his parents had given birth to twelve children not of any value. They could have been avoided. Rabindranath could have been their first child. And who knows how many other Rabindranaths are not making their way into the world? We need a very scientific approach about the outside and a very meditative approach about the inside.

You are saying, "...while silence and serenity are automatically associated with boredom and excessive accumulation of energy which results in tension and anxiety." If things remain the same then this is a truth. If you don't exert your energy... With your food, your continuous breathing, your drinking water, you are generating energy. It has to be used; otherwise it is going to become a tension, and finally it is going to become anxiety. But if my idea is understood... I am saying you are half outside, half inside.

Use your energy in the outside world in creative activities, not in football. There is so much to create, so much to discover, such a vast universe is standing there as a challenge to explore. Use your energies to make the world more beautiful, more poetic, more healthy.

When you feel that you are exhausted, tired, move withinward. Rest. And your rest will become your meditation because meditation does not need any exertion of energy. On the contrary, it conserves, it preserves; it makes you a pool of great energy. When you feel that your serenity, your silence, your joy inside wants to dance outside, then both are yours – then sing, dance, create. If your creativity comes from your silences of heart, it will have a different quality, a different flavor. It is only a question of a little intelligence and balance. Inside is the source of your energies; outside is the world, to let that energy create. Be a creator. But you cannot be a creator unless you are a meditator.

My sannyas has a new definition; it is not the old definition. In the old definition, sannyas meant renouncing the world. My sannyas means rejoicing in the world. But before you can rejoice, you should accumulate so much energy that you start overflowing with love, sensitivity, creativity, poetry, song, dance.

And certainly these things will have a very compassionate quality. They will not be violent. I cannot conceive of a meditator playing football. I cannot conceive a Gautam Buddha having a boxing match. But a Gautam Buddha can create a beautiful garden of roses. A Gautam Buddha can paint, and his paintings will be far superior to the paintings of Picasso because Picasso is almost insane. If you look at the paintings of Picasso, you will feel a kind of sickness that needs to be thrown out. Just keep a painting of Picasso in your bedroom and you will have nightmares because those paintings have come from the nightmares of Picasso – air-conditioned nightmares.

There have been meditators who have created. You can see the Taj Mahal; it has been created by the Sufi mystics. Just watching it in the full-moon night, you can suddenly fall into a deep silence which you have never touched within yourself. If you can sit silently by the side of Taj Mahal in the deep night, the beauty starts changing something within you. The Taj Mahal does not remain just there on the outside, it starts becoming a part of your own being.

I lived in Jabalpur for twenty years. I had a professor, and I loved him very much. He was an old man; he had taught me in my post-graduation classes and I had asked him many times to come to Jabalpur. Jabalpur has something which is unique and is to be found nowhere on this earth.

The old professor was very stubborn in the sense that he had been around the world, he had seen everything; he had been a professor in many countries. He could just not believe that there was something which he would be surprised to know. But I am also very stubborn. I made that old fellow agree, "Remember, I am going to take you to my place. You think you are stubborn? I am going to prove to you that although you are stubborn, you are number two."

And one day while I was driving him to his home, rather than going to his home… He started shouting, "Where are you going?"

I said, "I am going to the place I have been telling you about for almost two years."

He said, "This is strange. It is my car. Stop!"

I said, "No one can stop this car. And sit silently; otherwise I will take the car with speed!"

He was very afraid of going full speed, and when he saw that the car was going a hundred miles per hour, he closed his eyes and remained silent – because the car could go to one hundred and forty miles!

I took him to the famous marble rocks in Jabalpur. They are thirteen miles from Jabalpur, and even when you have reached the point, you don't know that just within two minutes you are entering another world. A beautiful river, Narmada, flows for two miles continuously between two mountains of white marble. In the full-moon night, if anything defeats Taj Mahal it is the marble rocks of Jabalpur. For two miles continuously, high rocks of white marble are reflected in the river. Absolute silence prevails, not even a bird. I took him in a small boat without an engine because that engine creates a disturbance. As he entered, he looked at me, he could not believe...

He said, "My God! If I had died without knowing this place, I would have lived without meaning. But please take me close to the rocks – I want to touch them, to feel that they really exist because it is so dreamlike."

I had to take the boat close to the rocks. He touched the rocks, he felt the rocks and said, "Now I am convinced that you have not created some delusion, that you have not given me some drug. I am perfectly in my senses." And he pinched himself to see whether he was in his consciousness or not.

There are temples in China, in Japan, in India, created by meditators. Just sitting there and you will find that what has been so difficult for you, to stop your thinking, stops itself. The whole atmosphere of the temple, the fragrance, the incense, the statues are all creating a certain space within you. Once humanity learns both things together – meditativeness and a scientific approach about the world – we will have entered a new phase, a totally new phase discontinuous with the ugly, unhealthy, sick and insane past.

I don't want to leave you in this silence...

Mendel Kravitz is a fitness freak; he lifts weights and jogs five miles a day. One day, he is admiring his body in the mirror. He notices that he is really suntanned all over, except on his prick, so he decides to do something about it. He goes to the beach, undresses, and buries himself in the sand, except for his prick which he leaves sticking out.

Two little old ladies are strolling along the beach, and one looks down and says, "There really is no justice in this world!"

"What do you mean?" her friend asks.

The first old lady says, "Look at that! When I was ten years old, I was afraid of it. When I was twenty years old, I was curious about it. When I was thirty, I enjoyed it. When I was forty, I asked for it. When I was fifty, I paid for it. When I was sixty, I prayed for it. When I was seventy, I forgot all about it.

"And now that I'm eighty, the damn thing is growing all over, wild!"

14

The Philosophy of Yes

Osho,
As you greet us, and again as you leave, you are pouring your energy on us. How come my body doesn't gracefully bow down to you? I know my heart does. Am I a rock among the waves?

Deva Ashu, I myself have been watching. There is some stoniness on your face, and you stand out because everyone is bowing down and you remain stiff. Now you yourself have asked the question.

The first thing: it is very difficult to know your heart, and it is very easy to say anything about your heart. It is something invisible, nonobjective. But your face, your eyes, your body, give indications of your heart. So please, don't be deluded that your heart is full of grace and the body seems like a rock in the river. The heart is part of your body. If the heart is graceful, the body is a very obedient servant. It simply follows the heart. But you have not mentioned anything about your face, naturally, because you cannot see it. I have seen your face.

You have been deeply connected with me. Deva Ashu has been my personal dental nurse. That's where the problem is – you must have come with unconscious expectations that you would be received in the same way as you have been received for many years.

But life stops for no one; now someone else is functioning in your place, and that must be the basic wound in your being.

I know you love me, but your love is not unconditional. It is not just a pure gift. Unconsciously it wants to be replied to, recognized – you have been important in the sense that Devageet, my dental surgeon, was working and you were participating. You are not finding that closeness any longer; you are feeling as if you are no longer significant or important. This is how the mind creates stupid expectations and then suffers from them.

Looking at you, I have remembered all the days you have been here. You are showing the face of a martyr. And there must be some jealousy too because now another nurse has replaced you. If your love is unconditional then your concern is not who is helping me to remain in the body – your concern should be that it is more than enough that I *am* in the body.

It may look hard to you, but there was no other way. You will be surprised to know that when Nityamo replaced you, because you were not here, the first thing I said to Nityamo was, "For years I have been accustomed to Ashu, and when I am in the dentist's chair I may use the name "Ashu" for you. Don't feel offended because my dentist chair is not just a dental affair..." With me everything is a little strange. From the dental chair, I have created three books! It must be absolutely unprecedented because people are so afraid of the dental chair and the dentist. I have enjoyed it so much – but it created difficulties for poor Devageet because you cannot work on the teeth while I am talking. What he could have done in ten minutes would take two hours!

You are missing that privacy, that intimacy, when I was talking to only two people, Devageet and you. And I have my own games to play. I had put you against Devageet – you are his dental nurse. I can experience whatever is happening, even under a high dose of laughing gas, and I used to remind Ashu again and again, "Don't listen to Devageet. As far as this dental room is concerned, I am still your master." Even with closed eyes... Because they tried that too. They blindfolded me so I could not see what was going on, but I could see that the gas was not at the maximum. And I was beating Ashu continuously: "You are listening to Devageet!" Devageet stopped talking. He managed to give messages by signal.

It was a beautiful time, and many things I talked about in the dental chair, I would have never bothered to talk about. I was creating difficulty for them. Because how can you work inside the mouth when I am speaking? But my sensitivity is such that just a lower degree of gas and I would hit Ashu immediately. She was in great difficulty because she has to listen to the doctor, but as far as I am concerned the doctor and the nurse are both my disciples. I have beaten Devageet so much that sometimes I feel sad about the poor fellow. He has been doing his best, but he was doing it according to his medical understanding. With me, things cannot be in any way ordinary.

Ashu has been here – as far as I am concerned there is no change. My love is as available to you, but because you are no longer in that intimacy, where you were even put in charge of the doctor to take care that he did not interfere in whatever I wanted to do… It is against medical practice; the doctor should not listen to the patient. But here the situation is totally different – I am the doctor and you are the patient, it does not matter!

So just a little understanding, Ashu, and your stoniness will melt. I know you have a graceful heart, but because of your mind you are feeling almost a foreigner here. Drop all this nonsense. You are the same to me.

Even if people have betrayed me, my love for them remains the same because I had not given my love with any condition. People have lied about me, have written books with complete fictions, but my love for them still remains the same. All that I know is that they are unconscious people, and they don't know what they are doing.

You have to be a little conscious. It is good that you asked the question. There is something more you have made part of your question which needs a totally different dimension of answer. You are saying, "As you greet us and again as you leave, you are pouring your energy on us. How come my body does not gracefully bow down to you? I know my heart does. Am I a rock among the waves?" As for your own psychology, I have said everything that you needed. Relax – you will remain in my heart just as any sannyasin, with the same love, with the same compassion because I don't ask anything from you. I have such an abundance flowing that I don't know what to do with it. I have to share.

But the second part of the question takes a totally different dimension. In a flowing river, a few rocks have their own beauty. A river without rocks loses sound. A river with rocks is a singing and dancing river. If your heart feels graceful, flowing, don't be worried about a certain stony feeling in your body. That too has its own place. Rather than fighting with it, rejoice in it. You are not an ordinary river but a river that sings, a river that dances. Without rocks, rivers are very poor.

I loved the place where I stayed in Kulu Manali for the simple reason that the river passing by was so full of rocks. Day in, day out, there was music, there was dance. But as you know about me, even in my own country I am a foreigner. The government to which Kulu Manali belongs started freaking out. They had made a law that a man who is not born in their state cannot purchase any land, just to prevent me. But I needed a vast land for my commune, and it is as retarded a part of the country as you can conceive – uneducated, poor, completely in the grip of the politicians.

You will be surprised that the day I left Kulu Manali, the arrangement was that they were going to arrest me on a very fictitious, absurd account. To them it may have looked like very solid ground. As I left Kulu Manali, just within one hour the arrest warrant reached the place I had been living in. The arrest warrant was hilarious – and makes me feel about our experts that they are donkeys loaded with knowledge.

The reason for the arrest was that I had paid four hundred thousand dollars in fines in America, so I have to pay tax and I have to explain from where I got the money. I have never paid any fine anywhere in the world. I don't know even the names of the people who paid the fine. Even my jailer was surprised because they were not expecting it, knowing perfectly well that I don't have a single cent to pay. And imposing four hundred thousand dollars... It is nearabout sixty lakh rupees. From where am I going to pay it?

But I am not a man who worries about anything. Not for a single moment did the idea even arise in me that this could be a strategy: to keep me in jail until the fine was paid. And I never think of tomorrow. Today is too beautiful and too fulfilling – who cares about tomorrows which never come?

As I was fined... It is a strange thing but it has to be stated publicly to the whole world. In America I had thirty-four charges against me, all fictitious, and they agreed with my attorneys that if two of the crimes were accepted, I would be freed. My problem is, what about the other thirty-two crimes that I have committed? The government of America is deceiving their own nation. If I have really committed those thirty-two crimes, then there is no other way; I should be punished. But for the first time I realized that in America, justice is part of business. Accept two crimes and the other thirty-two crimes disappear – and *any* two crimes; they were not even insistent about what crimes. The two crimes were so stupid that no one can think that a person should be fined even if he has committed them.

Four hundred thousand dollars... And to ask a man, knowing perfectly well that he has not touched money for almost thirty years – I had been in America for five years, and I don't know what a dollar bill looks like. But I have thousands of people who managed it immediately, within ten minutes. Even Judge Leavy was surprised that they paid the fine. If you look into the crimes, they are not even worth paying two rupees for.

One crime was that I had inside me an intention to become a resident of America. I never thought that people had yet found any way to know the intentions, the dreams, the imaginations of people's minds – and when I am saying that I don't have any intention to live in this most ugly and obscene society.

Another crime was that I have arranged thousands of marriages. I was silent for three and a half years, not speaking, not meeting any sannyasins except my secretary, just to be informed how the commune was going. I have not told anyone to get married because fundamentally I am against marriage. And if I can manage one thousand, or thousands of marriages, why can I not manage a marriage for myself? If that is the way to get residence, I could have married as many American women as they want! But I am absolutely against marriage, and the man who was making all these charges said such a hilarious thing – that I have arranged thousands of marriages which are fake, but certainly I have arranged at least *one* marriage.

Now, the man is only certain about one marriage. On what logical grounds does he stretch it to thousands of marriages? He himself admits that he is certain only about one marriage. Strangely enough, all the other marriages were not recognized – only that marriage was recognized, and given a green card for employment and residence. This is strange. This is bribery – they have purchased those two people, and neither of them has ever talked to me. And as far as marriage is concerned, not even the word had been uttered by those two people or by me. They had no way to meet me.

On these two flimsy grounds, four hundred thousand dollars as a punishment! I don't know who paid those four hundred thousand dollars because hundreds of sannyasins were there in the court. The court was almost *my* court. Strangely enough when I entered the court people stood up, and when the judge entered it was announced, "Stand up; the judge is coming in." Sometimes I wonder, who is the judge?

And now the government of the state of Kulu Manali wants to arrest me. I don't even know the names of those who paid the fine. I have nothing to do with it, I have never paid a single rupee to anyone. In the first place I don't have it – and a very logical thing has to be understood: I always left at the right time. That's what I say: existence manages things if you leave it to existence.

I left Rajneeshpuram in America. The next day they were going to bring four helicopters – their helicopters were coming every day to find my house, and from the helicopters they were going to drop paratroopers to arrest me. Just a few hours before they were to arrive, I left Rajneeshpuram to go to a beautiful mountain resort that belonged to my sannyasins. They had been insisting for two years. And it is strange that on that day I decided that okay, two years is enough. They had prepared the place; they just wanted me to rest there. And the government was in shock – their whole program had failed.

I left Kulu Manali just one hour before – I was still at the airport when they reached the hut where I had been living near the river. And now again the Indian government is continuously sending letters saying that I have to pay taxes. It is such a stupid and illogical step – in logic they call it infinite regression. If I pay the tax, then I have to pay tax on the money that I am paying as tax. Naturally… Where is it going to end? Whenever I pay tax, I owned that money – on that money I have to pay the tax again. It will go on infinitely. Either you stop at the first step or there is no way to stop. And they know perfectly well that I don't have any money, I don't have any possessions. Everything that the people who love me allow me to use belongs to them.

But governments are always stupid. In fact, if you are not stupid you are not qualified to be in the government. Can't they see the point? If someone else has paid the fine, and I don't even know their names, how can I be asked to pay tax? But the same foolishness prevails over the whole world in all the bureaucracies. It seems the moment they become bureaucrats their minds stop functioning.

I have heard…

A politician was going through mind surgery. But when the doctors opened his mind, it was so full of crap that it needed a dry cleaning, so they took out the whole brain and brought it to the other room. While they were cleaning his mind, a man came rushing in and said to the politician, "What are you doing here lying in the hospital? You have been chosen as president!" And the politician disappeared.

When the doctors had finished cleaning they could not find the man. They came to know from the newspapers that he had become the president, so they approached him saying, "You have left your brain with us."

The president said, "To be a president, the brain is no longer needed. You can keep it. When I am defeated or when I am no longer in power, perhaps I may need it."

There is a law, which is a very significant law, that all our bureaucracies and governments function in such a way that the most inefficient, inadequate person finally reaches the top. Hearing it for the first time it seems, how can it be? But if you see the whole process... A clerk is doing perfectly well, and because he is doing perfectly well as a clerk, he becomes the head clerk. He knows nothing about being the head clerk, but if he still has some sense left he will function better than other head clerks. He will become the superintendent.

You are moving people from places where they are efficient because of their efficiency, but you don't understand a simple thing, that to be efficient as a clerk does not mean that you will be efficient as a corporation commissioner. So all the heads of the bureaucracy are absolutely inefficient. They had been efficient in some area, and that has taken them to higher posts. The higher they go, the less efficient – until they reach to the ultimate inefficiency. Then they become the presidents, the vice-presidents, prime ministers. The whole world is being dominated by all kinds of idiots.

Deva Ashu, you should not feel at all tense; my love is not love that disappears. It goes on growing – whether you are close to me or far away, it does not matter. And remember that your body is a very significant signal. To know about the heart is a difficult job.

Your body indicates that your heart is no longer graceful, no longer loving. Listen to the body first because that is the most visible sign. Then move inward. The body has to be graceful, the body has to be beautiful, the body has to be deeply alive, and only then can you find the grace of the heart and ultimately, the grace of your being.

But start from the door and then enter the temple. Don't be disturbed because you have recognized that the body is not so graceful, is not so receptive – it is a great insight. Look around at all the causes that have made it so, and immediately the ungracefulness will disappear.

And whenever you can manage here, you can be my dental nurse because Nityamo was very graceful when I said to her, "If I sometimes call you Ashu, don't feel offended." She said to me, "Ashu is my friend, and if you call me Ashu it is perfectly good."

Nityamo is not your competitor. Here, no one is a competitor. Only once in a while some idiot enters.

A German has written a letter to me. Only a German can do it. He says, "You have been pouring so much juice over Deva Amrito, why don't you declare him your ambassador?" But he is not aware that there are three Amritos here. And as far as his suggestion is concerned, although it is coming out of jealousy, the suggestion is perfectly right. Even before receiving his letter I had told Deva Amrito that he is going to be my ambassador in Holland.

Once in a while someone brings the outside world into this oasis of different consciousnesses. Certainly he is not aware that he has become jealous, but I have my own reasons why I have answered Amrito's questions. He is writing a book. I don't have time to answer all his questions because he wants it to be his whole pilgrimage, the seeking and the search, and he wants to end it by finding me. He has already written eight books on me and he thinks this book is going to be very comprehensive – answering everything, destroying all lies that have been spread by governments, by politicians, by journalists, by all kinds of criminal people who are around.

It was because of this reason that I took his questions and answered them, and his questions were significant for you too. But the German mind becomes tense. Don't be worried. Meditate so that you are no longer a German. The day I see that you are no longer a German, I will also make you the ambassador for Germany.

In fact, every sannyasin is my ambassador. To make a certain man responsible is not making him a dictator for you. It is making him a help, a contact center because the fight is going to be all over the world. Twenty-five countries have prevented me from entering. Now I have to find my own ways to enter. And in each country I am going to have my embassy. For the first time, a single individual is going to have embassies around the world. Those embassies will be your meeting places because the fight is going to become more and more intense. And because I cannot enter every country, sannyasins have to fight their own governments and their stupidity.

The fight is so total that I disagree with the past on every point. It is not a question of choice – it is a question of breaking away from the past completely and creating a new man. I can see on the horizon the new man arising in you. And with this new man a new humanity, a new vision, and a new way of life will be born.

I am not interested in creating a religion, which is a very simple affair. I am interested to create as many religious people as possible – an atmosphere of religiousness, with no organized church but every individual having his own individuality as his religion. Man has never been given that freedom. I want every individual to have his own religion – in other words his own lifestyle, his own philosophy, and to live according to his own deepening insight.

You have to be alert of a tremendous responsibility that I am handing over to you. You have to be the harbingers, you have to be the dawn of a new, totally new humanity, completely discontinuous with the past. The past has played tricks with you to keep you encaged. Every religion condemns jealousy and every religion creates jealousy. I am surprised that for thousands of years no one has seen the connection. If you are competitive, you cannot drop jealousy. Jealousy is the energy in you – ugly, stinking, but it keeps you competitive. And every religion teaches you to be competitive, to be more "good," to be a greater saint, to be a more moral person. But then when you come across a person who is a bigger saint than you, jealousy will be the by-product. And they all condemn jealousy.

All the religions have condemned stealing, but no religion has condemned people accumulating riches. These are two sides of the same thing. If people go on accumulating riches, they are forcing people to be poor, to such an extent that the poor has only one choice if he wants to survive: he has to become a thief. All the religions are against sex, but they all preach celibacy. And celibacy makes sex unnatural, perverted.

The responsibility that I am giving you is to see clearly how the past has destroyed man – beautiful names hiding ugly realities. And unless you drop those beautiful names, you cannot discover those ugly realities. They live together, they are part of one another.

Each sannyasin has to be a revolt in himself – transforming his own being, cleaning his own mind, and spreading the message of freedom. Not of Christianity, not of Hinduism, but simply the dignity of the individual and his total freedom. Unless we can create this planet consisting of free individuals, we cannot survive any longer. The old, the past, has come to its very end. It can only manage a global suicide. I am fighting against the global suicide of a beautiful planet which has evolved more than any other planet in the world, which has come to some consciousness that can be increased very easily.

My teaching is very simple: the whole man, inside a meditator and outside a creator. But if you get into small jealousies that you have been carrying from your heritage… Rather than making it a problem simply drop it; it has not helped you, it has only made you more miserable.

Paddy is on his deathbed, groaning, when his wife Maureen walks into the room and asks if he has any last requests.

"Yes dear," says Paddy, "there is one thing I really would like before I go off to that great shamrock patch in the sky." And then he whispers, "A piece of that wonderful chocolate cake of yours."

"Ah, Patrick," says Maureen, "have a potato instead. I am saving the cake for the party after the funeral."

Five of the most important men in a woman's life are:

The doctor: he says, "Take off your clothes."

The dentist: he says, "Open wide."

The hairdresser: he says, "Do you want it teased or blown?"

The interior decorator: he says, "You will like it once it is in."

And, the milkman: he says, "Do you want it in front or in the back?"

Paddy and Sean are watching Molly being chatted up in the pub. When she leaves with the man, Sean turns to Paddy and says, "I can't understand it. Molly is one of the ugliest girls around, and yet all the men seem to find her attractive."

"It's because of her speech impediment," says Paddy, sagely.

"Her speech impediment?" asks Sean astonished.

"Yes," says Paddy, "she can't say 'no.'"

Ashu, you have to learn to say yes. Yes to the rocks, yes to the flowing river, yes to your totality as you are. And your song and your dance will return to you. In my vision there is no greater word than yes. Yes to existence without any conditions, and you will find relaxation; you will find a communion, you will find both the worlds: the inner and the outer.

You can call my approach the philosophy of yes. All other philosophies and all other religions are more interested in teaching you no. I teach you, without any conditions, to say yes to yourself in whatever situation you find. And each situation is changed miraculously the moment you are capable to say yes.

This silence is immense. But when I leave you I always like you to be in as hilarious a mood as possible. I know the trees also understand the jokes, and I have a deep compassion for them because they cannot laugh. Man is the only being on the earth who has come to understand laughter. Buffaloes don't laugh – they are very saintly. Donkeys don't laugh – they are too philosophic. Idiots don't laugh because they are afraid of being caught doing something that they don't understand.

The Englishman laughs only once, not to let anyone understand that he has not understood.

The Frenchman laughs twice – once to accompany other people out of courtesy and then, in the middle of the night when he gets it.

Germans simply don't laugh. On the contrary, they are worried, "Why are people laughing?" They inquire of others, "What was the matter?"

Jews don't laugh; on the contrary they say, "Shut up, it is an old joke and moreover you are telling it all wrong."

But I want my people to understand that because only man is capable of laughing, that means laughter is the highest point of consciousness, the highest point of understanding, the highest point of evolution. That's why I have started calling laughter "prayer time."

Waking up with a terrible hangover after the office party, Paddy turns to his wife Maureen and says, "Jesus! Would you believe, I can't remember a thing that happened last night!"

"It's just as well," replies Maureen. "You got into an argument with the boss and he fired you."

"He did?" shouts Paddy. "After all I've done for him? Well, screw the bastard!"

"I did," says Maureen. "You go back to work tomorrow."

Moishe Finkelstein is walking down the street one night in New York. Suddenly a man jumps out from the side alley and puts a gun to Moishe's head.

"Give me your money," he threatens, "or I'll blow your brains out!"

"Blow away," says Moishe. "In America you can live without brains, but you can't live without money."

15

Just to Be Is Enough

Osho,
The more I trust in meditation, the more I feel my heart opening and vastly present. At the same time I lose knowledge about who I am, why I am here and for what. I can't do anything about it except watch, cry, laugh, sing, giggle. Something is happening for which I have no name. It is just throbbing. The other night I woke up suddenly knowing, "Oh, I'm just human, a human being." It sounds funny, but it's been such a joy feeling so accepted. Would you please help me understand what is happening?

The question you have put is not coming from your mind; that's why it looks a little strange. The mind is very clever – it knows how to ask a question. It does not know any answer as such. Whenever such a thing happens to a meditator – which is bound to happen if you don't stop before reaching your inner being – that you suddenly feel a change of climate… The questioning mind is no longer there and you are standing before the answer; it certainly feels very weird that you don't have a question, so what is this answer all about? Our very training is that the question should come first and then the answer.

But existence is absolutely, fortunately, uneducated. It brings the answer first and then you have to start questioning: "What is happening? Where am I?" You see things are happening; there are tears of joy, there is a song in the heart, there is a rejoicing which cannot be named but can certainly be experienced. And you are surrounded by all these mysteries without any explanation. One thing certainly you *can* see, that the knowledge about who I am, why I am here and for what, has completely disappeared. It is happening for the first time, so you are still looking for it. But trust me – you will never come to know.

I don't know myself. Just think about these questions, firstly, "Who am I?" Do you think you can know it? The very process of knowing involves a duality between the knower and the known. And you are the knower, you can never be the known. It takes a little time to relax and accept the fact that "I am" without ever bothering about "Who am I?"

Why am I here? Why are the trees here? And why is this whole sky with the stars here? Why is anything in this universe here? And because people could not relax in this innocence, they manufactured fictitious answers: "God made the world; that's why it is here." But they forgot that sooner or later someone is going to ask, "Why is this God here?" The ultimate – and the ultimate is the immediate – is simply here for no reason at all. The day you can accept it without any kind of effort you will find a tremendous opening, of a totally new vision and perception, in which everything is accepted.

The question is really a way of not accepting things as they are. First you want to know why they are here. You may not have thought that this urge to know why is a kind of mental scratching. The more you scratch, the better it feels, but finally it starts bleeding. In the beginning it gives a sweet feeling. You can try – scratch. But don't scratch too much. That sweet feeling is leading you in a wrong direction.

The relaxed approach toward life is not to be worried about why I am here, who I am, and for what. If you can drop these "What? Why? Who?" – these three are the Christian God, the Holy Ghost and Jesus Christ. They are haunting you. They have haunted the whole of humanity's past. All your philosophies and all your theologies are born out of these three.

I am not a philosopher. Neither am I a theologian, nor am I interested in any kind of stupid mind gymnastics. I simply want you to know I am here, you are here. There is no reason why we are here and there is no purpose, and this is the beauty of existence. Now you can laugh and no one can ask why you are laughing. You can dance and no one has the right to ask why you are dancing.

I am reminded of Pablo Picasso…

He was painting a beautiful flower, sitting by the side of a rose bush, and a man was watching very intensely, knowing perfectly well that Pablo Picasso is not an ordinary man. But he could not contain his curiosity and finally he asked Picasso, "Forgive me. I should not interfere, but I am helpless. I can't understand what you are painting and why you are painting – what is the purpose of it?"

Picasso looked at him and said, "Do you think I know?"

The man was even more surprised. He said, "If you don't know, then why are you doing it?"

Picasso said, "Knowing has nothing to do with doing. Look at the rose bush – no one asks these flowers, 'Why are you here? What is the purpose?' And if you were not here, no one would have felt your absence. No one asks the trees, no one asks the clouds, and yet all the idiots are after me. Wherever I go they start asking me, 'What is it?' If the whole existence has no answer, from where can a poor Pablo Picasso find the answer?"

It looks absurd. But it looks absurd because we are looking for the meaning. The moment you drop the whole process of asking the meaning of things, everything is perfectly beautiful in its absolute absurdity.

A very rich woman asked Pablo Picasso, "I have never seen a portrait made by you and I am ready to pay any amount you ask. I want my portrait to be painted by you."

Picasso said, "I have not painted portraits because then I will have to answer so many questions for which I don't have any answer. If you promise me that you won't ask any question after the portrait is made, and simply give me the check, then I can do a portrait for you. This will be my first and last portrait."

The woman was very proud, having the only portrait in the whole world by Pablo Picasso. She was ready to pay any amount and she said, "You need not be worried about the check; I will give it to you in advance and I promise not to ask any question." Ten million dollars, and the woman gave him the check immediately.

Pablo Picasso painted her portrait for almost a whole week, every day a two or three-hour session, and the woman forgot the condition. In fact anyone would have forgotten the condition, seeing the situation of the portrait. She could not find any relationship either to her face or to her clothes or to her body, and the man was painting madly. But she must have been a very controlled and disciplined woman. She waited – at least let him finish first.

The seventh day he said, "The portrait is complete."

The woman said, "I have just a very small question."

Pablo Picasso said, "You have forgotten the condition! That's why I never made any portrait before. What is your question?"

She said, "It is not a big question. I simply want to know where my nose is? Because if I can find my nose in the portrait, I will start figuring out where my eyes are, where my mouth is. But I don't see my nose anywhere."

Picasso simply returned the check and said, "Get out of my house. I had made it clear from the very beginning. Why should I paint your nose? What purpose is the nose going to serve in the portrait? The portrait is not going to breathe."

Never again in his lifetime was he asked for a portrait. It was good, he could go on doing any kind of painting; at least if he is painting the clouds you cannot ask him stupid questions like, "Where is the nose of the cloud?"

I am in absolute agreement with Pablo Picasso. He was one of the most existential geniuses mankind has produced. He does not paint for any purpose. Painting is his dance with colors. Painting is his joy expressed with colors. You never ask when you see the sunset and the beautiful colors on the horizon – Pablo Picasso's paintings belong to the same category. They are immensely beautiful but absolutely irrational. Existence is irrational, it is not Pablo Picasso's fault.

You had entered a beautiful space, but you carried your old habits with you. You are saying, "I can't do anything about it…" There is no need to do anything about it. Doing anything will be a great disturbance; the whole beautiful space will disappear. Yes, you are allowed to watch it. You are allowed to cry, to laugh, to sing, to giggle; you are allowed to do anything that happens in the moment without ever bothering about the rationality of it, the relevance of it.

Bodhidharma entered China fourteen hundred years ago. Emperor Wu had come to receive him at the border; it was an extraordinary situation. Up to now, China has remained the biggest land in the world. The Chinese empire was the most vast empire you can conceive, and for the emperor to come to receive a beggar… Because in Buddhism the word for a sannyasin is bhikku. *Bhikku* means the beggar. It does not have the condemnatory tone which it has in English; it has, on the contrary, tremendous respectfulness. A bhikku is not one who has nothing, a bhikku is one who has renounced everything because what he has inside himself is so valuable he cannot carry unnecessary luggage with him.

The emperor had heard so many strange stories about Bodhidharma that finally he became so excited that he could not wait for him to enter the capital. On the contrary, he traveled hundreds of miles to receive him on the borders of China. But he could not believe his eyes. He remembered those stories… "They were right! I should have believed those stories rather than traveling so far, taking unnecessary risks."

Bodhidharma was coming toward him with one shoe on his head, and one shoe on his foot. Obviously curiosity arises, although the Chinese emperor and the whole Chinese culture is based on Confucian etiquette. Wu tried to avoid noticing the shoe on his head because it is not mannerly for a man like him to point to the shoe. But it was very difficult. He remembered that even Confucius in his *The Analects* has no mention of it – that if you see a man with a shoe on his head...

You should not ask because it is unmannerly; it might make the other man feel embarrassed, and that is not right for a man who is cultured. But the shoe was so prominent that everything else that he had thought about on the way – he was going to ask Bodhidharma about the lotus paradise, what is enlightenment, what is the essential teaching of Gautam Buddha – became secondary and the shoe became primary. In spite of himself he blurted, "Why are you carrying a shoe on your head?"

Bodhidharma said, "I will not enter your empire's territory. If a man is not even free to have his own shoe on his own head, this is not the place for me. This shoe was simply to check you out." He never entered the Chinese empire. He remained outside in a mountain cave.

Wu was very disturbed. Certainly he was right: the shoe was his, the head was his, and who are you to ask? This is interfering. He had to go to offer an apology, "I am absolutely sorry and I will never be able to forgive myself for interfering in your freedom."

Bodhidharma said, "I am not very far away from your boundary. Whenever you have any essential question to ask, you can come to me."

Wu said, "I have an essential question. So many Buddhist monks have arrived before you and I have opened many monasteries, many temples. I have put the whole empire's treasure into translating all the Buddhist scriptures into Chinese. Thousands of scholars are working. What will be my reward for all these virtuous acts?"

Bodhidharma said, "It is better you do not come near me because your question has not changed, it is still the shoe. Do you think you are doing anything virtuous? The very idea that you are doing something virtuous and you are inquiring about what reward you are going to get shows the mind, not of an emperor, but the mind of an ordinary businessman. You are trying to do business with existence, and existence is not available to the businessman's mind. The businessman is always trying to have more by giving less. That is simply the whole economics of business. Give less and get more – that is the profit."

Bodhidharma continued, "Existence is not for people like you. Existence is for those who can give everything without asking for anything in return; knowing perfectly well that what they are giving already belongs to existence, it is not theirs."

Do you think you have anything that has not been given to you by existence? And in returning it, you want some reward? You want some respectability, some prestige, some power? You have not understood even the *ABC* of the communion with nature. When you know that you don't exist as a separate entity, then there is no question of giving and taking. You are in existence, you have been in existence, you will be in existence. And this very understanding that "I am an essential part of this vast beautiful universe" will make you dance, will make you celebrate. There is no need to have any reason for dancing, for singing, for celebration. Just to be is enough. Out of this being all your joy, all your laughter, all your gratitude, all your prayers will flow.

I teach you this simple religiousness which has no doctrine, which has no reward for virtue and which has no punishment for sin. All those are fictions created by cunning priests and cunning founders of your religions. I want to erase the whole insane past of humanity completely, as if we are here for the first time.

You had touched a beautiful space, but because of old habits... It happens to everyone. Old habits follow you just like a shadow. You couldn't enjoy laughing because your old habit was standing by the side asking, "What are you doing? Have you gone mad? I don't see anything or any reason to laugh, and you are laughing. Why are you crying? There seems to be no reason for tears." Old habits have to be understood and renounced. All the world's religions have taught you to renounce the world. I teach you to renounce your old habits.

And then you say, "In the night I woke up suddenly knowing, 'Oh, I am just human, a human being.' It sounds funny…" It does not sound funny, it *is* funny! You and a human being! Still the old categorization that you are human beings, others are animals, and there are others which are trees. Why make these categories? Can't you simply experience *being*, in its purity, without putting a label on it?

I am making it emphatically clear to you because one label will follow another label. Labels have that habit. First you will say "human being" and then you will say, "A human being? I am an American, I am not a Black African. And I am a Catholic Christian, I am not a Hindu. And particularly, I am a woman, I am not a man." And there is no end to this long process. Simply accept that you are. This pure isness without any labels is the inner unfolding of your potential. There is nothing more you can aspire to. It is all in all. And it is so much that it is difficult to contain it; one starts sharing the joy.

One day a drunk is standing at the bar, when he turns to the man on his right and says, "Did you pour beer in my trouser pocket?"

The man says, "I certainly did not."

Then the drunk turns to the man on his left, and says, "Did you pour beer in my trouser pocket?"

The man says, "I most certainly did not pour beer in your trouser pocket."

"Just as I thought," says the drunk, "an inside job."

You are asking me what is happening? It is an inside job. Enjoy! It is our mental training always to look for some cause somewhere outside. Our whole training is meant to be for outer exploration. Even if the stars are so far away that there seems to be no possibility ever to be in contact with those faraway stars, billions of light years away; still there are thousands of scientists around the world who are wasting their lives finding out some way to have contact with other planetary beings.

In America – I have just remembered what I am going to say to you – sitting in the court, listening to the government attorney… He had a list of thirty-four crimes that I had committed. The truth is, I cannot even remember those thirty-four crimes. In fact many times I forget whether there were thirty-four or thirty-five. One time I even reached the number sixty-five!

The man was very seriously insisting to the judge, and finally he said the first crime was that I had come to America as a tourist, but with an inner intention to remain there forever. I wondered, in what way can anyone know my inner intention? And if my inner intention is a crime, then what about the dreams in which you have killed people, raped women? There is no way to prove what my inner intentions are.

The second thing he said was that I had arranged thousands of marriages in America. For three and a half years I was silent and I was not meeting people; I was living in isolation. I wondered from where is he getting these figures? I have arranged thousands of marriages and I have not been able even to arrange my own marriage? This man seems to be absolutely mad! A man who has failed even to arrange his own marriage is being charged with arranging thousands of marriages.

I looked at the man, and he realized the fact that he had exaggerated the thing. If I should ask him for the evidence, he would have to produce thousands of husbands and thousands of wives in the court. So he immediately said, "At least this man has arranged one marriage, certainly." Now I wondered: from one "certain" marriage, this government attorney can go on creating a fiction of thousands of marriages! And I had no knowledge even about that one marriage.

In fact, I am the only person in the world who is against marriage. I don't want a single marriage in the world. Because to me, unless marriages disappear, prostitutes will remain; you cannot get rid of them. Homosexuals will remain; you cannot get rid of them. All kinds of sexual perverts will remain – and psychoanalysts say almost ninety percent of their patients are psychopaths, but their psychopathology is rooted in their sexual perversion.

And there are millions of divorces. Children become orphans, unnecessarily. Their mothers are alive, their fathers are alive, but because of the divorce they have become orphans. The root cause is marriage. Just remove marriage and you will have removed almost half the miseries of humanity. It is not a small percentage. There will not be any need of prostitutes, there will not be any need for every husband and wife to fight every day. There will be no need for children to learn the behavior of married life from their fathers and mothers. There will not be homosexuals and there will not be any need of diseases like AIDS.

Strangely enough, a man who is preaching against marriage is being charged with arranging thousands of marriages. Sitting there, I was not allowed by my attorneys to say anything because they were worried about me. Every day they tried to convince me, "You should not speak because a single word from you and the case will become very complicated. It will take twenty or thirty years to solve it, so simply remain silent."

There were moments when I had to tell them, "It is going to be very hard because such stupid charges are put against me and I have to remain silent. And you don't have any courage to stand up and say something." I said, "I have thought many times in these twelve days that it would be better to fight in the court for thirty years. These courts of which America is very proud have to be put right."

Even the judges were sitting wrongly. A judge has to sit facing both parties. And I said to my attorneys, "Don't stop me. It is intolerable for me to sit there the whole day, seeing the judge changing the position of his chair and just looking at the government attorney. Is he a judge or just part of the same government? He should not behave as part of the government; otherwise there is no question of justice." Those judges were not even looking at my attorneys, they were not even listening to their arguments. Even if they stood and wanted to raise an objection, the judge would not listen to their whole sentence. Just in the middle of a sentence he would say, "Overruled!"

I said, "It will be better for me to suffer thirty years in jail, or a crucifixion. But seeing such unjust behavior… You are asking me to do the impossible. I would put that judge immediately right. He will have to turn his chair because he cannot sit this way and he cannot behave this way."

But slowly I felt the problem was that my attorneys were also Americans. Perhaps deep down they were also wanting the commune to be destroyed, and that I should not by any chance be victorious in the case. I am not saying that they were intentionally or consciously doing that, but the unconscious plays so many games. They were paid, highly paid, so they were fighting for me, but they were fighting for money. They were not fighting for truth. They believed that they were fighting for truth. But I did not see a single instance, except my own sannyasin, Niren, who is also an attorney. He was my attorney, but he is a younger man and some of those attorneys were his professors, some were nationally famous people. So obviously he could not fight against them.

But there came a moment when even he felt… Because once a person is a sannyasin, he is no longer an American, he is no longer an Indian. He came to me in the jail to say that one of our most important attorneys – and he had been Niren's professor; he is the head of the law department of the University of California, Peter Schey – was not ready to make a statement under the oath of truth. He was ready without the oath, but if the oath had to be taken then he would not make a certain statement.

I cannot conceive that an oath can make any difference to any man of understanding. This was simply a strategy to not make the statement because that statement would have changed the whole course of things. I told Niren, "Pull Peter Schey back and you go on the stand and make the statement."

What is an oath? In fact an honest man will refuse to take the oath. I myself have refused to take the oath. The reason is clear. If you ask me to take the oath you are certainly insulting me; you are telling me that without the oath I cannot speak the truth. You are telling me that only under oath am I reliable. And that means my whole life is a life of lies. No one is taking an oath every moment – before making a statement, first he takes the oath, touches the Bible and says, "It is nine o'clock."

The first time I appeared in an Indian court, I refused. The magistrate was shocked. He said, "Why are you refusing?"

I said, "There are many reasons. First, on what book do you want me to put my hand? – the Bible? Even the contemporaries of Jesus did not believe him, and the man was put on the cross. He was considered a greater criminal than any other criminal by his whole contemporary world. And you want me to put my hand on his book?"

He said, "No, you can put your hand on the Bhagavad Gita."

I said, "Then you are going from bad to worse because this man Krishna has stolen sixteen hundred wives from people, married women, and he himself was not a man of his word or promise. He has broken his promises, he has gone against his own word, and you want me to put my hand on his book? Then I will have to wash my hands!"

The magistrate said, "Then forget about the books. Simply say yourself that whatever you say will be true."

I said, "You don't understand even simple logic. If I am a man of lies, what is the problem for me to say that whatever I say will be true? It is still going to be a lie. Either you accept me as a man of truth...but don't ask for an oath."

This is the world that we have created – where in the name of justice all kinds of injustices will be done, where in the name of truth all kinds of fictions will be invented, imposed, conditioned. And you are carrying the whole past, so whenever you really touch an original space in your being, your whole past will try to distract you. You have to be very alert and very conscious not to be corrupted by your own past, not to be corrupted by your own scriptures, not to be corrupted by your own history. Unless this awareness is there, you may come around the right point many times and again you will go astray, far away.

It is very rare to come to such moments, but you went very easily satisfied, feeling, "…I am a human being…" Do you think that has solved the question of who you are? If you had felt that "I am a monkey," would that make any difference? Because the monkey also has consciousness, just as you have. No – no answer has to be accepted because any answer is going to come from your past conditioning. It is better to remain without an answer, utterly silent, and learn a totally new perception that is without labels. Just pure joy, pure consciousness, a communion with existence and a dance for no reason at all – a dance simply as a prayer of gratitude.

One Sunday afternoon, Pope the Polack is working on a crossword puzzle. He stops for a moment or two, scratches his forehead and turns to one of the cardinals.

"Can you think of a four-letter word for 'woman,'" he asks, "which ends in *u-n-t*?"

"*Aunt*," replies the cardinal.

"Ah, thanks," says the pope. "Do you have an eraser?"

Just old habits. You may become the pope, it does not matter.

The priest and the rabbi are sitting next to each other on a flight from New York to Chicago, when the captain announces that there is some engine trouble. Then he announces that they are going to fly through some rough weather.

Finally he suggests that anyone on board who feels religiously inclined should say their last prayers.

The priest falls on his knees in the aisle and starts kissing his crucifix. And then he notices that the rabbi is crossing himself.

As it happens, the plane levels off and things begin to look more hopeful. The priest turns to the rabbi. "So," he says, looking smug, "when you truly fear death, you turn to Almighty Jesus for help!"

"Not at all," says the rabbi, crossing himself again, "just the usual check: spectacles, testicles, money and cigars."

It does not matter who you are. Only one thing has to be remembered, that every impression on your being left by the past – and the past is very long, millions of years of experiences and they are all present in you. And your own space has become smaller and smaller because the junk goes on gathering more and more every generation. The greatest problem for the meditator is to cross the boundary of the past and to enter the present moment, in your purity of consciousness, without asking any question. Because the answer will come from the past. Just wait. Let your present experience itself become the answer.

It will take time. Just a little patience on your part, and a tremendous explosion... And your whole being becomes free from all chains, from all prisons, from all conditionings, and you are for the first time yourself. Strangely, the moment you are yourself you are the whole existence. Then you are flowering in the roses, dancing in the trees, singing in the rivers, roaring in the oceans. Then the silence is yours and the beauty of sound is yours.

Once you are finished with your past, the whole of existence suddenly becomes your own kingdom. I call this the Kingdom of God. There is no God – *you* are the god of this kingdom. And no effort is big enough. If you are an honest seeker, you will be able to pass all these hindrances and relax into the silent pool of your being.

16

Psychology: The Science of the Soul

Osho,

What is the psychology of the buddhas? It sounds like a science only for enlightened beings who need to pull, push, seduce, hit or kiss their disciples at the right moment, so that they don't wobble, get stuck or fall into traps. Can you please reveal some of your findings of the past thirty years?

The question you have asked is fundamentally unanswerable. But a few indications, a few hints can certainly be made available to you – with absolute certainty that you will not be able to get the point, but that is not my problem. I will try my best.

On your part, if you can be just a passive, silent mind, simply listening as if you are listening to the sound of the birds, not interpreting them, perhaps a certain door may open for you. It all depends on you. The process is not very difficult. It is just an old addiction – we cannot simply listen the way we listen to music; we immediately start reacting, interpreting, trying to find the meaning of it. We get lost in our own minds and the music passes by.

The first thing: I have used the term "the psychology of the buddhas" not to mean what it means. The man of enlightenment has gone beyond the mind. In fact, the mind has faded just like dreams fade away. All the psychologies in the West are concerned with figuring out the functioning of the mind, how it works, why it sometimes works right and sometimes wrong. They have accepted one basic hypothesis which is not true: the hypothesis is that you are no more than the mind; you are a structure of body-mind. Naturally, physiology looks into your body and its functioning and psychology looks into your mind and its functioning.

The first point to be noted is about those who have come to know a different space in themselves which cannot be confined by the mind and which cannot be defined as part of the functioning of it. That silent space with no thoughts, no ripples, is the beginning of the psychology of the buddhas.

The word *psychology* is being used all over the world absolutely wrongly, but when something becomes conventional we forget. Even the very word *psychology* indicates not something about the mind but about the psyche. The root meaning of psychology is "the science of the soul." It is not the science of the mind. And if people are honest, they should change the name because it is a wrong name and takes people on wrong paths. There exists no psychology in the world in the sense of a science of the soul. You are, for arbitrary reasons – just to be able to understand – divided into three parts. But remember, the division is only arbitrary. You are an indivisible unit.

The body is your outer part. It is an immensely valuable instrument that existence has given you. You have never thanked existence for your body. You are not even aware what it goes on doing for you, for seventy, eighty years, in some places one hundred and fifty years. And in a few faraway parts of the Soviet Union, even up to one hundred and eighty years. That leads me to make the statement that the ordinary conception that the body dies at the age of seventy is not a fact but a fiction that has become so prevalent that the body simply follows it.

It happened…

Before George Bernard Shaw reached the age of ninety years, his friends were very puzzled as he started looking for a place outside London – the place where he had lived his whole life. They asked, "What is the point? You have a beautiful house, all the facilities; why are you looking for a new place to live? And in a very strange way – a few people think you have gone senile." Because he would go around the villages, not into the towns but to the cemeteries, and he would read what was written on the gravestones. Finally he decided to live in a village where he found a gravestone where it was written: "This man died a very untimely death – he was only one hundred and twelve."

He said to his friends, "As far as I am concerned, it is a worldwide hypnosis. The idea of seventy years has been insisted on for so many thousands of years that man's body simply follows it. If there is a village where a man dies at a hundred and twelve and the villagers think he died 'very untimely,' that this was not the time for him to die…"

He lived in that village during his last years, and he completed the century.

In Kashmir, the part that is being occupied by Pakistan, people live up to a hundred and fifty without any problem. It is just that the idea of seventy years has not poisoned their minds. In Azerbaijan and in Uzbekistan, faraway corners of the Soviet Union, people live at least one hundred and eighty years, and not just a few people – thousands of people have reached that point and they are still young. They are still not retired, they are working in the fields, in the gardens.

I had told this to one of my professors – he did not believe me. He said, "I am a professor of philosophy and psychology, and I cannot agree with your idea that the whole humanity is dying because of a psychological conditioning."

I said, "I will show you."

He said, "What do you mean?"

I said, "Just wait a few days because no argument will prove it. You will need evidence."

One day... He used to live almost one mile away from the philosophy department in the university campus. He was perfectly healthy; he used to walk every day to the department and back to his home. I went to his wife and said to her, "You have to do me a favor. The next morning when Professor S. S. Roy wakes up you just say, 'What happened? Could you not sleep well? You look so pale, do you have some fever?'"

And when it happened, he simply refused to listen. "What kind of nonsense are you saying? I am perfectly okay. There is no fever and I have slept well. I am feeling perfectly well." I had told his wife to write down exactly what he said in a note and later on I would collect that note.

I said to his gardener, "When he comes out, simply say, 'What has happened to you? You look so sick.' And remember to write down what he says." And to the gardener he said, "It seems that I could not sleep well in the night."

After his house was the post office, which he had to pass. The postmaster was a friend of his, and I said to the postmaster, "You have to do this..."

He said, "But what are you trying to do?"

I said, "It is an argument between me and Professor S. S. Roy, and I am going to prove something to him. I will tell you the whole story later on. Just do one thing: when Professor Roy passes the post office, come out. Just hold him and say to him, 'You are wobbly, don't go to the university today. I will inform the vice-chancellor that you are not well.'"

And the professor said, "I was also thinking not to go. Something certainly seems to be wrong with the body."

Finally I had to persuade the peon of the philosophy department because he used to sit in front of the department. It was very difficult to convince him, but he knew that Professor S. S. Roy loved me so much, I could not mean any harm. I said to him, "The moment he comes, simply jump up and take hold of him. Even if he resists, don't bother; make him lie down on the bench and tell him, 'This is not the time for you to walk a mile, you are absolutely sick.'"

He said, "But I am a peon, a poor man."

I said, "Don't be worried. I give the guarantee that you will not be disturbed. Just remember to write what he says, and remember also whether he resists or not."

He did not resist. He simply followed the peon's idea, lay down on the bench and told the peon, "If you can bring the departmental car and tell the driver to take me home. I don't think I will be able to manage walking one long mile again. I am utterly sick."

I collected all those notes. S. S. Roy was lying down on a couch like the ones psychoanalysts use for patients, looking as if he had been sick for months. Even his voice showed that he could only whisper. I said to him, "You are certainly very sick, but how have you managed in just one night to be so sick that you look as if you have been sick for months? Just last evening when I left you, you were perfectly okay."

He said, "I am also puzzled."

I said, "There is no need to be puzzled, read these notes!"

Reading the notes – from the wife to the peon – he suddenly became perfectly okay. He said, "You are such a fellow that it is better not to get into an argument with you! You could have killed me. I was already thinking to make my will."

I said, "This is the answer to what I have been talking about with you a few days ago – that the body follows the ideas the mind gets."

Seventy years has become a fixed point, almost all over the world. But it is not the truth of the body. It is a corruption of the body by the mind. And strangely enough, all the religions are against the body – and the body is your life, the body is your communion with existence.

It is the body that breathes, it is the body that keeps you alive, it is the body that does almost miracles. Do you have any idea how to change butter or a loaf of bread into blood and sort it out into its different constituents and send those constituents where they are needed? How much oxygen your brain needs – have you any idea? Just in six minutes, if your brain does not get oxygen, you will fall into a coma. For such a long time the body continues to supply the exact amount of oxygen to your brain.

How do you explain the process of breathing? Certainly *you* are not breathing, it is the body that goes on breathing. If you were breathing, you would not have been here. There are so many worries, you could have forgotten to breathe, and particularly in the night – either you can breathe or you can sleep. And it is not a simple process because the air the body takes in consists of many elements which are dangerous to you. It sorts out only those which are nourishing to life and breathes out all that is dangerous to you, particularly carbon dioxide.

The wisdom of the body has not been appreciated by any religion of the world. Your wisest people were no wiser than your body. Its functioning is so perfect – its understanding has been kept completely out of your control because your control could have been destructive.

So the first part of your life and being is your body. The body is real, authentic, sincere. There is no way to corrupt it, although all the religions have been trying to corrupt it. They teach you fasting which is against nature and against the needs of the body, and a man who can fast for longer becomes a great saint. I will call him the greatest fool who has been dominated by the foolishness of the crowd.

The religions have been teaching you to be celibate, without understanding the mechanism of the body. You eat food, you drink water, you breathe oxygen. Just as blood is created in you, your sexual energy is also created – it is beyond you. There has not been a single celibate in the whole world. And I challenge all the religions who pretend that their monks are celibates to have them examined by scientists. They will find that they have the same glands and they have the same energy as anyone else.

Celibacy is a crime – it creates perversions – just as fasting is a crime. Eating too much is a crime; not eating enough is also a crime. If you listen to the body and simply follow the body, you don't need Gautam Buddhas to teach you, or Mahaviras or Jesus Christs to teach you what you have to do with the body. The body has an inbuilt program, and that inbuilt program you cannot change. But you can pervert it.

I have come across so many saints of different religions, but I have not come across a single saint who seems to be intelligent. He cannot be. His whole discipline destroys all intelligence. There are thousands of people in this country who are standing on their heads – and now the disease is spreading to the outside world. And they don't know that too much blood reaching the head destroys the very subtle nervous system that creates your intelligence. Hence you will not find an intelligent yogi – it is impossible. He has destroyed the very possibility.

Man became intelligent because he was not moving like other animals, horizontally. When the animal moves horizontally, as all the animals move, then the blood is circulated all over the body in the same amount, including the head. If you stand on two feet, because of the gravitation of the earth, the head is the last place where the blood will reach, fighting against gravitation. This is the reason why man became intelligent, started being poetic, creative: painters, dancers, mystics. But you are not aware of it. It has been kept outside of your control; otherwise there is every danger you will destroy yourself.

So I teach you, first, a deep respect, love and gratitude for your body. That will be the fundamental of the psychology of the buddhas, of the psychology of the awakened ones. The second thing after the body is your mind. The mind is simply a fiction. It has been used, in fact used too much, by all kinds of parasites. These are the people who will teach you to be against the body and for the mind.

There is a mechanism called the brain. The brain is part of the body, but the brain has no inbuilt program. Nature is so compassionate – leaving your brain without any inbuilt program means existence is giving you freedom. Whatever you want to make of your brain, you can make. But what was compassionate on the part of nature has been exploited by your priests, your politicians, your so-called great men. They found a great opportunity to stuff the mind with all kinds of nonsense.

The mind is a clean slate – whatever you write on the mind becomes your theology, your religion, your political ideology. And every parent, every society is so alert not to leave your mind in your own hands, they immediately start writing the holy Koran, the Holy Bible, Bhagavadgita. By the time they call you adult, capable to participate in the affairs of the world, you are no longer yourself.

This is so cunning, so criminal, that I am surprised that no one has pointed it out. No parent has the right to force the child to be a Catholic a Hindu, a Jaina. Children are born through you, but they don't belong to you. You cannot be the possessors of living beings. You can love them, and if you really love them you will give them freedom to grow according to themselves; without any persuasion, without any punishment, without any effort by anyone else.

The brain is perfectly right – it is the freedom given by nature to you, a space to grow. But the society, before you can grow that space, stuffs it with all kinds of nonsense.

There was a man I knew, Professor Bhansali…

He lived in Mahatma Gandhi's ashram. It is not much of an ashram, just a few widows and a few weirdoes, not more than twenty. But free food, free clothing, free shelter, and all they have to do are some stupid things. They call it worship, they call it prayer.

Professor Bhansali was an educated man, but it does not matter. Before your education you are already contaminated, polluted. He went on eating cow dung for six months, drinking cow's urine – that was his whole food, and this made him a great saint. Even Mahatma Gandhi declared that he had attained enlightenment. If enlightenment is to be attained by eating cow dung, then better enlightenment will be attained by eating bullshit, obviously! And when Mahatma Gandhi says that he has become enlightened, the whole country simply believes it. I have not found a single man criticizing it.

I said to Professor Bhansali, "As far as I am concerned, you are the most stupid man in this country." It is a very difficult competition, but look at all your religions, what they have stuffed in your mind. Every Hindu when he goes to urinate has a thread around his body. That thread ceremony is almost like the Jews circumcising their children. And will you believe that I have come across a statement by a rabbi that the reason Jews are so intelligent is because of the circumcision? Mohammedans do the same but at a later age.

The Jews have their own baptism. The Hindus have their way of introducing the child into the Hindu society with a thread ceremony. Just a thread is put around his neck, and he is surrounded by people chanting from holy scriptures. And every Hindu is expected, when he goes to urinate, to take the thread out of his shirt and wrap the thread around his ear. I have seen professors, vice-chancellors doing the same stupid act.

I caught the vice-chancellor, Dr. Tripathi red-handed. I threatened him, "Either you take this thread off your ear, or I will not allow you to urinate."

"But," he said, "it is my religion." And he was a well-educated man.

I said, "Can you give me any rationalization for it?"

He said, "Certainly. If you put the thread around your ear, it keeps you away from sexual ideas, sexual dreams. It protects your celibacy."

I said, "You are a man, perfectly educated in the West" – and he had been teaching in the West – "you will have to come with me to the medical center."

He said, "What do you mean?"

I said, "I want it to be confirmed by medical scientists that putting the thread around the ear protects a person from becoming sexual."

He said, "You always come with strange ideas."

The simple proof was that he had thirteen children. I said, "With this thread, you have produced thirteen children; without the thread you would have threatened the whole humanity! And still you have the nerve to say that it protects your celibacy?"

But everywhere, you will find the same kind of ideas forced into the brain. I want it to be clearly understood that the brain is natural; the mind is what is stuffed into the brain. So the brain is not Christian, but the mind can be; the brain is not Hindu, but the mind can be.

The mind is the creation of the society, not a gift of nature. The first thing the psychology of the buddhas will do is to take away this whole junk that you call the mind, and leave your brain silent, pure, innocent, the way you were born.

All around the world, modern psychology is doing something stupid – analyzing the brain, analyzing all the thoughts which constitute your mind. In the East we have looked into the innermost parts of humanity and our understanding is that the mind needs no analysis. It is analyzing junk. It needs simply to be erased. The moment the mind is erased – and the method is meditation – you are left with a body which is absolutely beautiful, you are left with a silent brain with no noise. The moment the brain is freed from the mind, the innocence of the brain becomes aware of a new space which we have called the soul.

Once you have found your soul, you have found your home. You have found your love, you have found your inexhaustible ecstasy, you have found that the whole existence is ready for you to dance, to rejoice, to sing – to live intensely and die blissfully. These things happen on their own accord.

The mind is the barrier between your brain, your body and your soul. You can see the difference. The psychology born in the West is concerned with the most nonessential part of you; it goes round and round analyzing the mind. The psychology of the buddhas, in a single hit, will drop the mind and accept only that which existence has given to you, not the society you were unfortunate to be born in.

But every society is unfortunate, every religion is unfortunate. This is the greatest calamity under which humanity has lived up to now. What is the difference between a Mohammedan and a Christian, except the mind? What is the difference between a communist and a spiritualist? – just the difference of the mind. Each has been cultivated differently.

So the first and the most basic thing is that the psychology of the buddhas has evolved methods of meditation which are really nothing but surgical methods so that the mind can be removed – it is the worst cancerous growth in you. Other than the mind, everything is absolutely beautiful. Only the mind is man-manufactured; everything else comes from the eternal sources of life.

You are asking, "It sounds like a science only for enlightened beings who need to pull, push, seduce, hit or kiss their disciples at the right moment so that they don't wobble, get stuck or fall into traps." It does not appear as a science to the enlightened person, but just like a spring cleaning. For the unenlightened it appears to be what you are describing: "…to pull, to push, to seduce, to hit, to kiss their disciples in the right moment…" This is how it appears from the outside. As far as the master is concerned, every moment is the right moment. There are no wrong moments in the world.

And certainly it is not a science in the sense you understand because science remains confined to the mind. It is more like an art. The master watches the disciple, goes on making every possible effort to wake the disciple. The moment the disciple is awake there is no difference between the master and the disciple – and he can use any kind of arbitrary method. But the methods are arbitrary, they are not scientific. I will give you an example to show that science is a very much lower phenomenon…

One morning Chuang Tzu sat up in his bed – which was strange because he used to get up and get out of his bed. Why is he sitting and looking so sad? He was not a man of sadness.

In fact, I have not found anyone else in the whole world of literature who has written such beautiful absurd stories. They don't make any sense, but they are beautiful. He was again creating a situation.

The disciples were worried; they came and asked, "What is the matter?"

Chuang Tzu said, "I am in a very great fix. Last night I slept, and I knew perfectly well that I was Chuang Tzu. But in the night I had a dream that I had become a butterfly."

The disciples laughed.

He said, "Shut up! It is not a matter to laugh about, my whole life is at risk!"

They said, "Master, it was only a dream!"

He said, "First you should listen to the whole thing. Then in the morning I woke up and the idea arose in me that if Chuang Tzu can become a butterfly in a dream, what is the guarantee that a butterfly cannot become Chuang Tzu in a dream? And now the question is, who am I? The butterfly dreaming, or...?"

Certainly the situation he has created is almost insoluble. Do you think there can be any rational solution to it? His question is very pertinent. If Chuang Tzu can become a butterfly in a dream, perhaps the butterfly has gone to sleep and has become Chuang Tzu. The problem is that Chuang Tzu is losing his identity. He told the disciples, "Meditate and find a solution. Unless you find a solution I am going to sit in my bed without eating because it is a question of life and death."

They went out and discussed it. "This is absolutely absurd! We have also dreamed, but this idea..." But the idea is such that there is no way out of it!

Then came Lieh Tzu, Chuang Tzu's chief disciple, and all the disciples asked him what to do. He said, "Don't be worried," and rather than going to Chuang Tzu, he went to the water well.

They said, "Where are you going?"

He said, "Just wait. I know my master." He pulled up a bucket of water – it was a cold winter morning – and he brought the bucket of water and poured it on Chuang Tzu!

Chuang Tzu laughed and said, "If you had not come, my life was at risk. You saved me!"

Lieh Tzu said, "Just get out of the bed, or I am going to bring another bucket of water. All that you need is to be brought out of your dream. You are still dreaming."

He said, "No, I am going to get out!"

The masters cannot create a science because science can only be objective. At the most you can call it an art because the art has more flexibility, more different approaches.

Now, what do you call Lieh Tzu's bringing a bucket of water? – a scientific method? Just a clear insight, and out of that clear insight arises an arbitrary, artful, but intelligent method.

In fact, Chuang Tzu was waiting for some disciple to *do* something – it was not a question to be solved by sitting and pondering over it. It was a question that someone has to *do* something and show by his act, his clarity. This was the moment Chuang Tzu declared Lieh Tzu to be his successor. All the other disciples could not understand what had happened: What kind of solution is this?

The psychology of the buddhas is not a science, is not a philosophy. At the most we can call it a very flexible art. Hence, there are no fixed answers for anything.

I will give you another example…

One morning, it must have been such a beautiful morning, a man comes to Gautam Buddha and asks him, "Does God exist?" Everyone is curious to know what Buddha answers.

Buddha said to the man, "There is no God – not only now, there has never been. It is simply a fiction to exploit the fools." The man was very shocked.

In the afternoon, another man came and he asked, "What do you think about the existence of God?" Again the same question.

Buddha looked at the man and said, "Yes, there is a God and there has always been."

And in the evening, another man came and said, "I don't know anything about God. I am absolutely ignorant. Knowing that you are here, I have come to be enlightened about the subject."

Buddha looked at him and then closed his eyes. No answer – and strangely, the disciples saw that the other man also closed his eyes. One hour must have passed when the man opened his eyes, touched Gautam Buddha's feet and said, "You have answered it, and I am immensely grateful."

Ananda, who used to be the attendant of Gautam Buddha twenty-four hours a day, became very confused. Anyone could have become confused – in the morning he says one thing, in the afternoon he says just the opposite, and in the evening he says nothing and the man gets the answer, touches his feet with tears of joy and leaves! When everyone was gone, Ananda said, "I cannot sleep tonight until you tell me which one is the true answer."

Gautam Buddha said, "The first thing you have to remember if that none of the questions were yours. Why should you be worried about the answers? You have been with me for forty years. If you had any question, you could have asked. Those were questions of three different people."

Ananda said, "I am sorry, it is true. None of them was my question, but I have ears and I heard. All three questions and the three answers are so contradictory that it has become a turmoil in me."

Buddha said, "You don't understand another thing. The first man who had come to see me was a believer in God. He was a theist, and all he wanted was not an answer but a support to his belief. I cannot support anyone's belief. My function is to destroy all beliefs, so that you yourself can see what is the truth. That's why I denied absolutely that there is any God, and said there has never been any God.

"The man who came in the afternoon was just the opposite; he was an atheist. He did not believe in God and he had also come to be supported so that he could tell people that 'Not only I am an atheist – Gautam Buddha himself is an atheist.' But this was also a belief, not an experience, because the experience never asks questions. It is always the belief that goes on creating questions."

Your mind is full of beliefs, with no experience at all. That's why Gautam Buddha said, "I had to be very strict with the fellow, and I told him there is a God and there has always been a God."

These are arbitrary methods to destroy different kinds of beliefs. But the basic purpose is to destroy belief so that you can find your own heart, your own trust.

"And the third man was a very innocent man because he accepted his ignorance, and he did not propose any belief. He had not come to be supported, he had come to be really helped. And there is a difference in being supported and being helped.

"Because he had no question, there was no need to answer. I closed my eyes, and he understood that he had also to close his eyes. Perhaps this is the way Gautam Buddha is going to answer him. And he was right – innocence is always right. In that one hour, my silence infiltrated his being. My presence surrounded his being. He was immensely fulfilled, contented.

"God is no one's business – certainly it was not the business of that man. All he wanted was a certain communion with existence, whatever name is given to existence. I gave him the taste, I gave him the experience; I shared myself with him – that's why he was so grateful. You are puzzled that the man said, 'I have received the answer' although I had not answered in words. And in gratitude, he touched my feet, with tears of joy. But in each case I had to use a different, arbitrary method because those three people had three different minds."

The psychology of the buddhas cannot be a science. Science is always objective, it is about the other. It is never about your own being. It is extrovert, it is never introvert.

But the man who has become awakened finds ways to shake you from your sleep, to wake you from your mind, which is your coma, which is your blindness. That's why different masters in different countries have used different methods. No method is scientific. It depends on the person who has to be operated upon. The surgery cannot be a definite science. As far as the psychology of the buddhas is concerned, it is going to be very flexible.

Yes, sometimes the master may hit you and sometimes the master may hug you. But it all depends on what kind of mind he is working on, and he is working on different kinds of minds. You don't have the same minds; otherwise the same method would have been enough.

Traditionally there are one hundred and eight methods of meditation. I have gone through all those methods – not just by reading them; I have tried every method. My search was to find what the essential core is of all those one hundred and eight methods because there is bound to be something essential. My experience is that the essential of all meditations is the art of witnessing.

And then I created my own methods because I had found the essential core. Those one hundred and eight methods have become, in a way, out of date. They were created by different masters for different kinds of people, to transform different minds. The contemporary mind did not yet exist; the contemporary mind needs new methods. The methods will differ only in nonessentials. The essential core, the very soul of the method, is going to be the same.

This silence is beautiful, but each laughter makes the silence go deeper. Have you observed it or not? After each laughter, there is a deeper layer of silence revealing itself to you. It is almost like being on a road and a car passes with its headlights on. Suddenly there is light where there was darkness. But once the car has gone, the darkness becomes darker.

Something almost similar happens; hence I have started calling my jokes "time for prayer."

Herman Levinsky is standing in front of the gorilla's cage in the zoo one day, when the wind blows a piece of grit into his eye.

As Herman pulls down his eyelid to remove the particle, the gorilla goes crazy, bends open the bars and beats the poor fellow senseless.

When Herman regains consciousness, he explains to the anxious zookeeper what happened. The zookeeper nods sagely and explains that in gorilla language, pulling down the eyelid means, "Fuck you!"

This explanation doesn't make Herman feel any better, and he swears revenge.

The next day, Herman arrives at the zoo with two large knives, two hats, two whistles and a large sausage. Putting the sausage in his pants, he hurries to the gorilla's cage, into which he throws a knife, a hat and a whistle.

Then Herman puts on his hat. The gorilla looks at him, looks at the hat, and puts it on.

Next, Herman picks up the whistle and blows it. The gorilla looks at him, looks at the whistle, and then picks it up and blows it.

Then Herman picks up the knife, whips the sausage out of his pants, and slices it neatly in two. The gorilla looks at the knife in his cage, looks at his prick, looks up, and pulls down his eyelid.

17

Variety Is the Beauty of Existence

Osho,
I heard you saying that we are all enlightened. If so, why am I waiting for something to happen? Is it an old habit?

It is one thing to hear; it is another thing to understand. You certainly heard me saying that we are all enlightened, but you did not trust it – at least you excluded yourself. "Perhaps everyone else is, but I am enlightened?" This was too much for you to accept; hence the question. Your question shows your innermost turmoil. You are saying, "If so..." I had not said that your enlightenment is some probability – perhaps you are enlightened, perhaps you are not. There were no ifs and no buts; it was a simple statement. I repeat again: "You *are* enlightened and you cannot be anything else."

But I can understand your difficulty. You have been told you are ignorant and you have accepted it. You have been told you are unworthy and you have accepted it. You have been told you are not beautiful and you have accepted it. Just look at how many things you have accepted without creating ifs and buts, without even asking a question.

When I was a student in the university, my philosophy class consisted only of three people. Two were girls and I was the third.

And a certain Professor Bhattacharya – a little cynical, as is almost expected from professors of philosophy – had a certain idea of celibacy. He used to teach the class with closed eyes. When I saw this on the first day, I could not figure it out: What is the problem? After the class I approached him and asked him.

He said, "I cannot see women."

I said, "If you cannot see women, why do you close your eyes?"

He said, "You don't understand me. I don't *want* to see women."

I said, "Even then, you have seen them; it does not matter whether you want to or not. Women are all around. Just by closing your eyes, do you think you are not seeing women? Then what are people doing in their dreams? I insist on the point that if you are keeping your eyes closed because of the women, you will be consistently reminded only of women. And remember that no woman is so beautiful with open eyes as she becomes when your eyes are closed. Then the woman becomes a romantic dream. Reality is not so romantic. With your eyes closed you are taking a very dangerous step."

The next day I also closed my eyes. He looked at me and thought perhaps I had also become convinced of his ideology of celibacy. After the class he asked me, "So it seems you are also convinced."

I said, "The reality is that I slept the whole hour. And now I will sleep every day. If you are free to close your eyes, I am also free to close my eyes. It does not matter what happens with closed eyes – you dream, I sleep."

He said, "But then what is the point of attending the class?"

I said, "There is no point at all, it is just that one has to be somewhere. Do you mean to say that wherever I am, I have to answer the question, 'Why I am here?'"

And I told him an old story…

A man comes home, finds his wife naked on the bed, sees the shoes of his friend by the side of the bed, looks all around, and suspects he must be in the cupboard. He opens the cupboard; certainly the naked friend is standing there. He is really angry and he says, "I used to think you were my best friend."

He said, "I am."

He said, "Then why are you standing here in the cupboard?"

The man said, "This is strange – everyone has to be somewhere, and this cupboard of yours is very cozy. And this is not the first time that I am standing here. It is my usual habit."

I said to Professor Bhattacharya, "Never ask me again about any reason because I don't believe in rationality. I simply mean, things are and there is no reason for them to prove why they are, where they are, who they are."

But from your very childhood, you have not been given the right vision. You have always been pushed and pulled this way and that way. "Become this, become that." No one ever thought that if existence wanted only Gautam Buddhas, it could have manufactured Gautam Buddhas just the way a Ford factory produces Ford cars: on an assembly line, all exactly alike, with tremendous efficiency. Each minute a single car comes out of the assembly line, twenty-four hours around the clock.

But existence does not believe in a situation where everyone is like everyone else. The enlightenment of Gautam Buddha is going to be his enlightenment. Your enlightenment is going to be your enlightenment. The problem arises out of comparison. You started thinking, "If I am enlightened, then why am I not a Gautam Buddha or a Jesus Christ or a Bodhidharma? I am just Veet Vigyanam. No one worships me. I go around, no one even takes any note of me. What kind of enlightenment is this? Certainly I have yet to achieve it. Certainly it has not happened yet, it has to happen."

The idea that enlightenment is an achievement has been propagated with such consistency, for so many thousands of years. I say unto you that enlightenment is not an achievement, it is your very nature. If you are missing it, the reason is not that you have not achieved it, the reason is that you are looking for it all around in every place excluding yourself. Going to every temple, reading every holy scripture, visiting all kinds of stupid people who are pretending to be masters.

I want you to declare this very moment that you *are* enlightened. It does not matter, it is not needed that everyone should worship you. Why should anyone worship you? You are making unnecessary conditions for enlightenment. This is not only your problem, it has been a problem for many. The Buddhists cannot accept Mahavira as enlightened because he is naked and Gautam Buddha is not naked. Because Gautam Buddha has beautiful hair and Mahavira pulls out his hair, how can both these men be enlightened? We have, without contemplating, accepted an idea that every enlightened person is going to be the same. It is absolute nonsense. In existence, variety is the beauty of it.

I would also like everyone to be enlightened in his own way and express his enlightenment in his own way. Otherwise this whole life will become a boredom. Just think – as Jesus says to his disciples – "Everybody has to carry his own cross." Just look around, imagine everyone carrying his own cross. There are not even people to crucify them because *they* are carrying their own crosses! The whole thing would be so hilarious. Existence never produces the same person again. Similarity is not the rule of this beautiful universe, but uniqueness. And the moment you accept uniqueness, you accept a tremendous respect for others as they are.

Let me say it in a different way. The moment you respect yourself as enlightened, you cannot do anything other than respect everyone as enlightened, as they are. There is no need for everyone to fit into a certain category. Enlightenment is not a category that you have to eat the same kind of food. If there was a certain rule like this, rather than eating spaghetti, I would have renounced enlightenment. It is good that no holy scripture says that spaghetti is absolutely the characteristic of an enlightened man.

If you understand me, what I am saying… I am saying that in your very ordinariness you are perfectly good. Nothing needs to be added to you. And if you can relax in this ordinariness, this very ordinariness – because of your relaxation – will become radiant, will start blossoming. Your acceptance, your self-respect will be a nourishment, will bring the spring to your being, and the flowers will start opening their petals.

But you are never at home. You are looking in other people's homes. Someone is in Gautam Buddha's, someone in Lao Tzu's, someone in Jesus Christ's, someone in Moses'. It is a very strange situation that you have been diverted in such a way that everyone is somewhere else, where he is not expected to be, and he is not where existence wants him to be.

I teach the immediate and ultimate ordinariness. It is the most beautiful experience because now there is no desire, no tension, no search, no inquiry, nowhere to go. You are already where you wanted to be.

And you are asking, "If so, why am I waiting for something to happen?" Now, do I have to answer this? Perhaps this is your unique enlightenment, that even though you are enlightened, still you are looking for some happening. A little crazy, but that does not destroy your enlightenment. And a few crazy people are also needed. They bring salt to existence. Existence without crazy people will lose something very interesting.

But you cannot even accept that. You go on, asking, "Is it an old habit?" Just trying to console yourself, that although you are enlightened, just because of the old habit you go on looking here and there. But the more you will look here and there, the more you will be nourishing the old habit. You will be practicing the old habit.

It is very difficult to see that eating your food silently and joyously, sleeping with as much blissfulness as you can contain, having an ordinary life of being a carpenter or being a shoemaker, or being a painter, a poet, a dancer, and relaxing in whatever you are without making ideals… But man cannot be destroyed without ideals, and he cannot be enslaved without ideals. He cannot be condemned, he cannot be made to feel guilty if there is not an ideal that he has to become. And no one ever becomes the ideal that he has tried his whole life to become.

Have you ever seen any Christian becoming a Christ? Almost half of humanity is Christian and for two thousand years these people have been trying hard to fulfill the ideal of being a Christ. Why do they go on failing? And it is not only the Christians – the Jainas, the Hindus, the Buddhists, the Mohammedans, no one has been successful. The reason is so fundamental that you cannot go against it. You can either be yourself or just a wastage. These are the only two alternatives.

Love Gautam Buddha for his uniqueness, but never imitate him. He himself never imitated anyone, that's why he is enlightened. It is strange that a simple fact has not been recognized. Mahavira never imitated anyone and that's why he's enlightened. You show me a single enlightened being who has ever imitated anyone.

I am reminded of a very beautiful man, Kabir…

In India, Hindus believe that the Ganges is a holy river, and if you die near the Ganges then your paradise is absolutely guaranteed. Then it does not matter what crimes you committed, what sins you committed, what immoralities; everything is washed out by the Ganges. Naturally, not all the Hindus can live by the side of the Ganges. That will be too much of a crowd. Those who live there are fortunate; those who cannot live there at least go in their old age to live there, when they see death is coming. In cities like Varanasi, you will be surprised to see – why are there so many old people, so many old women? No other city can compete in that matter. All these people have come there to die and now they are waiting for their death; it may come any moment.

Sometimes it happens that in some nearby village… Varanasi is costly, it is available only for rich people to live there to die; the poor people live in nearby villages. Naturally it happens that they die in their villages, but immediately their friends and their relatives take their dead bodies to the Ganges. It doesn't matter, just a few minutes or half an hour or one hour. God cannot be so cruel. He will also forgive even these people.

Kabir lived all his life in Varanasi, the holiest city of the Hindus. Just on the other side of the Ganges, there is a small village called Maghar. I don't know how the idea became prevalent that anyone who dies in Varanasi goes to paradise and anyone who dies in Maghar becomes a donkey. And Maghar is just on the other side of the Ganges.

Before Kabir felt that now his time had come, he told his friends, "Take me to Maghar."

They said, "Are you mad? No one wants to die in Maghar. People who are living there are continuously afraid – before death they have to escape from there. And you have lived your whole life in Varanasi and now, when the right moment has come, you want to go to Maghar? You know perfectly well that people who die in Maghar become donkeys."

Kabir said, "If you don't listen to me, I will have to walk down to Maghar. But I don't want any obligation, either to the Ganges or to any God. If I am enlightened, I am enlightened in Varanasi, I am enlightened in Maghar. Let me set the precedent because the poor people of Maghar have been condemned for centuries. Let me die in Maghar because after me it will be difficult for anyone to say that anyone who dies in Maghar becomes a donkey. At least that cannot be said about Kabir."

Kabir died in Maghar. He changed it; now no one says that if you die in Maghar you will become a donkey. On the contrary, many people who love Kabir live in Maghar; Maghar has become a holy place for the followers of Kabir.

It happened that Meera, another woman mystic, had come to Varanasi just on a pilgrimage. And Varanasi has the highest council of Hindu scholars, the so-called wise, and the saints. There was trouble because many of those people wanted Kabir to be invited to their annual conference, but Kabir was a weaver; not only that, it was suspicious whether he was a Hindu or a Mohammedan. His name was Mohammedan – *Kabir* in Arabic means Allah, another name of God. And he was found on the bank of the Ganges by a Hindu monk, Ramananda – left by his parents, a small child. And the story is very beautiful…

It was dark, early morning, when Hindus take their bath before their worship of the sun. As Ramananda was coming down the steps, a small child took hold of his robe. Surprised, he said, "Who is there?" He looked and saw a small child, not more than four years old, sitting on the steps. What to do with this child? There was no one else around; the parents had abandoned the child there.

Ramananda was a man of courage. He took the child, although all his disciples said to him, "You are taking an unnecessary risk. You will be renounced by the Hindus, by the same people who worship you. You are not supposed to do such things. Moreover, on the hand of the child is written in Arabic "Kabir," his name, which is an absolute proof that he is a Mohammedan. A Hindu monk is not supposed to have children, he has renounced life."

But Ramananda said, "I have not done anything in respect to gaining worshippers, followers. If they have come, they have come on their own. If they go, they go on their own. No one dictates to me what I am to do because I have never dictated to anyone what he has to do." So Kabir was brought up by Ramananda. Because of Ramananda, people think he must be Hindu, and because of his name, people think he must be Mohammedan.

And now, because he has become known as the wisest man of his times, a few people wanted him to come to the holy conference of the Hindus. He was a weaver. There was great opposition. But they did not want any split in their council, so finally they came to the agreement that they would invite him. But when they went to invite Kabir he had a condition: "You have to invite Meera also because she is staying with me. You can leave me out. Invite Meera in my place."

But that was even more difficult. She was a woman. No woman was ever invited into the wisest council of the Hindus. A woman is not accepted as pure; basically she is impure and unless by arduous disciplines she becomes born as a man, she will not be able to reach paradise. There is no direct way from the woman to paradise. She has to go via man. Now Kabir was making a condition which was even more difficult.

They told him, "It has been very difficult for us even to invite you, and you are making an even more difficult condition."

He said, "I never change what I say. If Meera is not respected by you, then you don't understand anything. And I don't want to mix with ignorant people."

Kabir's followers said to him, "It is a great opportunity. No weaver" – weavers are the lowest Hindu class – "has ever been accepted by the brahmins as wise. Don't miss this opportunity."

And Kabir said, "I am wise or unwise on my own accord. I don't depend on anyone else's acceptance. But I am making this condition because for centuries Hindus have behaved with such ugliness with women that the time has come to change it."

Because of Kabir's insistence, Meera was the only woman – for the first time – who entered the Hindu council of wise people. It was a very uneasy conference. One Mohammedan was there, one woman was there. The whole Hindu idea of their purity and their superiority was absolutely destroyed.

Kabir continued to be a weaver his whole life. Even kings were his disciples and they asked him, "We feel ashamed that you go on continuously weaving in your old age and then you go to sell your cloth in the market. We can manage everything that you want. There is no need."

Kabir said, "That is not the question. I want the future humanity to remember that a weaver can be enlightened, and even with his enlightenment he can continue to weave. The ordinary profession of a weaver is not a distraction from enlightenment; on the contrary, his weaving becomes his prayer. Whatever he does is his prayer; whatever he does is his meditation. Whatever he does is his expression of gratitude to existence. He is not just a burden on the earth, he is doing whatever he can do.

"I cannot be a sculptor, I cannot be a great painter, but I can certainly say that no one can weave the way I weave. I weave with each breath full of prayer and gratitude. And the cloth that I make is made not just to sell but to serve God, to serve existence in the way in which I can serve it the best."

The Hindu word for God is *Ram*. And Kabir used to address every customer who came to his shop by the same name, "Ram." He would say, "Ram, I have been weaving for you. Take care, this is no ordinary cloth. Each fiber in it is vibrating with my gratitude, my love, my compassion, my prayer. Be respectful to it."

Sometimes it would happen that he would wait, late, when the market was closing. People would ask, "For whom are you waiting? The market is closing."

And he would say, "I am waiting for my Ram, who has not come, and for whom I have made the cloth." A certain man had asked him and he might not have been available on that day, or might have thought that he would go on the next market day. But Kabir was waiting there.

People would inform the man, "What are you doing? It is getting late and Kabir alone is sitting in the marketplace waiting for you because he says, 'I cannot accept the fact that Ram would have forgotten or that Ram could have given me his word and go against it. I have to wait even if I have to wait for seven days.'" Because in India, in villages, the market day is only once a week, four times a month. "I will wait for seven days; perhaps he is in difficulty, perhaps he is sick. But I cannot move from this place. If he comes and finds that I am not here it will be sheer ingratitude on my part."

Now, Gautam Buddha lived in a totally different way. Meera lived in a totally different way. Meera danced all over the country, and she reached Mathura, where stands the greatest Krishna temple. The priest of the temple was a fanatic celibate. I used to tell Professor Bhattacharya, "You are an incarnation of that fanatic, and unless you drop this fanaticism you are not going to be relaxed and relieved from the wheel of life. You will have to born again and again and again."

No woman was allowed in the temple of Krishna. They could worship only from the outside. The priest had not seen a woman for thirty years – he never used to go outside, and no woman was allowed inside the temple. When he heard about Meera he was worried because she would certainly come to the greatest temple of Krishna. He had put two guards at the gate saying, "Prevent that woman if she comes dancing here."

But when Meera came dancing, those guards completely forgot their purpose, why they were standing there. The dance was so beautiful and Meera was so beautiful, so radiant, that without anyone noticing she entered the door, dancing. The priest was in the middle of his worship. The plate that he was holding in his hand, a golden plate full of roseflowers… Seeing Meera dancing and entering the temple, the plate fell from his hands. He was very angry and he said to Meera, "It is against the rules of this temple – no woman can enter here!"

And you will be surprised to know the answer of Meera, which stands out in the whole history of the mystics with a strange flavor, an aliveness. She said, "My God! I used to think that only Krishna was the man and everyone else is a woman, a lover to Krishna. Today I have found two men. You are also a man!" And the way she spoke to the priest, the priest trembled. Perhaps she was right.

There are only two ways for the devotees to conceive of God. Either God is conceived, like the Sufis, as a woman – she is the beloved and the mystic is the lover – or God is conceived, like the Indian mystics, that they are women and God is the man. He is the lover and they are the beloveds.

Meera said, "The thing has to be decided here now. Either you have to declare yourself a man or you have to declare yourself also a woman."

Under the impact of Meera that poor priest had to accept, "I am also a woman."

Meera said, "Then from now onward the rule is changed. *Only* women can enter this temple. Those who think they are male cannot enter."

If you look into the lives of these mystics, these enlightened people, you will not find any similarity. You will find only utter uniqueness. Sometimes they are so ordinary that you may not even recognize them. Sometimes they are so radiant that even those who are blind will see their light. But there is no general rule and there are no fixed characteristics. You don't have to fulfill certain ideals.

My own approach is to take away all ideals from you and to take away the very idea that enlightenment is going to happen to you in the future. The future does not exist! In fact the idea that it is going to happen in the future is simply to avoid the self-respect that you can have only in the present.

There have been teachers – they were not masters, they were as unconscious as you are. They were not aware of their own enlightenment. They were teaching morality, discipline, methods, how to become enlightened. But do you understand the inner logic? If you can become enlightened, then there is every possibility you can also become unenlightened again. If there are methods to become enlightened, there can be methods to make you unenlightened. This is a simple thing. If you can become sick, you can become healthy, and you can also become sick again.

Enlightenment is not something that you have to attain because that which is attained can be stolen. That which is attained can be robbed. That which is attained can be lost. I say unto you, "You *are* enlightenment itself." I don't want you to attain enlightenment, I want you to live it. From this very moment, whatever you do, do it in the way enlightenment is bound to do it.

I love one statement of one of the most important people of the West, Alan Watts. He was a drunkard, but he was the man who introduced the most essential parts of Zen and enlightenment to the West. He wrote not as a scholar, but as a master. Before he was dying, he was still drinking and a disciple asked him, "Have you ever thought that if Buddha had seen you drinking alcohol, what do you think he would have thought about it?"

Alan Watts said, "There is no problem. I always drink in an enlightened way."

The question is not what you do, the question is how you do it. Yes, I accept Alan Watts' statement. There is a possibility of a man to drink alcohol in an enlightened way. Enlightenment should not have any limits. And it should not have a particular formula, a particular pattern that you have to follow. Enlightenment should be an individual experience – the most individual experience, incomparable and unique to everyone. Once this is understood, all the clouds that surround you with darkness start dispersing.

Veet Vigyanam, I will go on repeating again and again, until it sinks into you, that you are enlightened. And you are not to do anything special for it; you have just to be as you are, totally relaxed, at ease with existence. Not going anywhere, no achievement, no goal. All goal-orientation is what is making people miserable.

Disperse all the goals and you will start dancing this very moment because you have so much energy involved in your process of achieving. Moving far away in your imagination, you don't have time, you don't have space, you don't have energy to be here. If you can gather all your energy in this very moment, just the accumulation of that energy will become a dance in your heart. And that dance transforms everything, not your efforts.

A Polack walks into the travel agent and books for a special sea cruise to Hawaii. The travel agent directs him to the next room to fill out some forms. Just as the Polack walks through the door, someone hits him over the head, throws him into the corner and mugs him.

Later the same day, an Italian enters the travel agency to book for the special Hawaiian sea cruise. As he is directed to the next room, he too gets hit over the head and mugged.

When the two of them wake up, they find themselves floating in the middle of the ocean on a small raft. The Italian looks over at the Polack and says, "I wonder if they will fly us back?"

"I doubt it," replies the Polack. "They didn't last year."

Father Murphy is chosen to do some missionary work for the Catholic church, and is sent to a remote part of the Arctic. After a few months, a bishop comes to visit.

"How do you like it here," asks the bishop, "among the ice and polar bears?"

"Just fine," says Father Murphy. "The Eskimos are very friendly people."

"And what about the weather?" asks the bishop.

"Ah," says the priest, "as long as I have my rosary and my whiskey, I don't care a bit about the weather."

"I am glad to hear of it," says the bishop. "Speaking of whiskey, how about a glass or two?"

"Great idea!" says Father Murphy. "Rosary! Can you bring us the whiskey?"

Hymie is a little drunk when he comes home. "Becky," he calls to his wife in the bedroom, "start nagging, or else I won't be able to find the bed!"

Just enjoy your life. It is perfect as it is. The whole idea of perfectionism creates only neurosis, pathology and a derangement of the mind. I teach you the ordinary. I teach you the simple, the natural, I teach you that you are where you have been trying to reach, exactly at home. Don't waste your time running here and there.

But you have been told always to become something, someone – that's why every religion is against me, all the moralists are against me. I can understand because if I am right, all the traditions and all the teachings that have been driving humanity toward some faraway goal are proven absolutely criminal. They have taken away people's chance to live, to love, to sing, to dance. And in the ultimate sense, the very opportunity to feel the divine in the herenow. Unless you can feel the divine in the mundane, you are not an intelligent person. If you cannot manage in your small things an expression of gratitude, joy, awareness, then you are bound to remain miserable – not only in this life but perhaps for many lives.

I can't see much opportunity for you to find a man like me again. You will meet all those religious teachers, missionaries; try to find one and you will find a thousand. But I am absolutely respectful to your ordinariness. My reverence for the mundane is absolute; I don't want to improve on anything. For centuries people have been improving and improving and improving, and nothing is improved. Just give me a chance. Stop improving. And you will be surprised to know that the energy that was involved in improving becomes your dance, your celebration.

18

Love Dissolves Identity

> Osho,
>
> As you glide into Buddha Hall, slowly turning toward where I sit waiting for your gaze to touch me, a strange overwhelming fear grips me. I say to myself, "Darshan, after all these years of being with him, why this fear?" Then as your eyes caress me, the fear melts immediately, I melt and something lovely starts dancing within me. Beloved Osho, please speak a little about this crazy partnership of fear and love that takes me so completely by surprise again and again.

Deva Darshan, your question is much more comprehensive and complex than you may have realized. Man is an organic unity. And the moment I say an organic unity, I mean you are love, you are fear, you are anger – the whole panorama; all the colors of the rainbow. But it is very rarely realized because our minds try to dissect things, divide things, arrange things. And as far as the parts are concerned, they are in a way very clever and intelligent. The moment the whole arises in your view, the mind freaks out. It cannot understand that even in fear, all the rainbows of your being are involved.

In schools they use a device to explain a simple fact. They make a fan with seven wings of all the seven different colors. When the fan is not moving you can see what is red and what is blue and what is green. There are just two colors you will not find in those seven colors: black and the white because they are not really colors. It is just from long usage that we have grown accustomed to calling white and black colors. Then they plug the fan into the electricity and the wings start moving as fast as possible. A strange phenomenon – you see all those different colors disappear; only white remains.

When you see the white color, it means all the rays that create colors are being reflected back, so you cannot find any color. White is an absence of all colors. Black is just the opposite of white; the black absorbs all the rays of color, not allowing a single ray to go back. Hence you cannot see the color because your eyes can only see reflected rays.

Black became – strangely enough, even before it was discovered by science – the symbol of greed, the symbol of the Devil, the symbol of all that has to be avoided. And white became a symbol, around the world, representing renunciation because it rejects all the rays. It has also become the symbol of compassion because it is no longer greed but only sharing. It does not take anything in, but only gives you back everything. White also became the symbol of innocence.

Poets became aware of it perhaps centuries ahead of the scientific research. It has been happening all the time, although no one gives the credit to the poets because they were thought crazy by their own contemporaries. They could not produce any scientific argument for what they were saying. But centuries afterward, science was amazed that without using any instruments, without any scientific facilities, how did these people come to certain conclusions? It is very mystifying.

I have told you about Van Gogh…

He always painted his stars as spirals. No other painter in the world has made stars as spirals; naturally even the painters, his own colleagues, said to him, "You are not aware of the fact that stars are not spirals."

But Van Gogh said, "What can I do? My innermost intuition is that they are, and I believe more in my intuition than in my physical eyes." Just recently, a hundred years after Van Gogh, it has been found by science that he was right and everyone else was wrong. Stars only appear not to be spirals because of the distance. And the distance is vast. But now with more accurate instruments, they can see that the stars *are* spirals.

A strange question arises. How did Van Gogh, a man who was not only thought to be crazy but was forced to live in a madhouse…? And his best paintings are those which he painted in the insane asylum. Seeing that he was a harmless fellow, it doesn't matter if he paints things which are not according to the common-sense view of things. It harms no one. You need not agree with him, but to force him to live in a madhouse is going a little too far. He was released from the madhouse – he was only thirty-three – and he committed suicide.

His suicide stands against the stubborn insistence of common humanity that every individual should agree with their conceptions. He wrote a small letter to his brother before committing suicide, saying, "I am not committing suicide out of any depression, I am simply committing suicide because perhaps the society in which I can live as a sane man is yet to come."

Your question makes it clear that in your mind you go on dividing things into categories: this is love, this is fear, this is anger. Just for a change, don't divide. Whatever arises in you is part of your total individuality. The division has come into existence because parts of you have been condemned and parts of you have been appraised. Naturally, the condemned parts should be repressed – at least should not be allowed to surface – and only the appreciated, the valued, the respectable parts of your being should become your personality. This has created such a split in you that with this split you can neither love nor can you sing nor dance. For all that celebration, your whole being is needed.

Let me tell you the truth, with absolute frankness because it has not been told to you even by courageous people like Gautam Buddha or Jesus Christ, or even Socrates, Pythagoras, Chuang Tzu. They all went a little beyond the crowd, but not far away. They always remained on the boundary line – any moment they could slip back into the crowd.

The most difficult problem is not that your fear is against your love; your fear is simply an indication that love is going to absorb you and your ego starts trembling. What you are calling fear is not the authentic fear but just a phony American fear. The ego is afraid that you will fall into an unknown space again. Naturally, the mind asks, "Are you aware that you are moving into the unknown? Is it possible for you to find the way back to your own identity?"

Love dissolves identity. In love, I am not and you are not; only love is. Love does not happen between two people. What happens between two people is only fight, in different names. It may be in the name of love, it may be in the name of something beautiful, but as long as two people cling to their identities, to their personalities which they have cultivated their whole lives… Naturally, there is a great investment. Love comes like a wild breeze and takes away all your cultivated identity. You are left just a pure silence, a serenity. You cannot even say that "I am." Even that will be a disturbance. There is tremendous isness, but there is no identity left.

I will read your question, "As you glide into Buddha Hall, slowly turning toward where I sit, waiting for your gaze to touch me, a strange overwhelming fear grips me." On the one hand, your innermost core is waiting for the taste of not being, for the immense joy of merging, melting, dissolving into the whole. But your personality is there, which immediately creates a fear, an unknown fear. You have to understand that this fear is natural because you have not been left innocent and natural by your society and culture. They have substituted a personality around you. Your whole religion, your whole education, your whole upbringing is involved in a single effort – to create a personality around you. That personality starts trembling and becoming afraid.

It is this personality which is destroying people's love. Everyone says he loves – husbands say they love their wives, wives say the same thing. Parents say they love their children and force their children also to say that they love their parents. Teachers say they love their students. If this were true in every nook and corner of your world, that everyone is loved in so many ways by so many people, this world would have been a totally different world. It would not have been a world always preparing for war, it would not have been a world divided into nations.

To divide the earth into nations is to take away freedom of movement. We ordinarily think we are free, but this idea of being free is created because the jail is so big. Your whole nation is your imprisonment. Just try to get out of the boundaries and suddenly you will realize the freedom was fake. You have been deceived. Even birds are more free because they don't have to carry their passports; more free because they can go thousands of miles, the whole sky is theirs. But unfortunately the whole earth is not ours. The structure, the way a personality is created, needs all these discriminations.

The American has his own pride, the Indian has his own pride. The Indian does not think that anyone else in the world is spiritual; only they have the monopoly on being spiritual. And as far as I know, I have rarely come across an Indian who can be said to be spiritual. They are the most materialistic people in the world. But the personality not only deceives others, it finally deceives you too.

The Americans think they are the richest people in the world. But I created a simple joke with ninety-three Rolls Royces and all their pride was gone. Even the president became jealous, the governors became jealous, the bishops became jealous. Every Sunday the bishop of Wasco County may have forgotten Jesus Christ completely, but he could not forget ninety-three Rolls Royces. He would bring up some way to condemn them. And you will be surprised that when I was bailed out of jail, he wrote a letter to me. He asked, "Now you will be going back to your own land, what about donating at least one Rolls Royce to my church? It will be a great act of charity."

Now, you can see the mind... I was teaching meditation to thousands of people; America was not interested in it. Thousands of people were coming to the commune; America was not interested in it. Each festival, there were twenty thousand people coming from all over the world; America was not interested in it. The whole of the news media were continuously talking about ninety-three Rolls Royces.

I used to think that perhaps in a poor country this could be accepted, but I destroyed the pride of America! I don't need ninety-three Rolls Royces. It was a practical joke, and not even a single so-called intellectual of America could realize the fact that I cannot use ninety-three Rolls Royces simultaneously. And all were of the same model, the latest model; there was no difference between one car and another. Even the president of the Rolls Royce company came to visit because this was the first time that in a single individual's garage there were ninety-three Rolls Royces. But I never went to that garage.

The director of the garage, Avesh, is here. I was telling him, "Soon I will be coming." He wanted me to see... He had made such a beautiful garage, and even the president of Rolls Royce appreciated it and said, "Your cars look in far better condition than our newest cars in our garages." Naturally, Avesh wanted me to come someday. And the garage was not far away, it was in the campus of my own house. I used to pass by the garage every day, but I never went in.

People have been cultivating all kinds of discriminations. The white man thinks he has something more special than the black man, that he carries the burden of the whole earth. But the black man does not agree about it. He has his own ideas.

When Marco Polo went to China on his world travels, he noted in his diary, "I have always suspected that there is some truth in Darwin's theory that man is born out of the monkeys. Seeing the Chinese, I am convinced." But you should also remember, when the Chinese emperor gave an audience to Marco Polo, he could not believe that he was a human being. In his biography, it is stated that he thought that there must be subspecies of human beings around the world; of course the Chinese is the highest expression – the same kind of stupidity.

All religions give you the idea that you have the truest religion in the world. But the basic mechanism you are not aware of is that all these things are created to nourish your ego and replace you from your center, which is your authenticity, to a false center which is just an artifact created by all kinds of methods.

Love is a danger to the personality. The personality starts trembling. But the difficulty is that your innermost being is waiting for it. It is imprisoned and it is waiting for a fresh fragrant breeze from the outside. Perhaps it may bring a few songs of the birds, a few rays of the sun. So you are in a duality: the personality is afraid but your reality is absolutely inviting, waiting, watching for the moment when it happens. You have to be very decisive to renounce your personality completely. It is your falseness. Being a Hindu, a Mohammedan, a Christian – drop all that nonsense. Just be a pure consciousness. That is your nature. And then there will not be any conflict.

You are saying, "I say to myself, Darshan, after all these years of being with him, why this fear?" You can be with me for lives – that is not going to change the fear. But a single instant of understanding, just like a flash of lightning, that you are carrying a load of false ideas about yourself, and the transformation will come.

It is a complex thing. Sometimes it happens to people who are very new. And sometimes it becomes more difficult the more you are with me because the more you start taking me for granted, it becomes an everyday experience. You know that the fear will come, the love will come, and it has become a routine. You will have to get out of this trap. And when I say you have to get out of this trap, I don't mean you have to make any effort. Because what has to be dropped is false; it has no roots in you. You can do it in a single moment of awareness.

I am giving you these moments of silence for a single purpose. I don't have a teaching, I have only strategies for transformation. I speak to you not to convey anything in particular, I speak to you so that I can give you a few gaps of silence. Listening to me, there are two possible ways: the way of the scholar, he will listen to my words; the way of the seeker, who will listen to my silences. My silences are my communion with you.

My words are only to divide small pieces of silences for you. One word is being used only so that before I utter another word, you can feel a silence sweeping over you. No one has used language in this way. Language is just creating possibilities for silence. Alone, your chattering mind does not allow you to be silent. But with me, I am chattering and you are freed at least for a few moments because in those moments you are waiting for what I am going to say. Naturally, waiting gives you an experience of silence.

As you become more and more aware of the false in you and the real in you, there is no need to make any effort to drop the false. Just being aware that "This is false," the false disappears. But there are stupidities which go on and on. Just the other day, Anando brought me a news clipping. Perhaps England is the most ghost-haunted country in the world. It is easy to conceive that in a primitive society, a house is haunted by ghosts. But in England, a ship was found to be haunted, and the ghost was creating continuous trouble. Something was going wrong again and again in the ship, and the people who worked on the ship finally became afraid because it was not natural. They abandoned the ship; they said their lives were in danger.

The vicar was called to investigate whether the ship was haunted. Do you think it is the twentieth century? The vicar came and he found that it was haunted, but the ghost was not of a man but of a fish. And there was no need to be worried – he did some ritual with the crucifix and baptized that ship into Christianity.

The most amazing part is that since then, nothing wrong has been happening. The ship is going perfectly well. Naturally, anyone will conclude logically that whatever the vicar did has helped because the ghost has left the ship. The reality is that the idea of the ghost was disturbing people. But because they were all believers in Christianity and Jesus Christ, when they saw that the vicar had done the whole ritual and now their ship was protected by Christianity, by Jesus Christ himself, immediately there was no fear. Religion has existed in the world because of false things.

Religion is almost like homeopathy. If you are a hypochondriac – finding this sickness, that sickness – then allopathy cannot help you. On the contrary, it may disturb you because if the disease itself is false, you don't need a real medicine for it. The real medicine will create its own effects in your body which are going to be disturbing. If there were a real disease, it would have destroyed the disease. It is because of false sicknesses that things like naturopathy, homeopathy, continue to exist.

In a recent survey it was found that seventy percent of sicknesses are just fictions of the mind. So all these homeopathic sugar pills, if you believe in homeopathy… The question is belief. Homeopathy cannot help me, but homeopathy can help you if you believe in it. Then that false pill, which has no effect, will cure you. Your personality is a false disease. It does not need actual methods to destroy it; all that it needs is the awareness that it is false. It is enough – to know the false is to finish the false. And the moment the false is gone, the real asserts itself without any effort on your part.

So when I say to you, "You are enlightened," I simply mean that you are believing you are *not* enlightened and that is creating the trouble. That is giving you a false idea of an unenlightened sinner, an ordinary person. And all the religions have been exploiting you on that point. If you drop the idea of unenlightenment and you simply accept your natural being – relish it, sing it, dance it – you will be surprised that this is what you have been seeking all your life. And it was prevented because of your seeking.

Jesus says, "Seek and the doors shall be opened for you." I say to you, "The doors are always open. There is no need to seek, simply enter." Jesus says, "Ask and the answer will be given to you." And I say to you, "You *are* the answer. Don't ask; otherwise you will get thousands of answers and you will forget the answer that you are."

Jesus says, "Seek and ye shall find it." And I say to you, "Seek and you will never find it. Why start with seeking? Why not start with finding? Find it and there is no need to seek!" But all the religions, all the priests... And the greatest exploitation and slavery of man has existed with the small idea that you have to seek, that you have to go somewhere else, that you have to be someone else. They have distracted every human being from his natural self.

Insist, because unless you insist, the crowd is going to push you here and there. Insist that you are what you are, and you are absolutely happy to enjoy yourself. You are not going to waste time in seeking, searching, and reaching your grave. I want to make your *this very moment* the explosion.

Darshan, you are saying, "Then as your eyes caress me, the fear melts immediately. I melt and something lovely starts dancing within me." If you have been experiencing it, then why not drop that fear? Because you know already that it melts and you enjoy that melting. Then why go on nourishing the fear again and again? Then it becomes a vicious circle. Jump out of the circle. Tomorrow when I come in, start enjoying even before I have entered the hall. Why should you wait for me? And why create unnecessary diseases, fear – fear of what? What have you got to lose?

There is a Sufi story about Mulla Nasruddin...

He is traveling in a train and the ticket checker comes, and he looks in all his pockets – except the pocket in his coat on the left side. He opens all his luggage, looks in every suitcase, perspiring because the ticket is lost. And it is an obvious fact – all the other passengers are waiting... The ticket checker says, "You have looked everywhere. Why are you not looking in your left coat pocket? Because I see that is the only place you have not looked."

Mulla said, "Don't mention it."

The ticket checker said, "What do you mean?"

He said, "That is my only hope, that perhaps the ticket may be there. I cannot look in it."

You are searching, you are seeking, you are opening all kinds of luggage. Why don't you look into yourself? That is the only hope. You don't want to destroy even that hope. And I say to you that it is not just a hope, it is a reality. The ticket is there.

Now a few moments for prayer…

An Englishman, an American and a Polack go together to Africa on safari. On the first day, they decide to hunt alone and go off in different directions. That night they meet again back at the camp and exchange hunting stories.

"I had a great day," says the Englishman. "I shot a lion, two elephants and a hippo."

"That's nothing," says the American. "I shot two lions, three rhinos and a giraffe."

"I did better than both of you," says the Polack. "I shot seventy-five no-nos."

The two other men look at each other and then ask the Polack what a no-no looks like.

"Well," says the Polack, "they walk on two legs, have black skin and curly hair and when you point a gun at them, they shout, "No, no! No, no!"

Hamish and Maggie MacTavish are queuing for a movie called *The Miracle*. The girl selling the tickets tells Hamish that there are no cheap seats left, only a few of the ones costing six dollars each. Hamish hesitates and consults with Maggie and at length produces two five-dollar bills and a handful of loose change. Hymie Goldberg steps out from the queue and says to Becky, "We can go home now, I have just seen the miracle!"

One night, after their owner is asleep, the parts of the body are arguing about which has the toughest job. "I've really got it rough," moan the feet. "He puts me in these smelly sneakers, makes me jog until I have blisters – it's awful!"

"You've got no reason to complain," says the stomach. "Just last night, I got nothing but beer, spaghetti, and aspirin. It's a miracle I kept it together."

"Ah, quit bitching, you two," moans the prick. "Every night, he sticks me up a dark tunnel and makes me do push-ups until I throw up!"

19

Simply Singing My Own Song

Osho,

There is nothing I need to know – I just love the sound of your voice. Please comment.

Deva Pagalo, it is not a coincidence that I have given you a name which means "the madman." It is a very rare and unique situation to be meditative and to be mad. There have been millions of mad people but their madness is a sickness; their madness means they have fallen below the mind and they have to be brought back at least to the normal state of mind. That's the whole profession of the psychoanalysts, the psychiatrists, the therapists.

But there have also been very few mad people who have not fallen below the mind but who have gone beyond the mind. As far as the mind is concerned, both are out of the mind. Both are mad, but the man who has gone beyond the mind has come to a state which is the ultimate blessing in this existence.

When I gave you the name Deva Pagalo, I had seen the possibility in your eyes that you can be one day a madman of the highest quality, a divine madman. It is not sickness, it is the ultimate in health. What you are saying actually needs to be understood by everyone. You are saying, "There is nothing I need to know…"

Certainly, there is nothing that one needs to know. In a deeper sense, there is no one who can have the need to know. You are an utter emptiness, silence, serenity.

This silence is not ignorance; hence the need for knowledge is not there at all. Knowledge is needed by ignorant people – this is so simple – and the more ignorant they are, the more knowledge they need. It creates a vicious circle. The more knowledgeable they become, the more they become aware of their ignorance. As they advance in knowledge they become aware of a tremendous space which has not been traveled yet, and a vast possibility of knowing more. It is unlimited, and they will never come to a point where they can say, "Now I have known all."

These are the scholars, the pundits, the rabbis. These people have dominated humanity simply because they have more information than you have. They have made a tremendous treasure of their information. For centuries, they have been defending the citadel of knowledge and not allowing everyone to enter their realm.

For example in this country, for ten thousand years the brahmins have not allowed one fourth of the population of the country to read or to learn to write. It was the greatest crime for these simple, innocent people even to hear a few words of the Hindu Vedas, which are the Hindu *Encyclopedia Britannica*. It hurts and it makes me utterly sad to say to you that even a man like Rama, who is being worshipped by the Hindus as an incarnation of God, punished a poor young sudra because the brahmins reported that while they were reading the Vedas he was hiding behind the trees trying to listen.

In the first place, even if he was trying to listen he could not have understood because brahmins never allowed their language, Sanskrit, to become the language of the people. It has remained a language monopolized by the brahmins, by the learned, by the scholars. Even though he could not understand, Rama punished that young man by pouring melted, burning hot lead into both his ears. The young man was killed. And no one has even objected against Rama, that even this single act is enough to prove that he is a murderer – the murderer of a man who has not committed any crime. But instead of being condemned as a murderer, he is worshipped as God – of course by the brahmins. And when the brahmins worship him as God, everyone else follows. This is the case not only in this country; in every country of the world, all kinds of information has been monopolized.

Lord Acton was right when he said later on that power is the reason why people have tried to monopolize knowledge. Because knowledge *is* power. Perhaps it was not such a great power in the past, but today science has become the greatest power. And the word *science* simply means knowledge. Only a man of silence, innocence, has no need for knowledge. He is not sick; hence he does not need any medicine to cure him.

To go beyond the mind is to go beyond all pathology that the mind creates. To be in the mind, you can be either normally mad or abnormally mad. If you are abnormally mad, you will be in the minority. The normally mad, who are the majority, will bring you back into their fold. It is strange to say, but it has to be said that all the branches of psychology are in the service of the normally mad. Their function is only to bring the abnormally mad back into the normal fold. But there is a totally different kind of madness which is not of the mind; hence no psychiatry, no psychoanalysis is needed – neither can it disturb it. Meditation takes you beyond your mind into a deep innocence which has no need to know, and which is absolutely blissful as it is.

Your saying, "There is nothing I need to know…" makes me immensely happy. Don't fall from this state. The mind will try to pull you back by creating new questions, new queries – persuading you, seducing you to explore new areas. Be very alert. And be on guard because there is no treasure which is more valuable than innocence. That needs no knowledge. In other words, this is your second childhood. You are born again. Your eyes are no longer filled with the dust of knowing. But this not-knowing is a tremendous perceptivity, a great clarity. It does not need to know because it feels, and feeling is a higher state than knowing. As the clarity becomes more and more transparent, instead of feeling, it becomes your being.

The moment your very being is nothing but a simple, silent clarity, perceptivity, you don't need even to feel. Let me say that the man who knows is a scholar; the man who feels is a poet, a painter, a dancer. But the man who simply is, is a mystic. He has entered the mystery of existence – not as separate from it, but as a dewdrop slips from the lotus leaf into the ocean; he has also slipped into the oceanic that surrounds you. Now, in a sense you are no more, and in another sense you are the whole ocean. There is no knower and there is no question to know.

Your second statement is also important to be understood. You are saying, "...I just love the sound of your voice." I really want you not to take my words the way they are being ordinarily taken and understood – as meaningful, as imparting some information to you. I am not teaching you anything. I don't have any message. I am not converting you. I am simply singing my own song. The meaning is not in the words, the meaning is in the silences between the words.

So many times people have wondered how I can go on speaking for four hours a day. And I have stopped reading for fifteen years. I don't know what my next sentence is going to be and I don't know why I am going to say it. I am not speaking out of knowledge; I can go on speaking for eternity. Knowledge is very small.

The man of knowledge is really repeating something which he has accumulated in his memory. He is behaving like a computer. I am speaking because I simply enjoy to see the moments of silence when you are waiting and I don't know what I am going to say. It is a miracle that somehow sentences make themselves, somehow the whole appears to have some interconnection, but I am not making any effort.

Even if people find contradictions, it is perfectly good because only a very ordinary knowledgeable person is concerned about consistency. A man who is speaking, using speech as a means to convey not meaning but poetry, not meaning but some significance, not meaning but some fragrance, not message but presence... I have nothing to say to you, but I have much to share with you. Speaking to you is just an arbitrary method to be with you and to allow my heart and your hearts to dance in the same rhythm, in the same wavelength. The moment your heart starts dancing in the same rhythm, I have reached you. Without converting you, I have transformed you; without even touching you, I have brought a new light and a new joy to your being. I have sown the seeds which, in the right time, are going to blossom into beautiful madness.

If I can create as many people as possible who can dance madly, laugh madly, sing madly, who can make every moment of their life just a celebration, then I have introduced you to the authentic religion for which man has been searching for centuries, but has not been able to find. I have found it and I want you also to be partners in this immense finding: religion without words, religion without creeds, religion without fictions of God, heaven and hell. A religion without sins and virtues, a religion with no condemnation, no appreciation. A simple religion that transforms each moment into a glory, into a gratitude, into a prayer.

I have not said anything to you, although I have been speaking for thirty-five years continuously. And as long as I live – or even a few minutes afterward – I am going to speak. If I see a moment when there is still an opportunity for someone to be involved in the universal madness, I can even speak after my death, it doesn't matter. Death can wait a few moments. I have been keeping it waiting for thirty-five years, so there is no problem. Just a few minutes more. As far as I understand, thirty-five years is such a long time that death itself may have forgotten. It has to take care of so many people, it will take too much time for death itself to discover a file that has been hidden for thirty-five years.

One thing is certain, whether I live or I die, my every gesture, my every word has a single purpose: to help you get rid of knowledge, to help you to become again a small child with eyes of wonder and a heart which cannot believe. Wildflowers, clouds in the sky, the sun rising and all the colors that the rising sun spreads over the horizon… This amazement is the authentic religious element, and if you can keep this amazement fresh without being covered by any experience and dust, you have attained that which was your birthright – what I have called enlightenment.

At his annual checkup, Solomon Finkelstein is given a clean bill of health. "It must run in your family," comments the doctor. "How old was your dad when he died?"

"What makes you think that he is dead?" asks Sollie. "He is ninety and going strong."

"Aha, and how long did your grandfather, old man Finkelstein, live?"

"What makes you think that he is dead, Doc?" replies Sollie. "He is a hundred and ten years old and getting married to a twenty-two-year-old next week."

"At his age?" exclaims the doctor. "Why does he want to get married to a twenty-two-year-old?"

"Doc," says Sollie, "what makes you think he wants to? He *has* to!"

Grandma Schieferstein is a feisty old bird. So when she gets admitted to the old people's home, she is constantly in trouble. One morning, just for a laugh, she comes downstairs stark naked and letting out a wild shriek, runs through the entire length of the dayroom before disappearing into the garden.

Old man Finkelstein and old man Kravitz are watching TV at the time. And Fink turns to Kravitz and says, "Who was that Mendel, making all that noise?"

"I don't know," replies Kravitz, "but whoever it was, her clothes need ironing."

And the last…

One day Herman Horowitz goes into a pet shop and says, "I want a parrot. I don't care what it looks like, as long as it talks."

"Okay, Sir," says the assistant. "I have got just the bird for you. That blue and green one talks very well."

Herman likes it, but the assistant warns him that it does not have any feet. "No feet?" cries Herman. "Then how does he stay on his perch?"

"Simple," says the man. "You may have noticed, he is a male bird. He just wraps his prick around the perch and stays up that way."

So Herman takes the parrot home and has a very long talk with him. The next evening, when Herman gets home from work, the parrot says, "Thank God you are back, I have got something to tell you."

"What is it?" asks Herman.

"Well," begins the parrot, "when you went to work, a man came to the door and your wife let him in and they sat on the sofa together."

"What happened next?" cries Herman.

"And then he opened her blouse and sucked her tits," says the parrot.

"And then what?" cries Herman.

"I don't know," says the parrot, "I got an erection and fell off my perch."

20

Love Has No Limits

Osho,

Can you please talk about the art of nourishing oneself with love? I feel so much love for you. Is this enough?

Love is never enough. There are mysteries in existence which don't have any limitation. Love is the closest experience to understanding all those mysteries because as far as the mind is concerned, it imposes limits; it cannot accept anything that is unlimited. Just think of the whole universe. The mind can conceive of it as very vast, perhaps the boundaries of it are not available to us, but the mind finds it intrinsically impossible to conceive that there may be no boundaries at all, anywhere. The universe has no boundaries; life has no boundaries.

Love is our closest experience of this unbounded, unlimited pure space, extending and extending and you never come to the point where it is written, "This is the end." And because of this intrinsic incapacity of the mind, it always inquires, "Is it enough?" It wants it to be enough so that it can create a boundary around it. Anything that can be limited by the mind becomes an object. Love is not an object. You cannot put it on the scientist's table to dissect it, to find out what basic elements it is made of.

Because the scientist cannot make love objective, there are only two possibilities for him. If he is authentic and sincere, he will say, "I do not know love." Because his way of knowing is only objective and love cannot be reduced to an object. But if he is not a sincere scientific mind but a fanatic, rather than accepting his own ignorance he will deny the existence of love itself. He will say it is all imagination, it is all emotion, it is all sentimentality; it is not even worth considering.

There is not even a single treatise on love written by any scientist. But that is his general attitude about love, life, consciousness – anything that he cannot hold in his hand, he simply denies its very existence. You cannot ask a scientist, "Does beauty exist? Is there something like blissfulness? Is there a possibility of an inner ecstasy?" His answer is going to be consistently "No." Basically, he denies the inner world of man. And the most hilarious part is that scientists fall in love, scientists feel hurt if insulted. If there is no one inside, what does it matter whether someone insults you, abuses you? And if love is not existential, then no scientist should dare to fall in love. But the scientist is not just a one-dimensional being; science is not his whole life, and cannot be.

Life contains many dimensions. The most important is the fact of the interiority of man. And the interiority of man is as infinite as the exterior universe. Love is part of the interiority of man; it has no limits. But there are misunderstandings which have to be clarified. Your question is, "Can you talk about the art of nourishing oneself with love?" There is no art because there is no need of any effort. Love *is* the nourishment. But humanity has been so confused by its leaders that one does not know the most inner realms of one's own being. Love is nourishment in itself. The more you love, the more you will find untrodden spaces where love goes on and on spreading around you like an aura.

But that kind of love has not been allowed by any culture. They have forced love into a very small tunnel. You can love your wife, your wife can love you; you can love your children, you can love your parents, you can love your friends. And they have made two things so deeply rooted in every human being. One is that love is something very limited – friends, family, children, husband, wife. And the second thing they have insisted is that there are many kinds of love. You love in one way when you love your husband or your wife. Then you have to bring another kind of love when you love your children, and another kind of love when you love your elders, your family, your teachers, and then another kind of love for your friends.

The truth is that love cannot be categorized the way it has been categorized throughout the whole history of mankind. There were reasons for them to categorize it, but their reasons are ugly and inhuman because in this categorization they killed love. Either you can have a loving heart… It has nothing to do with who you are loving. The emphasis of existence is that you are loving. It has not to be directed toward a certain person because that is accepting that, if someone is not part of the direction in which you are forcing your love to move, you become indifferent to them; you become even unloving to them. There are possibilities that you may even become hateful to them.

The reason why all the cultures have insisted on categorization is because they have been very afraid of love, and if there is existential love, it does not know boundaries – then you cannot put Hindus against Mohammedans, you cannot put Protestants against Catholics. You cannot draw a line saying that you cannot love this person because he is Jewish, Chinese. The leaders of the world wanted to divide the world, but to divide the world they have to do the basic division which is of love. Love is only for *our* people.

And it has to be insisted so deeply in your unconscious that in wars, in riots, when you kill other people who don't belong to your clan or to your country or your tribe, you don't feel anything. It is simply the way things are. A German killing an Italian will not think, "I don't have any personal enmity with him, and just as my wife will be waiting for me, my old mother may be praying for me, my children will be hoping that soon I will be back home, the person I am killing is in the same situation. He also has a wife, he also has old parents, he also has children, and they are waiting for him to come back. I don't have any reason to kill him; neither has he any reason to kill me, except that some idiotic politicians are not satisfied with the power they have. They want more power. They want to be world conquerors."

Because of this lust for power, love has been completely destroyed. They cannot exist together. I want it to be absolutely clear to you that the lust for power and the beauty of love cannot exist together. Religions would like you only to love people of your own religion – others are foreigners. Countries would like you to love only the people who live in that country. And you can see, there are divisions upon divisions.

India became independent in 1947. I was very young, but I had kept my eyes clear and uncontaminated by the older generation. From my very childhood I have insisted on having my own insight, my own intelligence, and I don't want to borrow any knowledge from anyone. My whole family was involved in the struggle for the freedom of the country. Everyone had been in jail. Although I was never in jail because of the liberation movement, I suffered as much as one can suffer because all the earning males were forced into jail and the family was left without any source of income.

I asked my father, "Are you aware that once you are liberated from the British Empire… And it is going to happen because now Britain is burdened. They have exploited the land to the maximum; now the situation has reversed – they have to help the country to survive. It is better for them to escape from here and get rid of a burden which has become absolutely unnecessary." They were not here to serve the people, they were here to exploit. And that's exactly what happened. The revolution happened in 1942 without any effect. It was quashed completely within nine days, and with those nine days all hope of freedom disappeared. But suddenly in 1947, out of the blue, Britain decided to make the country free.

I said to my father, "Don't think that your freedom movement has succeeded. Between the freedom movement and the actual coming of freedom there is a five-year gap. This is not logical. You are being given freedom because now you have become a burden and a trouble – just your existence." And I have come to know that researchers, looking into the whole history of the British Parliament and their decisions, found out that the British Prime Minister Attlee sent Mountbatten with the message, "Do it as quickly as possible." He had given him a set time, that "By 1948 we should get rid of this burden." Mountbatten proved even more efficient. He managed it one year earlier. But I said to my father, "You have been fighting, not knowing that once this country is free it will start having new fights, within itself."

Now the Mohammedans have taken Pakistan – it was part and parcel of the freedom because the Mohammedans refused to live with the Hindus. They had lived together for almost fourteen hundred years and there was no problem. In my childhood I have participated in Mohammedan celebrations; Mohammedans were participating in Hindu marriages, Hindu celebrations. There was no question of fighting because everyone was fighting the British empire. Once the British Empire was leaving, suddenly the Mohammedans and Hindus became alert – a new division. They declared that they could not live together because their religions are different. Mohammedans became adamant: "Either the British Empire remains… We can risk freedom, but we cannot live with Hindus in an independent country because they are in the majority. They will rule, and Mohammedans don't have any chance of ruling."

The situation became so ugly that there were only two alternatives. Either accept the slavery – which the British Empire was not ready to continue – or accept the division. The division was accepted; the country was divided into two parts. The Mohammedan part became Pakistan. But they were not aware, and neither were the Indians aware, that the Mohammedans got two parts – one part in the east, Punjab and Sindh, where they were in the majority, and another part far away, thousands of miles away in Bengal. Half of Bengal was Mohammedan.

So Pakistan became a strange country. Immediately, both parts were Mohammedan, but Bengalis saw that they were being dominated by the Punjabi Mohammedans. The shift away from the division of religions was immediate; now it became a question of language. Bengali Mohammedans speak Bengali; the Punjabi speaks Punjabi. Now they forgot completely that they were together in the fight to gain Pakistan. Finally, the Bengalis separated from Pakistan and created a new country, Bangladesh. The distance was so great that it was impossible for Pakistan to keep control over it. But the same situation goes on happening every day.

Forty years ago the constitution decided that Hindi should be the national language. But it has not been implemented because in India there are thirty languages. Taken as a whole the Hindi-speaking people are the majority, but if those twenty-nine languages are against it, then *they* are in the majority. Each single language is not capable of fighting against Hindi, but those twenty-nine languages together are a tremendous force. Now, you cannot believe it – they are all Hindus, and they have been killing other Hindus because they speak different languages! It is not a question that you can give all these thirty languages the status of a national language. Then suddenly you will find… For example Hindi is spoken in one way in one state, a slightly different way in another state. And there are five states – soon they will be fighting, "Our Hindi is the *right* Hindi and the others are only distortions."

Man has been trained to cut humanity into so many pieces on any excuse: religion, country, language, color. But the basic root is in teaching human beings that love is a limited phenomenon, and secondly, that love has varieties. I am trying to say to you that love has no varieties. It may have different expressions – certainly the love between husband and wife will have a different expression than the love between the couple and their children. It will have a different expression, but the expression does not change the quality. It is the same love.

And its center is not the other – that's what we have been told, that the center of love is the other: you love someone. The emphasis has to be completely changed. It is not a question of loving someone, it is a question of being a loving human being. Love should not have an address; it should be simply a radiation of your being. Whoever comes in contact with you will find the immensely nourishing energy of love.

You are saying, "I feel so much love for you." I would like you to feel the same love for the whole existence – for the trees, the birds, the oceans, the stars. Your love should not be confined. You can love me as much as you want, but that does not mean that I should become the only object of your love. Then it is not nourishing. On the contrary, it starts becoming a poisoning force.

Love is a nourishing force if it spreads all around just the way the sun rises, and it showers its light, its rays, to all the trees without any discrimination. Not thinking that "This is just a poor marigold, just a little bit less will do. This is a beautiful rose, a little more. This is a lotus, shower as much as you can." No, the sunlight showers over the whole planet without any discrimination. Your love should become subjective, not objective. It should become a radiation from the center of your being in all directions. Then it is nourishing and then it has a certain quality which can only be called divine.

Our so-called love only creates jealousy, only creates conflict, only creates two people living in intimate enmity, judging, looking, watching. Just look on the street and you can decide without asking anyone whether the couples who are walking together are husband and wife, or just boyfriend and girlfriend. I have never seen a husband and wife smiling together. What kind of love is this? Yes, they are both detecting each other. The husband cannot look around if a beautiful woman passes by. Just looking at that beautiful woman can create so much harassment that it is not worth it. What kind of society have you created? Is it human? It is absolutely human that if a beautiful woman passes by, the husband should tell his wife, "Look, a beautiful woman!" Beauty should not be made a question of jealousy or comparison. You can say that the roseflower is beautiful and your husband or your wife will not object to it because you can't have any relationship with it.

Just the other day I was listening to a song of one of the most beautiful singers of India. The meaning of the song is, "I was just passing by here and I thought just to say hello to you, although I know if my wife comes to know about it, this hello is going to be very dangerous. Because her insistence is, 'You should not look at anyone else except me. Your whole love is monopolized by me.'" And the singer Jagjit Singh says, "That is her insistence. But my hobby is that wherever there is beauty, I should at least be respectful to it." We have created an idea of love as a possession. And all kinds of possessions ultimately turn into poisons. One should live a life nonpossessive, available, open, respectful. There is so much beauty around you and so many different ways the beauty is expressing itself; to confine you is to destroy you.

And remember, anyone who confines you, you are not going to be loving to that person. Husbands don't love their wives, wives don't love their husbands. How can a wife love a husband who has confined her infinite capacity of radiating love, who has forced her: he is the only one that all her love should be directed to? This is insulting and this is against nature, against existence.

But religions have been doing everything to destroy the individuality of man. It seems to be that without destroying man, they cannot exist. Either man can exist in his dignity or your so-called churches and popes and priests can exist, with great power.

Just the other day...

I could not believe it, but I have to believe because it is a fact. Anando brought me the news that the Catholic church has decided that there will not be any other kind of music in the churches other than that which is absolutely devoted to the church. Even at weddings – and it has been going on for centuries; it is not something new. Even the classical music and the geniuses of the past are no longer allowed in the church. In a church wedding the music should be only what is approved by the church, and its function should be religious – no other music.

Why are these people afraid of people becoming light, rejoicing, enjoying? They have a certain investment in your misery. The more miserable you are, the better, because only miserable people go to church. Only the miserable people are in the bondage of the past. Only the miserable people are under the domination of the dead. A man who is alive can be alive only if he is allowed total expression of his individuality.

Who are these people to decide? On what authority do these people go on deciding things for millions of people? A very strange strategy has been used. First they invented God, then they invented his son Jesus Christ, and now they have imposed themselves as his representatives. Only they have the direct line to God.

A few months ago the Catholic church has prohibited that no one should confess to God directly. He has to confess to the priest; everything through the right channel. Then the priest will inform Jesus Christ, then Jesus Christ will persuade God the Father, "Let this poor man be freed from his sin." But you cannot confess to God directly. And not a single Catholic in the whole world revolted against the idea. At least man should be given the freedom to be in direct relationship with existence.

But the business point is clear: unless you confess to the priest, the priest cannot punish you. And what is the punishment? Five dollars, ten dollars – and I don't understand how these dollars reach Jesus Christ. And then he gives the bribe to God the Father, "Just forgive this man, he is a good man. Just look, he has sent ten dollars." Those ten dollars disappear in the pocket of the priest. They have nothing to do with Jesus Christ or with God.

I have heard…

A rabbi and a bishop were very friendly. The friendship had arisen because both were golf lovers, and they decided that on the next Sunday they were going to the golf club.

The rabbi waited and waited outside, but it was getting late so he entered the church. The bishop was in the confession booth – it is a small room, partitioned. On one side sits the bishop with a small window; on the other side sits the confessor. The strategy is that the confessor should not be made embarrassed; his face should not be seen, so that he can confess wholeheartedly because unless he confesses wholeheartedly he is not going to be contributing dollars wholeheartedly either.

The rabbi entered the booth and said to the bishop, "We are going to be late."

The bishop said, "I am doing everything as quickly as possible, but there is still a queue."

The rabbi said, "I don't know what this confession is, just let me see what you are doing. And then you can get ready while I function in your place because no one can see from the other side."

The bishop said, "It is very simple; just watch."

One man came and he said, "I have committed a rape."

The bishop said, "Don't be worried. Just contribute ten dollars to the charity box and I will pray for you."

The rabbi said, "It *is* very simple. Now you go and get ready." He sat in the bishop's chair. Another man came and he said, "I have committed two rapes this week."

The rabbi said, "My son, don't be worried. Thirty dollars."

The man said, "Thirty dollars? Has the rate increased? Just in front of me, for one rape you asked ten dollars."

The rabbi said, "Don't be worried. Just put thirty dollars in the box – ten dollars are in advance."

These are the people who have destroyed everything that is beautiful in man. But they are exploiting and they will cling to their exploitation to the very last. Otherwise, there is no reason for all these organized religions to exist.

Each individual should have a direct contact with the universe, its beauty, its tremendous glory – which creates without any effort a gratitude, a prayer, perhaps a song, a dance. If we can remove all these organized religions, organized nations, from the world, and allow each individual his dignity and respect, there will be immense love, immense respect, immense understanding. We can change this ugly world which has been created by the past, into a beautiful garden where everyone can rise to his potential height, can shower his flowers and can release his fragrance. I stand for the individual. All organizations have proved criminal. There is no need of any organization either in the name of politics or in the name of religion or in any other name. And the world will be an ocean of love, an ocean of beauty.

But this needs a tremendous courage to revolt and assert your individuality, whatever the consequences. We have been exploited long enough, sucked, destroyed. And the end result is this miserable world – where once in a while perhaps you can smile, but even that smile does not come from your deepest core; where once in a while you can love, but even that love is surrounded by all kinds of fears. Nothing in you has been left in freedom. The people who have done this greatest crime are the people you worship. That makes it more difficult to take humanity out of their clutches. You have to learn to love yourself first, to respect yourself first. And then certainly it will give you tremendous nourishment and it will start spreading around you.

Osho,
Why does spontaneity create so much fear in me? Having no structure feels like a death. How can I turn this fear into a let-go, a welcome, a rejoicing?

Perhaps you are not aware that you are again asking for another structure. I will read your question so that you can become conscious of what you are asking. "Why does spontaneity create so much fear in me?" – it creates fear in everyone because spontaneity means you are taking the responsibility for your act, whatever it may be. If you rely on the conditioning you have been given by your parents, teachers, professors, priests, leaders, and instead of being spontaneous just act out of your past conditioning, there is no fear. Because you know you are not alone; you know your action is approved.

The fear arises when you find yourself alone and you are doing something which goes against the whole training. You know you are revolting; you are going against your parents, you are going against the whole heritage of humanity. The weight of the past is so big and huge, so Himalayan, and you seem to be such a small individual, afraid of going against it. You may be crushed.

In my childhood I loved having hair as long as possible. My father had a shop and the house together, and I used to go in and out through his shop. He felt very embarrassed because people asked him, "Whose girl is this?" Such long hair in India is allowed only for girls, and naturally he felt embarrassed and angry that I was creating trouble every day. Finally he became so angry that he took his scissors, caught hold of me and cut my hair.

I said, "You can cut my hair but remember, I am not going to leave it at that."

He said, "What do you mean?"

I said, "You will see tomorrow."

And I went just on the other side of the road, where all the hair-cutting salons were. I had a friend, an old opium addict. I loved the man because sometimes he would cut half of someone's mustache and say, "Wait, I have to go somewhere." And he would be gone for hours, and the man would be caught because he could not leave with only half a mustache. Sometimes people would ask him for a shave and he would shave their heads. And by the time they became aware, he had already done some work – now there is no point in preventing him. He was such a nice man; he would say, "There is no need to worry. If you don't like it, don't pay me anything."

I used to sit in his small salon discussing with him because it was a joy. He used to come up with really original ideas. One day he said to me, "If all the opium addicts of India were organized, we can take over the whole country."

I said, "The idea is very good."

He said, "But you will have to help because these opium addicts don't listen to anyone."

I said, "First, I will try to contact all the opium addicts in this town. Let us create a small organization here. If it succeeds in taking over the municipal corporation..."

So I went to him because he was the only man who could have done this. In India a child's head is completely shaved only if his father dies. So I said to him, "I am tired of this long hair. Simply shave my head completely clean."

For a moment he hesitated. He said, "Your father will be very angry, I am telling you!"

I said, "Don't worry. It is my responsibility. And you are the only man of guts; no other barber is going to cut my hair."

So he said, "Okay."

He finished cutting off all my hair and I entered my father's shop. Looking at me, immediately his customers asked, "What happened to this poor boy? Has his father died?"

Now it was even more embarrassing for him to admit, "I am the father."

He came inside the house and said to me, "This is too much."

I said, "I have warned you. Whenever I do anything I do it totally. From now onward if you interfere with me, remember, I can move to the other extreme."

People from the neighborhood started coming to inquire, and when they saw my father they said, "What is the matter? You are alive? And I have seen with my own eyes that your son is completely shaved."

My teachers, my headmaster from my school seeing that my father must have died were very sorry. They said to me, "We are going to your house to express our sadness and our mourning. Your father was a good man." I allowed them to go, and when they saw my father sitting there they were in such a strange situation – what to do? Because it had never happened.

And my father would ask, "Why have you come? There must be some reason."

They said, "There was… But your son is so strange, we were telling him, 'He was a good man' and he did not even tell us that you were still alive."

That was the last time he interfered with me. He knew perfectly well that it was going to be dangerous.

Spontaneity means you are acting in the moment – not reacting, but acting. That is the difference between those two words. When you react it comes from your past accumulation of knowledge, experience. But when you respond, it is a pure act out of your present consciousness – not from memory. These are two different sources within you. Memory is comfortable because everyone will appreciate that you are doing the right thing because they also have the same memory. But if you act on your own, you are taking a risk. It may not fit. Most probably it is not going to fit with the structure which has been created around you. Hence, fear arises.

But I would say to you that it is better to suffer fear rather than remain a slave of those who had no idea in what situations you are going to be. They have given you fixed ideas, answers to questions and they don't know in what form the question is going to arise in your life.

Five thousand years ago, they wrote Rig Veda, and the Hindus are still following the structure. It is no longer relevant. But the situation is the same everywhere. Mohammed allowed Mohammedans to have four wives. It was perfectly right at that moment. In Arabia the proportion was exactly one man and four wives because men were continuously being killed. They were continuously fighting; war was their life. They would rape the woman, but they would not kill her. To kill a woman was not according to their culture. So there were four times more women than men, and naturally it was creating a very difficult situation. If three women remained unmarried, there was going to be great prostitution, corruption of all kinds. To avoid the situation, Mohammed suggested that every man marries four women. It was perfectly right in Saudi Arabia fourteen hundred years ago, but they are doing the same in India even today.

Now India wants fewer people. It is already past the limit; it has never been so crowded in the whole of history. In 1947, when India became independent, the population was four hundred million, and just in forty years the population has gone to nine hundred million. By the end of this century it is going beyond one billion. For the first time India will have a greater population than China. But Mohammedans insist that it is their religion and the government cannot interfere with their religion.

It is difficult because in India the proportion of men and women is almost equal. They go on raping women who are not Mohammedans. And once a woman, whether raped or not, has been kept in a Mohammedan house – Hindus are following another tradition five thousand years old – she has fallen, she is no longer acceptable. Neither her parents will allow her into the house nor her own husband. She has to become a Mohammedan or commit suicide.

And when Mohammedans go on marrying four women, naturally they produce four times more people than Hindus. Soon this country will have more Mohammedans than Hindus. Already, you will be surprised to know, India has the largest Mohammedan population in the whole world. There are Mohammedan countries – Egypt, Iraq, Iran, Afghanistan, Pakistan – but no country has a greater Mohammedan population than India. The reason is simple because in those countries there are only Mohammedans and the proportion between men and women is equal. It is very difficult in a Mohammedan country to find four women. What will happen to the three other men whose wives you have taken? So it is only in India where they have a good pasture around to get more and more women and more and more children.

To respond to the situation that is facing you needs intelligence, not memory; needs awareness, not your past heritage. So even though it creates fear, which is natural, decide to be spontaneous in spite of all the fears. Soon those fears will disappear. It is only a question of acting out of spontaneity more and more, and then you will see your individuality becoming more integrated, more solid, free from all the chains that the past has put around you. The fear will disappear, but it will take a little time. If you listen to the fear you will never be able to gain your dignity as an individual.

Even trees have their individuality. Every animal has his own individuality. It is simply shameful that man has lost his individuality. So in spite of all your fears, take the risk. Be courageous and act according to your own consciousness. And soon you will see that whenever you act spontaneously you *are* right because you are answering the situation directly.

But you are asking, "Having no structure feels like a death." There is no harm. Die! Your life is not much more valuable. Rather than be a prisoner of all the dead, it is better to die spontaneously. At least you will have the dignity to say, "At one point I am at least free from the whole past and all the prisons of religion, nation, race, color."

Then you are asking, "How can I turn this fear into a let-go?" Do you understand? *How* means again filling your memory with a new structure. But no structure can be spontaneous. You cannot know what is going to happen the next moment. You cannot conceive of what tomorrow is going to bring to you. So whatever structure you make, whatever homework you do, is going to be irrelevant to the situation.

I have never done any homework. In my schools, colleges, universities, I made it absolutely clear to all my teachers and professors, "Never ask for any homework from me."

And they said, "But this is so strange, no one has ever said such a thing."

I said, "I don't care whether anyone has said such a thing or not. One thing is certain: you can answer me, you can question me, you can do anything you want – I will be spontaneous, I will not be prepared."

Homework is preparation; you have already prepared everything. In my final post-graduate examinations, the professors who loved me very much were so afraid because I was not preparing anything for the examination. I was still reading whatever I wanted to read in the library. It had no concern with the examination. I was asking questions in the classes and one professor had to say to me, "Now only one month is left, and you should not bring such questions which have no relevance to your examination."

I said, "I am not here to be worried about an examination which is going to happen one month later. My concern is this moment, and this is my question."

One of my professors was so concerned that he gave me one of the questionnaires, telling me, "I have made this so that you can at least be ready for these five questions. They are going to be asked because I am the composer of the paper."

Without reading it, I threw it away and said, "You should not insult me in this way. I want to live life unprepared. Whether I fail or succeed, it doesn't matter."

He used to come to my hostel room just fifteen minutes before the examination was going to commence. Everyone had gone into the examination hall. He would pick me up in his car and tell me, "Unless you enter the examination hall, I cannot feel at ease. I am always afraid you may be sleeping, you may be discussing things which have nothing to do with the examination, or you may be reading things." He used to say to the superintendent of the examination, "Don't let him out before three hours."

I used to answer those questions in one hour or one and a half hours. The superintendent would say, "I am sorry but I have promised your professor that I will not allow you to leave."

I said, "It is up to you. If you don't allow me to go out... Has he told you that I cannot even sleep here?"

He said, "He has not said anything about sleep."

I said, "That's okay. Take this paper; I am finished with it. And for one and a half hours let me rest."

When my professor came to know, he said, "It is impossible to deal with you. I prevented you from going out but you managed to go out! And how can you answer those five questions in three hours? Others find that they have answered only four; someone has answered only three."

I said, "They are prepared people. They have done so much preparation that they want to impress the examiner with how much they are informed. I am absolutely uninformed. Sometimes I simply write one sentence as an answer and sometimes I ask another question because I cannot agree that the question is right. But I am absolutely free. I have no preparation."

One professor had asked the question, "Can you define Indian philosophy?" and I simply answered him, "There is no such thing as Indian philosophy so the question of defining it does not arise. There is *Western* philosophy because the very word *philosophy* means a search for knowledge, a search for wisdom, a love for wisdom." In India we don't have any word which can be translated as philosophy.

The Indian word is *darshan* and its approach is totally different. It means an inquiry to see the truth. Darshan means seeing. It is not a question of thinking. A blind man can think about the light and can be a great philosopher, can propose hypotheses about light. In India there has never existed anything like philosophy. What has existed is seeing. We want to see the light, we don't want to philosophize about it.

Just by coincidence that paper was sent to a very eccentric retired professor, Dr. Ranade of Allahabad. Basically he belonged to Pune. And he gave me ninety-nine percent out of one hundred, with a note to the vice-chancellor saying, "I always wanted someone to answer spontaneously, and I always wanted someone to answer as sharply as possible." He had never given a first class to anyone else in his whole life. With him, even to pass was a difficult job. But he wrote the note and he also wrote, "What I am writing you should show to the student. I loved his answers and I loved the way he made me aware that Western philosophy is one thing and there is no equivalent in India for it."

He has written books on Indian philosophy and he said in his note, "I am too old now to change it, but your point is absolutely right. We don't have anything similar to what has happened in the West."

It is because of this difference that Western philosophy has never come to meditation. It was always contemplation. And the Indian counterpart has never bothered about thinking, contemplation, concentration; its whole concern is meditation. In fact they are two such different directions that a single word cannot describe both.

My professor was amazed. He said, "I was thinking you were going to fail, you were so unprepared."

I said, "Your whole idea is preparation and my whole idea is to be simply spontaneous." I got the gold medal, topped the whole university, shocking everyone. And as I came out of the auditorium I threw that gold medal into the well.

A professor was standing by my side. He asked, "What are you doing?"

I said, "I have nothing to do with gold, and I don't want to be appreciated as topping the whole university. I would love it if someone appreciated that spontaneity has its own beauty, freshness. Whether it fails or succeeds is irrelevant."

You should not ask, "How can I turn this fear into a let-go?" Because whatever I say to you will be your structure again. Just be simple. Whenever you find a situation, act! Put the fear aside and rejoice in the spontaneous response. It is only a question of a few times and you will find the fear has disappeared. Because the spontaneous response gives you such a joy, such an opening of the heart, such freshness – as if you have just taken a shower. But don't ask for any strategy for "how to be spontaneous." Because *how* simply means a structure. Just *be* spontaneous. Don't ask how. Try it. Without knowing, innocently, respond to a situation and out of it you will learn the great experience of let-go. And you will rejoice because you have attained your freedom from all kinds of fears.

In my childhood I had a friend whose father was a magician. They had a very good business – the business was that they had a few snakes. Being continually in their house, slowly I learned that ninety-seven percent of snakes don't have any poison. Only three percent of snakes have poison, and only one percent, the cobra, is very dangerous. Once the cobra bites you it is very difficult to save you. Death is almost certain. But the snakes all look alike.

The father used to have nonpoisonous snakes, and he would send his son – who was my friend, and I accompanied him many times – to someone's house. There we would leave two or three snakes around the place and then the father would come with his special musical instrument that was used for snakes. He would announce, "If anyone has snakes in his house, I can catch them."

As he started playing on his instrument, the snakes that we had left around the house would start coming, and for that service the housekeeper had to pay. He would say, "It is very good of you – once in a while you should come back because we were not aware that there were snakes in our garden."

Knowing that there are snakes which don't have any poison, I would enter my class with a snake in my pocket. I would just leave it on the teacher's table and he would stand on his chair and shout, "Save me!"

The other students were running out, so who is going to save him except me? I would say to him, "I will save you, but remember that I have saved your life. You should not be nasty with me. Promise?" And with that snake sitting on his table, you could have taken any kind of promise.

Finally it was reported to the principal that a strange thing was going on. But a principal is just the same as anyone else. When he called me, I went there with two snakes. I left them on his table and he stood on his chair, and everybody in the whole school was looking through the windows: What is happening? I said, "Now do you have something to say to me?"

He said, "No. Just don't bring these things in my office!"

I said, "I have not come on my own, you have called me. Now I cannot go without your promising me that you will not be nasty to me."

He said, "This is strange, but I promise that I will not be nasty to you."

I said, "That's okay; then I can persuade the snakes."

People have lived with such fear. Fear always seems to be around them – anything can create fear. If the man had been a little spontaneous, he could have seen that if I can manage those snakes, certainly there must be some trick and there is no need to be afraid. But the very word *snake* is enough to trigger all the fears of centuries of humanity that you are carrying within you.

It was reported to my father, "Now your son is becoming more and more dangerous."

My father said, "I have promised him, just as you have promised, not to interfere. Otherwise he will start bringing those snakes in the house!"

What are your fears? What can you lose? The only thing that you can lose is your life. And that does not belong to you, that belongs to the universe. One day you are going to lose it, so what does it matter? In a week there are only seven days. Either you will lose your life on Monday or on Tuesday… So it is only a question of seven days. But I have never thought for a single moment that I have anything to lose. I don't have anything to lose. That has given me a tremendous freedom to act spontaneously, to act without any fear, to say whatever I want to say – to be against all the governments of the world, to be against all the religions of the world. And I don't think that even a shadow of fear arises in my heart.

On the contrary, the more I hit these idiots the more I rejoice because according to me they are criminals. According to me they are the greatest calamities that have happened to humanity. There is nothing to fear from these people. There is nothing to be afraid of in the ghosts who are lying in their graves. But everybody is injected with fear from the very beginning, so that his whole blood becomes full of fear. This fearfulness helps all these criminals to dominate you, to destroy you, not to let you live your life of love and blissfulness.

As far as my sannyasins are concerned, fear should not be at all a part of their being. The fear exists in the darker corners of your being – bring more light. Bring more consciousness, bring more awareness, and the fear will disappear.

A lady health inspector, after checking the sanitary conditions in Boccala's Bakery, summons the proprietor.

"Listen," she complains. "One of the bakers back there is throwing the dough against his bare chest to flatten it out for pizzas!"

"That's-a not-a so bad-a," says Boccala. "You should-a be here yesterday when he make-a the doughnuts!"

The newlywed Greek couple are in a deep embrace. While kissing and caressing her, he whispers, "My love, now I will put it where nobody else ever has!"

In a frightened voice she cries, "No, no! In my ears? Never!"

What is there to fear? There is everything to laugh about and there is nothing to fear. Laughter has to be our sword to cut all these heads who have been torturing humanity for centuries.

21

The Meeting of the East and the West

Osho,
It is so good to be back again. Sitting in your discourse I find myself connecting with my inside to an extent that doesn't happen in the West. What is this alchemy?

Your question can be answered only if you can understand the phenomenon of energy fields. Every place in the world has its own energy field, created by thousands of people who have lived there. The way they have lived, the way they have loved – they are gone, but they have left behind them a throbbing energy that continues to exist for centuries. And if it has been a continuous reinforcement of the energy, the way it has happened in the East… The whole genius of the East has been devoted to a single purpose: for thousands of years they have been trying to look inward – not one or two people, but millions and millions, generation after generation. It has created a certain vibe which is missing in the West.

Here in the East, meditation is something that you can float in. The whole energy around you is just like a river; it is already going toward the ocean. You don't have to swim, you have just to float. In the West you have to fight against the current because for centuries the extrovert mind has created a totally different kind of energy

– not just different but absolutely contrary to the East – the outgoing, the extrovert.

If you are working as a scientist in the West, you will find an invisible support from the whole atmosphere. In the East this happens only to those who are going on an inward journey; then the skies, the air, the trees, everything starts helping you. Not that they have any intention, but simply that for centuries this is how they have been pulled again and again – toward the inward center.

There are beautiful stories, which may not be factual, but I insist on saying that they are true. I want to make a clear-cut distinction between the fact and the truth – something may be factual and still may not be true. Your dreams are factual. When you kill someone in a dream you really kill them, but they are not true. When you wake up you suddenly find it was just a dream. Just as something can be factual yet not true, the opposite has also to be understood – something may be true, absolutely true, but may not manifest as a fact. The fact is a lower phenomenon. I can explain it only in a way…

On a full-moon night, sitting by the side of a silent lake, you can see the full moon in the lake. It is factual, but not true. And you might not look at the real moon which is far away in the sky; it might not become part of your factual knowledge, but its truth is indubitable.

The beautiful stories that have surrounded people of inner growth create a problem for the historian but not for the meditator, because the historian is concerned only with the factual. The mystic's concern is far deeper, far higher. He is not interested in the factual, he is devoted absolutely to the truth.

I would like to give you a few examples…

It is said that whenever Gautam Buddha moved – and he was continuously moving, for eight months of the year except the four months of the rains. It would be the time of the fall and he might come to rest under a tree whose leaves had fallen, whose branches were standing naked against the sky. But it is related that, seeing Buddha resting under the tree, it would seem very shameful to the tree that there is no foliage, no shade, no flowers rejoicing and welcoming a man who has reached the ultimate peaks of consciousness. And in the morning when Gautam Buddha would wake up, all his disciples would see a miracle: the tree which had been absolutely without leaves, without flowers, has suddenly become so green, such beautiful foliage around it and hundreds of flowers. They had seen it just the evening before – the miracle has happened in the silences of the night, and the flowers are showering on Gautam Buddha.

This incident is repeated so many times, in so many different sources, that it cannot be simply denied as symbolic, as poetic. As far as I am concerned I take it for granted to be a true and an existential experience. Whenever I have read such things – and there are so many instances – I have always remembered the incident in Jesus Christ's life, for which Christians cannot give any explanation. They try to hide it. But before you can understand the incident in Jesus' life I have to give you some relevant information.

Jesus came to India when he was fourteen, and he lived in India for almost fourteen years. Gautam Buddha was still in the air, he had lived just five hundred years before, and he left behind him hundreds of enlightened people. The air was so full of his fragrance that young Jesus must have been tremendously influenced by it. And the route Jesus followed for his traveling proves it. He went to Ladakh, which is where one of the oldest Buddhist monasteries is still functioning, and then to Tibet, which had become more in tune with Gautam Buddha than India itself.

This attraction was pulling him into the very unknown and dangerous spaces of Ladakh, Tibet. The reason was that he wanted to know as much as possible about this strange man, Gautam Buddha, who had transformed the whole atmosphere in the East. He must have come across these stories that when Buddha passed by, trees blossomed even though it was not the season for them to blossom.

Just one hundred and twenty years ago, a Russian traveler remained in Ladakh for six months, studying the old records. He reported that those old records remember Jesus as a young man but of immense silence, beauty, and a great search; who had come to the monastery and lived there for three months. They described Jesus exactly. The old records stated that he was coming from Judea, a faraway country; that it was very difficult for him to understand because of the language barrier, but he tried hard and accumulated as much honey as he could from every possible source which was still available. After Gautam Buddha the air was still full of remembrance, although five hundred years had passed. The mountains had not forgotten. And there were hundreds of people who could have been called contemporaries of Gautam Buddha as far as their consciousness was concerned.

I am telling you these facts because now Christian missionaries have removed all those records from Ladakh. There were records in Tibet which were destroyed by Christians in the time of the British Empire. They tried to remove any possible evidence that Jesus had been in the East learning the art of inward-going. But in spite of all their efforts, there are intrinsic proofs. And now I come to the story in Jesus' life…

For three days he and his disciples had gone hungry because the towns they were passing through were very fanatically Jewish and they would not give them shelter. On the contrary, they stoned them and threw them out of their towns. And Jesus came to a fig tree and he was very angry with the tree. He was not a man of anger, certainly. He was a man of immense love and peace. But this incident stands, on its own, without any explanation.

In the first place it is absurd to be angry with a fig tree because they are hungry and the tree is not welcoming them with figs – and it is not the season for figs! It looks simply absurd and insane; Jesus cursed the tree. Now, for Christians it is very difficult to explain what happened. A man like Jesus cursing a tree without any rhyme or reason because it was not even the season. And even if it were the season, the tree has no obligation to anyone. You cannot expect that the tree should welcome you.

From where did he get the idea? In the whole Jewish tradition there is not a single instance from where he could have got the idea. The only explanation is that he got the idea from the Buddhist stories in which trees are welcoming Gautam Buddha with flowers, with fruits. Even whole forests forgot about the season, the climate; they become green, they rejoiced in the enlightenment of Gautam Buddha. They rejoiced in the company of Gautam Buddha and they showed in their own language their joy, their appreciation, their blissfulness. Because if even a single man recognizes his enlightenment, a part of the universe becomes enlightened. Just because of a single man, the whole level of consciousness in the universe rises.

This has been a recognized truth in the East. Without being in the East, Jesus could not have dared to expect the fig tree… But he forgot completely that the fig tree also needs a certain climate, a certain vibration and a certain tradition. Unless the fig tree knows that for thousands of years its ancestors have always welcomed the buddhas, that this vibration is enough for the tree – a provocation to dance and to express itself in all its beauty.

Neither was the fig tree aware nor was Jesus an enlightened man. He had heard about enlightenment, he may have sat at the feet of enlightened people in the East. He may have created a desire in himself to become enlightened, but enlightenment and its language was so foreign to his own people in Judea. They had never heard the word, they had never heard that anyone becomes self-realized. They had lived a totally different kind of religious tradition – one of prophets, saviors, messengers, claimers saying that they are coming from God and if you believe in them you will be saved.

The whole Judeo-Christian tradition takes away the responsibility from every individual of becoming enlightened. And people unconsciously think that it is far easier to believe in someone and to be delivered from misery, from this dark night of the soul; rather than to take the responsibility in their own hands. But they are not aware that the moment you give the responsibility to someone else, without your knowing you have also given your freedom.

Responsibility and freedom are two aspects of the same coin. You cannot give one and save another.

You cannot say, "The responsibility to save me is that of some prophet, and I am still free to be myself." The moment you become a believer and you give your responsibility to Jesus Christ or Moses or Ezekiel, you have already given your freedom too. Now it is no longer an urgency for you to realize your being, or even to bother about who you are. It all depends now on the prophet you believe in, it is his responsibility. You think that you have become free from responsibility, but you have forgotten that you have also denied your freedom. With your responsibility gone you have reduced yourself to a slave.

Jesus could not speak the language of the East. He had to speak the language of his own people. But here and there the influence of the East is clear. For example, the Jewish God in the Old Testament says, "I am not a nice fellow. I am a very jealous God, I am very violent, and whoever is going to disobey me is going to suffer indefinitely. Remember." Finally he says, "I am not your uncle."

When for the first time I came to the part where he says, "I'm not your uncle."… He is reminding you, "I am your father! And obedience is the only religion." That's the whole story of creation in Christianity and Judaism: man was thrown out of the Garden of Eden – not for committing any sin, not for murdering anyone, not for raping; he was thrown out of the garden of God because he disobeyed. That makes the thing absolutely clear, that the Judeo-Christian tradition believes basically that obedience is religion and disobedience is the greatest sin, the original sin.

And it is strange to know what things Adam and Eve disobeyed. If you are impartial, not prejudiced, you can see a very strange scene. God says to Adam and Eve, "In this vast garden you can eat the fruits from any tree; just two trees are prohibited." It is a parable, but immensely significant. It may not be factual but is certainly true. One is the tree of wisdom, which God is denying you. You can translate it. One is the tree of enlightenment that God is denying you because enlightenment is nothing but wisdom. And the second tree is of eternal life. He is forbidding man to eat the fruits from these two trees.

He has taken away everything that can make life an ecstasy. He has taken away your enlightenment and he has taken away your experience of the eternal. What else is left? He has taken your very dignity. He has destroyed your freedom. He has taken away even the urge to go inward because those two trees grow inside you. The tree of wisdom and the tree of eternal life are not really two trees. It is one experience with two fragrances.

Unfortunately, Jesus became acquainted with words which don't fit the tradition from where he was coming. He went back when he was nearabout twenty-eight; it took two years for him to travel back to Judea. It is natural that he would have to speak the language that could be understood. For example, if he talked about nirvana, enlightenment, inner ecstasy, he would not have been understood. He had to translate it into a language that might have some meaning to the people he was talking to. He talked about the "Kingdom of God" and he tried his best to manage somehow to bring in the flavor that he had learned in the East.

That's why he is the first man in the West to say, "The Kingdom of God is within you." It is not in the Old Testament. No one had ever heard that the Kingdom of God is within you. This was simply a very clever translation to say that you *are* the god. "The Kingdom of God is within you" is a way of saying that looking outside is not the way of the seeker; you have to go inward. This created the whole trouble. The Jews could see that he was using words from their tradition, but he was giving them some strange meanings. It was absolutely clear. The Jewish God says, "I am a jealous god, a very angry god, and I will not forgive you if you commit any sin." And it is proved by the expulsion of Eve and Adam because they committed the sin of eating the fruit from the tree of wisdom. They were not quick enough to eat from the other tree too. They were caught red-handed on the first tree. That is the only sad part in it.

Sometimes, if you are unprejudiced, you can see things which prejudiced minds are absolutely incapable to see. Eve is persuaded by the Devil to eat from the tree of wisdom. Eve is naturally afraid – God has prohibited it – but the reasoning that convinces Eve is very significant. The Devil said, "You don't understand *why*. He has prohibited you from the two most significant experiences. He has prohibited you from wisdom, he has prohibited you from immortality because he is very jealous. If you are also enlightened, and you are also immortal, you will become a god in your own right. And that is his jealousy. He wants to remain as the *only* god and does not want anyone else to attain that position." I am surprised that no one has appreciated the Devil because what he is saying is more significant – in comparison to God's orders, which are fascist. God looks like any Adolf Hitler.

I should remind you that the word *devil* and the word *divine* both come from the same Sanskrit root. Both mean the same. Perhaps the Devil is the first great revolutionary. His fault was that he had revolted against God; otherwise he himself used to be an angel, but because he had the mind of a revolutionary he was thrown out of the company of God, condemned as evil. But the way he persuaded Eve makes me deeply respectful to the man. He is teaching exactly what all the enlightened people of the world have been teaching, that you can become a god. You are essentially a god, it is just that you have forgotten it. Perhaps you are asleep and you don't know who you are; all that you need is an awakening.

Jesus tried, and that very effort became the cause for his crucifixion. He was not yet enlightened; that can be said without any difficulty because he still believed that he was superior – the only begotten Son of God, and every other human creature is inferior, needs support. No one can become part of the Kingdom of God without believing in him. Now, this is not the way of an enlightened man.

The moment Gautam Buddha became enlightened, the first thing that he suddenly became aware of was that the whole existence is enlightened – just unawareness, people are just fast asleep. Perhaps trees are more deeply asleep; perhaps mountains are in a coma, but the essential core of every being – asleep or awake – is the same. There is no qualitative difference.

Jesus could not be enlightened because he still believes in the phony ideas of virtue. What is virtue? – obedience, slavery. And what is sin? – disobedience, revolt. He was teaching the same things, but he got mixed up. Being in the East he could not say that God is jealous. That was impossible. He had seen a totally different atmosphere in the East. He had seen godly people and he had seen millions of people who did not have any idea of a ruling God.

Existence has been accepted in the East as autonomous; it is not a creation. Long before Charles Darwin, very long, thousands of years before, the East had come to understand that existence is an evolution with no beginning and no end. And you will not believe that Ronald Reagan is trying to prohibit Charles Darwin in America – he has already prohibited. Books on evolution have been burned, universities have been forced to teach the idea of creation, not evolution. Charles Darwin's name is no longer mentioned in American universities, in American colleges. Strange! And the whole world is simply silent; no one says anything.

We have become accustomed to think that we are already civilized and cultured. Now, what Ronald Reagan is doing is so uncivilized and so uncultured that even a primitive society will be ashamed of it. We have heard stories that in the Middle Ages, Mohammedans burned libraries, the great library of Alexandria. That library was so big that it took six months for the fire to settle down. It contained all the ancient scriptures from Atlantis, the continent that had drowned. And we have thought that this was absolutely primitive behavior, but it is being done in the most pretentious country of the world – which thinks it is democratic, which thinks it allows freedom of speech, but there is no freedom for Charles Darwin. Books have been burned this very year! Whole educational systems have been completely cleaned of the idea of evolution. And creation should be taught. Why? – because creation is the Christian idea.

There is no scientific evidence for creation. There is every evidence for evolution. The Christian idea of creation is so foolish that one feels not angry but that it is hilarious: God created the world four thousand and four years before Jesus Christ was born. That means the world has existed for only six thousand years. It is such utter stupidity.

And because of this idea they have not much space, so they have to fix everything within six thousand years. They cannot accept the Hindu idea, which has absolutely scientific grounds, that the Rig Veda was written ninety thousand years ago. How can it be arranged in the Christian compass? Everything has to happen within these six thousand years. At the most, Christian scholars have agreed, the Rig Veda can be five thousand years old.

They are not aware that the Rig Veda contains intrinsic proof that it is ninety thousand years old. It describes a certain constellation of stars which happened ninety thousand years ago. Astronomers of all the world are absolutely agreed that that kind of constellation has not happened since. And if it is described in the Rig Veda, that means the people must have seen it, there is no other way. The description is in such detail that there is no need for any other proof. The book must have been written when the constellation happened.

Fifty-thousand-year-old skeletons of human beings have been found in China. Christian theologians have been in such a great difficulty: How to manage...? But there are always great idiots. One great theologian has proposed a theory that God created the world exactly as it is described in the Bible four thousand and four years before Jesus was born, but he also made things look like fifty-thousand-year-old skeletons simply to test your faith. Now, these are the great idiots of the world.

And Ronald Reagan is forcing the idea of God creating the world on America – against the constitution of America because the constitution wants the state and the religion to be kept absolutely separate. But he is being cunning. He is saying, "This is not a religious idea, it is a scientific idea." The idea of evolution means existence is eternal. It has never been created. It has always been here and it goes on evolving to new peaks of consciousness.

Now, it was very difficult for Jesus to say such things, but he managed a few things. He said that God is love. Now, that is absolutely against the Jewish tradition – God is not even your uncle and you are saying God is love! Of course for Gautam Buddha the ultimate consciousness is nothing but pure love. Jesus has taken those ideas and tried to give them a Jewish flavor, but he could not deceive the Jews. They immediately suspected he was bringing foreign and strange ideas which would corrupt their tradition, their religion – particularly their younger generation. Jesus was crucified because he was the first man, according to me, who was trying to introduce a few Eastern experiences into the West. The climate was not ready. The climate is not ready even today.

I have been to the West and I have seen the difference in the climate. I have seen a different vibe, one in which meditation is fighting against the current. It is not a let-go; it is not easy simply to flow *in*. All the forces around you are pulling you *out*. This idea that we are surrounded by different kinds of waves is a little difficult to comprehend. The people who are outgoing will find meditation the most difficult thing. The people who easily relax inward will find scientific projects, experiments with objects, very difficult and against their innermost desire to relax. They will become tense and will feel a certain anguish. It is unfortunate that this is so, and it has to be changed.

Man is both, in and out, and humanity should have both kinds of small pools of energy. For example there can be universities absolutely devoted to outer exploration, and there should be universities absolutely dedicated to the inner exploration. Then those universities will slowly become more and more different from each other and finally completely separate from each other.

In India there have been universities – long before Oxford or Cambridge existed. Nalanda, was one such university. Every professor in Nalanda – and Nalanda had almost one thousand professors – had to be a meditator. Unless a person had meditated for years there was no possibility for him even to become a student in Nalanda. Nalanda had four gates. And it is beautiful to remember that at these gates, the gatekeepers were no ordinary people. Unless a person was able to answer their questions, unless they were satisfied that he had a possibility to become a meditator, the person was refused entry at the very gate. There was no question of entering and having an interview with the professors. The gatekeepers were as much meditators as the professors.

And once you were accepted by the gatekeepers into Nalanda, it was more than you could have ever expected. A great opportunity opening before you. The whole university was concerned with only one thing, that everyone has to be reminded of enlightenment. All the scriptures indicated toward it, every sermon, every act, every exercise, was meant purposefully to take you inward. There were a few other universities, Takshila was one, and they were all concerned with the interiority of man. We can create a world where each university can have two different areas. There is no need for any conflict; both areas can become complimentary. But something has to be done urgently to destroy this difference between the East and the West.

Rudyard Kipling was one of the great English poets, who was recommended by the British Empire as the royal poet, the poet laureate. He lived mostly in India, and his experience of India and England is condensed in his two lines: "East is East and West is West and never the twain shall meet." I can see that he had a certain insight, and what he was saying was factual. But if what he is saying becomes the prophecy of the future, if it is forever going to be a fact, then there is no hope for humanity to survive. Then humanity is going to remain schizophrenic.

I would like to say that at least in this temple, West is not West, East is not East, and the twain are already meeting. I don't see that there is any existential reason for their not meeting. We have lived wrongly in the whole of the past and this is the ultimate consequence of it. Our whole reasoning about man has to be completely transformed. If man has an inside – and certainly he has an outside – then any worldview, any lifestyle must be inclusive of both; nothing should be excluded. In this possibility of a whole man, of man as an organic unity of the inner and the outer, of the mundane and the sacred, is the whole hope of allowing this beautiful planet to survive. Otherwise we are already on the brink of committing a global suicide.

You are right that you find it difficult in the West to go inward and here it happens easily. There is certainly this alchemy: the East is vibrating with so many enlightened people that when you meditate here, everything around you invisibly helps you. We are aware now of radio waves; radio waves are always passing all over you, although you cannot hear them. Just a mechanism, a receptive mechanism is needed, a radio, and immediately you can catch almost all the broadcasting stations in the world. Do you think when the radio is tuned to a certain station, then the waves start coming here? The waves are already passing by; it is just that there is no receptive center for them, so you remain unaware of it.

It happened in the last world war…

A man was very badly injured, and as he regained consciousness he felt a strange thing. He felt as if he were listening to a broadcast from a radio station. He could not believe it. He looked all around – there was no radio. He finally told the doctor. The doctor laughed and said, "You must have imagined it."
He said, "It is not imagination. The exact time is announced; the broadcasts, the news…"

At first no one believed him, because how can it be? But finally they had to try in some way to figure out what was happening. They put a radio in another room and said to the man, "Just go on writing down whatever you hear." The man wrote down exactly everything that was being broadcast!

But it was a very difficult situation. It opened a new door; it made it clear that our ears *are* capable to receive radio waves. Perhaps one day we may have some mechanism, just a small mechanism attached to the ear. However, the man was going mad because he could not sleep. And as he became more and more clear, it was not only one station that he was hearing; he was receiving many stations simultaneously. He was going mad. He said to his doctor, "Stop your experiments and your findings; otherwise I am going to commit suicide! Fix my ear back as it used to be, normal." An operation had to be done.

But an accident suddenly made it clear that we *are* capable; all that we need is a switch to turn the radio on or off. Or just a small mechanism so that we can fix which station we want to listen to. One day it can be – it has to be. It has been delayed because radio has almost become out of fashion. The television has taken its place. But what has happened with radio waves could also happen with your eyes. We may have to wait for some accident, but the possibility is there because those are also certain kinds of waves that are bringing pictures to your television screen. Why couldn't they bring them directly to your eyes?

Scientists say that our capacity to see is very limited. We can hear only certain wavelengths, we can see only certain areas. For example, the owl can see more than we can see; its capacity of seeing is far bigger, far stronger. That's why it can see at night when we can see only darkness. And because of this, his eyes have become so delicate that he cannot open them when the sun is out. He can catch only the very delicate rays; the sun is too much, too harsh. We are perfectly aware that when we think it is day, for the owl it is night. The owls have lived for millions of years, perfectly capable of seeing in the darkest night. The darker the night the more receptive the owl becomes because his eyes are so delicate.

There are other waves of which a few people become aware of, and they are thought to be a little crazy, nuts. But they are not nuts. They may not be normal... For example in India, medical science developed in a totally different way, with the Indian medical science, Ayurveda. Even its name is indicative of its difference. *Medicine* simply means that you have accepted the disease and you are trying to cure it. Medicine is curative. *Ayurveda* means the science, or more accurately, the "wisdom of life." It has nothing to do with disease. Its emphasis is that life should be made stronger so that disease cannot happen. It is not curative, it is preventive.

Just a few days ago, a Japanese sannyasin was here. He is a great scientist, particularly about atomic radiation. He has been working for twenty years in Hiroshima, and he has discovered... He has brought a few things and he is going to bring more. He discovered these things by chance because for twenty years he has been working in Hiroshima, where the radiation is becoming less and less.

The bomb was thrown on Hiroshima forty years ago. In forty years the intensity of radiation has become very much lower. And he was surprised because when he came back from Hiroshima after twenty years, his colleagues in the university could not believe it. He had gone there when he was forty-five and when he came back again he was still forty-five! His colleagues were already retired.

That made him aware that a small amount of radioactivity, atomic radiation, cannot be destructive to life, but on the contrary can be immensely protective to life. So he has created a few things. He has created belts – you can wear the belt twenty-four hours a day. The belt is filled with radioactive material, and it goes on radiating into your body. A few of the sannyasins here have used it and they all say it feels just great. One feels younger, one feels more energetic. He has made small plates to put in your bathtub while you just rest in the bath. And that radioactive material will make the water radioactive around you.

His understanding is that life can be prolonged; many diseases can be prevented, those which have already happened can be cured.

And he is making many different kinds of things. He has been reading me, and he was very interested when he heard that I have been poisoned by the American government. That was the reason for his coming, to bring a few things which according to him can take the poison out of the body. He has made those things for the emperor of Japan, Hirohito. He has made a special tea with radioactive material. One of those small belts costs two thousand dollars, but they look just like a belt worth not more than five rupees. The real material is inside; it can simply be anything that has been exposed to radiation. It can be earth, it can be any rubbish, but because it is still radiating, it is costly.

This scientist was told by America's biggest manufacturer of nuclear bombs that they wanted to purchase – whatever the cost – all his inventions and their patents. He refused because he knew that the idea must not be to let those inventions reach the market for everyone to use. Because if everyone is using radioactivity and radiation, people will become less and less receptive to any dangerous amount. A certain wall will be created within them; they can survive any atomic explosion. There will be enough atomic energy inside them.

There are other spheres of energy, and particularly you can try some small experiments. You can plant a few rose bushes of the same height, in the same soil, using the same fertilizers, taking the same care, but do one thing: with one bush, be very loving. Just talk to it, sit by its side. And you will see a strange phenomenon. They are all receiving the same nourishment, same food, same soil, same water, but because this bush is receiving something which the others are not receiving, this bush will become bigger, with more foliage, greener, and it will bring bigger flowers than the others. You have created a certain energy field of love around the bush. You can neither see it nor are there scientific instruments available to judge, but your eyes can see the difference.

If for thousands of years a country has been producing meditators, it is filled with invisible vibrations. It is not a coincidence that for centuries, seekers of the inner have come toward the East. A certain pull, a certain magnetic energy has accumulated, and it is still functioning. Although the East has fallen into dark days of poverty, slavery, hunger, famine, not even water to drink – but still the vibrations of Mahavira, Parshvanath, Gautam Buddha, Bodhidharma, continue to reach those who are ready to receive them.

It all depends on you. If you have an honest search, then the East is the place for you. Here you can blossom more easily, more spontaneously, more effortlessly. This may not be possible anywhere else – you will have to fight for it, you will have to struggle against forces that you cannot see.

An Englishman, an American and a Frenchman are on a sea cruise, when the ship hits a rock and begins to sink. "Women and children first!" cries the Englishman. "Women and children first!"

"Fuck the women and children!" shouts the American.

"*Oo la la*!" says the Frenchman. "Do we have time?"

An Englishman goes to visit his doctor. "Doc," he says, "I'm madly in love with this Polish girl. You've got to help me become a Polack."

"Are you sure?" says the doctor. "In order to do that, we've got to surgically remove half your brain."

The man says that it doesn't matter what it takes, he wants the operation anyway.

Afterward, when he wakes up, he finds the doctor standing beside his bed. "I'm terribly sorry," says the doctor, "we made a bad mistake. We removed three quarters of your brain."

The man slaps his forehead and cries, "Ah, mamma mia!"

22

The Silence between Two Sounds

Osho,
The other night you were like a master musician playing a beautiful melody on the strings of my heart. Beloved Osho, is this your secret in letting me sing my song more and more?

Music is the only language that comes very close to silence, the only sound which is able to create the soundless. It has to be understood that music has no meaning. It is sheer joy, celebration. It is the only art that can somehow impart the inexpressible.

The ancientmost tradition of music is that it was born out of meditation. The people who meditated could not find any way to impart their experiences. They invented different instruments so that something can be said without creating a meaning in you but certainly a joy, a dance.

It must have been a tremendously valuable revelation for those who in the beginning discovered a language which is not a language. Sounds in themselves have no meaning. Meaning is man's imposition on sounds. Sounds are natural. The wind blowing through the pine trees has a sound and a music of its own. Or a river, descending from the mountain through the rocks, has its own sound and its own music.

It is my assumption that meditators, listening to the inner silence, must have felt the tremendous difficulty of how to share it. It was in those beginning days that music was discovered. The discovery is simple: take away the meaning from the sounds and instead of meaning, give the sounds harmony, a rhythm which penetrates to the very heart. It says nothing, but it says the unsayable too. The ordinary idea of music is that it consists of sounds, but that is only half the truth – and of lesser importance. As the music becomes deeper and deeper, it consists of silences between two sounds.

An ancient proverb in China: When the musician becomes perfect he throws away his instruments. Because instruments can only create sound. The silence is created by the musician. But at the perfection, the same sounds that were creating small pieces of silence start becoming a disturbance. A strange idea, but perfectly meaningful, significant. It applies to every art. When the archer becomes perfect he throws away his bow and his arrows; just his eyes are enough to look at a flying bird and the bird will fall to the ground. The bow and arrows were only a preparation. The same applies to music, to painting, to all the arts which man has discovered. At the ultimate peak, you don't need the steps, the ladder which has helped you to reach the peak. It becomes irrelevant.

The classical music was devoted to silence and to meditation. A beautiful story is told about a nabob of Lucknow. For centuries Lucknow remained the most cultured, sophisticated city in this country. The arts were respected, wisdom was highly prestigious.

The nabob, the king of Lucknow, was certainly a man of tremendous courage, insight. But these are the people who become misunderstood by the common man. Before I tell you the story about the musician, it will be good to know about the king who invited him to Lucknow, to his court. He was the last king of Lucknow, and when the British armies invaded Lucknow he was listening to music. He was informed that the British armies were coming closer and closer. He said, "Just welcome them. They are our guests." Perhaps nowhere else in history has there been a king who accepted his enemies as guests. And he told his people, "Make every arrangement for their comfort, and tomorrow I will receive them in the court. If they want to remain here, they can remain. If they want the power, they can have it. There is no need for unnecessary violence. Things can be settled in a more cultured way. But as far as this moment is concerned, I will not disturb the musicians just because a few stupid people are attacking the city."

This nabob was very concerned that all the great musicians had played in his court except one. He inquired, "What are the reasons?"

His people said, "His conditions are absolutely insane. He says that no one should move while he is playing his music. If anyone starts moving or swaying with the music, his head has to be immediately removed from his body. He will come only if this condition is fulfilled."

The nabob said, "You should have told me before! Invite him and tell him the condition is accepted. And declare to the whole beautiful city of Lucknow that those who want to hear the musician should know the condition; otherwise they should not come."

But almost ten thousand people came to listen to the musician. And the nabob was not a man to go against his word. One thousand soldiers with naked swords were surrounding the listeners. The order was that they should note down whoever moved because to remove his head in the middle would be a disturbance.

Only twelve heads moved. They were noted. In the middle of the night, the musician asked, "Has my condition been fulfilled?"

The king said, "Yes, these are the twelve people who moved and swayed and forgot the condition. Now it is up to you. What do you want? Should we behead them?"

To everyone's surprise, the musician said, "These are the only people worthy to listen to me. Now let the whole crowd go. They were not listening to me, they were simply protecting themselves. Just an accidental movement could cause death, just a change of position could be dangerous. They were too concerned with their lives. Music is not for them; let them go. Now I can play the *real* music for you in the remains of the night, and for these twelve people." It took a strange turn!

The nabob said, "But this is a strange way to find the right people."

The musician said, "That is the *only* way to find the right people. These are the people for whom music means something more than life itself."

In fact, they had simply forgotten all about the conditions. Music touched their hearts and they started swaying, a kind of dance entered their beings. He played his music for those twelve people in the remains of the night. And he told the nabob that he did not need any reward. This was enough reward: to find the right people who could listen to music. "I would pray to you to reward these people because these are the people to whom music is meditation."

Looking at this story, there are two possibilities. Either the meditators found music, or the musicians found meditation. But they are so immensely and deeply connected with each other. My own experience is that because meditation is a far higher, a far deeper experience, music must have been found by the meditators – as a language to bring something from their inner dance, inner silence, to the people they loved.

The ancient music in the East needs not only training for the musician, it needs immense training for the listener. Everyone cannot understand the ancient classical music. You have to be capable of falling in tune with the harmony. In a certain way you have to disappear and let only the music remain.

It has been the experience of all great musicians, dancers, painters, sculptors, that while they are deepest in their creativity, they are no more. Their very creativity gives them the taste of disappearing into the universal. That becomes their first acquaintance with meditation. So both are possibilities: either music has led people to the point of meditation, or meditation has tried to find a means to express the inexpressible. But in any case, music is the highest creation that man is capable of. Meditation happens. Music is your creativity.

But we have lost contact with the authentic music. And slowly, slowly, as humanity has become less and less interested in the inner world, its music has become lower and lower. The contemporary music is absolutely the lowest that has ever existed. It touches you, but it touches you at your lowest center of sexuality. The contemporary music is sexual, and the classical music is spiritual. I would like my people to create music on the path of meditation – or create music if you have found meditation, as a language to express the silence of it.

Many mystics have done that. The mystic Nanak was always accompanied by a musician, his disciple Mardana. Before he would speak, he would tell Mardana to play on his veena and create the atmosphere for him to speak. And as he would stop speaking, he would again ask Mardana to create music as beautiful as possible. "So that these people who have come to listen to me understand perfectly well that words are impotent. The beginning is music and the end is the music. I have to use words because you are not aware that there are higher ways of communicating."

Mardana followed Nanak. And Nanak is the only mystic who stands aloof in a way because he traveled the most. He traveled all over India; he went to Sri Lanka. And finally, he traveled to Afghanistan, to Saudi Arabia, and reached the holy place of the Mohammedans, Kaaba.

It was evening time when he arrived. His fame, his name, had already reached ahead of him. But the people, the priests of Kaaba, could not believe that a mystic of the quality of Nanak, as they have heard about him, should behave in this way. The night was falling and he prepared his bed and told Mardana to make arrangements for sleeping. And they both kept their legs toward the Kaaba! That was absolutely insulting to the Mohammedans. They are so touchy about it that even the graves of all the Mohammedans in the world are made in such a way that their heads in the grave are pointing toward Kaaba. They don't allow even the dead people any freedom!

Certainly, they were offended. They said to Nanak, "You are not a mystic and you don't know even how to behave in a gentlemanly way. You are insulting us."

Nanak said, "Don't be annoyed with me. I have my own troubles. My trouble is, that wherever I keep my feet they are always pointing toward the divine. Because except the divine, nothing else exists. I have not knowingly done it, but if you feel offended, you can move my legs in any direction you want."

The story is so tremendously beautiful. And as Nanak's legs were moved in all directions, the priest became puzzled – the Kaaba started moving in the same direction where Nanak's feet were moved! Perhaps that is a parable. Kaaba is only a stone, and stones are not supposed to be so sensitive. But one thing it indicates clearly – that the whole existence is full, throbbing with only one music, one dance, one godliness.

So if you can feel the sound of silence in my words, my purpose is fulfilled. Because my words are not being used in the same way they have been used by everyone. I am using words just as instruments of music. I am not a musician, but I can create the same situation with words and the silences in between. Those who cling to my words miss me because they start interpreting. They start finding contradictions, they start an agreement or disagreement, but certainly a process of judgment starts in their being. That was not my purpose. My purpose was to start a silence, a music, a fragrance in you.

You have to change the gestalt. From words – which is the ordinary way humanity has used words forever, and no one has insisted on changing the gestalt – listen to the silences. Read between the lines and you will find a tremendous explosion of silence, music, celebration. And flowers go on growing in your being.

Your question is, "The other night you were like a master musician, playing a beautiful melody on the strings of my heart." For thirty-five years I have been doing that every morning, every evening. But the other night was special for you. I am a very stubborn person; I will go on hitting you on your head till you get the point. Last night you got it – now don't lose it. These are such subtle experiences, you can get them and you can lose them. Once you have got any insight, remember not to lose it.

Yes, whatever I am doing is closer to music than anything. It is not philosophy, it is not religion, it is not theology. What I am saying is not in my statements, but just in those small spaces which remain utterly silent, empty. But they are neither empty nor silent. Once you have stumbled on those small pieces of silence and emptiness, you will be surprised that the silence is not silence; it is full of music, it is alive, it is a dance. And the emptiness is not emptiness; it is the only fullness that exists in the universe.

So there are two ways of listening: one is jumping from one word to another word and another is jumping from one silence to another silence. Those who are following the second way will be immensely rewarded by existence with great blissfulness, with tremendous ecstasy, and with an immortality, an eternity. The treasures are incalculable. But if you are listening only to the words, you will end up at the most in a certain system of thought. This makes me sad because I am not here to create systems of thought. Millions of people have done that and distracted people from their inwardness. All thought systems exist in the mind, and all silences exist beyond the mind. My simple message to you is to transcend the mind, transcend the word.

I have found so many places to argue against in the Bible. From the very beginning, it does not appeal to me. The Bible says, "In the beginning there was the word, the word was with God and the word was God." I absolutely disagree with this stupid beginning. How can there be a word in the beginning? Because a word means a sound with meaning, and meaning can be given only by someone else. The sound itself is meaningless. It would have been better if they had said, "In the beginning there was sound." But even that would not have been the perfect beginning because even for sound to exist you need some ears. Without the ears, there are no sounds. The best and the most perfect would have been, "In the beginning there was silence." That statement in the Bible already starts in a wrong direction and goes on moving in that wrong direction. Silence is the greatest spiritual experience.

And the universe consists only of silence. Silence can become as expressive as sound if there is someone to listen to it, and the sound can become meaningful if someone is there to give meaning to it. But silence is absolutely and utterly pure, untouched by human hands. Its purity is its godliness. Its purity is what every meditator comes to know. Every meditator stands in the beginning of existence. It is not a question of time. If you can fall into silence, each moment can be transformed into the beginning of existence. Silence does not divide people because it is not an ideology, it is an experience.

So whatever happened the other night to you, I have been hoping that it will happen sooner or later to everyone. I don't want you to belong to any belief, and not to belong to any idea, but simply to relax into the universal silence. And you will taste the sweetness of music and you will come to know that existence is not a misery but a mystery – a mystery that can be lived, loved, but can never be made part of your knowledge. You can become part of it, but it cannot become part of you.

You are asking me, "...is this your secret...?" Yes, this is my secret. This silence.

The Jesse James Gang holds up a train in the Wild West. When they have overpowered the guards, Jesse and the gang burst into the passenger compartment.

"Okay!" says Jesse. "You folks had better get ready, we are going to rob all the men and rape all the women."

"Look here, you outlaw," says a pretty young woman, "you can go ahead and try to rape me, but you'd better not lay a finger on my old aunt Sally."

"You hold your tongue, young lady," says old Sally. "Jesse knows what he's doing."

Alvin Pimpleburger turns sixteen years old, so his proud father gives him twenty dollars and sends him off to the local whorehouse.

On his way into town, Alvin passes his grandmother's house and she calls him in. He explains where he is going, and his granny insists that he saves the twenty dollars and makes love to her instead.

Alvin returns home with a big smile on his face. "How was it?" his father asks.

"Great!" replies Alvin. "And I saved the twenty bucks."

"How did you do that?" asks his father.

"I did it with granny," Alvin explains.

"Do you mean to say," screams his father, "that you fucked my mother?"

"And why not?" replies Alvin. "You have been fucking mine!"

And the last...

Moskowitz, Horowitz and Shapiro go on safari, where they are captured by a large tribe of fierce and hostile savages. Bound and helpless, they are brought before the chief. Pointing to Moskowitz, he says, "You have a choice: death or *chi-chi*."

"What could be worse than death?" cries Moskowitz, "I'll take *chi-chi*!"

There is a loud cheer and he is seized and viciously sodomized by the entire tribe.

The next day, the chief says to Horowitz, "Death or *chi-chi*?"

Horowitz trembles and says, "*Chi-chi*!" and he too is abused by the whole tribe.

The next morning, Shapiro is summoned to the chief and is asked the same question: "Death or *chi-chi*?"

Shapiro, who has watched the fate of his friends, looks the chief right in the eye, and says, "Death!"

"Terrific!" says the chief, and turning to the assembled tribe, yells, "Death by *chi-chi*!"

Just be silent and you will discover an immense laughter that is going on all around the earth. The trees are laughing, the birds are laughing. Except man, there seems to be no one who is sad. This sadness is because of your clinging to the words. Let your life be a life of a dancing and laughing silence, and you have entered the only authentic temple of godliness.

I am not interested in what kind of ideologies you are carrying in your head. They are all bullshit. I want you to drop them all, irrespective of what they are. Let your whole being be filled with laughter. Let each of your cells be singing, let each fiber of your being be a part of the universal dance. To me, this is the only revolution, the only transformation which can bring this earth millions of joys.

It is our own stupidity that we have been listening to idiots of all kinds. Their whole purpose is to make us sad because if they succeed in making humanity sad and serious, they have taken away the possibility of your being in tune with the tremendous festivity that surrounds you. And now that you are taken away from the universal festival, you can be exploited, enslaved, oppressed. Every possible kind of crime can be done to you, and you will not revolt.

Only laughter can be a revolt, a revolution, a transformation. Start laughing against your so-called religious pretenders, hypocrites. Start laughing about your politicians, who have been deceiving mankind for centuries. Don't pay any attention to this whole gang of criminals, and we can enter an absolutely new era, where everybody is joyful, loving, laughing. And everyone is carrying his own guitar – no need to carry any cross. I want to change every cross into a guitar. Right?

23

Cut the Roots of Misery

Osho,
Would you like to comment on the differences between being withdrawn, being introverted and turning in?

Western psychology has created a very schizophrenic situation by dividing man into extroverts and introverts. Man is one. This division has been destructive of all humanity and its whole past. The moment you divide any organic unity, it dies. You can divide only mechanical unities, but not organic ones. You can take a bicycle apart and you can put it together again and you will not lose anything. But if you take a man apart and put him together again, you won't have the same man you had divided; you will have only a corpse. This division is of utmost importance to understand, that organic unities cannot be divided – neither into higher and lower, outer and inner, sacred and mundane, material and spiritual. Man is all. To those who understand, what appears to be contradictory is only complementary. Your question raises great implications.

Just a few days ago a Japanese scientist was here to attend a world science conference. He became aware about me only at the last moment, but before rushing to the airport he came here. He had not more than fifteen minutes, and I was asleep. He wrote a letter stating many important things. The first one was that no one understands him. He has been around the earth in search of a man who can understand him.

Looking at his letter I could not contain myself from laughing because this is a much lower stage, when no one understands you. I have also been around the world – everyone *mis*understands me. I have invited the scientist, his name is Fukuoka. [*Somebody giggles at the name, and the laughter becomes contagious. Osho waits for it to subside.*] You can laugh in English, but not in Japanese!

I have written to him, saying, "Most of the things that you are saying cannot be understood because you yourself don't understand that they are based on a dual conception of reality. On one hand you condemn the famous philosopher Descartes, saying that he is responsible for dividing science from religion, and his division has created tremendous trouble for the whole humanity." I can understand. But Fukuoka himself goes on continuously talking in his letter about the inner man and the outer man.

Man is not divided into the inner and the outer. You are both. You can open your eyes and you are outside, and you can close your eyes and you are inside. Just small eyelids – that is the only division. Not much of a division. But the blindness of man is such that although Fukuoka understands that Descartes is wrong, he himself goes on doing the same thing without being alert at all. The materialist, the spiritualist – he wants the whole world to become spiritual. He goes on praising Gautam Buddha, and that makes me laugh because if you go on dividing man into lower and higher, into material, into spiritual, you may have changed the direction of division but division is there. I stand for the whole man – to be accepted, appreciated, loved in its total organicity.

Your question is, what is the difference between "...being withdrawn, being introverted and turning in?" All belong to the extrovert man. There is not much qualitative difference. Being withdrawn means simply being indifferent, aloof, uncaring. But you are still outside. Being introverted simply means you have closed all your doors and windows, and you will not receive the fresh breeze, the sun, the moon, the stars; you have become closed to reality. An introverted man is just vegetating, not living. Life needs both – a tremendous balance between the inner and the outer, between the day and the night, between life and death. They are not separate. Nowhere is there a demarcation. The introverted man is a dead man, a corpse.

And the third – turning in. There is no need to turn in. It is the philosophers, the people who are too concerned with words, language, and not at all concerned with experience, who go on creating such ideas as "turning in." You have never been out – how can you turn in? You have always been there; from there you can radiate outward, but there is no question of turning in. "Turning in" means you had gone out of the house, roamed around and finally you have come back home. But you have never left the home – you cannot because you *are* the home.

Wherever you go, it will be the same: your inner and your outer will be balancing wherever you are. You cannot leave one behind and go ahead with the other half; that's an impossibility. But the professors and the philosophers are more concerned with words, never bothering to look into reality and existence itself.

I have heard…

There is a commune in Poland which has only four members. Their names are Everybody, Somebody, Anybody and Nobody.

One day there is an important job to be done and Everybody is sure that Somebody will do it. Anybody could do it, but Nobody does it. Somebody gets angry about that because it is Everybody's job. Everybody thinks that Anybody can do it, but Nobody realizes that Everybody won't do it. It ends up that Everybody blames Somebody when Nobody does what Anybody could have done.

Here in this place, all those four are present – and enjoying immensely! There is no need to condemn anybody. Everybody is what he is supposed to be. But man has been dominated by the idea of condemning this, condemning that; this is right, that is wrong. It has created so many layers, so many categories, that some way or other it has made everybody guilty – guilty in so many ways. It has wounded everybody's psyche and destroyed man's dignity, his individuality.

Fukuoka is not understood because he is asking things which are only symbolic, symptoms. He is not raising questions about the roots – he himself *believes* in the roots. He was here attending an international conference. Naturally, just out of etiquette, he praised India so much saying, "This is the only land which can save humanity." It is not capable of saving itself! And you are putting the responsibility on the poor human beings of this devastated, destroyed, enslaved, hungry, uneducated, uncultured people to save the whole humanity.

It reminded me of an old Jew who was praying his last prayer before dying. Someone heard, and could not believe what he was saying. The old Jew was saying to God, "God, it is time you should choose someone else as your chosen people. We have suffered enough." Jews would have never suffered if God had not named them as his chosen people. Who bothers about ordinary people?

This country is being praised and this country feels very comfortable with all this praise, without looking at the reality.

Fukuoka mentions in his letter that the world needs an ecological change. It is true – the world needs deep ecological understanding. But the way he expresses it destroys the whole truth it contains. He says, "I loved the Indian roads, where cows are sitting." This is ecology – where men and animals are together, drinking water, taking baths, doing all kinds of stupid things together.

This is not ecology, this is nonsense, and he was very impressed when he saw it. But he does not understand that these cows are hungry, they are dying; their owners have disowned them because their owners cannot feed them and they are of no use anymore. Neither can they give milk nor they can give more young, more cows and bulls. They are not resting on the streets, they are simply waiting for death – hungry, uncomfortable. Death will come to them not in a natural way, it will come through the traffic. They will die and they will take a few more people with them. They will not die alone.

And when he saw a temple of the monkey god Hanuman, he was immensely impressed. This is ecology – man worshipping hungry, mangy... All kinds of animals are being worshipped in India, elephant gods... I have always been sad that Charles Darwin never came to India. Otherwise he would have found the most valid reason for his theory of evolution, that man has evolved out of monkeys. The worship of the monkey proves that they are your forefathers.

That reminds me of Ronald Reagan. He has tried to stop the teaching of Charles Darwin's theory of evolution in all the universities, the colleges, the schools of America. Not only that, Darwin's teachings have been taken out of libraries. The books have been taken out and burned because the theory of evolution goes against the theory of Christianity, which proposes not evolution but creation. But the real reason to me seems to be that Ronald Reagan does not want to accept monkeys as his forefathers. But just burning those books does not change anything.

Fukuoka cannot be understood by Ronald Reagan. But he is proposing something which is not even worth proposing. He is not hitting at the roots. Whether monkeys are worshipped or not, is not going to change the fate of the coming humanity. But the problem about hitting the roots is that it is dangerous. It immediately annoys the vested interests. I went through his whole letter. He seems to be a sincere and nice person; he really wants a better future. But he has not the insight that by pruning the leaves of the trees nothing is changed. You will have to cut the roots. And the moment you start on the roots you will be in difficulty because the politicians are in the roots, the organized religions are in the roots, all the races are in the roots.

You cannot change anything in this world unless you cut these roots completely. Unless there is only one world government and no divisions of nations and freedom of movement; without any need of passports and visas and all kinds of idiotic conditions, you cannot do anything to change the ecology. For example, Bangladesh is suffering every year with great floods. It cannot do anything about it because the roots are in the division of nations. Nepal is the poorest country in the world and it has nothing to sell except its ancient trees. Two-hundred, three-hundred, five-hundred-year-old trees – it has sold them to the Soviet Union and now the Soviet Union has cut so many trees that for miles and miles the land is without trees.

The trees used to slow down the flow of the rivers. Now there are no trees; the waters from the Himalayas come with such a force that the ocean cannot absorb them in so much quantity, it has never done it. It turns them back, and every year Bangladesh suffers. Thousands of people die, thousands of houses are destroyed. It is beyond the power of Bangladesh to do anything. If Nepal sells its trees, who are you to say anything to Nepal? And if you say anything then you have to understand that Nepal has nothing else to sell. Then feed Nepal.

The ecology is so interdependent. It became clear that if anything goes wrong in the Soviet Union, in their nuclear plants, then the clouds of nuclear radiation will spread wherever the winds take them – and winds don't think about national boundaries. Now the problems are international, and your solutions are national. Unless humanity is one there is no hope.

But the politicians will not allow humanity to be one because it is their whole power trip. If there is only one world government, it will not satisfy so many people's egos to be presidents, to be prime ministers, to be ministers, to be governors. To fulfill these people's egos, we have to suffer. Everyone has to suffer.

In India there is enough coal and not enough wheat. But Russia has burned wheat in its railway trains instead of coal because it does not have coal. It could have been a simple understanding, but the barriers of nations prevent a bird's-eye view of the whole situation. And although this country is so poor, it has been selling its wheat to purchase more atomic plants, more nuclear technology – and almost half the country is hungry and starving.

Every six months the European Common Market goes on drowning billions of dollars' worth of food in the ocean. And in Ethiopia, every day one thousand people go on dying, but that food cannot be given to them. The European market has its own problems: its economy will collapse if it starts giving things free to people. Then its own people will ask, "Then why should we pay? We create – Ethiopia eats. We work hard and you are throwing our earnings to other countries. We have nothing to do with them." America goes on drowning food in the same way – mountains of butter and other foodstuff. The last time it took millions of dollars just to carry that foodstuff to the ocean; that is not including the price of the food. Now, do you think we are living on a sane planet? The roots have to be hit hard. But the moment you hit any root you become dangerous.

My attorney, Swami Prem Niren, is sitting here. He is now doing deep research into what was going on behind the scenes when I was arrested in America. And such hilarious facts are coming out that one cannot figure out whether this world is sane or a big madhouse.

The politicians and the church leaders were trying to force the Supreme Court of Oregon to arrest me, send me to jail, or at least deport me. But it was difficult for them to find any legal, constitutional reason. They knew perfectly well that it was not going to be a small thing. So first, a preparation was needed. And you will not believe that just to arrest me, they wasted five and a half million dollars in research work to find something that I might have committed so that my arrest could be valid. They were at a loss because I am such a lazy man – to commit a crime is such an impossibility. In my whole life I have not even prepared a cup of tea for myself. Most of the time I am asleep. The few hours I am awake, I am talking to you.

After five years of research, wasting five and a half million dollars in the research… And the pressure was increasing. But this is strange – a man cannot just be deported because then you would be afraid that he will fight up to the Supreme Court. On what grounds are you deporting him? Neither can you allow him to live there – not because he is doing any harm to anyone, but you cannot allow him to *be*, because he is hitting your very roots. I don't have to go anywhere to hit the roots. I can hit those roots from here.

The Christian fundamentalists were angry because I said that to me, Jesus Christ is not a man of enlightenment. He may be good entertainment, but he is not… And to crucify a man who has not done anything except making statements which are simply stupid… For example, "I am the only begotten Son of God."

Now anyone you meet in the street who says to you, "Listen, I am the only begotten Son of God," do you think it is right to crucify him? At the most you can say, "It is perfectly good." What is criminal in it? If he was saying, "I am the one who can save the whole world," so who is preventing you? Save! But I don't think that he is worthy of a cross. And when I said this, the more I look into Jesus and his psychology, I see only a crackpot and nothing else.

But that I can do from here. I *am* doing it from here. America is not that far away. Neither is Italy that far away. And the Italian Consul is here, just by my side. He wanted to see me alone, and because my secretary insisted that I never see anybody alone, because whatever I say has to be recorded, he started perspiring. He became so nervous, he said, "Then cancel the appointment." What could be the fear?

The fear is that for one year, the Italian government, without any reason, has been trying to prevent my entry into Italy. The whole of the Radical Party of Italy is fighting continuously. Eighty-four prominent citizens of Italy – Nobel Prize winners, poets, painters, professors – have protested. The government goes on saying that next week they are going to issue a visa for me, and this has been going on for one year. And this is because of the fear of the pope, the fear of the Catholics. What just happened in America is happening in twenty-five countries. Sitting in my room, mostly sleeping, I am fighting in twenty-five countries.

In spite of the Supreme Court, the politicians, and the church, the head of the FBI refused to arrest me because he said there were no valid grounds. Otherwise they are very famous people for doing anything wrong – even *they* could not think that it was right to arrest me. Then they asked the CIA, and the CIA chief simply refused. He said, "There is a limit to some things; innocence is not crime." And you will not believe that the research that is being done by my attorneys in America has brought out a very strange fact: finally, the Supreme Court asked the army to arrest me! They could not find anyone else to arrest me because everyone wanted evidence. The head of the army laughed. He said, "This is unprecedented. The army is being called to arrest a single individual who is not even a citizen of this country, who is just a tourist? The whole world will laugh at it." He simply refused.

Finally, when I was arrested they had no arrest warrant because no one was ready to issue one. Even the immigration department – which had put five and a half million dollars into research – their head refused to issue an arrest warrant because he said, "Your research shows nothing. There is nothing that you can call a crime for which an arrest warrant is needed."

They must have persuaded the city police of Charlotte to arrest me without an arrest warrant. They had nothing even verbally to tell me about what the reasons were for my being arrested, and six of my friends were also being arrested. They had only a list saying that these people had to be arrested. And strangely enough, the names of these six people were not on that list. We told them, "Our names are not on your list. You are doing simply an absurd act. You can look at our passports. Your list contains other names; we are not the right people."

And because they were not yet ready for evidence, finally they managed what they could have done in the very beginning.

They simply fabricated thirty-four charges against me – just pure fiction. Obviously, they had to give some result; they had wasted five and a half million dollars. And you will not believe what the government attorney who was fighting for three days continuously in the court against me, finally said: "I have not been able to prove anything, but neither has the other party been able to prove anything."

Can you see the stupidity of the statement? Does innocence also need to prove that it is innocent? No constitution of any country requires that innocence needs to be proved. But these politicians are so afraid that if the roots are opened and cut, then their vested interests will be gone. If there is no God, and Jesus Christ is a crackpot, then what is the pope? – just a representative of a crackpot! And it is not only in one country. Today I have received news from Germany that one of the major political parties, the Green Party, has asked the government, "It is now two years continuously you have been keeping this law, the order that Osho cannot enter Germany." Not only that, I cannot even land on any airport of Germany – even for refueling the plane – because I am a dangerous man.

Now their own party, a major party, is asking the government, "You have to explain. What is the danger? For two years you have been avoiding the issue. You should appoint a commission to do the research. What is the danger?"

And if I am a danger, are there other people also in Germany who are in the same category? Just now, a German psychoanalyst has published a book after many years of research which says that Christianity has created more crimes in the world than any other religion. Now the Green Party is asking, what are you going to do about Christianity? It is basically a question of bringing out the roots of all our misery, of all our torture. But those who are in power will not allow you even to know where the causes lie. You have to fight only with the effects. That's why up to now, no revolution has been successful.

Now, why should this Italian Consul be so insistent to talk with me alone? What is the fear that the talk should be recorded? From where does this fear arise? What was the fear in America? Because when they deported me, the United States Attorney admitted that I had not committed any crime. "But our purpose was to send him out of America because he is dangerous." Dangerous to what? Dangerous to morality. And the man who was most emphatic about this point – his name is Michael Stoops, and he is a fanatic fundamentalist Christian – today I have heard that he has been charged with child abuse, sexual child abuse. And this was the man who was in favor of my being deported because I am dangerous to people's morality. Who are these people and what is their morality?

Just a few weeks ago in America there was an international conference of homosexuals. One of the men from Britain, a member of the Parliament, represented the homosexuals of England in the conference – obviously, he must be a homosexual. And he said, "I know at least fifty-six members of the Parliament in England who are homosexuals." It is absolutely confirmed that one of the popes before this Polack pope was a homosexual. Who are the people whose morality has to be saved? In fact, a deep research is needed into who has already destroyed people's sense of purity, integrity, responsibility.

The roots are very strange because they remain hidden underneath the earth. You only see the flowers and the trees and the leaves – you don't see the roots. All the religions of the world are responsible for homosexuality. To find out why they are responsible, you will have to go a little deeper. Because they insisted that celibacy is very spiritual, and that without being a celibate you cannot be spiritual.

Now, celibacy is absolute nonsense. It is against nature, it is against medical science. I am amazed that not a single medical institute stands up and says to the world that celibacy is not possible, it is not in your program. In your body, everything has been programmed by the sperm and the egg of your parents. Celibacy is not in the program, and we don't yet know how to change the program. So anyone who claims to be a celibate is a hypocrite – he will find some perverted ways; one of them is homosexuality, another is sodomy.

Who has created all these prostitutes? If you dig up the roots, you will be very surprised to know that to protect marriage, prostitutes are an absolute necessity. Because the man gets fed up with the woman, the woman gets fed up with the man. Then just for a change… In the past, women were not courageous enough and not educated enough. That's why there have not been male prostitutes. But now you can find male prostitutes in London, Chicago, San Francisco, New York. This is a by-product of the women's liberation movement. Obviously, if men can go to prostitutes, why not women? And the whole thing is to protect marriage.

Protecting marriage is one of the causes of homosexuality, it is one of the causes of child abuse. And then all the monasteries – Christian, Hindu, Buddhist – are full of homosexuals. I am not condemning their homosexuality. I am simply saying that they are victims of a stupid ideology, teaching celibacy. And the governments are still doing the same. Now they are making laws against homosexuality – not against celibacy. You can make laws against homosexuality but that will make homosexuality go underground. Or, men will start finding new ways to express their sexuality – maybe plastic women; they are in existence already.

But no court in the world has thought to cut the very root: make a law against the celibacy which drives people into perversion. But that will go against all the religions, and religions are tremendously powerful – from the outside and from the inside because you are conditioned by them. The whole of human history is full of violence, full of war, and we know perfectly well that it is because of the existence of nations. There is no need of nations. This whole planet is one. Its problems are one, its solutions have to be one. But why is it not being implemented? And anybody who says this…

Yesterday I received a letter from a sannyasin, Ma Prem Madhu from England. She has won the first prize in a competition for creating better and more beautiful neighborhoods, more in tune with nature. Prince Charles gave her the prize – and she went there in orange clothes with my mala. Everyone was shocked. All the celebrities must have been there, all the idiots and all the lords – and Prince Charles looked at my picture and said to Prem Madhu, "This is dangerous." Now, what danger am I causing the world? Princes find me dangerous… When the Prince of Wales came to India, Queen Elizabeth insisted to him, "You can go everywhere in India, but not to Pune." He himself confessed it to his cousin-brother Vimalkirti, who was my sannyasin, and his wife, Turiya. Both were present in Mumbai to meet him, and he was so interested in me, but the Queen had told him not to go because it is "dangerous." I have been wondering what this word "danger" means. I have never killed a fly in my life.

Twenty-five countries have prohibited my entry into their land. The grounds are the same, that I can destroy their morality, religion, tradition. And these people don't even consider a simple fact that, if a man who comes as a tourist for three weeks can destroy your morality of two thousand years, then your morality is not worth saving. It should be destroyed. You are accepting defeat by refusing my entry for just three weeks. Your religion is not courageous enough to answer me, your politicians are cowards.

Where does this cowardliness come from that is in all the politicians and all the priests? – it comes from a root that Friedrich Nietzsche has called "will to power." Anyone who suffers from an inferiority complex, feels in some way inferior – it may be intelligence, may be strength, may be beauty; it can be anything. If one feels inferior… And a kind of inferiority is bound to happen to almost everyone because our whole educational system is based on competition, comparison. And the moment you compete and you compare, naturally you have to put yourself somewhere; you are inferior or superior.

The moment you feel yourself inferior, your whole being takes a certain route: will to power. Somehow, you have to prove to yourself and to the world that you are not inferior. Your presidents, your prime ministers, your ambassadors, your kings, your queens, are all in the same boat: just trying to prove they are not inferior, that they are great leaders of men. And I have seen many of these great leaders of men – just phony. If you look inside, you will find nothing but bullshit.

Otherwise I cannot see how a man who does not even have a paper knife needs the army to arrest him. And all the agencies of the government refused to arrest me because they didn't see any point. They would look stupid. And finally that happened.

The United States Attorney from Oregon who was fighting the case – because he could not manage a crucifixion or something more contemporary… It was not his fault, it is my fault. I have not committed anything; what could that poor man do? He tried his best. Now the reward for that man is that he has been fired. He tried his best, but for fictions.

He said in the court that I had arranged thousands of marriages, just for the purpose of getting residence – at least certainly *one* marriage. Just look at the point. I have arranged thousands of marriages and he himself ends with the conclusion that at least one marriage *certainly*. Then from where do those thousands of marriages come? He could only bribe one couple. He tried to persuade many couples that they should say that I had arranged their marriages, and they said I had not been speaking for three and a half years; I had not been seeing anyone. It would look simply stupid. Out of five thousand sannyasins, perhaps they managed to bribe someone – to give him a job, to give him a green card. That was the only proof.

And the head of the army laughed at the point. "If he has married just one couple, it does not require the army! For such a small, messy affair!" But everywhere, politicians are basically hollow people, utterly empty and completely in fear, in paranoia because their position is never certain. Today they may be the prime minister and tomorrow they may not be. Today they have so much power and tomorrow they will be just a beggar on the streets. The man who was the prime minister in Russia before the revolution, a man named Kerensky, fled the country. He died in 1950 in New

York. People had completely forgotten about him. He was one of the most powerful men of his times, being the prime minister of the czar of Russia, one of the greatest lands. And he died as a grocer. He had been running a grocery store in New York since the revolution, hiding in disguise.

The politician originates out of an inferiority complex. He wants to have more power, more power so he can fill his emptiness. But strangely – by the side – as he goes on climbing ladder upon ladder, more and more fear also grows on both sides. The fear that he can be pulled down because so many people are pulling his legs, so many people are competing for the same position. He cannot remain forever in power – that fear is the reason why a man like me becomes dangerous. Because I simply want to say that two and two are four.

Religions have made men's minds retarded by creating beliefs from fictions. And politicians have destroyed man and created as undignified a life as possible because their power depends on your slavery. Unless we cut these roots... This earth has the capacity to feed at least five times more people than exist today – that is a scientific calculation – and these barriers should be removed. Science should be employed not in the service of death and destruction but in the service of life and love, affirmation, celebration.

We are in such a situation today that either we will let these rotten politicians and priests destroy the whole humanity and the earth, or we will take the power from their hands and decentralize it to humanity. No army is needed because no nation is needed. No destructive weapons are needed because no war is needed. And if this whole energy – right now fifty percent of our energy goes to war – if a hundred percent of the energy and a hundred percent of the intelligence of humanity goes together hand in hand to create a better society, a more scientific education, a better humanity, which for the first time we are capable of...

It was not possible in the past. Today it is possible. Much of the work can be done by robots; there is no need to destroy human life in unnecessary work. Much of the work can be done by computers; there is no need for small boys and girls to burden their memories unnecessarily. They can just carry a small computer in their pocket which contains everything that they want to know. And to me, it is even more significant because if the whole memory is shifted to the computer, meditation will become such an easy job. Then you don't have to fight with any thoughts and memories; you just have to turn your computer off, deposit it at the gate and enter the temple! You need not be worried about anything.

And according to the people who work in the realms of physiology, biology, genetics, a better man is possible, better than any who have ever existed on the earth. It is a confirmed fact that man can live at least three hundred years without any difficulty, without even becoming old. Three hundred years – the implications are great. If Albert Einstein can live three hundred years, his contribution will be tremendous, to physics, to mathematics. If a Mozart can live three hundred years, certainly his music will become more and more meditative, more and more silent. If a Rabindranath can live for three hundred years, his poetry will become pure fragrance of the beyond.

It is within our hands to choose what kind of people we want. It is in our hands to decide how many people we want. But we have to remove these barriers of politicians and religions – otherwise they are going to force humanity to commit suicide.

I would like Fukuoka to know that he is in a better position because no one understands him. He should feel some sympathy for me – everyone misunderstands me. And I am making everything as clear, as logical, as rational as possible. Fukuoka is not logical or rational in his statements. He has a beautiful heart – that I can see from his statements. But he has not worked out interconnections. For example, he thinks that if we move back to nature, all problems will be solved. This is not new. Leo Tolstoy was teaching "back to nature." Rousseau was teaching "back to nature." In this country Mahatma Gandhi was teaching "back to nature." And all three were in the same trouble as Fukuoka, that no one understood them.

The problem is very complicated. First, there is no way to go back. And even if some way can be found to go back, where is the line? Where will you think you have gone back enough? It will certainly be when the first monkey jumped on the earth and stood on two legs – against nature. The first scientist, the founder of civilization... I don't think that before that, you can stop. And I don't think anyone would like to go to that state again. It will be very difficult.

In these thousands of years, your body has changed so much. You cannot jump on trees, naked in the rain, in the cold, in the heat. And you cannot live on just fruit. Most probably everyone will be having fractures, multiple fractures, and there will not be any ambulances because Mahatma Gandhi does not allow even railway trains. He is even against something innocent like telephones. I know one thing is wrong in the telephone. That is the last part of it, *phone*, because from that phone has come *phony*. But otherwise, it is innocent. You can change the name.

He was against telegrams. He thought that if man goes back – as Fukuoka also thinks, without having a clear-cut conception... At the time of Gautam Buddha, twenty-five centuries ago, the population of the whole world was twenty million. Even then there was poverty. Even then there was crime, murder, rape. People don't find it in history books, and when I first said it, a Buddhist scholar, Bhadant Anand Kaushalyayan, stood up and said, "From where have you found out these things?"

I said, "From the teachings of Gautam Buddha! Because he is teaching people they should never commit a rape. That simply means people were committing rape. He is telling people, 'Be content in your poverty.' If there was no poverty, there was no need to make such a statement." And for forty-two years continuously he was telling people not to steal, not to murder, not to be violent. To whom is he talking? Either he is mad or I am right."

Now, just as India became free in 1947, forty years ago, the country's population was four hundred million. And Mahatma Gandhi, Mother Teresa and all the *shankaracharyas* insisted that birth control is against God. In the first place there is no God. In the second place, if it is against God, let it be! It is his problem, not our problem. But no one listened, and just in forty years' time, from four hundred million, India's population has reached nine hundred million. By the end of the century, India will have more than one billion people. For the first time, India will be the most populated country. Up to now, China had that privilege; now India has defeated China in stupidity.

By the end of the century, the whole world will have five billion people. And what do you think will be the result of going back to nature? Even twenty million people cannot live, going back to nature. There will be simply corpses all around. This is being taught by people like Mahatma Gandhi who think they are nonviolent. What can be more violent? Genghis Khan killed four million people. Nadir Shah killed three million people. Adolf Hitler killed eighteen million people. But if Mahatma Gandhi and Fukuoka are to be followed, they will kill at least five billion people. The whole earth will be full of corpses.

Back to nature is simply back to death. If humanity decides to go back to nature, I will suggest to them to first do one thing: dig your grave, prepare it because there is going to be no one else to prepare it. Everyone will be dying himself. So right now, prepare your grave and lie down in it and then go back to nature.

All that you have, ninety-nine percent of it is because of science and technology. It is true that science and technology have taken a wrong turn. Descartes was wrong when he said that man and nature are enemies; Bertrand Russell was wrong when he said that we have to conquer nature. These people have given a wrong direction to science. Nature and man have to be friends. There is no question of conquering. We are part of nature, and the part cannot conquer the whole. The part can only dissolve into the whole, rejoice in being one with the whole.

Science has to be given a new turn so that it becomes a bridge between man and nature. And the same science that has created atom bombs and nuclear weapons can also create a far greater consciousness for man, far healthier human beings, more beautiful trees, bigger flowers. This planet, although it is very small, contains the potentiality of being the richest planet in this vast universe where millions and millions of stars are surrounded by more and more planets.

Right now the count is three million stars, but they don't say that is the end. That is as far as our scientific instruments can see. There is beyond, unlimited, with no boundaries. But in this whole expanse, only this small earth has evolved to the point of consciousness, love, beauty, music, poetry, sensitivity, meditativeness.

It should be a determination in every intelligent being that we are not going to allow any vested interest to destroy this planet. This planet has to remain. And there is a golden future just ahead on the horizon – but we must cut the roots, whatever the cost. This is the only revolt I teach. All revolutions have failed because they were cutting the leaves and branches. I teach a total revolt against the past, against all vested interests.

The question is of tremendous importance: to save man is to save the greatest creation of the universe. It has taken four million years for this earth to create man. It is so precious, and the future is much more valuable because inside you the possibility of a Gautam Buddha, the possibility of a Zarathustra, the possibility of a Lao Tzu is there. You can also blossom in the same silence, in the same peace, in the same beauty, in the same ecstasy.

I forgot to look at my watch!

Ronald Reagan, his cabinet members, and his wife Nancy, traveled to the Rocky Mountains for a skiing holiday. Waking up one morning, Reagan opens the curtains and there in the snow, in yellow letters, someone has pissed the message: "Reagan is a wimp." Enraged, Reagan orders an analysis made of the urine to find out who the culprit is.

An official returns with the results and tells Reagan, "I have some bad news and some terrible news. The bad news is that the urine belongs to your attorney general, Ed Meese."

"What?" shouts Reagan. "I will shoot that bastard! And what is the terrible news?"

"Well," says the man, "the terrible news is that it is written in Nancy's handwriting."

24

Understanding the Desire for Power

Osho,
All my life I have been intrigued by power and the recognition I can take from it. Now that seems very confined and petty. Yet, I sense also that there is a more authentic type of power, not dependent on other people or their reactions – more within myself. Can you please talk about my attraction toward this?

Your question needs deep scrutiny because I can say yes to it and I can also say no to it. Yes, I will not say; the greater possibility is for the no. And I will explain the reasons to you. This is how the mind goes on playing games with you all. You are saying, "All my life I have been intrigued by power and the recognition I can take from it." This is a truthful recognition, sincere. Many of the power-oriented people are not even aware of it; their will to power remains almost unconscious. Others can see it, but they themselves cannot see it.

As I said last night, "This will to power is the greatest sickness man has suffered from." And all our educational systems, religions, cultures, societies are in absolute support of this sickness. Everyone wants his child to be the greatest man in the world. Listen to mothers talking about their children, it's as if they have all given birth to Alexander the Great, Ivan the Terrible, Joseph Stalin, Ronald Reagan.

Five billion people are rushing toward power. One has to understand that this tremendous urge to power is arising from an emptiness within you. A man who is not power-oriented is a man fulfilled, contented, at ease, at home as he is. His very being is an immense gratitude to existence; nothing more is to be asked. Whatever has been given to you, you had never asked for. It is a sheer gift out of the abundance of existence. And these are the two separate paths: one is the will to power, the other is the will to dissolve.

You are saying, "Now that seems very confined and petty." Not only confined and petty, but also sick and ugly. The very idea to be powerful over other people means taking their dignity, destroying their individuality, forcing them to be slaves. Only an ugly mind can do that.

You continue the question, "...I sense also that there is a more authentic type of power, not dependent on other people or their reactions – more within myself." There is some truth in what you are saying, but it is not your experience. There is certainly a power which has nothing to do with domination over others. The power of a flower opening its petals... Have you seen that power, that glory? Have you seen the power of a starry night? – not dominating anyone. Have you seen the power of the smallest leaf dancing in the sun, in the rain; its beauty, its grandeur, its joy? It has nothing to do with anyone else. It does not even need someone to see it. This is true independence. And it brings you to the source of your being, from where your life is arising every moment. But this power should not be called power because that creates a confusion.

The very word *power* means "over someone." Even people of great understanding have not been able to see the point. In India, the religion Jainism exists. The word *jaina* means "the conqueror." The original meaning certainly must have been what you are talking about: the power that arises within you as a petal opens and the flower releases its fragrance. But I have looked deeply into the tradition of Jainism. When they call a man a conqueror, they also say that he has conquered himself. *Someone* has to be conquered.

Mahavira's name was Vardhaman. They changed it to Mahavira. *Mahavira* means "the great conqueror," the great, victorious man. But the very idea that Mahavira has conquered himself, if reduced to simple psychological terms, means that he can stand naked in the rain, in the cold; that he can remain hungry in the name of fasting, continuously, for months. In twelve years of discipline and preparation, he ate for only one year; for eleven years he was hungry. Not in a continuity – one month he would remain hungry, then one day he would eat; two months he would remain hungry, then for a few days he would eat. But in twelve years the number of times that he ate comes to a total of only one year. For eleven years he tortured his body.

It needs a deep insight to understand that whether you torture others or you torture yourself, there is no difference at all – except that the other can defend himself. At least there is that possibility. If you start torturing yourself, there is no one to defend you. You can do anything with your own body. This is simply masochism. It is not, in my understanding, finding the source of your inner being. Hence I would not like to call it power because that word is contaminated.

I would like to call it peace, love, compassion. You can choose the word. But power has been in the hands of violent people; whether they were violent with others or with themselves does not matter. I think the people who were violent with others were more natural and the people who were violent with themselves were absolutely psychotic. But the people who have tortured themselves have become your saints. Their whole contribution to the world is a discipline of how to torture yourself.

There are saints who have slept on a bed of thorns. They are still there; in Varanasi you can find them. It may be good showmanship, but it is ugly and has to be condemned. These people should not be respected. These are criminals because they are committing a crime against a body which cannot even go to the court.

So the second part has to be understood very well; otherwise your first desire, of being intrigued by power, will be there again in a different disguise. Now you will start making an effort to find power over yourself. And that's what it seems to be.

You say, "…a power not dependent on other people or their reactions – more within myself." Even the reference to other people and their reactions implies that you are not thinking in a very different way. First you were interested that people should give you recognition; that you should be a powerful man, a world conqueror, a Nobel Prize winner, or some other kind of stupidity. But not everyone can be Alexander the Great. Neither can everyone become a Nobel Prize winner, nor can everyone be greater in some sense than others.

This takes a turn: finding yourself in a situation where this is not possible, or perhaps there is too much competition and you will be crushed – there are far bigger people, far more dangerous in the competition… It is better to withdraw within yourself and try to find a power that has no reference to other people, a power that is independent of other people. Even this much connection is enough for me to conclude that now you are going on another trip of the same kind. First you were trying to dominate others, now you will try to dominate yourself. That's what people call discipline.

I am reminded of Aesop's very famous fable…

The mango season has come, and a fox is trying to reach the ripe mangoes, but they are too high. The fox's jump is not high enough to get them.

She tries a few times; then seeing the impossibility she looks all around to see whether anyone is watching or not. A little rabbit has been watching the whole scene. The fox walks away, not showing her defeat, but the rabbit asks, "Auntie, what happened?"

The fox says to the rabbit, "My son, those mangoes are not yet ripe."

If you change your desire for power, it should not be like Aesop's fable. You should first understand from where the desire to power has been arising. It has been arising from your emptiness, inferiority. The only right way to be freed from this ugly desire to dominate is to enter your emptiness, to see exactly what it is. You have been escaping from it through your power trips. Now put your whole energy not into torturing yourself, not into making any discipline of masochism, but simply entering your nothingness: What is it? And there, roses blossom in your nothingness. There, you find the source of eternal life. You are no longer in the grip of an inferiority complex and you don't have any reference to other people. You have found yourself.

Those who are intrigued with power are going away and away from themselves. The farther away their minds go, the emptier they will be. But words like *emptiness*, *nothingness*, have been condemned, and you have accepted the idea. Rather than exploring the beauty of nothingness… It is utter silence. It is soundless music. There is no joy that can be compared to it. It is sheer blissfulness.

Gautam Buddha called his ultimate encounter with himself *nirvana*, because of this experience. *Nirvana* means nothingness. And once you are at ease with your nothingness, all tensions, conflicts, worries, disappear. You have found the source of life which knows no death. Still, I would like to remind you not to call it power. Call it love, call it silence, call it blissfulness because that *power* has been so contaminated by the past that even the word needs tremendous purification. And it gives wrong connotations.

This world is dominated by people who are basically inferior but are trying to cover up their inferiority with some kind of power, any kind of power. They have created many ways. Certainly everyone cannot be the president of the country – then divide the country into states. Then so many people can be governors, chief ministers. Then divide the work of the chief minister – then many people can be cabinet ministers, and just lower than them, many people can be state ministers. This whole hierarchy consists of people suffering from an inferiority complex. From the lowest peon to the president, they all have the same sickness.

Indira Gandhi remained in power for a long time. When she was in power, she told my secretary many times that she wanted to see me and meet me, and that she had a few questions. At least six times the date was fixed and just one day before, the message would come that "An emergency has arisen and she will not be able to come this time." When it happened six times – that an emergency arises, exactly! – I asked my secretary to ask her what was the real thing. This emergency is not the real thing. And she was honest enough to say, "The problem is that my cabinet ministers, my colleagues in the parliament prevent me. They say, 'Going to Osho can be disastrous to your political power.'"

Then she was defeated and my secretary said to her, "Now there is no problem. Use this opportunity. You are no longer prime minister of the country, you can come."

She said, "It is even *more* difficult. Now my people are saying, 'If you go there, then forget forever about becoming a prime minister again.'"

Her son Rajiv Gandhi was a pilot and he told my secretary many times that he wanted to meet me and to have my guidance about his future career, whether he should enter politics or remain a pilot. Since he became the prime minister, he has not asked for any guidance. Now, the same fear.

I have become such a danger that if you come to me, all those who are against me will be against you! I have such a great company of enemies around the world – I enjoy it really. A single man without any weapon is at war with twenty-five countries! And those great countries, having all the power, seem to be absolutely powerless.

In Germany, in two courts, my people have filed a case against the government because in the parliament they were calling Christianity a religion and my movement a "cult." In the Christian theological world, the word *cult* is condemnatory. In two courts we appealed that either they should also call Christianity a cult or they should call our movement a new religious movement, but they cannot call it a cult. And two courts have given their verdict in our favor, saying that the government has no right to condemn and use condemnatory words for people who have not done any harm in the country. It is a religious movement. But the government goes on using the same word, *cult*.

I am informing my people that those two courts should make it clear to the government that they are destroying their constitution, their law, themselves. And if anyone in the parliament again calls my religious movement a cult, against the court's ruling, he should be treated as a criminal. It may be the chancellor of Germany itself, it does not matter. These people are all trembling inside, worried that they can collapse; just a push is needed. They know that inside there is nothing, and outside a great competition for power.

It is not a coincidence that all the twenty-four tirthankaras, the masters of Jainism, came from royal families. Gautam Buddha was a prince. What happened to these people? Rama and Krishna, the Hindu incarnations of God, are also in the same category, belonging to royal families. It seems no one else can become enlightened. Only royal blood is needed for enlightenment!

The point that I want to make clear to you is that these people were at the top already. They had power and that power they experienced did not destroy their inner emptiness. They renounced power to find out what their interiority was. Finding it, they blossomed – in beauty, in truth, in a statement to the whole world that "I have come home."

People have not recognized the fact of why these people renounced their kingdoms. They had all the power that they needed, but just that situation: all the power that they need, all the money that they need and still, inside there is no one. The house is full of money, comforts, luxuries, but the master is missing. It was out of this urgency that they renounced power and went in search of peace.

Naturally, ordinary people don't have the power. They only look at powerful people from far away and think, "If I was also given the same honor, the same recognition, I would also be someone. I would leave my footprints in the sands of time." They become intrigued with power. But look at the people who were born in power and renounced it, seeing that it is an exercise of absolute futility. You still remain the same inside. Even if you have billions of dollars, it will not make any change within you. Only a change, a transformation within you, is going to give you peace. Out of that peace will come your love; out of this peace will come your dance, your songs, your creativity. But just avoid the word *power*.

Right now you are only thinking about it. Thinking will not help. Thinking is perfectly good if you want to compete in the world for power, money, prestige, respectability. But as far as settling in your being, the mind is absolutely useless. Hence, the whole effort here is how to help you get out of the mind into meditation, out of thoughts into silence. Once you have tasted your inner being, all greed, desire for money, power, will simply evaporate. There is no comparison. You have found God himself within you. What more can you desire?

Osho,
What is this universe made of, besides this silence which I don't know, and with which the sages are overflowing?

This universe is certainly made of silence. But the silence is not dead, it is not the silence of a cemetery. It is the silence of a temple. It is alive! It is a song without words. It has gestures, and in a thousand and one ways those gestures show what this universe is made of. Look at the roses, look at the lotuses, look at the birds on the wing. Look at the stars and the trees and the mountains. These are all gestures of silence. This whole existence is the dance of silence. It takes unique forms, it melts from one form into another form, but silence is its fundamental constituent. These words you listen to are not saying anything. Just gestures of silence, alive.

You have asked a beautiful question. "What is this universe made of besides this silence which I don't know...?" How can you know the silence? You can *be* the silence, but you can never know it. For knowing, a distinction, a distance is needed. You have to be the knower and the silence has to be the known. You are also made of silence. It is just that you have not looked deep enough in your own being. Then it is not a question of knowing, it is a question of being.

And you are saying, "...this silence which I don't know and with which the sages are overflowing." You are also overflowing. It's just that you are intrigued with all kinds of stupid things, so you remain unaware of your overflowing silence. Sages drop all nonessential things and then only the silence remains – and the overflow of it. The whole world is flooded with silence.

Now even the scientists are turning into mystics because they are saying that stars disappear into black holes, symmetrical to our death. We also don't know the dark tunnel of death. But scientists have also observed that not only do old stars simply disappear, new stars are continuously being born. And stars are not small things. The idea has entered the scientific world that everything arises out of nothing and finally collapses back into the nothing to rest. Perhaps it may arise again. It looks illogical. How can the whole existence with such variety come out from nothing? But it is not a question of logic. What can I do? It is the way things are.

And to make it logical we have made things unnecessarily idiotic. We could not conceive how this world, this universe, can come out of nothingness. We created a fictitious God to console our hearts and our logic that "God created the world." It gives a little satisfaction to the mediocre minds. Those who are a little more intelligent will find the question remains the same: "From where does God come?" Finally you have to accept the fact that God comes out of nothingness. Why bring in poor God unnecessarily? Then he gets so many hits – for centuries he has been hammered by all sides. There is no problem. From nothing, everything comes.

For example, I am speaking to you and I am fully aware from where these words are coming; they are coming from my nothingness. I don't find any other place from where they are coming. Nothingness is not nothing. Nothingness is all. And to recognize nothingness as all, as an experience, is the only way to find your unity with the universe. In life, in death, there is no fear. You have been here many times and then rested. Rest *is* needed, one gets tired. Every day you work and in the night you rest, hoping that in the morning you will wake up again.

I know a man who does not go to sleep and keeps the whole house awake by knocking and asking people, "Are you asleep?" Now, if they answer, their sleep is disturbed. If they don't answer, he will shake them asking, "What happened, are you asleep?"

I was a guest in that family and everyone said, "Somehow this man is driving us crazy. Neither he sleeps nor does he allow anyone else to have a restful night."

I said, "What is his logic?"

They said, "He used to be a professor of logic, and you cannot argue with him because he says, 'What is the guarantee that if I go to sleep I will wake up? I will not go to sleep.' And he quotes ancient Upanishads which say that death is like sleep."

I talked to the man. I said, "Death is certainly like sleep. And sleep is such a restful period; after every day you need a small period of rest. After your whole life, you need a longer period of sleep.

"You have been here – where else can you be? This is the only universe there is. So when you are rested, you can wake up again, fresh, rejuvenated. Don't be worried about death. Death is a tremendous relaxation into the universe, into its nothingness."

Only a meditator can understand. As his meditation becomes deeper, he comes to explore the whole world of nothingness within himself. But it is a nothingness to be rejoiced in – so restful, so peaceful, so cool, so alive, so overflowing. You will have to enter your nothingness. That is the only real temple.

Gautam Buddha, in his tremendous compassion, said to his disciples, "While you are going deeper into yourself, if you meet me on the way cut my head off immediately! I should not become a barrier. Your nothingness should remain absolutely yours; it cannot be shared, cannot be divided."

You have to go into absolute aloneness. Just the very idea of being totally nothing brings a shower of flowers. Just being alone, utterly alone, brings such a fresh breeze, such fragrance. But the experience is a million times more than you can conceive of with the mind. If this world needs anything, it is an experience of nothingness. Not an experience of a God, not an experience of a Jesus Christ, not an experience of Gautam Buddha. It needs only one experience: of a purity, uncontaminated, unpolluted even by the presence of anyone else. A pure presence, of your own being. To me, that is liberation. To me, that is the ultimate flowering of your being. Your eyes will show it, your hands will indicate it, your dance may become the part of the overflow. You will be a transformed human being.

And at this juncture of time we need millions of transformed beings who can fill the whole world with joy, with roses of consciousness, with the light of awareness, with the music of the soul. Only that can prevent the idiotic politicians from destroying this world.

Perhaps you may not have noted that destruction also gives a certain power. Just as creation gives a tremendous well-being, a dignity, those who cannot be creative have all become destructive – in the name of politics, in the name of religion, in the name of education.

I want my sannyasins to stand against the whole ugly past of humanity. Only then can we see a new sunrise, a new world overflowing with love. Otherwise, we have come to the point where the greatest criminals of the world are joined together to destroy it. They may destroy it in the great names of democracy, equality, communism, socialism, but these are just names. Behind is the reality that these uncreative people are taking revenge against those who have created. They could not be a Mozart, a Wagner, a Michelangelo. At least they can be an Adolf Hitler. They can be in some way destructive because they could not convert their energies into creativity.

Only a man of inner silences becomes a creator. And we need more and more creative people in the world. Their very creativity, their very silence, their very love, their very peace will be the only way to protect this beautiful planet. Yes, this existence consists only of silence and laughter.

One day, Jesus wakes up in a bad mood. He is feeling depressed and lethargic. In fact, a typical Monday-morning feeling. He wanders around heaven looking for someone to cheer him up and finally arrives at the Pearly Gates where Saint Peter is interviewing the new arrivals.

Suddenly he sees an old man with a long white beard whose face looks familiar. He goes up to him. "Excuse me sir," says Jesus, "but your face seems familiar. I am sure we have met. What did you do on earth?"

The old man smiles. "As a matter of fact," he says, "I am a carpenter and lived a full and happy life until my son left home and became world famous. I never saw him again."

Jesus looks at him with astonishment and says with delight, "Dad!"

The old man opens his eyes wide and rushes forward with outstretched arms, crying, "Pinocchio!"

Little Ernie accompanies his parents to a nudist beach for the first time. After looking around for a few minutes, Ernie asks his father why some men have big ones and some men have small ones.

Rather than go into a long explanation, his father replies, "The men that have big ones are smart and the men that have small ones are stupid."

Accepting this explanation, Ernie goes off to explore the beach. Time passes and he finally comes across his father again, "Have you seen your mother, son?" asks his dad.

"Yes," says Ernie, "she is behind the bushes talking to some stupid guy who is getting smarter by the minute."

25

The Art of Trusting

Osho,
For years now, I have been sitting by your side. Knowingly and unknowingly, an inner mountain has been climbed, effortlessly for the most part. Just today I looked down and it frightened me how far off the ground I am. A fear that I could fall grips me. The road is getting smaller and smaller, and I feel the danger. Would you speak to me about this?

David, the path back home is certainly a razor's edge. As you come closer and closer to yourself, the path goes on becoming narrower and narrower. At the very end of this path you are going to find your pure aloneness. The crowd has never found any truth. On the contrary, whenever anyone has found the truth, the crowd has rewarded him with crucifixion. To seek truth is the most dangerous, but a very exciting, challenging, experiment.

An ancient Tibetan proverb says: "One hundred seekers start; ninety-nine are lost somewhere on the way, go astray. Only one – that too, very rarely – reaches the goal of his search." With this proverb is attached a small story…

Deep in the mountains, far away from Lhasa is a monastery. The chief monk is getting old and he wants a master from Lhasa to replace him.

He sends a messenger, a young man, to the main monastery in Lhasa to ask them, "Our master is getting very old and he wants a man to replace him." After long, long difficulties of mountainous paths the young man finally reaches the main monastery.

An audience is given to him. And the master says to him, "I can understand. I will send one hundred people with you."

The young man said, "But I have asked only for one."

The master said, "Have you forgotten the old proverb? A hundred should go; rarely, one reaches."

The proverb was certainly known to the young man, but he could not trust that a hundred people could go and only one would reach. But he could not argue with the chief of all the monasteries of Tibet. And one hundred monks followed the young man.

They had not gone very far when they were stopped by a few soldiers with naked swords, who said, "Our small kingdom has lost its master. We need a master urgently. The pay is good, a palace to live in, and you will be the only religious man in the whole kingdom. We are simply conveying to you the orders from the emperor. Refusal can be dangerous – you can see the naked swords."

Many of those hundred monks started thinking, "This is a good place. Why unnecessarily go deep into the mountains? It is close to Lhasa, the kingdom is rich, the monastery is rich, all the facilities are available, and you will be the high priest of the kingdom." So not only one, but many wanted to go.

The young man said, "Have you forgotten?"

They said, "We have not forgotten. *You* forget it – all of it! We are going to stay."

The soldiers said, "We need only one, but the monastery is big. If many of you want to come, you can be part of the monastery and the emperor will be immensely happy."

Half of the crowd disappeared. The young man could not believe...

Just a few miles further they were again prevented to go any further, this time by a crowd. They needed four priests because the richest man's daughter was being married, and the reward was going to be great. "It is only a question of a few days, and then you can go on wherever you are going." Immediately, more than four were ready, but the crowd said, "We don't want more than four."

The other monks tried to ask them, "What are you doing? We have been sent for a certain purpose, because of a certain message."

They said, "We are not going astray. It is only a question of a few days. Soon we will finish the marriage and we will come a little faster and join you. Your journey is long. The path is tedious. We cannot miss this opportunity of earning, getting rewards from the richest man." And again four people disappeared.

It went on in this way, and the young man started feeling, "Perhaps I am the only one who is going to make it back!"

As they were passing a river, a very beautiful young woman with tears in her eyes said, "You are all compassionate people. My father is a famous hunter – I live with my father, my mother is dead. He was supposed to come back this morning and it is evening and he is not back. I am immensely afraid in this lonely part of the Himalayas. Won't you be kind enough, at least one of you stay with me for the night? And in the morning you can go as soon as my father comes home."

Immediately a young man… In fact many were ready, but a young man said, "I am coming. This is the essential teaching of Gautam Buddha – compassion!"

And this continues… It is a long story, and people went on disappearing. Finally only two monks and the young man remained. They were passing the last village and soon they would be arriving at the monastery. It was already in view shining in the morning sun on the mountains.

In that village there was an atheist who challenged those monks saying, "If you have any guts, first accept my challenge for a debate. I don't believe in Gautam Buddha and I don't believe in his teachings; I am ready to fight on each and every point."

The young man said to the remaining two fellows, "Don't get involved in this. Our monastery is there, you can see it – so beautiful in the eternal snows of the Himalayas."

But one of them said, "I cannot move an inch. My master Gautam Buddha has been challenged. I am going to remain here. However long it takes, I will either convert this man to Buddhism or I will be converted to his disciplehood." So he was left in that village.

Only one monk and the young man reached the monastery. The young man said, "I have passed through an immense experience. I had never thought that proverbs are so accurately true."

The old master said, "I knew he would send at least one hundred people because I had asked for one."

The young man said, "But you never mentioned it to me."

The old man said, "There was no need to mention it. This is how things go on happening in this world. We are fortunate that at least one has arrived. There is no certainty; there are so many bypaths, so many allurements, and once you have gone astray it is not easy to come back to the right path."

The crowd consists of people who have all gone astray. Once in a while a courageous person comes out of the crowd and starts searching a path of his own. It needs daring, it needs courage, it needs intelligence. It needs trust in yourself, and also a deep understanding that you will be condemned by the crowd. The crowd never likes people to be individuals. Individuals irritate the crowd very much. The crowd wants you just to be a part of the crowd, a Hindu, a Mohammedan, a Christian. The moment you declare, "I am myself; neither a Hindu nor a Christian nor a Buddhist, and I am going to search the truth of my being on my own," all the crowds around you will become antagonistic.

There is a deep psychology behind it. Your standing aloof and alone and moving in the direction of the unknown – without any companion, without any guide – irritates the mind of the crowd because you are showing them that they are cowards clinging to each other like sheep, not moving like lions. But truth is not for sheep. The sheep are not courageous enough to allow truth to reveal its mysteries and its glories to their minds. The glories are so immense, so boundless, the mysteries are so infinite, that only the heart of the lion can rejoice, dance, sing.

Yes, there are moments when even the heart of the lion trembles, feels fear because the path is so alone. And it goes on becoming narrower. As you are reaching higher and the path is becoming narrower, naturally, you look to the side and your whole being goes into trembling. Just a single wrong step and you will be finished. On both sides are such depths.

But strangely enough, although the path is of the razor's edge, no one has fallen from it. Everyone has felt the fear, but existence supports those who are in search of truth. Its support is unconditional. Existence does not support those who are nothing but living lies. They may have great power, but their own power will destroy them. Many civilizations have existed on the earth and they destroyed themselves by their own power. We are not the first civilization in the world. Atlantis drowned – perhaps the people of Atlantis had reached a far higher civilization than we have.

In India we have the story of Mahabharata, the great Indian war that happened five thousand years ago. In minute detail, the story describes weapons which can only be nuclear. The civilization had certainly reached the same point where we are. But power in the hands of ignorant, retarded crowds is self-destructive.

Crowds upon crowds have come and disappeared, but not a single individual seeker has ever fallen from those heights where, David, you are feeling – "What will happen?" I have been watching you. This is perhaps your first question to me. For all these years you have been silently with me. That is the only right way to be with a master – not to ask, and the answer will be given to you. Wait, and you will be showered with all the blessings possible. Don't be in a hurry; otherwise you will miss the whole point.

Patience is the only prayer by the side of a master. Utterly relaxed, in deep love, in great gratitude, something goes on growing in you without any effort. Something goes on maturing, something goes on becoming more and more crystallized, without any effort on your part. You are just a watcher of the miracle that is happening to you.

David, your question is not just out of intellectual curiosity. You have been long enough with me; there is no point to remain silent so long and now suddenly become curious. Your question is coming from your existential experience. And only these questions are authentic.

You are asking, "For years now, I have been sitting by your side." In fact, that is the very meaning of the ancient word *upanishad*: sitting by the side of the master. Nothing else is expected, just sitting by the side. The master is radiating and if you are ready to receive silently, seasons will change, days will come and go, and slowly, slowly you will find you are no longer the same person who had first come.

And as your insight deepens, you start becoming aware that each and every moment you are changing, becoming something new, fresh, just born, and the joy of this freshness is immense. I have been watching you sitting by my side. In fact, if you are capable of just going on sitting, nothing else is needed. All the meditations will happen on their own, all the flowers of love and silence will blossom on their own, and once you have learned the secret, then there is nothing else to do in the world.

You are saying, "Knowingly and unknowingly, an inner mountain has been climbed, effortlessly for the most part. Just today I looked down and it frightened me how far off the ground I am. A fear that I could fall grips me. The road is getting smaller and smaller, and I feel the danger." There is no need to feel the danger because it is unprecedented; no one has ever fallen from the path that leads to truth.

No one has ever fallen from his own being. However big the mountain of being may be, you cannot fall. That is simply not in the nature of things. I have never heard that any seeker, any searcher, any honest inquirer has ever gone astray. Existence protects.

It is good you have asked it. Relax, because it is an absolute guarantee that existence supports you. The higher you reach, the more and more you become a beloved of this whole universe. This is my vision of a sannyasin. He has to become a beloved of this whole universe. And when you become a beloved of the whole universe, fear disappears – just as if it was nothing but darkness, and the light of love has come in and the darkness has disappeared.

Everything is going exactly right with you. Just remain in a let-go. Don't make any effort even to keep yourself on the path. Don't be worried that you may fall and at least you have to be alert not to fall. That will be unnecessary and will be preventing your growth, your evolution. You have come far away, certainly, from the earth. And it is natural to look and see the depths that are on both the sides of the path. I am not saying that fear is unnatural. It is natural because you are not aware of a far higher law, that existence protects those who are in search of truth. Slowly, slowly you will see that you cannot fall; the universe will not allow it.

The universe is not unintelligent. You are not living in a cosmos which has no intelligence. Existence is made of pure intelligence. Call it love, call it silence, call it nothingness, but in everything remember that the tremendous intelligence of existence is always there. Once you have learned the art of trusting, you are beyond all fear – you will learn it because there is no going back.

And when I am saying that it is absolutely guaranteed, I am saying it from my own experience. I have passed through the same fears. And as I became aware of a certain protection that surrounds me, I relaxed. Then I could move on this razor's edge, this narrowest path possible, with closed eyes. In fact, most of the people who have reached have reached with closed eyes! At the final stage the trust becomes so deep, who cares to look here and there? The eyes become closed on their own.

It is the fear that keeps them open. You may take a wrong step. But when trust becomes total you drop all cautiousness; you simply relax. Whatever existence decides to be your destiny, you are absolutely willing to relax in it. This is the only experience that has transformed people from ordinary, mundane mortals into immortal beings, has transformed them into luminous lights. The search for truth is the only search that makes you authentically human. Otherwise there is no difference between you and the animals – and the crowd remains at the level of the animals.

Never belong to a crowd, never belong to a nation; never belong to a religion, never belong to a race. Belong to the whole existence. Why limit yourself to small things? When the whole is available, only stupid people will cling to small things. Be oceanic.

Only then will you have the taste of what true life is. And a great gratitude arises, David, on its own accord. Not toward anyone in particular, but just toward this "whole" – all these stars, the trees, the birds, the mountains, the rivers, the oceans, the people. All that is. You simply feel a tremendous gratitude.

And when you open your eyes with gratitude, the same world becomes so psychedelically beautiful, so colorful – you could never have believed that the trees are so green; they have never been, and these are the same trees. Or that the winds passing through the trees are creating such subtle music – they have always been creating, but you were deaf. Or the sunsets and sunrises and the tremendous beauty they bring – you had missed them because you were blind. Your trust in the total opens all your sensitivities to their extreme. This whole existence becomes a sheer dance, a sheer celebration.

Little Ernie comes home early from school.

"What are you doing home?" asks his mother.

"I put a stick of dynamite under the teacher's desk," replies little Ernie.

"You march right back to school" says his mother, "and apologize!"

"Mom," says Ernie, "*What* school?"

David, what earth are you talking about? It is just a shadow, a dream, a memory. And you cannot fall into a memory, you cannot fall into a shadow, you cannot fall into a dream. Forget all about falling and the fear because this is the time: either you will become very afraid and stuck… You cannot go back, and you may not dare to go forward. That's why I am emphasizing the fact. Go ahead; there is nothing to be feared at all.

If a master cannot teach his disciples fearlessness, then that master is simply fake. I teach you in every possible way to be fearless, daring, courageous, risking, taking every challenge of life because this is the whole science of how to create a steel spine in you – which will be needed!

First, learn to drop small fears; then slowly, slowly bigger fears. Then finally, your whole energy which was involved in all kinds of fears, worries, tensions, anxieties, is released. The energy that is released is so much that it makes you dance, makes you laugh, makes you sing. Suddenly a deep feeling that you have arrived – arrived at the place which you have never left. It is just that you have gone astray into your mind, far away, traveling all over the world. You simply needed a good hit.

Just today, I loved the news from Germany…

A young man punched his girlfriend on the nose, and the girl reported it to the police. They were produced before the magistrate. The magistrate must have been a wise man, which is very rare.

He said, "Young man, you can slap her a little here and there, but don't punch her exactly on the nose." And with this advice he released them. He must have been a man of great understanding. A little slapping here and there is perfectly okay; otherwise life loses all juice. But punching on the nose; that is not for boyfriends – that is left for the masters!

A little pygmy living in the jungle in Africa gets a sore ass every time it rains. He goes to the witch doctor who offers him a cure which costs six chickens.

The pygmy catches the six chickens and receives an ointment from the witch doctor.

The next time it rains the ointment does not work, so the pygmy returns to the witch doctor. This time the witch doctor says that he will need a dozen chickens to make the cure.

With much effort the pygmy catches a dozen chickens and he is given some medicine by the witch doctor.

When it rains again the pygmy takes the medicine, but he still has a sore ass. So he goes to the missionaries. They cure him for nothing, and the witch doctor becomes very embarrassed.

The pygmy offers to tell the witch doctor how he was cured, but says it will cost him eighteen chickens.

The witch doctor catches the eighteen chickens and hands them over. "Okay," he says, "How did the missionaries stop you from getting a sore ass each time it rains?"

"The method is very simple," says the pygmy. "They cut the tops off my rubber boots."

David, take life very nonseriously. You are not going to fall; there is nowhere to fall to.

Pope the Polack is on a pilgrimage when his plane crashes in the Sahara. Only the pope and a nun survive. They are lucky to catch a camel and start to ride it toward the nearest town, a hundred miles away. But on the second day the camel drops dead.

As they wait for death, the pope sighs, "The only thing I regret," he says, "is that I have never seen a naked woman in my life."

"All is pure to a pure man," says the nun, and takes off her clothes.

The pope is amazed and blesses the nun for showing him. Then the nun confesses her desire to see a man's body before she dies.

Pope the Polack takes off his clothes.

The nun gazes at his prick. "What is *that*?" she asks.

"*That*," says Pope the Polack, "is the giver of life."

"The giver of life!" exclaims the nun, jumping up and down. "Well then, give life to the camel and let's go home!"

26

Peace Is a Fragrance of Your Being

Osho,

Often, when I look at the sunset, sadness arises from deep within. It feels as if the sun is my home – the place I will return to when "the work" is done. But now I have fallen in love with the work, this earth, this existence, these people. I do feel a deep longing to be free but I wouldn't want to go home alone. Osho, will the work ever be done? Will I ever be able to go home in peace?

It is one of the deep-rooted habits of the mind to always divide things. The moment you divide things you are in trouble – and the mind wants you to be always in trouble; otherwise it has no function. The greatest trouble the mind can create is the longing for home. I call it the greatest trouble because you have never *left* home. And the mind projects homes. They may be the moon, the sun, or some faraway quasar – these are new, contemporary substitutes for a faraway God. The mind is so tricky that if you drop the old division, it immediately replaces it with a new, more refined, more contemporary-looking, more intelligent division.

In the past, people were wanting to go to heaven, to paradise, to God to find peace. As you are, I don't think even if you meet God, you will find peace. On the contrary, the meeting with God will create so many problems, so many inquiries, so much anger and rage against God because he created you without your permission. He created a world full of misery and you had to live in it. He created all kinds of desires in you which do not seem to be fulfilled; every desire goes on asking for more and more and more, and there is no end to it. Do you think a meeting with God will be a peaceful meeting? It is going to be the greatest fighting encounter!

It is good that God does not exist. He cannot exist because of you – so many people with so many problems and poor God, alone with a crackpot son and a Holy Ghost. A strange company.

I remember one of the ancient stories…

At one time God used to live on M.G. Road. But people tortured him so much – and in no other language can you torture someone better than in Marathi. Even if two people are in a loving conversation, it seems they are fighting. Marathi is unique in that way. It has no music in it. It seems to have come out of anger, violence, war. It has not come out of people loving each other. Each language has its own stamp, from where it has arisen.

And people were continuously surrounding the house of God on M.G. Road, not bothering whether it was day or night. There are so many complaints to be made – to whom to make the complaints? Everything seems to be wrong in some way or other. Someone is too tall, someone is a pygmy, someone has accumulated all the riches and someone is a beggar. Someone is so beautiful and someone else is just on the other extreme; so ugly that people use his photograph to frighten children. Your passport photographs are also used for the same purpose!

God said to his company, "This is intolerable. You have to suggest some place for me to move away to."

Jesus said, "There is no problem. We can go to Everest, no one is going to come there."

God said, "You are still too young to understand and to see the future. I can see that it is not safe for many more days. Soon there will be people coming and we will have to move again. Find some place from where we cannot be forced to move."

The Holy Ghost suggested, "Then the moon is very good."

But God said, "You don't understand the problem. These mad people are going to reach Everest, the moon, Mars – for no purpose! But if they find me anywhere they are going to kill me because naturally they think I am responsible for everything."

Finally a man from the crowd, an old sage, came forward and whispered something in God's ear and God said, "That is the right place!"

He had said to God, "Don't go anywhere, just enter man's own being. There he will never go; that is the only place he avoids. You can be at peace."

You think that by finding home you will be at peace. Your very formulation of the question is based on a division, an assumption that you are not already at home. And peace is an art that you have to learn, not on some faraway sun – those are meaningless hopes – but right here, now.

When a great rabbi was dying, his wife continued to nag him, as usual, to the very end. Finally she said, "At least pray to God. Make peace with God."

The rabbi said, "I have never been in a quarrel with him. There has never been any conflict between me and him, so the question of peace does not arise."

It is not some faraway goal that is going to give you peace. That is simply a postponement. You will be the same wherever you are.

The first man who landed on the moon was asked after his return, "You must have felt very different." He said, "I am sorry to say to you, I felt just the same." Changing places is not going to help. But changing your understanding is certainly going to transform you.

You are asking me, "Often when I look at the sunset, sadness arises from deep within." That sadness is not something negative. It arises in all those people who have a deep sensitivity – such beauty and they are stunned. Beauty can be a great shock. But it happens only to very poetic, artistic, sensitive, vulnerable people.

It is a misunderstanding on your part that a sadness arises from deep within. It is not sadness, it is simply a deep silence. It's as if your whole being comes to a stop when you see a beautiful sunset or a sunrise. Time stops, the mind stops – and those are the things you are accustomed to. In the beginning, this silence of the heart, this new space of which you are not aware always looks like sadness. It needs a little more acquaintance with it and you will be surprised that it is not sadness, it is silence. You can experiment: just sit silently and someone is going to ask you, "Why are you looking so sad?" Silence is not a value accepted by the society.

Since my childhood, I have been sitting silently. By and by the members of my family became accustomed to it, but in the beginning they used to say, "Why are you looking so sad? Why don't you go out and play?" And when I said, "I have gone *in* and I am playing," they simply thought that something was wrong with my mind. People go *out* to play and this fellow goes *in* to play!

Just look at the silence that surrounds a calm and cool lake, the silent waters. In the beginning it will look like the lake is sad because you are accustomed to noise. If there is no noise, you will feel at a loss – what has happened?

I have heard a story, I don't know whether it is true or not. It has to be true…

Long ago, when humanity was not such a big crowd of five billion people, they decided to see what happens if on one particular day everyone laughs loudly, dances and jumps for no reason at all. At a certain moment, the whole world decided it was worth experimenting to see what happens. And what happened was very shocking because everyone thought, "When there will be so much noise and laughter dancing, singing, it is better to remain silent and watch and enjoy the whole thing." But everyone thought the same way. The mind functions the same way. For those five minutes that were chosen for rejoicing, shouting, jumping – whatever you felt you wanted to do to express your joy – the whole world fell completely silent. They could not believe it: What has gone wrong?

Nothing has gone wrong; it is the same mind. Everyone thought, "Let us watch it. It is going to be great entertainment. If you become a participant, you will not be able to enjoy all kinds of things that will be happening all around." But what came to their mind was that because everything stopped – there was such silence, as there has never been. But everyone said, "It looked so sad." No one could look deeper into the phenomenon of silence.

You say, "I feel sad whenever I see the sun setting." You feel silent. You will have to learn a new language. Spirituality is a new language. You will have to change the meanings of words, the nuances of words. Give them new flavors and new fragrances because they have been used in the marketplace. They are perfectly good in the marketplace, but when you are entering the beauty of existence, you cannot carry the same language. Next time it happens, just see the sunset and feel what you have been calling sadness more deeply – and there is going to be a transformation. The same sadness will become your silence.

If a man cannot be silent facing beauty, he is not aware of the beauty. At least you are halfway: a little aware of the beauty, but not aware of the impact of the beauty that is created in your heart. Silence and sadness have something similar, but they are not the same thing. Sadness is something dead and stale. Silence is something alive, a song without words, a music without instruments. And what has been understood by you as sadness will become a great spiritual ecstasy for you.

This whole universe is a temple, and the whole existence is trying to reach you in so many ways – through the sunrays, through the trees, through the birds. These are all messengers. These people who have pretended to be prophets, messengers, saviors, are just lunatics. There are messengers all around you. In the early morning when the birds start their song, when the flowers open their petals, and the dewdrop shines like any great pearl on the lotus leaf; when so many colors are spread all over the horizon in welcoming the new day – these are all messengers of existence. If you can be sensitive to these, you will not feel sad, you will feel immensely grateful, understanding, fulfilled. You will feel at home, you will feel at peace.

I have not gone to the sun and I don't know what it means not to be in peace. Peace is not something that has to be achieved, it is something that you are carrying always, but never giving it an opportunity to blossom. It is a rose within your heart. It is a fragrance of your being. It is a sense of immense freedom and joy and celebration.

Peace is not a very good word because it is associated with war, and peace seems to be a little sick, weak. No, I will not agree for peace. Unless your inner being has a tremendous dance of joy, which has nothing to do with war or peace; then you will be able to understand the difference between the words, between peace and silence. Peace is something dead. Silence is throbbing with a heartbeat in harmony with existence.

A woman journalist asked me in America – I was addressing a world press conference and she was the first one to ask a question. She asked, "Can't you live in coexistence with America?"

I said, "No."

The woman may not have thought that anyone would say no. She was so stunned that she left the microphone. Later on she met me again and I told her, "You did not listen to my whole answer, to why I said no. You must have misunderstood because I could see it on your face, but you moved away and another questioner came."

She said, "Can *no* have many meanings?"

I said, "Every word can have many meanings, many implications. What did you understand?"

She said, "I understood simply that you cannot accept coexistence."

I said, "You misunderstood me completely. I was saying that coexistence is still war. Coexistence means we will tolerate each other. Coexistence means, 'What else to do? – we have to live together.' All husbands and wives are living in coexistence. All nations are living in coexistence. All religions are living in coexistence. But this coexistence is not a joyful, celebrating experience. I was going to say to you that I want *one* existence, not *co*existence. Why divide?"

She said, "My God, I reported your answer on the television and I have done an injustice to you. Because that no is resounding all over America, and naturally with the same meaning."

Words are delicate people, and as you become deeper, you start giving new meanings to words. By saying no to coexistence I was saying that the whole idea of coexistence is ugly. It means we cannot be one – that we will remain enemies. We will not fight, but the antagonism is absolutely implied in the word *coexistence*. And this is the situation with the whole language. Don't call it sadness and you will see the change. It is silence. That is natural when you come across beauty.

And then you say, "It feels as if the sun is my home..." You will be simply burned there! It will be your grave, it cannot be your home. The sun is our life source, but we have to be at a certain distance. The sun's rays reach us in eight minutes, with the speed of light; it is a vast distance. One hundred and eighty-six thousand miles per second the light travels, multiplied times sixty – that means one minute – and then multiplied by eight. That will be the distance the sunrays travel to reach us. This much distance is absolutely necessary, neither less nor more. If the sun comes closer we will be burned, and if the sun goes farther away, again we will be dead because it will be too cold – unbearable.

It is a strange coincidence, why life exists only on the earth. It is because it is at the right distance from the sun. Life exists on no other planet. Some are closer, some are farther away. This beautiful earth is immensely fortunate to be at exactly the right distance. The sun is not your home. Your home is within you. And you are not to search for it anywhere. You *are* your home.

Your question goes on, "It feels as if the sun is my home – the place I will return to when 'the work' is done." What kind of work? You are having crazy ideas. First, the sun is your home. Have you heard that scientists are trying to reach Mars, they are trying to reach other planets? But no scientist has even mentioned that anyone is trying to reach the sun. [*From one of the trees surrounding the hall, a bird bursts suddenly into a loud insistent song. Many people laugh.*] You see? The bird has understood before you!

And the idea of "the work" has been imposed on you for centuries, that you are here to do a certain work. Naturally, people wanted you not to be just lazy and enjoy. They wanted work because your work is going to create wealth, your work is going to create Alexanders, your work is going to create wars. Everything depends on you. From the very beginning, every culture, without exception, has been imposing the idea on the child that "You have a certain work, a certain purpose to fulfill in this life."

It appealed to people, although it was absolutely absurd. What work are the trees doing, and what work are the birds doing? What work are the sun and the moon and the stars doing? Except man, no one is so insane to think that you have a certain great work to complete. This is how they have created the achieving mind. And for thousands of years you agreed with the idea because it was very ego-fulfilling. If you are not here to do any special work, then you are accidental. You may be here, you may not be here, it doesn't matter. That hurts the ego. The ego wants you to be indispensable to existence, that without *your* work, existence will not be complete.

The same teaching was given to me by my parents, by my teachers: "You have to do some work in your life; otherwise your life is just the life of a vagabond, a bum."

I said, "Perhaps that is the work I am here for – to be a vagabond! Anyway, a few people are needed to be vagabonds."

The teacher who was telling me about the work said, "It is very difficult to discuss with you."

And I said to him, "This is a very psychological trap to enslave people into some work by giving nourishment to their ego, to say that by fulfilling this work you will have fulfilled your destiny."

I said to the teacher, "I don't have any destiny because I cannot conceive that existence has any destiny. What destiny could existence have? When the work of existence is complete, that will mean an absolute death because there is nothing more to be done. Everything has been done, so drop the curtain. I cannot see any purpose in the flowers, any purpose in the trees, any purpose in the oceans, any purpose in the stars."

Existence is not a work, it is a celebration – a sheer dance of energy which will go on and on forever in different forms, but cannot disappear. The energy is eternal.

And I said to the teacher, "Never again mention work to me. Celebration is okay, but work? It is destroying the whole beauty of life. I am in tune with existence, not in tune with you. You can go on doing your work. What work are you doing? Just being a geography teacher. I cannot conceive why existence needs a geography teacher. The whole geography is of the existence; what is the need of a teacher?"

It is a very wrong conditioning that has created a workaholic society, which condemns people who are not participating. Yes, there are needs: you need food, clothes, shelter. Naturally, you will have to do something to create these small things. But this is not the destiny of existence, that you created a house, that you produced a few children, that you are fighting with your wife. I cannot see that against the vast panorama of existence, your small stupidities are fulfilling any destiny.

I want it to be emphatically understood by my people that we don't have any work here. We have to join in the celebration of existence. Those small needs are only survival measures. Don't brag about how big a bank balance you have; existence has no need of it. Don't brag about how great a politician you are, a prime minister or a president; existence simply knows nothing about you. Existence is more in tune with these small birds who start singing for no reason, just out of sheer energy. I want to destroy the achieving mind. That is your disease. I want you to relax and enjoy. Just do a few things which are needful, or manage someone else to do them for you. It all depends on your intelligence.

I have never done anything, but I have a strange insight into people who will do things for me. And they do! And my needs are fulfilled and their doing gives them immense joy. It is not easy to be chosen by me, I am a very fussy person. I simply make you happy by your doing something for me. And I don't think, "If I could manage it for more than half a century, I will manage a few years more." In fact, I don't do anything as far as management is concerned; that too is done by others. I am simply enjoying.

I am not a messenger to tell you that you have to do this and you have to do that. I don't have any discipline for you except freedom. I don't have any commandments; they have all destroyed the dignity of man. I want to give you the dignity of the trees, the birds, the oceans, the Himalayan peaks, the stars. They are all in celebration – dancing, rejoicing, overflowing with energy. No one is working except human beings.

I want to transform even your small work that you do. Make it more aesthetic, make it more creative. Make it a great joy because it is your life. It is going to give you food, it is going to give you clothes; so whatever you do, it is not work, it is simply to remain as long as possible in this body and celebrate existence.

I have loved only one American in my life, and that man is Walt Whitman. The reason I loved him is one of his small poems. The title of the poem explains everything. The title of the poem is "I

Celebrate Myself." Only when you can say, "I celebrate myself," is your work transformed into celebration and your life becomes a non-achieving, non-ambitious journey of beauty.

And you say, "But now I have fallen in love with the work..." That is the only good thing that has happened to you. The moment you love the work, it becomes creative. It takes on a totally different color, different beauty. You say, "...this earth, this existence, these people. I do feel a deep longing to be free, but I would not want to go home alone." The one good thing you have is that you have fallen in love – now spread your love. These people, these trees, these birds should also become part of the space that you call love. And then you will not ask, "I want to be free." You *are* free.

Love is the only alchemy that brings freedom. It is hate, anger, jealousy that keeps you in bondage. Just a pure love – unconditional, because what condition can you put on the birds? What condition can you put on the trees? Unconditional love, and you are free. Free from all jealousy, free from all anger because there is no enemy here. All are friends, all are lovers, all are part of one cosmic whole.

But this kind of confusion happens in the mind because the mind is carrying very contradictory, inconsistent, irrelevant information. Your mind has been completely destroyed because the society does not need you to have a mind. The society needs you to be a worker, a slave, and a slave is not supposed to have a mind of his own.

They have used a very cunning way to destroy your mind, so that you can remain satisfied that you have your mind and in fact, you don't have it. They have put all kinds of contradictory things in it. One has to attain freedom, and no one has told you that love is freedom. No one has told you that celebration is freedom. No one has told you that to be alone and contented, so utterly satisfied that you can say "I celebrate myself," is freedom. But you are even worried about going home alone. So who are you going to take with you? At least as far as I can see, no one except someone who wants to commit suicide is going to go with you to the home you have chosen – the sun!

You don't understand that the path that brings you to yourself – from where you have never gone away, just your mind has been projecting faraway goals... But you have remained in your home. The only thing that can bring you back, can withdraw your projections, is the joy of being alone. You don't know the purity of aloneness. You must be living in a great mess, because aloneness *is* your home. And aloneness is your freedom – freedom from the other, freedom from the need of the other, freedom from the dependence on others. Aloneness is your freedom and aloneness is your home.

But your mess is really deep. You ask, "Will the work ever be done? Will I ever be able to go home in peace?" Linguistically, your sentences seem to make sense. But existentially they don't make any sense at all.

First, there is no work; hence the question of when the work will be done does not arise. Otherwise, it would have been a very tedious, torturous world because the world goes on and on – the work is never finished. Every spring the flowers come and every fall the trees drop their leaves; every morning the sun rises and every night the sky is full of stars. And it is not that it is happening only now, it has been happening for millions of years. In fact from eternity, because there is no possibility of a beginning. It will continue till eternity again because there is no end conceivable.

If you become too attached to the work, you will be eternally in bondage. Enjoy the work, love the work, transform it and make it a part of your celebration. It is never going to end, so you need not be worried about when it is going to end. You will be gone; we all will be gone, and we will come back in another time, in another spring – rested, rejuvenated, fresh.

Perhaps we will meet here again – in this impossible world, everything is possible. Perhaps we have met in this place before, too. The same players go on playing different games. But once you drop the idea of work, then a load, a burden disappears and you don't have to go to any home. This celebrating existence, this celebrating consciousness is your home. It has always been your home.

Your question is a mess, but it is good because many people are carrying the same kind of messes. It will help you and it will help them, too; make life a very simple thing, utterly innocent. Do you think this silence needs anything more to be added to it? Or is not this gesture complete? Each moment has to be lived in beauty, in joy, has to be made a festival of lights.

Now some really serious things…

A farmer munching on a cookie is watching a big rooster chasing a hen around the barn, and gaining on her at every lap.

The farmer throws a piece of cookie in front of the racing pair.

The rooster comes skidding to a stop and gobbles up the piece of cookie.

"My God," says the farmer, "I hope I never get *that* hungry."

The elections come and Ronald Reagan is out of a job. He is sitting with Nancy Reagan in the Oval Office for the last time, working out some economy measures for his retirement.

"You had better learn to cook, Nancy," says Reagan, "so we can fire the cook."

Nancy thinks it over for a few moments. "Okay," she says, "but you had better learn to screw so we can fire the chauffeur."

Little Ernie is playing with his train set in the living room, while his mother is cooking dinner.

He lets the train go around the track ten times, then stops it and says, "All you fuckers who wanna get in, get in. All you fuckers who wanna get out, get out!"

He lets the train go around ten more times and then stops it and says the same thing.

At this, his mother comes storming into the living room and tells Ernie to go and stand in the corner for using such filthy language.

Half an hour later, his mother tells him he can go and play with his train again. Little Ernie sends the train around the track ten times, stops it and says, "All you fuckers that wanna get in, get in! All you fuckers who wanna get out, get out! Anyone got a complaint about the delay, go and see the bitch in the kitchen!"

27

The Difference between Expectation and Just Waiting

Osho,
When I first sat in front of you at Woodlands, fourteen years ago, there was an explosion inside. I don't know what it means, but I've often had the feeling that all I've been trying to do ever since is catch up with something that has already happened.

Krishna Prem, the question you have asked has tremendous implications for all the seekers of truth. It is a question which touches the very fundamental law of those who are in search of something inexplicable, something inexpressible. Let me first make the law clear to you. It may have happened to many; it is going to happen to everyone. But you may not have taken the whole, comprehensive view. The law is that when you first meet the master you come innocent, without any experience. You simply come as a receptivity, a sensitivity – ready to move into any dimension, willingly and totally. Hence, the first meeting with the master always brings an explosion.

The explosion happens because of your innocence, because of your unexpecting mind. You know nothing about spirituality, you know nothing about ecstasy. Your not-knowing is the cause of the explosion. But then begins a very troublesome journey. Then begins a nightmare. Then, each and every moment, you are waiting for that explosion to happen again. And you may wait for years – it will not happen because you are not fulfilling the basic condition for its happening. You have forgotten completely in what situation the first explosion has happened.

Now there is no way to be in that situation again. Whatever you do there will be the expectation, the experience. You cannot create that not-knowing; that is not within your hands, and that is not the way existence functions. So the first thing you have to do, Krishna Prem, is to forget all about that explosion. It was good that it happened, but there are far greater things. Why bother about something so primary, a kindergarten experience? [*A sound is heard as firecrackers are set off at a neighborhood wedding celebration.*] You see? Just like that!

Start waiting for something greater. Of course you don't know what that something will be. [*Another explosion, and the assembly collapses with laughter. Osho looks around, grinning.*] I am afraid that the moment I say anything more, it will happen again! [*A pause to let the hilarity settle.*] Start fresh. Sit by my side, not expecting but waiting.

Try to understand the difference between expecting and just waiting. In expectation there is a desire and there is a clear-cut object that you are desiring. And that is blocking your progress. When you are just waiting, you don't know for what, but the experience of just waiting is so precious, so valuable, so deeply transforming, that something greater than the first explosion is bound to happen.

It will not be the same explosion. In these fourteen years so much water has gone down the Ganges. Neither you are you, nor am I the same person. Nothing is the same. The whole situation is changing every moment. And you get stuck with some beautiful moment and go on missing greater beauties and greater ecstasies. Unhinge yourself. Unless you drop that explosion and the expectation for it, you will remain fourteen years back in time, and between me and you there will be a gap of fourteen years. Just understand that it happened because you were not expecting it, and now it is not happening because you are expecting it.

It is a simple law, but very fundamental. Everyone becomes a victim of it. Once you have tasted something you start asking for it again. Remember, existence is inexhaustible. It can give you so much, just don't ask for repetition. Existence hates repetition. It does not want you to have the same experience again. Even if it is the same experience, it will *not* be the same experience. Do you understand? Because you will know you have seen the film before. It is the same story. You know the end, what is going to happen. You know the dialogue that is going to be followed, the incident.

In my village, the father of one of my friends was a goldsmith. The wife had died and all the children had grown up and had gone to their own jobs, and he was left alone in the house. I saw him every day going to the movie house – and the village had only one movie house. I inquired of the manager and he said, "I am more amazed than you are because not only does he come to see the same film for seven, eight days, as long as it runs, he sees it three times a day!"

I had not thought about that. I had been puzzled that he went every day to the same film because every film in a small village will run for four days, seven days, at the most eight days – and he was going to the movie so religiously, so regularly! But when I heard that he was going to the movie house to see every show – and there are three shows – I thought I had better go to see the old man; something seemed to be wrong. His son, who was my friend, had become a bank manager and gone away; another son had become a teacher and gone away, and there was no one even to inquire about the old man.

I went to him and I asked him, "Is it true you go to see three shows of the same film every day?"

He said, "Who sees the films?"

I said, "What do you mean?"

He said, "That is the only place to sleep silently." Because he lived in the part of town where the goldsmiths were, and they are continuously hammering this and hammering that. There is noise the whole day long and it continues to the middle of the night. The old man said, "The only place where people are silently sitting for hours is the movie house. I have not seen a single film. I am not mad, you need not be worried about me."

I said, "Then it is perfectly okay. You can go on sleeping. I will make arrangements with the manager for special concessions for you because you are not watching the films. He can only charge for sleeping, not for watching!"

You cannot watch a film even twice; you cannot read a novel twice. Any experience when it happens twice loses the most precious thing in it – the newness, the freshness, the early-morning glory. If you can understand this, Krishna Prem, the first experience can be a tremendous help rather than a great hindrance. The first experience simply shows that you are on the right path, you have entered the door. Now be more receptive and more innocent, more not-knowing, and much more is going to happen every day.

A small understanding becomes a golden key which opens the doors of mysteries, secrets. But you can get hung up with the first experience and go on repeating in your mind, "When is it going to happen? It is not happening." These fourteen years must have been of sadness and you must have concluded everything absolutely wrong. You may have thought, "Perhaps Osho's presence is no longer available to me. Perhaps Osho has withdrawn his love toward me. Perhaps I have lost some quality, some sincerity, some immense longing." Whatever you have concluded is wrong. And because of all these conclusions your fourteen years have been a long nightmare. It is time to understand that the first was only the beginning.

Deep in the Himalayas from where the Ganges flows, the current is so small that you cannot believe that this small current – which falls from a marble face of a cow – is going to become such a tremendously big river, so vast that when it meets the ocean it is very difficult to decide which is the ocean and which is the river. When the Ganges meets the ocean, the place is called Gangasagar, the "Ocean of Ganges." It has become so big, you cannot see the other shore.

The moment you meet a master for the first time, something is bound to explode in you – is going to fill you with a light that you had never dreamed about. An experience that has never been a thought in your mind, and a beauty that you can only know but you cannot say anything about. I can understand your difficulty. It is the ancientmost difficulty of all seekers of truth.

The first experience either becomes a hindrance or becomes an opening. It all depends on you. If you cling to it, if you expect it again and again, you are turning it into a hindrance. If you feel grateful to the experience, with deep thankfulness in your heart, and move ahead with no longing, no desire for the first experience; it has given you the taste that you are on the right path.

Gautam Buddha used to say only one thing to every sannyasin after initiating him, for forty-two years continuously. And he must have initiated thousands and thousands of people. After accepting the person as his disciple, he would say only one thing: "*Charaiveti, charaiveti.*" It is a Pali word. It means, "Now walk on. Never stop; walk on. However beautiful the experience is, remember: much more is waiting for you ahead." *Charaiveti, charaiveti*. Just go on.

Experience everything, be thankful, but don't stop and never expect the same experience again because that is blocking your path for greater experiences. But nothing is lost. Those fourteen years can be forgotten; start fresh from this moment. *Charaiveti, charaiveti*.

Gautam Buddha's compassion is perhaps never expressed so clearly as in the statement, "Even if I meet you on the way, cut my head off immediately; don't stop." He's saying that there is no experience worth stopping for. Enjoy and go on. And the pilgrimage becomes a goal unto itself. This is very difficult for the logical mind to understand. The logical mind asks you, "Where are you going?" It wants to know about the goal, it is goal-oriented. And existence is not going anywhere, it is simply enjoying. It is simply enjoying the flowers, the birds, the people, the rivers, the clouds, the stars. It is not going anywhere. There is no goal. And if you want to be in tune with existence, drop the goal-oriented mind. Hence I say that the very pilgrimage is the goal.

You can dance, you can sing, you can rejoice because each moment in itself is complete and perfect. Never ask for it again. Existence is non-repetitive. You can see it. Twenty-five centuries have passed and not another Gautam Buddha, not another Zarathustra, not another Chuang Tzu. Such beautiful people, but existence is not a Henry Ford's factory to produce similar cars. Existence never repeats anything. It gives dignity to every individual because you have never been, you will never be; you are just unique. Nowhere is there anyone who is exactly like you. You are incomparable. This gives you so much grace, so much richness that you cannot be grateful enough to existence.

But the mind is mechanical. It always wants the same thing again and again because it feels secure with the familiar. But you are not the mind. The mind is a social product. You are existential, not just social. Your roots go into existence and you have to listen to the harmony and the laws that existence follows. It never repeats. It never brings the same experience again. It is always new. You will not find even two leaves in the whole world exactly the same, or two roseflowers exactly the same. What to say about human consciousness, which is the greatest flowering in the world. You can have millions of experiences which will be each time bigger, higher, greater, wider, but never ask for any experience to be repeated. Existence is not a film that you can see twice.

Old Heraclitus was right when he said, "You cannot step twice in the same river." One day somewhere I am going to meet the fellow. I have made a list of the guys I would like to meet someday because they have to be corrected. No one has criticized Heraclitus on the grounds I criticize him. I love him. He has made a tremendously beautiful statement, but I want to make that statement even more beautiful. I want to say that you cannot step in the same river even once because the water is continuously flowing. Once you understand the flow and you become in tune with the flow, so many treasures are available ahead.

Don't behave like an old Indian who had gone to see a movie for the first time in his life. A beautiful girl is undressing by the side of a lake, and just when she is going to drop the last part of her clothes a railway train passes by, and that blocks the view. The old fellow tries in every way – this way and that way, between the compartments, but the train is going so fast and when the last compartment of the train has gone, the girl has already entered the lake and she is swimming.

The old man is very frustrated. The first show is over, everyone has left, and the old man is still sitting in his seat. The manager comes and asks him, "Is there something I can do to help? Everyone is gone, the show is over. Now the cleaners will come and then the second show will begin."

He said, "I am going to stay here. Bring me a ticket for the second show!"

The manager said, "But people don't see two shows."

He said, "Don't bother me! I am already too annoyed and irritated."

The manager thought, "The man seems to be a little out of his mind, but there is no harm." He brought the ticket, charged him the money, and again the second time the same thing happened. The train came right on time. The old man could not believe that this is happening in India – the train was not even a few seconds late!

The second show was over and the manager came to the old man to say, "Now it is time. The third show is going to begin."

He said, "I am not going to leave this place unless I see what I want to see!"

The manager said, "But you have seen the same film twice."

He said, "You don't understand at all. It is India – the train cannot always come at the right time, and I am waiting for the moment when the train is late."

Life is not a film. Nothing is fixed, nothing is repeated. It is always original. I have been traveling in this country for almost twenty years continuously. I was waiting – because of this old man – perhaps some time I may find a train which was on time. And finally one day in Allahabad the train I was waiting for came *exactly* on time. It was such a surprise! I went to thank the driver and the guard saying, "In my whole experience of twenty years, this is the first time that a train has arrived at the right time." They both looked at each other.

I said, "What is the matter, why are you feeling so embarrassed? I have just come to show my gratitude to you."

They said, "We are sorry to say to you that this is yesterday's train."

At that very moment the stationmaster had also joined. We were all three in shock and I asked the stationmaster if this was the situation. "For twenty years I have been traveling, and for the first time a train has come at the right time and finally it is discovered that it is yesterday's train. Then why do you publish timetables?"

The stationmaster said, "They have to be published. Otherwise how will we know by how much the train is late?"

I said, "That seems to be absolutely logical."

Existence is original every moment. And to find a synchronicity with this originality, Krishna Prem, is all that one can experience. This is the ultimate ecstasy.

Old man Finkelstein and old man Rabinowitz are having a holiday in Miami, when they meet two young ladies considerably younger than themselves. They both fall in love and decide to get married in a double ceremony.

Following the wedding night they are both in their rocking chairs after breakfast when old man Fink says, "You know, Abie, I had better see a doctor."

"Why is that?" says old man Rabinowitz.

"Well," says Fink, "I could not perform last night."

"My god," says Abie. "In that case I had better see a psychiatrist."

"Why?" asked Fink.

"Well," says Abie, "I didn't even think of it!"

A cannibal child and his mother are walking together through the jungle when suddenly there is a roar from the sky above.

"Don't be frightened," says the mother. "It is only an airplane."

"What is an airplane?" asked the boy.

"It is something like a banana," explains the mother. "There is a lot you have to throw away, but the insides are delicious."

Fred Ruddel, the famous brewer, has an audience with Pope the Polack. He shakes hands with the pope and says, "Your Holiness, I have a request. I would like to make a small change in the Lord's Prayer."

"Change? In the Lord's Prayer?" screams the pope. "But we have been saying the Lord's Prayer for two thousand years!"

"I know, Your Holiness, but it is just a small change," replies Fred.

"Well," says the pope, "what sort of change do you have in mind?"

"What I would like to do," says Fred, "is to change 'Give us this day our daily bread' to 'Give us this day our daily beer.'"

"I am sorry," says the pope, "but we can't do that."

"You don't understand me," says Fred. "Your Holiness, I am a very wealthy man."

"But the Lord's Prayer is traditional," blurts out the pope.

"Listen," says Fred, "I am talking about one million dollars, cash, delivered to you personally!"

"I will have to pray about it," says the pope, "so come back in a couple of days."

When Fred Ruddel has gone, the pope calls in his secretary. "Look, Giovanni," he says. "How long until our contract with the bakers' union expires?"

Little Ernie the cabin boy asks Long John Silver the pirate how he got his wooden leg.

"Ah, it was a cannon ball, Ernie, my lad," says Silver. "Took my leg clean off at the knee."

"And why have you got a hook instead of a hand?" asks Ernie.

"Ah, a cutlass," replies Long John, "took my hand clean off."

"How did you lose your eye?" asked Ernie.

"Ah, I got seagull shit in it," says the pirate.

"But a seagull doing that can't take your eye out!" exclaims Ernie.

"It can," replies Long John, "when you forget you have got a hook for a hand!"

And the last....

Two Martians land on earth near a deserted gas station. They leave their flying saucer and waddle over to one of the gas pumps.

One Martian talks to the pump, "Can you take us to your leader?"

There is no reply and the other Martian whispers, "Be careful, this guy looks mean!"

The braver Martian points his ray gun at the pump and says, "Did you hear? Take us to your leader!"

Again there is no reply. "Let's get out of here," says the second Martian.

"No!" says his friend. "This time he will talk." He prods the gas pump with his ray gun and shouts, "Take us to your leader or I will shoot!"

He waits for a moment and then shoots. There is an enormous explosion. A minute later, a mile away, the Martians get up and one of them remarks, "I told you to be careful. Any guy that can take his prick, wrap it twice round himself and stick it in his ear, you don't want to mess with!"

28

Love Comes from Meditation

Osho,

Your silence goes so deep in my heart that it makes my love unconditional. Is this what *satsang* is?

There are two ways to look at life. One is the way of the schizophrenic. That has been followed by the crowds around the world down the centuries. It divides things. It is very uneasy without dividing them. And because for thousands of years the teaching has penetrated into every mind, it seems to be the only way. It looks neat and clean divided, but existence does not follow it. It has its own undivided melting, merging into each other without making any demarcations. I am against the first because it has destroyed so much that the crime is incalculable.

Just the other day an underground sannyasin has been sent to an insane asylum by the court in Germany. And all she has done is stick posters around the city saying that Christianity is the greatest crime against humanity. She was caught and brought to the court and the judge said, "It is criminal to hurt people's feelings."

The young woman must have been of immense courage. She said, "If truth hurts people's feelings, what are you going to choose? People's feelings or the truth? Whatever I have written on the posters, I can prove. And unless you disprove it you have no right to send me to jail."

It is a truth that Christianity has committed immense crimes, and goes on committing them. And Christianity is not alone in it. Hinduism, Mohammedanism, Jainism, Buddhism – even these soft religions, Jainism and Buddhism – continue committing crimes. Instead of sending her to jail the judge ordered that she should be put in a mental asylum. To speak the truth is the greatest crime. In fact the judge should have been put in the mental asylum. He has no grounds to refute her, and he cannot say that truth has to be repressed because it hurts some stupid people who are clinging to lies.

But this goes on happening around the world. Not a single protest has been made against the treatment of the young woman; neither has anyone protested against the judge. It has been taken for granted. We have taken so many things for granted which are not so. The old way, the wrong way, the ugly and the insane way, divides love from silence, divides silence from ecstasy, divides ecstasy from self-realization and so on, so forth. But they are not divisions. It is a simple flow of energy moving into different spaces.

You are asking, "Your silence goes so deep into my heart that it makes my love unconditional." To any logician, to any follower of the first path it will look absurd. What has silence to do with unconditional love? They seem to be worlds apart. But you gathered courage to say something which goes against your training of logic. It was possible because it is not an intellectual question, it is your existential experience. And logic cannot overrule existential experiences.

Man is a miniature cosmos, everything intertwined with each other. If your love deepens, your silence will deepen; your blissfulness will deepen, your innocence will deepen, your sensitivity, and your aesthetic potentiality will come to flowering.

Just as your hands are not separate from your eyes, neither are your feet separate from your head – you are an organic unity – the same is the situation in the inner world. Your love, your meditation, your silence, your blissfulness are all simply waves in the same ocean of consciousness. So don't be disturbed by the mind, which is pretending to be the master. Listen to the heart and you will never be on a wrong track. And the more you listen to the heart, the more and more your life will go beyond intellect, logic, dialectics, beyond all kinds of discrimination.

It is beautiful that you have brought it into a question, "Your silence goes so deep into my heart that it makes my love unconditional." Start from anywhere. You are a perfect circle, and so deeply interconnected with everything in your life. You can start by being more meditative, which is the simplest because it does not involve other human beings. The others are a little complex; it is better to let them come on their own.

My own understanding is not to start with love because your understanding of love is not the authentic love. It is simply biological infatuation, and if you start with that you have gone astray. Start with meditation because meditation is the only thing that biology has not given to you. It has a tremendous force of its own. That's why the physiologist or the biologist will account for everything, but will never mention the word *meditation*.

Meditation is the only bridge between you and the beyond. Start with meditation – and that's what is happening to you, effortlessly. Sitting with me, listening to me, a silence enters your heart and suddenly you feel springs of love unaddressed, radiating in all directions. It is not love to someone, it is simply being loving. But if it comes from meditation, from silence, it will have purity because it is not coming from biology. It is not coming from your past, it is not coming from all your conditionings; it is coming from the spontaneous experience of silence. And suddenly you see a great aroma of love around you. You have known love, but it was always conditional. Anything conditional is not worth a penny because the conditional will disappear. Once the condition is fulfilled there is no purpose in it.

Two small boys were talking seriously. One said, "It is strange, everyone else has a girlfriend and I cannot get one."

The other said, "You are fortunate because to get one is simple, but to get out of the love affair is a very messy thing. Enjoy your aloneness as long as you can. I am suffering from these girlfriends!"

Any love which has some conscious or unconscious conditions is bound to bring frustration because those conditions cannot be fulfilled. The very nature of conditions is such. Every girl hates her mother; she may not be conscious of it at all. But the thing becomes more complicated because she hates the mother and she imitates her too, because there is no other woman whom she can imitate and learn from. So she learns all those ugly ways that she hates! Every young girl loves the father, just as the boy loves the mother. It is very natural because the first experience of the other polarity for the girl is the father, and for the boy is the mother. That is their first experience of the other sex, and naturally there is a tremendous attraction.

But there is also a big, wide barrier. The boy hates the father, just as the girl hates the mother. The reason is the same: the boy hates the father because he is possessing his love object – the mother. And the girl is jealous because the mother is possessing the father whom she would like to possess. These things go into the unconscious realms of your being, and they remain with you for your whole life unless you become enlightened. This makes your love strangely conditional, which cannot be fulfilled.

Every man unknowingly is expecting his wife to be his mother; that is the image of the woman that he is carrying. Now no other woman can fulfill that image, and anyway the girl has not married him to become his mother! And things become more and more complicated because the girl is carrying the image of her father; she wants her husband to be exactly like her father, and certainly no man marries a woman to become her father.

The complexities go on becoming more and more difficult: the husband wants the wife to be like the mother, but she hates the mother. The wife wants the husband to fulfill the condition of being the father, but in the first place the poor husband has no idea what is expected of him and in the second place the wife also hates the father. Now things become so complex and complicated. The family has been, as long as we can remember back into the past, the basic unit of the society – a very insane unit, and it creates the whole society. Each generation transfers its cancer to another generation.

When I say that love has to be unconditional it means you are not expecting anything from the other. You are not expecting the other to be someone else. You are simply loving to the other, as he or she is. And your unconditional love will make you unattached to individuals; it will be just an aroma around you. You will be a loving person. You will love the trees, you will love the sunset, you will love a woman, you will love all that this universe provides you.

Right now, the conditional love is like an imprisonment. Two people who don't like each other are holding each other in imprisonment. It is a strange thing. If you don't like the other, say good-bye. But you cannot say good-bye because you are afraid he may enjoy himself somewhere else. It is not according to your jealousy, he has to be happy with *you*. A husband does not like his wife to be laughing, to be happy with another man. Neither does the wife like such a situation.

So it is a very strange situation in which we have placed humanity. And unless a great awareness happens that this is our fundamental misery, you cannot be freed from this hell that you have made of the earth. Lovers – I mean the so-called lovers – are more like detectives to each other than lovers. Jealously watching what the other is doing. Every letter is opened, every pocket is searched.

One night, a woman heard her husband, in his sleep, saying again and again, "Kamala, darling." The woman was listening to exactly what he was saying. The first thing she asked in the morning was, "Who is this 'Kamala darling'?"

The man said, "It is nothing, it is just the name of a female horse. I have been thinking to bet on that horse – you know the racing season is coming."

And then, just when they were talking about this, the phone rang. The husband ran toward the phone, but the wife said, "Stop, I will take it." She handed over the phone to the husband and said, "That female horse 'Kamala darling' wants to talk to you."

Even in sleep you are not free to say things. And people say there is freedom of speech! If there were a small window which God had managed to make in every head, the wife would have been looking through the window into your dreams. "What are you seeing? Who is this woman?"

I have heard…

Two young men were going to Alaska, far away from humanity, for some research work. In the last village, they purchased everything that they would need for at least three months. When their purchase was complete, the owner of the shop said, "I don't want to interfere, but I am more experienced and I have been giving things to all kinds of research workers who go deep into Alaska where you will not meet another human being."

They said, "What do you mean?"

He said, "I have a suggestion: I have a plastic woman, really great, glamorous…"

They both said, "This is nonsense. A plastic woman – what are we going to do with a plastic woman?"

He said, "Just keep it in case you need. There will be no woman available for thousands of miles."

One of them relaxed and he said, "I will purchase it."

The other said, "Are you mad?"

The first said, "I am not mad, but without a woman for three months, I may *get* mad. I am going to purchase the woman. Just show me."

The shop owner pumped the air into the woman, and it came out so beautiful because it was manufactured, and everything was perfect. The first man said, "You have been a great wise man to advise us."

He purchased the woman and he said to his friend on the way, "Remember, I don't like anyone to fool around with my wife."

The man said, "Have you already gone mad? It is a plastic woman, it is not your wife."

He said, "Whatever it is, for these three months in Alaska, watch out. Because I am a very angry man. If I see you with my woman, there is only one way that I know and that is to shoot you."

The man said, "What kind of nonsense are you talking? A plastic thing and you will shoot me – your best friend! And why should I get interested in your plastic woman?"

He said, "I have just made you alert about it. Don't ask me later on why I did not say it to you."

After two months, the man who had purchased the woman came back to the same village and thanked the shop owner, saying, "You gave me something that was immensely needed in that lonely place."

The owner asked, "But what happened to your friend?"

He said, "Don't ask me about that bastard. I shot him."

The owner asked, "For what?"

He said, "I caught him making love to my woman! And that idiot did the last thing as I came in and was going to shoot him – he cut the nipples of my woman with his teeth, so she immediately flew out of the window. I have lost the woman, I have lost the friend. I have come to ask if you have another pair."

This whole society is boiling with jealousy. No one says it, everyone hides it. But the more you hide it, the more it goes on like a cancerous growth, expanding in your interior being. Just look how many things you are jealous of: someone has a beautiful house, someone has a beautiful physique, someone has a beautiful strong body, someone is an intellectual giant, someone has the most wealth that one could ever think of. So on, so forth, there are people all around who will make you jealous. Instead of your life being in an oceanic love, it is suffering in a gutter of dirty jealousy. But unless you start looking inward and finding the roots, you will not be able to transform it.

You are blessed that, just without any effort, my silence reaches your heart. It will purify you, it will destroy all that is poisonous in you – jealousy, anger, greed, attachment, possessiveness. It will make you just a beautiful flower of love.

What is happening has been called in the East *satsang*: being with a man who has attained the truth. Yes, this is *satsang* – where, without any effort on your part, just the grace of your master starts alchemical changes; so silently that you become aware only when the work is done. And there are a few things – for example, if you have known unconditional love, you cannot undo it. It is so vast and it is so beautiful that what you used to think was love looks like just an ugly nightmare compared to it. You would not like to go back to it; your whole being will resist going back to it.

My speaking to you is not especially to give you any philosophy, dogma, creed, theology, religion. My talking to you is a device so that you can experience my presence, my silence. In an unaware moment perhaps you can come closer to my heart without any fear. This is a device for meditativeness. I am not interested in any kinds of doctrines; they have tortured humanity long enough. I am interested in a loving humanity, in a humanity fragrant with silence, rejoicing this immense gift of life and existence.

The madam watches anxiously as Gloria, her best girl, is about to be wheeled into the operating room for a heart transplant. She grasps the surgeon by his sleeve and asks, "What are her chances for recovery, Doc?"

"Ah, pretty good, I would say," replies the doctor. "After all, she has not rejected an organ in twenty years."

Mendel Kravitz, the wealthy Jewish businessman, has a very bad case of hemorrhoids. He goes to all the most famous doctors for a cure, but no one can help him.

One day he is glancing at a religious magazine when he notices an article explaining how Pope the Polack has a special holy cure for hemorrhoids. He goes to see the pope, who for a fee of ten thousand dollars gives him a series of massages, using special holy oil.

After the third session, Mendel asks the pope if he could buy some of the holy oil to take back to New York so that his wife Ruthie can complete the treatment.

Pope the Polack agrees, and the next day Mendel is sprawled on his bed at home while Ruthie massages his hemorrhoids. Mendel asks Ruthie exactly how she is giving the massage. "Well," says Ruthie, "my left hand is on your shoulder and with my right hand, I am massaging your ass."

"That's funny," says Mendel, "when the pope did it, he put both of his hands on my shoulders."

29

Authority and Authoritarianism

Osho,
I am a twenty-four-year-old German guy, and after doing a Primal group I know pretty well that I don't want to accept any other father or mother than me.

Now, I like your teaching, and your destroying of my old conditioning very much, but why should I change my name, be a sannyasin and accept a master who says that there is no need for any authority?

Peter Heidegger, the question you have asked is immensely interesting. Even if you had not said that you are a German guy, the question would have revealed it – the question is authentically German! I am going to analyze it because that is the only way a German can understand.

You have done only one Primal group and you have taken conclusions for your whole life. Do you see the stupidity of it? Do you see the impatience of coming to conclusions from a small Primal group – which is just a cathartic group, it is not meditation? It is not even the beginning of meditation. It is only preparing the ground, taking out the weeds and the grass roots before the seeds can be sown. Just this small group and you jump to far-reaching conclusions, without being aware of what you are asking. You don't know even the meaning of the words that you are using.

You say, "After doing a Primal group I know pretty well that I don't want to accept any other father or mother than me." Do you see the implication of it? Primal therapy, and other therapies also, want you to be freed from your childhood fixations. You have been brought up by a man and a woman. Naturally, you have become fixated on the father, on the mother, and these fixations affect your whole life, your whole lifestyle. And because your father is not going to live forever, you will find yourself in great trouble; without a father what will you do? Without a mother what will you do? You have become so dependent in your psychology.

It is out of this dependence that "God the Father" was created, that there are "Mother Goddesses." These have not come out of the blue; they are projections of your psychology. You need them. They are tremendous consolations. Your father may die, may abandon you, but the great father in the sky is going to protect you forever.

Even Jesus, a man who has created the biggest gang of criminals in the world, was tremendously father-fixated. All his prayers, hands raised toward the sky, are simply foolish because there is no one in the sky to answer your prayers. And he was so fixated that he denied his father Joseph; he insulted his mother Mary. A small incident will explain it to you…

Jesus is preaching in his usual way in the marketplace, where you can always find a few bums who have nothing to do, a few urchins, a small crowd. And then someone shouts from the crowd, "Jesus, your mother is waiting outside the crowd. She has not seen you for many, many days. She wants to see you."

And the way Jesus treated his mother is so ugly that just this incident would have been enough to condemn this man forever. He said, "Tell that woman that my father is above the clouds in the sky. Here on the earth, there is no one who is my mother and there is no one who is my father."

A poor woman... But from where does this insult come? – a deep fixation upon an eternal father, that "I am the only begotten Son of God," gives him this stupid idea to insult a poor woman who has just come to see her son. She had not seen him for many days. But he did not allow her into the crowd, and he did not go out of the crowd to meet her. He just shouted these words; that was the whole conversation. And Mary, with tears, went back home.

The implications of these fixations have many dimensions. People call their language the "mother tongue," their country the "motherland." Except Germany – Germany is rare in that it calls its country the "fatherland." That shows a more male chauvinistic idea. But why do people call their languages their mother tongues? I have heard one man explaining to me that the reason why the language is called mother tongue is because the child never hears the father; it is always the mother who speaks. The moment the father enters the house he is silent; then the whole conversation is a monologue. Perhaps this may be the reason.

But deep down, we want to be surrounded by "mother earth" as a protection, as our nourishment. We are so consoled by the idea that the sky is our father, the earth is our mother, and we are perfectly protected between the two. All therapies will destroy these fixations because these fixations are the roots of other stupid ideologies that you go on clinging to: the father race, the mother race, your superiority.

I have heard about two generals, one German, one English, talking to each other after the Second World War about what had happened. The German was saying, "We had all the power in the world, more than any country ever had. We went on winning continuously for five years. Then suddenly, everything collapsed. What went wrong? What made you victorious?"

The English general laughed. He said, "You don't understand. It is not just power that determines everything, it is God's blessing.

Before every attack, our armies went into prayer. Without prayer, we never attacked; that is the reason for our victory."

The German said, "But we also did the same; we also prayed before every movement of the army, so this cannot be the cause."

The English general insisted, "This *is* the cause. In what language were you praying?"

The German said, "Obviously, we were praying in German."

And the English general said, "Who has ever heard that God understands German?"

These kinds of stupid ideas are all over the world. In India, people think that the Sanskrit language is the only language God understands. That's why he has written the Vedas in Sanskrit, because that is the only language he can write. But Moses gave the same kind of idea to the Jews: "You are the chosen people of God, and your scripture is the holy book. It is written by God himself." Certainly he understands only one language, Hebrew. And you can go on asking around the world; everybody has this idea.

There is no God, and there is no one to understand what you are talking about. But it certainly gives a consolation – in depression, in suffering, in misery, just opening your heart and praying to God certainly gives peace. It is made of the same stuff as dreams are made of; it is nothing valuable. But man has lived on dreams, hopes, imagination: "If God has not heard today, tomorrow he will hear."

For the first time in the world, all these therapies have come with the idea that man's psychological troubles are rooted in his fixation on the mother, on the father. This fixation has to be cut completely; with it will disappear your gods, your mother goddesses. With this, many fictions, prayers, hopes, dreams will disappear. You will be cleaner, more unburdened, more clear, more perceptive.

But you have come to a wrong conclusion. You say, "I have done the Primal group. I know pretty well that I don't want to accept any other father…" The Primal group was not saying to you that you have to accept any other father. That's what religions have been doing – instead of a Hindu god accept a Christian god. That is changing your father, your fixation.

I was staying with a small aboriginal tribe in faraway central India. One of my professor friends used to go; he was an anthropologist and he was studying the aboriginals, their civilization, their mannerisms. And he said to me, "The place is so beautiful in the deep forest, so virgin." He showed me a few photographs of a cave which goes miles underground, and a small river that flows in the cave. He had been through the whole cave with torches, taking photographs. I became interested and I went.

The first night we were resting, and in the morning, we were going to explore that tremendously beautiful cave. But in the night, something happened that I want to tell you. A missionary had come to the village, and the whole village gathered in the clearing in the middle of their small huts, just a little ground for meetings. They all gathered; they were very interested in what this missionary was going to say.

The missionary said to them, "You have been in misery, in suffering because you have not yet found the right god."

One of the old men of the tribe asked, "How to find the right god?"

He said, "I will show you the way." But he continued to look at me, although I was sitting behind the crowd. Without disturbing anything, I wanted to see what he was trying to do. And he was afraid because he could see me and my friend, and the car behind. But still he went on; he brought out two statues from his suitcase. One was of Rama, who is being worshipped by the aboriginals of central India as a god, and one was of Jesus Christ. He had a bucket full of water and he said, "You can see for yourself how to find the right god. You can see your god, Rama, and my god, Jesus Christ. Now I will drop them into the bucket and you will see that whoever drowns is wrong, whoever floats is right."

They were painted exactly alike, but the statue of Rama was made of brass and the statue of Jesus was made of very soft wood, very lightweight wood. Naturally, Jesus was victorious. And the whole crowd of aboriginals looked at each other. They said, "Now, there is no way. We have to change. We have been worshipping a fellow who cannot save himself. How can he save us?"

At that moment I thought, "Now it is too much." I went into the crowd and I said to the missionary, "Before anything else happens, I want to ask a few questions of the crowd."

He said, "I have no objection."

I asked the crowd, "Have you ever, in the whole history of your race, heard of anything like a water test?"

They said, "We have never heard of it; we have heard only about a fire test." The missionary became afraid.

I said, "Make a bonfire here and then we will see who is the right god."

And they jumped up and enjoyed the idea, "In the first place that idiot is using a wrong method. 'Water test'! Who has ever heard of it? A fire test is a well-known thing."

The fire was built and I said to the people, "Don't let this missionary escape; he will try." So four or five young men surrounded the missionary and I said, "This is your duty because after the test about the gods we will test the missionary!"

The gods were tested and of course Jesus burned immediately. Rama came out without any problem. I asked the crowd, "Now what do you want? Should we test this missionary also?"

They said, "That's the right thing to do because he was trying to deceive us." And the missionary was almost in tears, nervous, trembling and he said, "You are an educated man – don't kill me! I have nothing to do with Jesus Christ or anyone, I am just a missionary; I just get a salary for it."

I said to the people, "Let the poor fellow go."

Who is telling you to change the father or the mother? All the religions have been doing that, arguing with each other – "Our god is better, superior, more powerful than your god." That's the whole idea of conversion. There have been only two religions, Judaism and Hinduism, which are non-converting religions. But not for the right reasons – they don't convert anyone because anyone who is not born a Jew is an inferior being; anybody who is not born a Hindu cannot be converted to Hinduism because by conversion you cannot purify him. He will have to go through a whole process of disciplining himself so that in the next life he is born as a Hindu; conversion is not possible right now. It is a long process of transformation.

But Judaism and Hinduism are the oldest religions of the world, and they never came in conflict because they were in separate parts of the world. New religions, out of necessity, had to depend on conversion. Otherwise from where are you going to get Christians, if you don't convert? From where are you going to get new converts other than from older religions? That makes the Christian the most fanatic, fundamentalist, fascist because he has to be very aggressive in his attempt to convert people to Christianity. And they have succeeded; almost half of humanity is Christian.

From where have these Christians come? – they have come from older religions which don't convert. But the whole game is the politics of numbers. The more people you have under your wing, the more powerful you are. There is no other priest in the world except the Catholic pope who is also a sovereign king of an independent country, the Vatican. Obviously he has the greatest number of people around the world; as Catholics they are his power.

These people have been trying to change you, but the new therapies are not trying to change your father fixation into a new fixation. Therapies are trying to help you drop the whole idea of a father and a mother. To be an individual, without any bondage, free, authentic and sincere.

But instead of that you are saying, "I don't want to accept any other father or mother than me." So you are going to be your own father? You are going to be your own mother? You are going to be in a tremendous confusion! I cannot figure out how you will manage your life. Inside you there will be a conflict: your father and mother will go on fighting. You will become a nervous wreck. You gained great insight out of your primal therapy! At least the father *was* faraway in the sky. Now it is within you; the danger has come even closer. And not only the father – the mother is also there! Just be a little saner.

And then you say, "I like your teaching…" Have you ever thought what my teaching is? The question of liking or not liking does not arise. There is no teaching at all. Neither is there a teaching nor is there a teacher. I am not preaching a certain doctrine to you, a certain system of beliefs, a philosophy or theology. I am not a teacher and I don't have any teaching because I don't have any belief: no God, no heaven, no hell. Just this universe, which is not a belief – which is your experience, my experience, everyone's experience. So don't get this wrong idea that you like my teaching. No such thing exists.

And then you go on being more and more stupid: "…your destroying my old conditioning, very much." You like my destroying your old conditioning very much, and still you are a German guy! Your being a German is simply a conditioning. If you have understood me, you cannot be a part of any nation and you cannot be a part of any religion and you cannot be a part of any kind of doctrinaire philosophical system. You can be only a silent human being, in tune with the universe.

And you go on saying great things: "…but why should I change my name…?" Why not? It will help you to forget that you are a German; that's why. The changing of the name simply means you are dropping the whole old personality that was indicated by the old name, and that you are beginning afresh with a new name. It is symbolic. You were not born with a name. The name was given by your father, by your mother, by your people. Now you have dropped all conditionings, why not drop the name those conditionings gave you?

You can choose your name yourself; anything will do. It is not necessary for a name to mean something, it is only symbolic so that you can be recognized in the crowd and called. You can make up your name yourself, but change you must! Your insistence on not changing it shows your inner idea: "On the surface, play the game that I have dropped all conditionings." And you are not even ready to drop a bogus name. I have no interest in changing your name. It is just out of compassion that I am saying, "Start a new life with a new symbol, so that you can be discontinuous with your past."

And then, "...why should I change my name, be a sannyasin...?" Do you understand the meaning of sannyasin? It simply means a seeker of truth. You don't want to be a seeker of truth? Then what the hell are you doing here? And further, "...why should I change my name, be a sannyasin and accept a master who says that there is no need for any authority?" Two things: first, the master accepts the disciple, not the disciple accepts the master. So you need not be worried about that. The disciple has to wait for that blissful moment when he can be accepted. Who has given you this idea that it is in your hands to accept a master or not?

I will tell you a small story about Junnaid...

Junnaid was a Sufi mystic who used to tell his disciples, "I had such a beautiful master that there is no way for me to explain to you his beauty, his grace. But I will tell a few stories that happened between me and my master." And he never named his master; that was disrespectful. So no one knows who Junnaid's master was because Junnaid never mentioned his name. He always called him simply "my master."

He was asked again and again, "Please tell us his name."

He said, "How can I say his name? That will be against gratefulness, against respect, against my love. Don't ask his name. Just the word *master* is enough."

"I lived with my master," he used to say, "for twelve years. As I entered the palace where he used to live he simply gestured with his hand, indicating to me, 'Sit down.' And for three years afterward he did not even look toward me. Every day I would come in the morning, sit down by the side. Other disciples would come – their questions, their problems, their difficulties on the path, their experiences, realizations. By the evening I would leave.

"After three years, for the first time he looked at me. And just that look went like an arrow into my heart. That very moment I knew I had been accepted. It took three years of waiting, but I was determined that even if it takes my whole life to wait, I am going to wait. Because every day I have seen more and more grace, more and more of the master's beauty, more and more the feel of his presence. I had already forgotten how many days had passed. When he looked at me, I remembered; three years I had been waiting.

"Then for three years again he never looked at me. After six years of waiting, he smiled at me. In his smile I knew I had been embraced, he had taken me into his heart. The first time he had looked I knew he had reached my heart; after six years I knew he had taken me into his own heart. And not a single word! Three more years passed and he hugged me, kissed my forehead and told me, 'Junnaid, now you are ready. You can go.'

"Not a single word of teaching, but initiation happened just by a look, and a deeper mystery opened just by a smile. A hug from the master became the certificate, and he has sent me into the world to teach. He has not said a single word to me about what to teach. So whatever he used to do, I am doing."

This was Junnaid's whole life, and he transformed hundreds of people. And all that he knew was: sit down – first, a gesture. Then after three years of waiting it becomes a growing intensity; waiting becomes almost your whole life. Then, suddenly he looks at you and your whole life is filled with a new light. You are bathed, you are purified. You have passed through the test; you have been accepted.

Junnaid continued to do the same, because he said, "This is all that I have learned from my master." And he created great people. The greatest of them was al-Hillaj Mansoor. He was of the same category as Gautam Buddha, Chuang Tzu, Basho, Bodhidharma. But he has nothing to say. He has something to convey – words are not necessary.

The seeker of truth has to show his credentials, his ability to wait, his capacity to be patient because the journey is long and the path is very narrow. A master accepts a disciple only when he can see the sincerity of the heart, the risk, the danger of going into aloneness. And when the master is convinced that the person is capable of all these, he is accepted as a disciple.

You don't have to be worried. It is not so easy to be accepted by a master. And if you don't want to be a sannyasin… Perhaps you thought that sannyasins are also a kind of religion; perhaps this is also a new movement, enrolling people. It is not. If you are searching for truth, whether you know it or not you are a sannyasin. If you are ready to drop all your conditioning, you are a sannyasin. If you meditate and raise your consciousness to its highest potential, you are a sannyasin. It does not matter whether you know the meaning of the word *sannyasin* or not.

The ancient meaning of the word *sannyasin* was: one who leaves the world in search of truth. My own meaning is: one who lives in the world and yet goes on searching for truth. Because where can you go? Everywhere is the world. I cannot understand where those people were going, leaving the world. To the Himalayas? It is also part of the world, part of our geography. Where are those people going to find a place outside the world?

There is nothing outside the world. Everything is inside the world, and there is no way to get out of it. The only way is to go into yourself, and you are out of it. If the world is not inside you – no desire, no longing, no will to power – if all this nonsense has disappeared from your inner world and it is utterly pure emptiness, you are out of the world. That is the only place which is not in the world. But as far as your body is concerned it will be in the world.

I have always wondered where those people used to go. Wherever they go, they will find some kind of world.

An old master was dying, and he called his successor, "My last message to you is, never, never allow a cat in your house." And the old fellow died.

The successor said, "My God, what has it to do with the search for truth? And now I am going to be on guard continuously that no cat enters the house? What kind of thing has he left me with and died? Now I cannot even ask, 'What do you mean?'"

But an old man who was there said, "Don't be worried, I know the whole story. I will tell you what he means. I have known him for many, many years..."

When he had become a sannyasin, he left the world and went out into the forest. But you need food, milk, clothing, you need some kind of roof. But he had left everything, according to the ancient formula; he had brought with himself only two pieces of Indian-type underwear. I emphasize the word *Indian-type* because that kind does not exist anywhere else in the whole world. It is just a single strip of cloth, long enough so you can wrap it around yourself. In the West you are becoming acquainted with mini-underwear, which show much and hides less – that has been done by the Indian sannyasins for centuries. It is nothing new.

So, he took two of these pieces of underwear, and left. But there was trouble. He managed to make a small hut with bamboo and grass, but those two pieces of underwear were creating trouble because rats would come and eat the underwear. He was in great difficulty. Again and again he had to go to the village to ask for new underwear.

Finally, the village got tired. They said, "You have left the world. If you had said that you would come again and again for underwear, we would have stopped you, saying, 'Don't go. What is the point? You had everything, now you are a torture."

He said, "What can I do? There are so many rats."

The people suggested, "Then do one thing. We will give you a cat."

He said, "What will the cat do?"

People suggested, "The cat will kill the rats and will protect your underwear." It was perfectly logical. So he took a cat with him. But now a new problem – the cat needs milk, the cat needs food. She certainly finished all the rats, but now he has to go to the town to ask for some milk for the cat.

The people said, "You are a constant nuisance. We were thinking that we had got rid of you. We have given you the cat, and now you have started coming for milk. Rather than giving you milk every day, we will give you a cow. Take the cow as a contribution from the whole village. But don't torture us any longer. This cow will help in many ways. It will give enough milk for the cat and it will give enough milk for you, too. So you need not come for your food either."

He said, "The idea is good," and he took the cow. But new problems – every solution brings new problems.

So those who are really men of understanding never solve anything. Look at me. I have never solved anything. I don't have any problem. Just... I simply saw the thing clearly, that the moment you have a solution, a problem comes.

Now the cow needs grass. From where to get so much grass every day? Finally, he had to go to the village again. He said, "You give me solutions and they create new problems! Now I go on searching for grass throughout the whole forest. I have gone into sannyas to meditate, but since I have been in sannyas – rats, cat, cow, grass... I was never in so much business when I was in the world. Now show me a way."

They said, "Don't be worried, every problem has a solution. There is a widow in the village. She is very poor. We hope she will be willing to go with you and live with you. She can take care of the cow, and we will come and clear some ground so you can grow grass. You can also grow some wheat. And sometimes you may be sick, sometimes you may be not feeling well, so that woman will take care of you, too."

He said, "My God, it seems the whole thing is… That's what I had escaped in the very beginning! A house, a woman, a cow; I had all these things. Everything is coming again from the back door."

But there was no other alternative, so he took the widow. And for many, many days he had been involved in such complicated problems that he had not thought about women. But now he saw the widow, and she was really beautiful. Deep down, dreams started arising: "This is great. Together alone in the forest…" And what had to happen, happened. Then children, then searching for a school.

The old man explained to the young successor, "That's why your master finally told you to never, never allow a cat in the house. Because it was the cat that destroyed his whole life."

But where will you go? I don't think there is any place anywhere, where you will not need essential things. And those essential things will bring you back again and again. Instead of becoming a sannyasin, you will become a beggar. Instead of becoming a creator, you will become just a burden on the society.

That has happened in the East, to the extent that in Thailand, the proportion has grown so much that out of every four men, one is a Buddhist bhikku who has renounced the world. Thailand is a poor country. It cannot manage so many people who do nothing except always ask for clothes, food, milk, medicine. Finally, just a few years ago, the parliament of Thailand passed a law that unless someone gets permission from the government, he cannot renounce the world. This is the strangest law you could have in any country. But in any other country the situation will be the same. There is a limit – how long can you tolerate these people who do nothing, and are ready to ask for everything?

The old sannyasin, the old concept of a sannyasin, is basically wrong. I don't teach you to leave the world, I teach you to live in the world but don't let the world live in you. Be a lotus leaf in the water – but the water cannot touch it. That's the only possibility, if we want the whole world to taste something of meditation; otherwise, the old sannyas cannot survive. And it is meaningless because it makes you dependent on people. You were independent, you had your own time; you worked for a few hours and then you had your own time. But these poor people who have left the world, their whole time is wasted in asking for small things, being rejected, being insulted, being told, "Go away, go somewhere else." These people were in search of dignity, and what they have found is utter indignity.

And the second thing: you don't understand – perhaps millions of people in the world don't understand – the difference between authority and authoritarianism. They both originate from the same root; in dictionaries they have the same meaning. But in experience, they are not only different, but diametrically opposite. An Adolf Hitler is authoritarian, but he is not an authority. Authoritarian means he has power to dominate. He has power to order you, to command you.

Authority simply means that whatever you are saying is your own experience. You are not dependent on any other source. You are not repeating the Holy Bible, the holy Gita, the holy Koran. You are saying what you have experienced within your own self. This gives you a deep authority. But it not the same authority as a commander has over the army, or a politician has over the country. It is not power over others, it is simply an experience arising, with absolute clarity, with no hesitation, without any doubts. It is your own experience. You don't depend on any scriptures. So these two things are totally different.

Jesus is authoritarian because his authority is derived from the God whom he claims is his father. The source of authority is the father. Moses is authoritarian; so is Mohammed, so is Krishna, so is Rama because they all derive their authority from outer sources. If those outer sources are proved to be fictitious – as they are – then the whole authority of Jesus, Mohammed, Krishna falls, collapses. If their God is proved to be nonexistent, then they don't have any authority.

But my authority cannot collapse because it is not dependent on anyone. Even my death cannot destroy it – it is my own experience. Only authority makes the master. And you can only learn something with a man of his own experience. You can imbibe his spirit. You can be overwhelmed by his love, by his presence. If you are receptive, you can be completely transformed. That's the meaning of the word *disciple*. It comes from the same root as *discipline*. A disciple is one who is ready to learn, who is ready to discipline himself into receptivity, alertness, awareness, patience.

Peter Heidegger, be here; let the atmosphere enter you a little deeper. Do a few more groups, do meditations. Sit here, just for the joy of sitting. You can ask questions later on. Right now, your questions will be absurd. Become well acquainted with this caravan of seekers; imbibe their spirit, merge and melt, and perhaps you may be able to find an authentic question that helps you in your search for yourself. But this question is too early.

There are a few more strange questions, but you will have to wait for them until tomorrow. Right now is the time to have a little fun.

Paddy and Maureen go fishing together in a boat. "Do you mind if I fish off the right side of the boat?" asks Maureen. Paddy agrees and starts fishing from the left side. He catches nothing all day, but Maureen keeps pulling up fish, one after the other.

The next week, they go fishing again, and this time, Maureen asks to fish from the left side of the boat. Paddy fishes from the right side and catches nothing, but again Maureen almost fills the boat with the fish she catches from the left side. At the end of the day, Paddy is really puzzled.

"Maureen," he asks, "how do you know which side of the boat the fish are going to be on?"

"Well," replies Maureen, "when I wake up in the morning I have a look at your prick. If it is hanging on the left side, I fish on the left side of the boat. And if it is on the right side, then I fish on the right side of the boat."

"That's amazing," says Paddy, "and what if my prick is right in the middle?"

"Well, Paddy," says Maureen mischievously, "on a day like *that*, who cares about fishing?"

30

A New Way of Science

Osho,

What is your vision of a World Academy of Sciences for Creativity?

Amrito, the world has come so close to a point of crisis that the so-called thinkers of the world simply avoid talking about the coming suicide. It is not far away; just by the end of the century, if we do not do anything. This has been the habit of all good people of the world – not to do anything, while the criminals and the evil continue to do all their crimes. This habit has to be broken at least this once.

You have raised a question which has tremendous importance and I would like to go deeper into detail about it. Science is a new phenomenon compared to religion. Religion has dominated the world in some form or other as far back as we can see. Science has a history of only three hundred years. This background has to be understood; only then can the problem be seen in the right perspective.

These three hundred years, science has had to fight inch by inch against the deeply rooted religions, which were vast empires of power, vested interest. Science was in difficulty on the smallest things: if it went against the religions, it was so young that it was not possible for it to fight.

I am reminded of Galileo, himself a Christian, not an atheist. But because he discovered that it is not the sun that goes around the earth but just the contrary, it is the earth that goes around the sun – and this statement is against the Bible – Galileo was condemned.

In his old age, sick, almost dying, Galileo was forced to the court of the Christian pope.

The pope said, "Do you think you know more than God? God has written the Bible and he says that the sun goes around the earth. You are making a statement which is dangerous to our whole structure."

Galileo asked, "What is the danger?"

The pope said, "The danger is obvious. If God can commit a mistake about his own creation, then what guarantee is there that he should he be taken for granted as right about other things? Your statement creates doubt. You have to cancel that statement; otherwise death will be the only penalty."

Galileo was certainly a man of great humor. He said, "There is no problem, I can change the statement – and I am not in a state to fight against the idea that God has written the Bible. But remember, even if I change my statement, neither is the sun going to listen to me, nor the earth. The earth will still go around the sun."

On such small matters science was continuously struggling against religion. That created a rift for which religions are solely responsible. But the rift had its own repercussions. Seeing the situation, science started moving more and more toward politics.

These have been the two powers holding humanity in their hands: religion and politics. If religion is against you, then the only way is to have some protection from politics. But again you will have to make some compromise. The compromise is that politics will provide labs, instruments, facilities – but its interest is in creating destructive weapons, which have resulted finally in nuclear weapons. Now the whole world is loaded. Right now there are only five nuclear nations, but by the end of this century there will be twenty-five nations with nuclear weapons. And nuclear weapons mean we have decided for death, we have decided to destroy this planet and ourselves.

At a late age, Albert Einstein understood that it had been a tremendous mistake to take shelter in the powerful hands of politics, just to avoid religion. It was not in any way helpful in creating a better humanity, a better planet, which science is absolutely capable of.

I have my vision, and I want my people to be aware of the vision. This ashram is not only for the old and the retired who don't want to do anything but need shelter and food. That has been the situation with ashrams in the East. According to Hindu tradition, a man should become a sannyasin after the age of seventy-five. That means perhaps after his death because seventy is the average age for death. But if seventy-five-year-old people gather together, it is just a home for the old, rejected, useless, somehow tolerated. I want to change the whole idea of an ashram. My sannyasin is not to wait for the age of seventy-five. The real sannyasin is a revolutionary, and youth is the authentic time to enter this inquiry.

All the ashrams of this country, all the monasteries of the world, are against this ashram for the simple reason that you are going against the traditional idea. Young men and women of intelligence are not just going to sit and do Transcendental Meditation; they have much more energy to be creative. I want this ashram slowly to develop into a World Academy of Sciences for Creativity. This will be perhaps the greatest synthesis ever. Your search for religious truth in no way hinders your search for the objective reality because both areas are absolutely separate; they don't overlap.

You can be a scientist and a meditator. In fact, the more you go deeper into meditation, the more clarity, the more intelligence, the more genius you will find flowering in you which can create a totally new science.

The old science was created as a reaction against religion. The new science I'm talking about is not a reaction against anything, but an overflowing energy, intelligence, creativity. Politics corrupted science because its own interest was only war. Religions could not accept science because they were all superstitious and science was going to demolish all their gods and all their superstitions.

Science has passed these three hundred years in a very difficult situation, fighting on the one hand with religion and on the other hand, unconsciously becoming a slave to the politicians. I want this place to grow and I am making arrangements for a world academy of sciences and arts totally devoted to life-affirmative goals.

The science that can create Hiroshima and Nagasaki and destroy thousands of people, birds, trees – without any reason; just because the politicians wanted to see whether atomic energy works or not – the same science can create more food, more life, better health, more intelligence in all fields of life. But it should be taken out of the hands of politicians and it should not bother about the religions. Scientists bothered about religions in the past because they themselves were conditioned by the same religions. Galileo could not say that the Bible was not written by God, it is just a fiction; he himself believed that it was written by God.

My idea in details about the academy is…

Just a few days ago Dr. Masashi Murakoshi from Japan was here. He has been working for twenty years in Hiroshima, experimenting. As the radiation of the atomic explosion becomes less and less, he has come upon a far more important discovery than Albert Einstein himself did. He went to Hiroshima and wondered at the fact that atomic energy, radiation, is destructive only at a certain quantity. At a lesser quantity it is very creative, very productive, immensely helpful.

He himself was forty-five years old when he went to Hiroshima. Now he is sixty-five years old, but looking at him you would not say he is sixty-five; he still looks as if he is forty-five. His colleagues are dead and those who remain cannot believe the miracle that has happened to him. Radiation in small quantities is life-affirmative. It is the higher dose that destroys.

I have been in contact with scientists, Nobel Prize winners, who have been fighting for my rights in other countries. In Italy eighty-four of the most eminent people have just signed a protest against the government. Among those eighty-four there are at least six Nobel Prize winners. The same is the situation in Germany and in Holland. These Nobel Prize winners, eminent scientists, artists of different dimensions, will constitute the academy, and they will make efforts to change science's whole trend of being destructive.

Our sannyasins – and there are many who are scientists, artists, physicians – will help the academy. We will arrange scholarships, and people from all over the world can come and study a new way of science, a new way of art that affirms life, that creates more love in humanity and that prepares for the ultimate revolution.

That ultimate revolution is a single world government because while the world does not have one government, you cannot stop wars. Each nation has to have its own military, its own defenses, its own weapons, and there is competition as to who has more destructive power. But once there is one world government there is no need of any armies, air forces or navies; all these can be transformed into services dedicated to life, to the whole of humanity.

The World Academy of Sciences will be the first step because if we can slowly take scientists from all over the world out of the grip of the politicians, all the power of the politicians will be finished. They are not powerful; the scientist is the power behind them. And the scientist is in a difficulty because there is no institute in the world which will give the scientist enough of the materials, instruments, machines that he needs to work with.

The days are long gone when Galileo could make a small lab in his own house, and scientists could work independently without any support from outside. Now science is so complex and has grown so many branches – and each branch has become a science in itself

– that unless he is supported by a government or a very powerful institution which has money, intelligence, dedicated students, the scientist cannot work.

It seems existence is arranging for the money that we will need to create the academy. Another very important man in Japan, who holds many foundations for humanitarian services, is also coming to see whether it is possible to bring money from those many foundations to create this world institute. And it will have support from all over the world, from all the scientists without exception because now everyone is seeing that they are serving death, not life.

We can have the greatest library for scientific research and we can have sannyasins working, studying. The synthesis will be that everyone who is working in the institute will also be meditating because unless meditation goes deep in you, your love sources remain dormant. Your blissfulness, your joy remain unblossomed. Man is not for science, science is for man. But science can be of tremendous help if all the scientists of the world who are creating destructive power are removed. They want to move, but they have no place to move to. We have to create a place for them. They are all feeling guilty.

Albert Einstein died feeling utterly guilty because he had helped to create atomic bombs and surrendered those bombs to President Roosevelt of America. Once those bombs were in the hands of the politicians, Albert Einstein went on writing letters saying, "These should not be used; they should be reserved as a last resort." But no one bothered about those letters – who cares? And the bombs were used without rhyme or reason.

Japan was coming to the point of accepting surrender because Germany had already surrendered, and without Germany's help Japan would not be able to continue. It is a small land, beautiful, brave, but this world has moved from braveness, from courage, to war which is mechanical. Even a weak man can drop bombs; there is no need for him to be a giant, a wrestler. There are even airplanes which can be directed by remote control, without any pilots, and they can drop the bomb and come back home.

War has gone beyond any conception of braveness, courage. Japan is a courageous country, but it was going to fall any moment, and every general – even the American generals – told President Truman, "It is absolutely inhuman to drop atom bombs now when the country is already ready to surrender."

But President Truman insisted, "This is the last chance, don't miss. Before they surrender, drop the bombs. We have to see what atomic energy can do so that we can go on creating more, bigger and more superior bombs." The bombs that were dropped on Hiroshima and Nagasaki were just toys compared to the nuclear weapons that we have now.

Scientists are in a difficulty. They cannot work individually; they have to work under a government. The government's interest is war, and no religion is going to support them because their findings go on destroying religious superstitions. There is an immense vacuum which I want to fill by creating a world academy absolutely devoted to life, love, laughter – absolutely devoted to creating a better humanity, a better and more pure, healthy atmosphere, and to restoring the disturbed ecology.

I have called these two people, and Dr. Murakoshi has already been here. He has already created a few things which radiate atomic energy, but in such minute doses that they help; they remove diseases, they give more well-being. He has made a small radiator disk for me, especially for my bathtub; just ten minutes and the whole bathtub becomes full of radiation. Just to check whether it works or not, I have used the bath; it certainly works.

He has made a few belts filled with radiating material, and sannyasins are using them and are finding immense energy that they have never found before. He is going to come with more gadgets that he has invented. He loves me so much that he informed me that it will be better if I move the ashram to Japan because there he has contacts with the emperor, with other scientists. And he is ready to found the academy and provide the money that will be needed. And it is going to be an enormous amount of money. But

I have informed him that Japan is running out of land. It is the most crowded country in the world. They have even made artificial islands in the ocean, and they have floated a few to create industries on them.

Secondly, Japan is very costly. Its currency is now the most valuable in the world. It will prevent my poor sannyasins from going there. And to be there for months will be too costly. I have called him and I am certain I will convince him that this is the right place. The whole of Koregaon Park is for sale! And we are finding sources of money to purchase the whole of Koregaon Park. Then all the gadgets can be used by every sannyasin. Mechanisms can be managed to purify water, to purify air, because Pune is utterly polluted. But one thing is good about India, and that is things are cheaper. People can come from every country, be here for three or four months, and then eight months back in their country they can earn enough and come back. There is no need for them to work here.

Here is their temple of meditation. And I want all the dimensions – the best musicians to teach you music, the best artists to teach you painting, the best poets to teach you the experience of poetry and the expression of it. I am an incurable dreamer. But I can say to you that whatever I have dreamed in my life, I have managed it, without doing anything. Just a proposal to existence…

If a sannyasin remains here for four months, he will learn much about natural cultivation, how to live in tune with nature, not against it; how to make your life free from all bondages that the past has imposed on you. And once all the branches of science… This is a strange fact that perhaps you may not be aware of: science has grown so many branches that one branch does not know anything about the other branches. And they go on researching and doing great work against each other. The most important thing for the academy will be to create pure science, just the way I am making every effort to create pure religiousness.

Man can have a pure religiousness inside him – that means love, silence, meditation – and also a sense of pure science, so that no branches of science go on doing work unnecessarily which is destructive to other parts.

The second great thing the academy has to do... Up to now science has developed accidentally. There has been no sense of direction; people just went on discovering anything without any idea for what. Moving accidentally, still they have created much, but it is in the service of destruction. Pure science will give the sense of direction and a unity of all the sciences, so that science works as a whole, not as different branches.

Right now the situation is hilarious. My ear was infected. I mentioned to Dr. Jog, a very prominent specialist, "You are just treating the ear without bothering about the whole body. The ear is not something separate; perhaps the reason may be somewhere else." For a moment he remained silent, and then he said, "I cannot say anything more. I know only about the ear and I will treat the ear. You are right, logically, that perhaps the ear is the weakest point and the disease, which is somewhere else, has found the weakest point to express itself." And that's what acupuncture knows.

It will be good to remind you how acupuncture came into existence. A man had been suffering his whole life from migraine; no treatment helped him. One day, just by accident, he was shot by an arrow in his knee. He was passing through the forest and some hunter misjudged; it was getting dark and he thought it was some animal. But the miracle was that as the arrow hit the knee the migraine disappeared forever. That was the origin of acupuncture.

So if you say to the acupuncturist, "My head is suffering very badly with a continuous headache, migraine," he will not touch your head at all. He will work on some other point with just a small needle. They have found at least three hundred and sixty-one points in the body – and they have been as successful as anyone else. The body is a whole organism; the disease comes from the weakest point. Man has to be taken as a whole. This is going to be one of the foundations of pure science: to look at man as a whole, to look at nature as a whole; to look at the whole cosmos as one organic unity. And work out ways how this organic unity can function in harmony in the different layers.

We have the source from where the money can be brought here; we just have to work out the process. This whole Koregaon Park is going to be turned into the World Academy of Creative Science and Art. It will be also a research body, and it will also have its nursing homes, hospitals. Without such a thing happening, this century is going to see us finished.

Dr. Masashi Murakoshi was concerned that if I leave the body, then who is going to materialize the dream: "They can work, but the whole dream..." He wants a written promise from me, and I have given it. This is twice that I have given a written guarantee that I will not leave the body. The first was to Nostradamus, that I will not leave the body before 2001, and now again the same guarantee is being asked. I am giving it. That does not mean that after 2001 I *will* leave! That simply gives him the guarantee so that he can bring all the scientists, the sources, the foundations, and the money. I can understand that without me, it will be impossible to create such a vast project.

But it is an absolute necessity, seeing the crisis that is coming closer every moment. And people are even avoiding talking about it, afraid because they don't have any answer; or forgetting all about it, believing that some miracle will happen. No miracle ever happens unless you make it happen. I want this ashram to be the first synthesis between religiousness and a scientific approach to life. This will fulfill my dream that the inner and the outer of man are not separate.

It is absolutely possible – there is no difficulty in it. I have found the right sources, so you can rejoice in the fact that soon this place is going to become the world capital of science and religion. And once governments see their scientists disappearing, the world government will become a possibility. We need three things:

First, a world government. The world government will be only a functional government because there will be no one to fight with, no need of armies, no need of any arms. Secondly, one humanity with no discrimination. The most dangerous consequence of discrimination has been that man has not been able to use a very scientific method – which he is using with the animals, with the trees – with himself. I mean crossbreeding. No one should fall in love just in the neighborhood because it is nearby. Fall in love, fall out of love, there is no problem, but find your girlfriend or boyfriend as far away as possible – some Martian… Only then can we create a better, stronger, more intelligent human being.

Genetics is going to be the most important part of the world academy. We have not looked at all at how we go on producing children – just accidental. How many geniuses we are missing every day is impossible to imagine. In a single lovemaking the man releases millions of sperm; only one of them – that too not always, only once in a while – will reach the mother's egg. Once one sperm has reached, the mother's egg closes. What happens to those millions of people standing in the queue? Their life span is only a few hours.

And my understanding is that the best, the most intelligent, will not rush into this race with all kinds of idiots and nasty people; they will stand by the side. But the criminals, the wrestlers, the politicians will do everything to reach the mother's egg. It is such a great competition, a marathon race in which certainly the best will not participate. It is just accidental that once in a while a Michelangelo, or a Socrates or a Rabindranath Tagore somehow managed to reach. My feeling is, somehow they got carried by the crowd, just pushed, and they could not get out; they reached by chance.

It is a long journey for the sperm. According to sperm size, the tunnel they have to pass through before they reach the mother's egg is almost two miles long. We could have missed lazy people like Lao Tzu, Chuang Tzu – and there is no way to know how many we have missed.

Genetics is going to be the most important science in the future. All our old habits have to be changed; they are absolutely out of date. You can go to the medical center and donate your sperm. And now we have ways to find the potentiality of the sperm in minute detail – how long he will live, whether he will be healthy, strong, intelligent or retarded. We can simply avoid nasty people like Adolf Hitler, Joseph Stalin, Benito Mussolini, Ronald Reagan. We can choose the best.

Just the small understanding is needed that the best sperm can be injected whenever society decides that we need a few children, a few scientists, a few poets, a few flute players, a few mystics – on order. For the first time we will be out of the prison of biology, which is accidental, blind.

There are so many things that the world academy has to do. The first thing is to spread around the world the idea that misery is unnatural, that sadness is sickness; that the lust for power needs psychiatric treatment, and that a man who goes on gathering money is mad. And once we make the whole of humanity aware of the dangers of our past ways of life and where the whole past is leading us – to a global suicide – it will not be difficult to convince the intelligent, the young, to drop the past and to welcome the future.

Amrito, the world academy, devoted in every sphere to creativity, is going to happen. I don't like to prophesize, but once in a while… This is my prophecy: the world is not going to be finished by idiot politicians. All over the world, that's all they are doing – preparing the funeral pyre for the whole of humanity. We are going to stop it. And if they insist, we will tell them, "Jump into the funeral pyre yourself!"

Once we can get rid of the priests and the politicians, the whole earth will become so full of peace, silence, love. And so many flowers, so many rainbows. We have been in the wrong hands; the world academy has to create an atmosphere so that these wrong hands are no longer powerful.

We have destroyed so many trees that the oxygen layer on the earth has fallen low. That is affecting everyone's health because without oxygen you cannot live. We have created industries, and the smoke from those industries has such chemicals that it has made holes in a certain layer around the earth, the ozone. It is oxygen, but just a little "thicker" oxygen, which was preventing any destructive rays from the sun reaching the earth. But our industries have created holes in the ozone layer and now destructive rays are entering. We have done the same stupidity by sending rockets to the moon; those rockets have also made holes. But perhaps it has all happened unconsciously. No one was aware what the effects were going to be.

The world academy is a conscious effort to do everything and be perfectly aware of what the consequences will be. Small experiments can be done which will give us the idea of the consequences. Right now there are thousands of inventions of scientists which have been purchased by the vested interests and are lying in their basements; they have never been brought into the market for the people to use. And because we are behaving so insanely, any invention is bound to change many things. Perhaps many industries will be closed because a better product, more life-affirmative, is available. Now those industrialists will try to purchase the rights and keep those scientific discoveries hidden from humanity.

Even Dr. Masashi Murakoshi was approached by the greatest nuclear manufacturer of America who said, "We want to purchase all your discoveries and all the things that you have made. Whatever the price, say it and you will be given it." But Masashi is a man of tremendous courage; he refused. He said, "That means all my life's effort will be lying somewhere down in your basements." He is not ready to sell his patents; he wants to give the patents to the academy so that millions of dollars can simply come here just from his small inventions.

The second man I mentioned is one of the most respectable men in Japan and has many foundations in his hands, with millions of dollars for any humanitarian purpose. I cannot think what more humanitarian purpose there can be than creating an academy of sciences and arts totally devoted to life and to enhancing life.

This is going to happen. When I am saying this is going to happen, I am not saying it; I am simply a vehicle for existence. I know perfectly well that when it comes from my absolute nothingness it is a message from existence itself. It is going to happen. No one can prevent it. And this is the only hope for the new man and the new humanity.

There are so many funny and strange questions which will have to wait – but a little laughter in the end will be good. It is the most healthy thing in the world. Just listen to it very silently; otherwise you will miss the point.

The little Toyota car comes to a sudden stop.

"Have you run out of petrol?" asks the girl sarcastically.

"No, of course not," replies the young man.

"Then why have we stopped?" she says.

"Well," he says, "you have probably noticed that we are parked in a quiet place in the forest miles from anywhere so I thought you might like a discussion about the hereafter."

"That's something new," replies the girl. "What do you mean?"

"Simple," says the man. "If you are not here after what I am here after, you will be here after I have gone."

About Osho

Osho defies categorization. Mystic and scientist, a rebellious spirit whose sole interest is to alert humanity to the urgent need to discover a new way of living. To continue as before is to invite threats to our very survival on this unique and beautiful planet.

His thousands of talks cover everything from the individual quest for meaning to the most urgent social, political and environmental issues facing society today. Osho's books are not written but transcribed from audio and video recordings of his extemporaneous talks to international audiences. And he tells them, "Remember: whatever I am saying is not just for you...I am talking also for the future generations."

Osho has been described by *The Sunday Times* in London as one of the "1000 Makers of the 20th Century" and by American author Tom Robbins as "the most dangerous man since Jesus Christ." *Sunday Mid-Day* (Mumbai) has selected Osho as one of ten people – along with Gandhi, Nehru and Buddha – who have changed the destiny of India.

About his own work, Osho has said that he is helping to create the conditions for the birth of a new kind of human being. He often characterizes this new human being as "Zorba the Buddha" – capable both of enjoying the earthy pleasures of a Zorba the Greek and the silent serenity of a Gautama the Buddha.

Running like a thread through all aspects of Osho's talks and meditations is a vision that encompasses both the timeless wisdom of all ages past and the highest potential of today's (and tomorrow's) science and technology.

Osho is known for his revolutionary contribution to the science of inner transformation, with an approach to meditation that acknowledges the accelerated pace of contemporary life. His unique OSHO Active Meditations® are designed to first release the accumulated stresses of body and mind, so that it then becomes easier to experience a stillness and thought-free relaxation which can be taken into daily life.

Two autobiographical works by the author are available:

Autobiography of a Spiritually Incorrect Mystic, St. Martin's Press, New York (book and eBook)

Glimpses of a Golden Childhood, OSHO Media International, Pune, India (book and eBook)

OSHO International Meditation Resort

Each year the Meditation Resort welcomes thousands of people from more than 100 countries. The unique campus provides an opportunity for a direct personal experience of a new way of living – with more awareness, relaxation, celebration and creativity. A great variety of around-the-clock and around-the-year program options are available. Doing nothing and just relaxing is one of them!

All of the programs are based on Osho's vision of "Zorba the Buddha" – a qualitatively new kind of human being who is able *both* to participate creatively in everyday life *and* to relax into silence and meditation.

Location

Located 100 miles southeast of Mumbai in the thriving modern city of Pune, India, the OSHO International Meditation Resort is a holiday destination with a difference. The Meditation Resort is spread over 28 acres of spectacular gardens in a beautiful tree-lined residential area.

OSHO Meditations

A full daily schedule of meditations for every type of person includes both traditional and revolutionary methods, and particularly the OSHO Active Meditations®. The daily meditation program takes place in what must be the world's largest meditation hall, the OSHO Auditorium.

OSHO Multiversity

Individual sessions, courses and workshops cover everything from creative arts to holistic health, personal transformation, relationship and life transitions, transforming meditation into a lifestyle for life and work, esoteric sciences, and the Zen approach to sports and recreation. The secret of the OSHO Multiversity's success lies in the fact that all its programs are combined with meditation, supporting the understanding that as human beings we are far more than the sum of our parts.

Cuisine

A variety of different eating areas serve delicious Western, Asian and Indian vegetarian food – most of it organically grown especially for the Meditation Resort. Breads and cakes are baked in the resort's bakery.

Night life

There are many evening events to choose from – dancing being at the top of the list! Other activities include full-moon meditations beneath the stars, variety shows, music performances and "meditations for daily life."

Facilities

At the Meditation Resort you can buy all of your basic necessities and toiletries in the Galleria. In addition, the Multimedia Gallery sells a large range of OSHO media products. For those who enjoy shopping, Pune provides all the options, ranging from traditional and ethnic Indian products to all of the global brand-name stores.

Accommodation

You can choose to stay in the elegant rooms of the OSHO Guesthouse, or for longer stays on campus you can select one of the

OSHO Living-In programs. Additionally there is a variety of nearby hotels and serviced apartments.

www.osho.com/meditationresort
www.osho.com/guesthouse
www.osho.com/livingin
Facebook: osho.international.meditation.resort

OSHO Books (English)

(OSHO books are available in Printed book and eBook formats, and most of them in audio format too. If a book is not available in one format, you can look up and buy it in another format.)

Early Talks

The Art of Living
Astrology
Breaking All Boundaries
Compassion and Revolution
Dimensions beyond the Known
The Eternal Quest
From Sex to Superconsciousness
The Great Challenge
Hidden Mysteries
I Am the Gate
The Independent Mind
Into the Void
Keys to a New Life
New Dimensions of Yoga
The Psychology of the Esoteric
Religion's Expiration Date
The Search for Peace
Woman and Rebellion
Work Is Love Made Visible

Meditation

And Now and Here
Body/Mind Balancing (Book & Audio)
Falling In Love with Darkness
In Search of the Miraculous
The Inner Journey
Just a Small Step
Meditation: The Art of Ecstasy
Meditation: The First and Last Freedom
The Path of Meditation
The Perfect Way
Silence: The Message of Your Being
Three Steps to Awakening

Buddha and Buddhist Masters

The Book of Wisdom
The Dhammapada: The Way of the Buddha (Vols 1-12)

The Diamond Sutra
The Discipline of Transcendence (Vols 1-4)
The Heart Sutra
The Great Secret
The Guest
The Path of Love
The Revolution

Indian Mystics
As if a Tree Starts Running (Yari))
The Beloved, Vols 1 & 2 (Baul Mystics)
Bliss:Living beyond Happiness and Misery (Shiva)
Die O Yogi Die (Gorakh)
Enlightenment: The Only Revolution (Ashtavakra)
Geeta Darshan Vol. 1 (Adhyaya 1-2)
Geeta Darshan, Vol.2 (Adhyaya 3)
Krishna: The Man and His Philosophy
The Last Morning Star (Daya)
Showering without Clouds (Sahajo)
The Song of Ecstasy (Adi Shankara)
The True Name (Vols 1&2) (Nanak)

Kabir
The Divine Melody
Ecstasy: The Forgotten Language
The Fabric of Life
The Fish in the Sea Is Not Thirsty

Western Mystics
The Art of Dying *(Hasidism)*
Come Follow to You, Vols 1-4 *(Jesus)*
Guida Spirituale (*Desiderata*)
The Hidden Harmony *(Heraclitus)*
I Say Unto You, Vols 1 & 2 *(Jesus)*
The Mustard Seed *(Jesus)*
The New Alchemy: To Turn You On (Mabel Collins)
Philosophia Perennis, Vols 1 & 2 (*Pythagoras*)
Reflections on Kahlil Gibran's *The Prophet*
Theologia Mystica *(Dionysius)*
The True Sage *(Hasidism)*
The Voice of Silence (Mabel Collins)
Zarathustra: A God That Can Dance (Nietzsche's *Thus Spake Zarathustra*)
Zarathustra: The Laughing Prophet (Nietzsche's *Thus Spake Zarathustra*)

Sufism
Just Like That

The Perfect Master, Vols 1 & 2
The Secret
Sufis: The People of the Path, Vols 1 & 2
Unio Mystica, Vols 1 & 2
Until You Die
The Wisdom of the Sands, Vols 1 & 2

Tantra

The Book of Secrets (Vigyan Bhairav Tantra)
The Tantra Experience (Saraha)
Tantra: The Supreme Understanding (Tilopa)
Tantric Transformation (Saraha)

The Upanishads

Behind a Thousand Names (Nirvana Upanishad)
Finger Pointing to the Moon (Adhyatma Upanishad)
Flight of the Alone to the Alone (Kaivalya Upanishad)
The Heartbeat of the Absolute (Ishavasya Upanishad)
I Am That (Isa Upanishad)
The Message beyond Words (Kathopanishad)
Philosophia Ultima (Mandukya Upanishad)
The Supreme Doctrine (Kenopanishad)
That Art Thou (Sarvasar Upanishad, Kaivalya Upanishad, Adhyatma Upanishad)
The Ultimate Alchemy, Vols 1 & 2 (Atma Pooja Upanishad)
Vedanta: Seven Steps to Samadhi (Akshaya Upanishad)
The Way beyond Any Way (Sarvasar Upanishad)

Tao

The Empty Boat (Chuang Tzu)
The Secret of Secrets (The Secret of Golden Flower)
Tao: The Golden Gate, Vols 1 & 2 (Ko Hsuan)
Tao: The Pathless Path, Vols 1 & 2 (Lieh Tzu)
Tao: The Three Treasures, Vols 1-4 (Lao Tzu)
When the Shoe Fits (Chuang Tzu)

Yoga (Patanjali)

Yoga: The Science of the Soul, Vols 1-10
- The Path of Yoga (Vol.1)
- The Heart of Yoga (Vol.2)
- Yoga: The Mystery beyond Mind (Vol.3)
- The Alchemy of Yoga (Vol.4)

- Yoga: A New Direction (Vol.5)
- Essence of Yoga (Vol.6)
- Yoga: The Science of Living (Vol.7)
- Secrets of Yoga (Vol.8)
- Yoga: The Path to Liberation (Vol.9)
- Yoga: The Supreme Science (Vol.10)

Zen and Zen Masters

Ah, This!
Ancient Music in the Pines
And the Flowers Showered…
And the Grass Grows By Itself…
A Bird on the Wing
Bodhidharma: The Greatest Zen Master
The Buddha: The Emptiness of the Heart
Christianity, the Deadliest Poison and Zen, the Antidote to All Poisons
Communism and Zen Fire, Zen Wind
Dang Dang Doko Dang
The First Principle
God Is Dead: Now Zen Is the Only Living Truth
The Great Zen Master Ta Hui
Hsin Hsin Ming: The Book of Nothing
I Celebrate Myself: God Is No Where, Life Is Now Here
Kyozan: A True Man of Zen
The Language of Existence
Live Zen
The Miracle
Nirvana: The Last Nightmare
No Mind: The Flowers of Eternity
No Water, No Moon
One Seed Makes the Whole Earth Green
The Original Man
Returning to the Source
The Search: Talks on the 10 Bulls of Zen
A Sudden Clash of Thunder
The Sun Rises in the Evening
Take it Easy
This. This. A Thousand Times This
This Very Body the Buddha
Turning In
The White Lotus
Yakusan: Straight to the Point of Enlightenment
The Zen Manifesto: Freedom from Oneself
Zen: The Diamond Thunderbolt
Zen: The Mystery and the Poetry of the Beyond
Zen: The Path of Paradox, Vols 1-3

Zen: The Quantum Leap from Mind to No-Mind
Zen: The Solitary Bird, Cuckoo of the Forest
Zen: The Special Transmission

Osho: On the Ancient Masters of Zen

Dogen: The Zen Master
Hyakujo: The Everest of Zen – With Basho's haikus
Isan: No Footprints in the Blue Sky
Joshu: The Lion's Roar
Ma Tzu: The Empty Mirror
Nansen: The Point of Departure
Rinzai: Master of the Irrational

Responses to Questions

Be Still and Know
Beyond Enlightenment (Talks in Bombay)
Beyond Psychology (Talks in Uruguay)
Come, Come, Yet Again Come
The Diamond Sword
From Bondage to Freedom
From Darkness to Light
From Death to Deathlessness
From Ignorance to Innocence
From Misery to Enlightenment
From Personality to Individuality
From the False to the Truth
From Unconsciousness to Consciousness
The Goose Is Out
The Great Pilgrimage: From Here to Here
The Invitation
Light on the Path (Talks in the Himalayas)
My Way: The Way of the White Clouds
Nowhere to Go but In
The Osho Upanishad (Talks in Bombay)
The Path of the Mystic (Talks in Uruguay)
The Razor's Edge
Sermons in Stones (Talks in Bombay)
Socrates Poisoned Again After 25 Centuries (Talks in Greece)
The Sword and the Lotus (Talks in the Himalayas)
Transmission of the Lamp (Talks in Uruguay)
Walk without Feet, Fly without Wings and Think without Mind
The Wild Geese and the Water
Yaa-Hoo! The Mystic Rose
Walking in Zen, Sitting in Zen
Zen: Zest, Zip, Zap and Zing

Osho's Vision for the World
The Golden Future
The Hidden Splendor
The New Dawn
The Rebel
The Rebellious Spirit

The Mantra Series
Hari Om Tat Sat
Om Mani Padme Hum
Om Shantih Shantih Shantih
Sat Chit Anand
Satyam Shivam Sundaram

Personal Glimpses
Books I Have Loved
Glimpses of a Golden Childhood
Notes of a Madman

Interviews with the World Press
The Man of Truth: A Majority of One

Meetings with Individuals
Above All Don't Wobble
Hammer on the Rock

Quotation Books
Gold Nuggets
More Gold Nuggets
Words From A Man of No Words

Letters and Writings
A Cup of Tea
Earthen Lamps
Flowers of Love
Life Is a Soap Bubble
Love Letters to Life
Seeds of Wisdom

For any information about OSHO Books, please contact:

OSHO Media International
17 Koregaon Park, Pune – 411001, MS, India
Phone: +91-20-66019999 Fax: +91-20-66019990
E-mail: distribution@osho.net
Website: http://www.osho.com

For More Information

The official website of OSHO International is www.OSHO.com

www.OSHO.com/AllAboutOSHO is a comprehensive portal to all things OSHO.

www.OSHO.com/AllAboutOSHO
www.OshoTimes.com
shop.OSHO.com
iOSHO.OSHO.com

YouTube:	OSHO/OSHOinternational
Twitter:	OSHO
Instagram:	OSHOinternational
Facebook:	OSHO.international
Facebook:	OSHO.international.meditation.resort

ALSO IN THE MANTRA SERIES